FL Studio Power!: The Comprehensive Guide

Steve Pease

Course Technology PTR
A part of Cengage Learning

COURSE TECHNOLOGY
CENGAGE Learning™

Australia • Brazil • Japan • Korea • Mexico • Singapore • Spain • United Kingdom • United States

COURSE TECHNOLOGY
CENGAGE Learning·

**FL Studio Power!: The Comprehensive
Guide**
Steve Pease

Publisher and General Manager, Course
Technology PTR: Stacy L. Hiquet

Associate Director of Marketing: Sarah
Panella

Manager of Editorial Services: Heather
Talbot

Marketing Manager: Mark Hughes

Executive Editor: Mark Garvey

Project Editor/Copy Editor: Cathleen D.
Small

Technical Reviewer: Scott Fisher

Editorial Services Coordinator: Jen Blaney

Interior Layout Tech: Macmillan Publishing
Solutions

Cover Designer: Mike Tanamachi

Indexer: Sharon Shock

Proofreader: Gene Redding

For product information and technology assistance, contact us at
Cengage Learning Customer & Sales Support, 1-800-354-9706

For permission to use material from this text or product, submit all
requests online at **www.cengage.com/permissions**
Further permissions questions can be emailed to
permissionrequest@cengage.com

All trademarks are the property of their respective owners.
All images © Cengage Learning unless otherwise noted.

Library of Congress Control Number: 2009933321

ISBN-13: 978-1-59863-991-9

ISBN-10: 1-59863-991-9

Course Technology, a part of Cengage Learning
20 Channel Center Street
Boston, MA 02210
USA

Cengage Learning is a leading provider of customized learning solutions with
office locations around the globe, including Singapore, the United Kingdom,
Australia, Mexico, Brazil, and Japan. Locate your local office at:
international.cengage.com/region

Cengage Learning products are represented in Canada by Nelson
Education, Ltd.

For your lifelong learning solutions, visit **courseptr.com**

Visit our corporate website at **cengage.com**

Printed in the United States of America
1 2 3 4 5 6 7 11 10 09

*For her love, patience, and a selflessness that
even the most benevolent of souls could learn from,
this book is dedicated to Alyssa.*

Acknowledgments

I must first thank Steve and Nancy Pease, my wonderful parents. You have each been amazing pillars of strength through transitions in my life and will always be unending influences. Dad, don't worry, they'll bring back Old Blue someday. Karen, I love you sis, and thank you for getting me into all types of music and helping me to keep an open mind. This really would not have fallen into place without the faith and support of Alyssa. Preston, the lengthy and legendary discussions on all things sound during our morning commute were more significant than a great deal of experiences I have had in this life—thank you, my friend. Eric, you keep me tough as nails and have always been a constructively critical voice and interested ear in all of my ventures (even when I talk too much), so cheers to you, captain. I want to send a resounding thank you to my good friend and mentor Paul Cox, who helped me get started on the path of digital recording. Ryan, you are a genius, and I thank you for always having a response to my inquiries on or off topic. Thanks to M-Audio and all the guys I worked with for their seemingly endless knowledge base. Mahalo to Greg for connecting me to this opportunity, and I must give big thanks to John and Les for causing me to froth at the mouth over recording equipment at an early age. Thank you to Mark and Cathleen for guiding me through this process. And finally, Scott, sometimes I wonder if your intelligence is human, because I don't think you can get stumped. Thank you so much for your help, and next time I am out your way, I owe you a beer, buddy.

About the Author

Steve Pease is a San Diego–based writer, composer, guitarist, and DJ. He has been playing the guitar most of his life and began getting into music manipulation as a DJ in Mexico. Eventually becoming a resident DJ in downtown San Diego, he began working with different versions of music software, and the digital recording fire was lit. After making a paycheck from online sales of simple soundscapes, he moved to L.A., where he furthered his knowledge for all things music while working at M-Audio. After leaving M-Audio, he returned to San Diego, where he currently composes soundtracks. You can check out tracks he is working on at myspace.com/friarfist.

Contents

Chapter 4
Recording Audio   109

Chapter 7
Effects Plug-Ins   227

Chapter 8
Extra Generators and Effects Plug-Ins
275

Introduction

FL Studio Power!: The Comprehensive Guide was written with the most important part of FL Studio in mind...you! This guide dives deep into every corner of FL Studio 9 and speaks to you as if one musician is talking to another, rather than using the jargon of your ordinary technical manual. In these pages you will find the necessary information for a beginner or tips and explanations for even the most seasoned veteran. This guide is designed for a more modern musician who demands speed and functionality. FL Studio will help to bring your ideas to life faster than you ever thought possible, with maximum control over how everything sounds. This guide was written to show you exactly how to utilize the tools available. Whether you are a home studio weekend warrior or a major label producer, you can bump your music up to the next level.

FL Studio

Everyone wants to be a producer, but the key is to be able to *produce*! In today's market, we need to be ever changing and quick to adapt. Styles change, trends change (although sometimes not soon enough), and even our music changes. Essential to being able to keep up with this whirlwind of musical evolution is having a tool that can seamlessly create these sonic changes. When we think of a great idea, beat, verse, or song, we would like to just open our head and pour it into a CD, shake it up, and voila! Instant music! Although I will someday figure out how to do this, Image Line Software has given us a program that has the tools for taking these ideas from simple thoughts to songs we can instantly hear and restructure any way we see fit—FL Studio!

The abilities of FL Studio far surpass many of the industry-standard names that we are used to seeing, because FL Studio takes a fresh approach to the music-making process. The software allows you to record audio and MIDI using a wealth of plug-ins already included and top-quality effects processors that will place your music well above the demo-CD level. The design is perfect for the musician who demands metronome-like perfection as well as the swing-style musician who likes to have that natural "live" feel.

Even more impressive, the software allows those who enjoy putting together live-performance songs an avenue to express their talent. With its built-in Live feature, you can take portions of your songs, rearrange them to your heart's content, and end up creating even more impressive compositions in front of an audience. This ends up becoming a fantastic tool for rearranging when you are putting together new music and auditioning different music samples.

What Is FL Studio?

FL Studio (originally known as FruityLoops) is a program that places creative control of many types of music in the hands of those who cannot get into million-dollar studios and use the overly complicated array of hardware gear they offer. It is a software-based sequencer that allows you to record any audio source or use the MIDI functions to create new, never-before-heard sounds with a wide range of software synthesizers and effects (see Figure 1.1).

One of the standout features of the program is the Stepsequencer, which is contained inside the Channel window. This is where artists can take a prerecorded sample or software synthesizer

1

Figure 1.1   This is a working project in FL Studio.

and then place it into any channel and select when that sound will play using the buttons on the sequencer. This is great for getting everything exactly on beat because it adheres to the project's master tempo, or the speed that the music is playing. The Mixer is great for routing sounds you have in the project to specific tracks that you can individually control. This broadens your flexibility for great mixing of volume, panning, and effects processing on each track. The Piano Roll window allows you to take MIDI data and either play notes live or draw them in so you can get your sound just right. You can even lay out preselected chords! The Playlist window is where the different patterns created in the Stepsequencer can be arranged alongside live audio and automation clips, which allow you to control any automatable parameter in FL Studio.

Where Did FL Studio Come From?

I remember back to the earlier versions of FL Studio, when a friend would demonstrate for me what he had made. It was an interesting setup, and it was not half bad for the time. Interestingly enough, I even found myself occasionally using it on his computer to try to make some little sequenced beats, but never taking anything too seriously. At that point I was DJing in the Gaslamp Quarter of San Diego, so I constantly had my hands on an eclectic blend of music and grooves unheard by many aside from my faithful following. When you listened to something put on vinyl, it towered in quality (arguably) over anything I could make with the program. I saw the basic idea of creation, but I didn't really know what tools they were using to get the music to breathe and come alive. The latest version has those tools and more.

FL Studio was not always the streamlined program that you see today. It began as a little sequencing program called FruityLoops that was MIDI only. The very first version (1.0) was not even released, but it is still available to the public if anyone wants to see just how far they have come. You can grab it on Image Line's website in their FL Studio History section. This program was developed in Belgium and created by Didier Dambrin. He holds the lead program-mer title and oversees all further development. It was his decision to write the program in Delphi, which is a complicated way to say that it will only work on Windows platforms. Fear not, Mac users—Image Line supports Boot Camp.

What Is This Program All About?

FL Studio is all about giving you seemingly limitless options in the way you create music. One thing you will notice when you open the demo projects included in the demo or full version is that not only are the projects different musically, but they also are different in the way they are organized. The program allows users to record and sequence in many different ways. I find that for the singer/songwriter, recording into the Edison (more on this in the "Recording Audio Clips into Edison" section of Chapter 4, "Recording Audio") is simple, effects and reverb can easily be added, and multiple takes can be layered to create a full sound. On the other hand, the hip-hop producer who wants to get that perfect sound can use the patterns to switch between different beats on the fly to see which works best with the associated lyrics (see Figure 1.2). For the elec-tronic artist, you can loop in different patterns and layer sections all while recording vocals or synths live.

Included in the most basic package of the program is a ton of plug-ins, add-ons, and instruments that put other programs to shame. Many programs are purchased barebones, without any add-ons, and only allow you to record audio and MIDI. Here's the problem with that: Without any add-ons, you can't give your music that wow factor we all seek. Furthermore, if there are no instruments included, when you record MIDI, it will just be nice little squares in the MIDI edi-tor, but no sound will play. (We'll look more closely at MIDI in Chapter 5, "Recording and Using MIDI.") To see just how many additional plug-ins are available in FL Studio, press Ctrl+F8 on your keyboard, and it will bring up the Plugin Picker (see Figure 1.3). Bear in mind that some of these are demos, and in some cases, they are entire programs themselves. Although they need to be purchased separately, they are functional minus an occasional audio dropout and the fact that they cannot be saved in a project. The demo plug-ins will say DEMO at the top of their window, and the information on any plug-in (even when it is a demo) can be accessed by pressing F1 when the plug-in is focused.

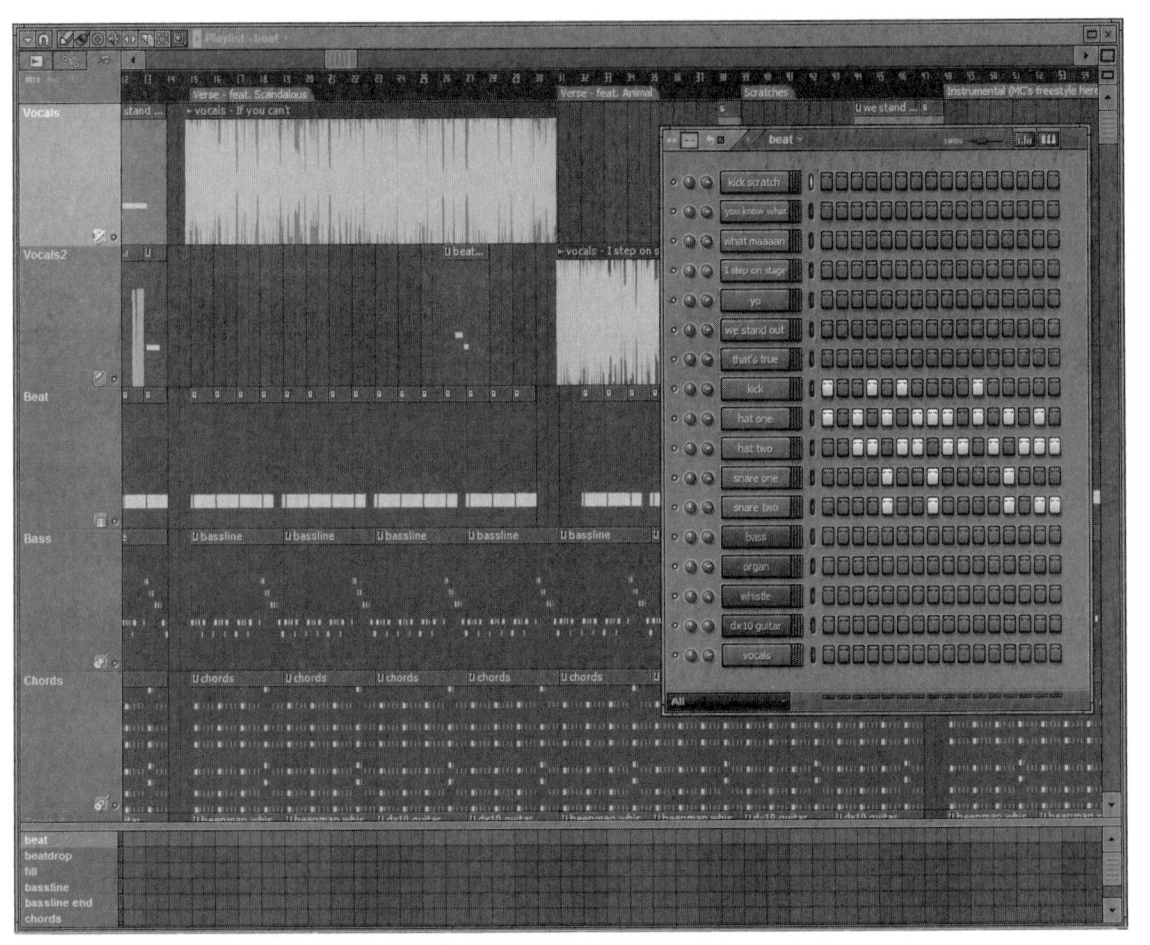

Figure 1.2 In this project, the Stepsequencer has a beat punched in, and the Playlist can be used to go over a section of lyrics to make sure the beat sounds right.

Just a few notable features of FL Studio include:

- **Recording audio.** Even if all you want to do is play the guitar and record, this program can give you everything you need for a full and complete sound.

- **Recording and manipulating MIDI.** Finally, those master pianists have their work cut out for them! Have you ever thought to yourself, "I can see those notes, but my hands just don't know where to go"? If you can imagine it, the Piano roll lets you place the notes wherever you like. This can be applied to any instrument loaded into FL Studio.

- **Looping.** Take parts of any number of patterns and place them in any order you wish. This is great for quick reordering when something just isn't sounding right.

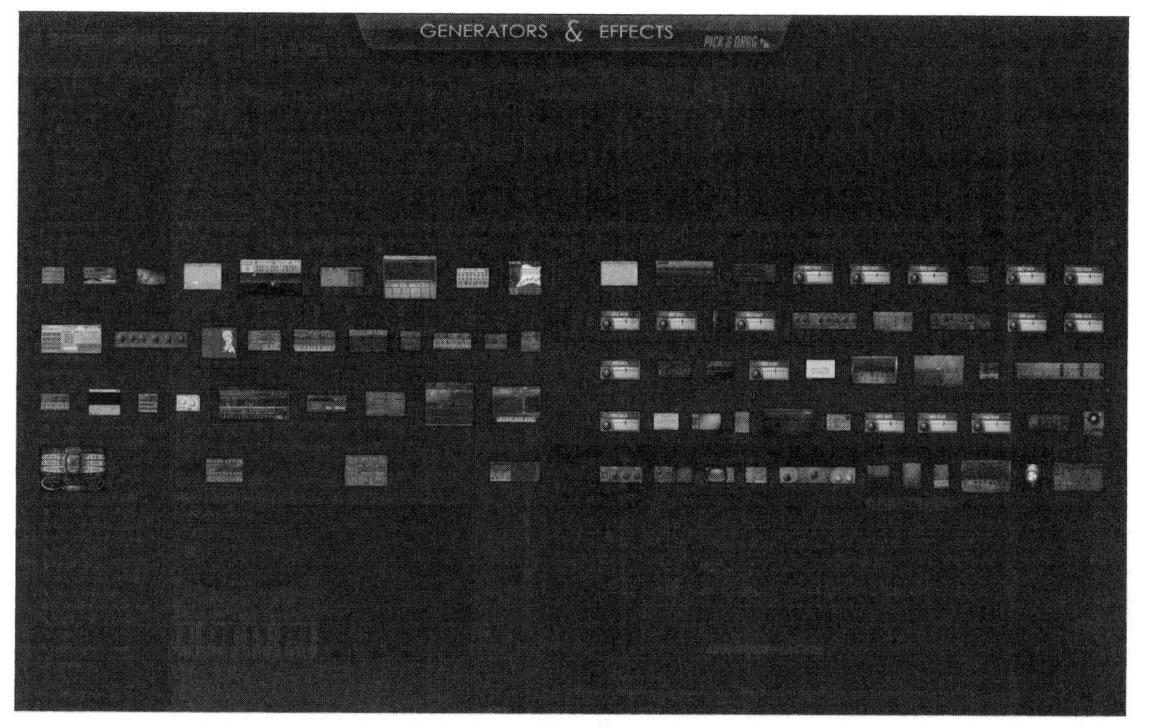

Figure 1.3 Ctrl+F8 will bring up the Plugin Picker, allowing you to browse FL Studio's plug-ins and generators.

- **Live mode.** The looping feature with touch control! You can assign a MIDI controller to skip to different parts of your composition.

- **MIDI Machine control.** FL Studio has added MIDI Machine control so that you can control parameters in FL Studio using your controller or control surface. This means if you have a keyboard with faders or a control surface, you can link your volume control, panning, filters, and so on inside FL Studio to a fader on your external device, giving you that hands-on feel of a studio.

- **Time stretching.** This is a big one for those remixer artists out there. Many times you can find yourself cutting and pasting for hours, trying to get a song to match a beat you have created. Now you can just click and drag, and the selection will adhere to the tempo you select.

- **Multiple routing.** In FL Studio you can send in up to 99 tracks of audio, although most soundcards will not be able to do this. You can send out different mixes simultaneously to hear one version of a song in one set of speakers and a completely different version in another set.

- **Effects routing.** I must praise the Image Line folks for setting up the ability to move plug-in effects ordering around. A simple click on your effect gives you the ability to reorder your effects.

- **Customizable interface.** Don't like where something is? You can move it! Practically the entire GUI (*graphical user interface*) can be moved around to suit your needs or computer screen area.

Who Is FL Studio For?

This program is for nearly anyone! If you are recording simple riffs, composing complicated pieces using MIDI, making the latest chart-topping beats, or even scoring to a movie, it can be done right here with this program. Any style of music that can be created can be catered to, and I have not found any limitations even within my own personal music preferences. I hold spanning interests in hip-hop, house/electronic, and acoustic guitar. I find that with the power of FL Studio, I can take a hip-hop beat, run it a few times, set it to loop, and add guitar. Speed it up, and all of a sudden I'm working with a breakbeat house track! Many artists have found FL Studio to be a great building program to create their masterpieces.

What makes the program so useful is its ease of use and how quickly you can create music and mold it into a professional-sounding piece. With the ability of a workflow like this, there is no limit to what you can accomplish. There is nothing worse than getting to a spot where the creative juices are flowing and then reaching a lull in productivity because using the program is cumbersome. Slowing you down in your creation, in my opinion, is the worst thing that can happen. Granted, there are those of us out there who do not run out of ideas, but for those people, now you can write twice as many songs, and that means twice as many Grammys!

So now the fun part begins: how, what, where, when, and why? The next chapter explains the setup of the program and what you need to look for when putting together your workstation. I will explain the system requirements and things you will need and even provide some suggestions on things you will want to have when considering your studio. Keep in mind the following questions when looking through the next chapter: What pertains to me? Do I need this? Will this make my life easier when recording and creating?

Setting It All Up

When it comes to not reading the manual and just wanting to get things going, I am just as guilty as the next person. "Pshh, I can do this! I don't need to read that piece of paper, right?" Well, in short, no, you don't *have* to read it. However, like a professional engineer friend of mine, Paul Wagner, would say, "It's not so much *can* you, but *should* you?" Originally, he was speaking of someone who buys a system so new that nothing is compatible with it; however, in this situation, his words of advice still ring true. In this example, I know that we all *can* pop in the disc and hope for the best, and sometimes things will just work, but we *should* make sure that things are set up properly. Systems falling beneath specification minimums or improperly routed sound can lead to the audio having pops and clicks, being distorted, or there being no sound at all!

In this chapter, I will explain the minimum requirements to run FL Studio properly, specifically with the computer and then with your hardware. Many times, you will find that taking the time to set everything up correctly will save you a ton of headaches, not to mention many calls to the people in the technical support call centers. When I was working at M-Audio, one of the most common complaints that we would receive from customers was about software running poorly, and it was because they were using computers that were less powerful than a typical cell phone. When you check these specifications yourself, not only will you know whether your system is up to speed, but if you need a new computer, you will know what you're looking for when you get to the computer store!

System Requirements

Something to bear in mind while looking at these minimum specifications is that they are intended for a computer running *only* FL Studio when it is properly installed, with no oddball programs running in the background. Different programs, plug-ins, and services can cause system performance to lag, and when it does, that can slow down workflow and even cause audio to drop out (no sound) or become distorted. Simple things, such as music players, can lock out the soundcard you are using and prevent FL Studio from being able to use the soundcard to play sound!

These are the minimum requirements as shown on the FL Studio website:

Minimum Requirements

- 2 GHz AMD or Intel Pentium III compatible with full SSE1 support or an Intel Mac with Boot Camp running XP or Vista.

- Windows XP or Vista (32-bit or 64-bit).

- 512 MB of RAM.

- 130 MB of hard disk space.

- Windows-compatible soundcard with DirectSound drivers. ASIO drivers are required for audio recording.

These are my personal recommendations to successfully run FL Studio:

My Recommended Requirements

- 3 GHz AMD or Pentium 4 processor or 2.0 GHz dual-core processors.

- Intel Mac is still fine running Boot Camp.

- 1 GB or more of RAM.

- Dedicated hard drive with 500 GB of storage running at 7200 rpm.

- An ASIO-compliant soundcard.

- Some type of MIDI keyboard or interface.

The Computer

This is one of the most important aspects to recording with FL Studio. Before music went digital, computers were used to sequence MIDI and not much else, so it was not important to have a powerful computer to run things. Now we are in the modern age, where an award-winning artist can write, perform, produce, and finish radio-ready projects all in an extra bedroom or even while riding in a car! Why is the computer important? It is the engine of your project and allows you to work as quickly as you possibly can. If you don't like to wait for something to load, or you hate not being able to record multiple inputs (due to computer power, not literal soundcard limitations), it is good to pay attention to this section.

PC versus Mac

The debate rages on! When considering a computer, which one is best? To be honest, when both are optimized and have identical specifications, you will find that they perform almost identi-cally. I have seen the good and the bad for both operating systems. It basically comes down to which operating system you prefer. In other words, if you like the way the Mac screen looks, or if Vista has that feature you can't live without, stick with your comfort zone. No need to hop over to an operating system where you can't even open up FL Studio! One thing to keep in mind is Boot Camp on a Mac. Although FL Studio supports Boot Camp on a Mac, that does *not* mean your soundcard does! It is very possible that your awesome, totally powerful computer can't utilize the inputs and outputs of your soundcard because Boot Camp can't see the soundcard. Check with the manufacturer of the soundcard to ensure that it supports Boot Camp if you are planning on using a Mac with FL Studio.

Processor

If the computer is your engine, the processor represents how powerful your engine is. Remember that in the digital audio world, more power makes life easier. I understand that we don't all have money to simply toss around like it's going out of style, but consider the statement "You get what you pay for." Although not 100-percent accurate, it does tend to ring true in most cases. A stronger processor allows you to run more effects and record more tracks simultaneously. A great thing about FL Studio is the real-time capabilities. In most cases you can make adjustments on the fly, such as adding low-pass filters, altering the pitch, and so on. Having to wait for these things to process or hearing a pause or click in the audio can be a little bothersome and can disrupt the creation process.

In my personal experience, I have noticed that the Celeron processor is notorious for performing poorly with audio applications. Many times while troubleshooting setups, I've run into someone with pops and clicks in his recordings, and after extensive system searching, optimizing, and turning off all background programs, it ended up being the processor's inability to run audio applications well. Don't get too down, though, because your music can have pops and clicks when playing in the program, and when you want to render the song to disk, FL Studio will slow rendering to remove the pops and clicks, allowing the processor to catch up. This means that when you burn it to a CD, the final sound playing on the stereo or in the car will not have the problem sounds your processor may have been causing. You can always make it work, regardless of how well, but for a better working environment, keep the processor in mind and always remember to optimize the computer.

RAM

The RAM (*random access memory*) in your computer is basically short-term memory of everything happening in FL Studio. For example, when you are working with a track, the audio that is there or the effects that are processing audio require RAM. FL Studio will utilize the amount of RAM you have, but the computer draws its memory usage from the physical RAM as well as the hard drive space used to create virtual memory. The computer will use both physical and virtual RAM as memory, but the more physical RAM you have, the more likely the computer will use it. You want FL Studio to be using the physical memory rather than the hard drive space because it is faster and performs better. While my personal recommendation was a gig of RAM, don't be afraid to go even further and grab more. RAM is easy to install, and it is just a simple stick that plugs into your motherboard. A stick of RAM (commonly called a *gig stick* when it is a 1-GB stick) is fairly inexpensive and will boost FL Studio's performance. Any program in a 32-bit environment can utilize up to 2 GB of RAM, but FL Studio allows you to increase that ceiling to 3 GB by installing the extended memory file. Again, this goes hand in hand with the physical versus virtual RAM usage, so installing more RAM than this limit can still benefit your performance. This can make FL Studio run faster, but use caution whenever changing anything about how programs react in your operating system. The instructions for this can be found in the help file (F1). If you are not sure how to install physical RAM, let a pro do it, because I have seen someone plug in a stick backwards, and the computer screen went blank upon booting. The RAM and processor go hand in hand when you're putting together your setup, and if you stay above the minimums, you should be able to perform most (if not all) functions seamlessly in FL Studio.

Hard Drive

Not all hard drives are created equal, and typically this is last on a checklist of "why things might be running slowly or oddly," but it is something to pay attention to. For optimal performance, I would suggest using an internal hard drive that runs at 7200 rpm. It is best to check with the manufacturer on these specs. Most will run at this speed, but there are some older ones that move along at 5400, and this can cause slow writing and reading (that is, writing to the drive and reading from the drive).

Is it possible to use an external hard drive? Yes, it is! I have been successfully using a USB external hard drive for months to run FL Studio directly from it. I did run into some wait times for things to load and occasional pauses in audio when changing effects parameters, but that was due to the particular unit I was using. If you have to use an external hard drive, use FireWire 800—it is extremely fast compared to USB. But the true victor in external drives is an eSATA drive. These perform like an internal drive and are just as fast, but they have the ability to be removed without taking an entire computer with you.

When recording your tracks, the more music you make, the more takes you have. These files build up quickly and start taking up massive amounts of space. Having a backup drive for speedy file transfer is a great solution (see Figure 2.1).

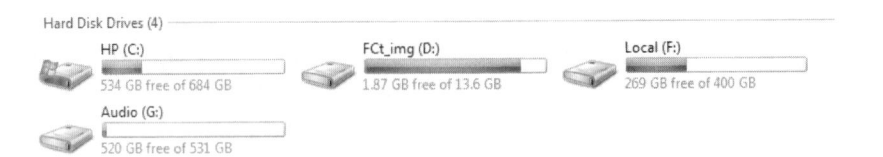

Figure 2.1 Here you can see that I have my C drive basically empty, aside from important operating files, while I have an entire drive dedicated to audio, and it has plenty of room for recording.

Ideally, never record to the same drive (or partition) that your system files are on. This way, you can leave your system files plenty of room. When the system drive (usually the C drive) fills up and has less than 10 to 15 percent free space, the entire system starts running slowly. By separating these, you don't have to worry about system space, but if you have an immense drive, you shouldn't experience any trouble regardless of where you save your files and recordings. The hard drive can affect your performance, but the important point to focus on is what *you* need from the hard drive. Audio files take up lots of room, so if you will be recording a ton and saving all of your takes, it is probably a good idea to get a larger internal hard drive. If that won't work, try an external FireWire hard drive and save your audio in there. Another solution could be to save your work on the external hard drive and drag the files onto the main drive when you want to work with that particular project. If your workflow stays streamlined and there are no hiccups in the creative process, you may find the effort well worth it.

Audio Interface

This part of your setup to me is extremely important, and although you can use the onboard soundcard of your computer, I highly recommend getting a soundcard that supports ASIO, which I will further explain in a couple paragraphs. To begin, you have many options when considering a purchase, and when I say "interface," a more generalized term would be the soundcard. Sometimes this can be a card plugged right into a PCI slot in the computer that has some inputs and outputs. Other times this can be a FireWire device that is no more than a cable plugged into the computer, and the interface itself is a unit that sits on your desk with all the controls right there, rather than inside a software application. My personal suggestion is a soundcard that gives you the ins and outs you want with ASIO support. Getting a soundcard that only has outputs (which is pretty rare) means that you won't be able to record! Take time with this one, and we'll explore some things to consider when getting your soundcard.

Cost versus Function. I don't advocate spending more than you need unless you are made of money, in which case it helps to get the top-of-the-line soundcard so it will last you for years to come. Most of us, though, can get a fully functional music-making station at a fraction of the cost of a modern professional studio. What will you be doing with FL Studio is the most important question to ask when considering your device of choice. If you are recording vocals and only use one mic, you can stick with a less-expensive device that has a single mic input and a stereo output for mixing. If you are recording multiple inputs at once, then you will need to get a device with those capabilities, but keep in mind that more inputs equal more parts, which means that it will be more expensive. Also remember to make sure your device will work with what you have. (For example, PCI devices will not work on a laptop because there is no PCI slot.) You will find a difference in prices, varying from less than $100 to well over $1,000, which allows for a great deal of selection and will help you get the exact interface you need.

Connection Types. What began as endless, tangled messes of cables and connectors has simplified into single cords! The connection you choose to work with will not make or break your projects, but there are a few good things to know about each.

USB. These days, many USB devices are available that simply plug into the computer and have built-in microphone preamps and speaker outputs. All you need is that device and a set of headphones or speakers, and you are ready to go. This is a great option for the mobile music maker or on-the-spot recorder. USB devices can be plugged into a laptop, and you can even come up with the latest chart-topper while on a cross-country road trip! USB devices are hot pluggable, meaning that they can be plugged into the computer when the computer is on and running. I don't recommend trying to plug in the device with FL Studio open, though, as the program most likely will not see the device until the application is restarted.

It's worth mentioning that when I refer to USB devices, I am mostly referring to USB 2.0. This is a standard that was developed in 2000, but due to computer manufacturers' lack of support, it really didn't gain popularity until 2004. There are still computers that will only put out USB 1.1, and this is something to take note of. USB 1.1 runs much slower than 2.0, and many devices simply won't work with the older USB speeds. Some devices will just lose functionality on inputs and outputs, or their sample rates will not be able to run at their maximum capability.

The Edirol UA-1EX, shown in Figure 2.2, is great for plugging a smaller dynamic mic with a 1/8-inch output (the same size as your iPod headphone jack) right into the interface. This little device is able to record at a higher quality than your CDs or MP3s can even play, but it is good to keep in mind that the quality of recording will be limited when using a 1/8-inch mic. A convenient feature is that it uses USB, and most computers have many USB ports to choose from, so finding where to plug it in is pretty straightforward.

Figure 2.2 The Edirol UA-1EX is a USB audio interface that allows 24-bit/96k recording and has both a headphone output and a 1/8-inch mic input.

PCI, PCI-X, or PCIe. PCI audio devices are great for transfer rate, and with the addition of PCI Express to the family of cards, those speeds have risen dramatically. Many interfaces still use PCI or PCI-X (both are *not* PCI Express) due to their design and production happening well before PCI Express was available. Also, many older computers do not have PCIe slots and only use PCI or PCI-X. When considering this type of interface, it is best to check with the manufacturer of your computer to see what type of interfaces it supports. (In other words, what slot does it have? This is important because if you only have PCIe slots, you won't be able to use PCI or PCI-X audio cards.) PCI cards have a large range in price, but there are many that won't completely clean you out.

The M-Audio Delta 44 (see Figure 2.3) plugs into the PCI slot on your desktop computer and is pretty stationary. It has four inputs and four outputs, allowing you to have two stereo inputs and route out two separate stereo outputs. This is great if you want to create different mixes for your artists. With this particular soundcard, though, there are no mic ins to send into the program. If that is the case, then you can give yourself nice analog control with a little mixer like the Behringer Xenyx series (see Figure 2.4). This way, you can mix multiple ins on the Behringer and send them into the different inputs on the breakout box of the PCI device.

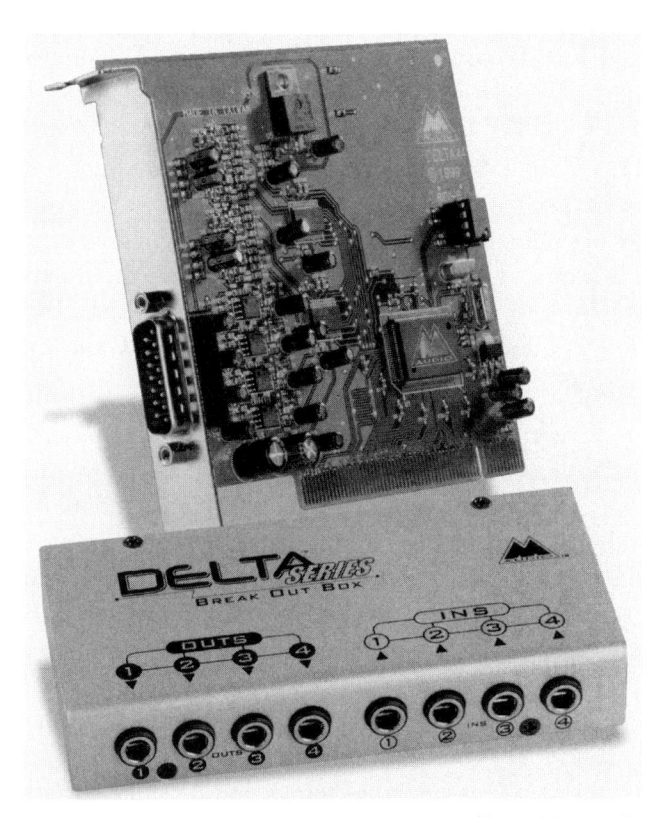

Figure 2.3 The M-Audio Delta 44 is an affordable PCI-based interface with four ins and four outs.

My initial draw to the PCI card was the functionality and quality alongside its value. With the array of USB devices now competing with the cards, it is more of a preference and need debate

Figure 2.4   The Behringer Xenyx series is a mixer that allows you to control many inputs and multiple outputs to send into your soundcard.

rather than performance and reliability. Many USB devices have all the inputs and outputs you could need and do not require any extra hardware for the music you want to create. You will probably hear me say this again, but all types of audio interfaces can have problems, and when it comes down to it, cost can and should be a factor. There are overpriced cards out there that claim the best conversion quality and can run at very high sample rates with high bit depth, but unless you have taken the time to acoustically tune your room so there is low noise and no reflections, it is not worth paying the price, in my opinion.

FireWire. FireWire devices offer a better transfer rate, and when considering computers, remember that all information—audio or otherwise—is just data to the computer. USB claims speeds up to 480 Mbps where FW 400, as you might guess, runs at 400 Mbps. Here's the funny thing: That 480 Mbps speed is burst! In other words, it doesn't sustain those speeds; it only reaches those speeds in occasional "bursts." In every benchmark test when the two were run side by side, FW 400 destroyed USB 2.0 in transfer rates. This does not mean that buying a USB interface will cause your performance to suffer, because the device you purchase will be designed to work with the number of inputs that it has. If you are recording drums or many vocals at once, and you need many inputs, I advise going with a FireWire device, such as the M-Audio ProjectMix I/O (see Figure 2.5). This device has eight mic inputs and has an ADAT connection to send in even more channels. This is on the more expensive end of things, but it can be a great asset with its capabilities.

FireWire has exponentially grown in popularity with the superior transfer rates and general abilities. I highly recommend searching around what it has to offer and seeing whether it fits your needs. Although there may be other forms of connections involving a device and computer,

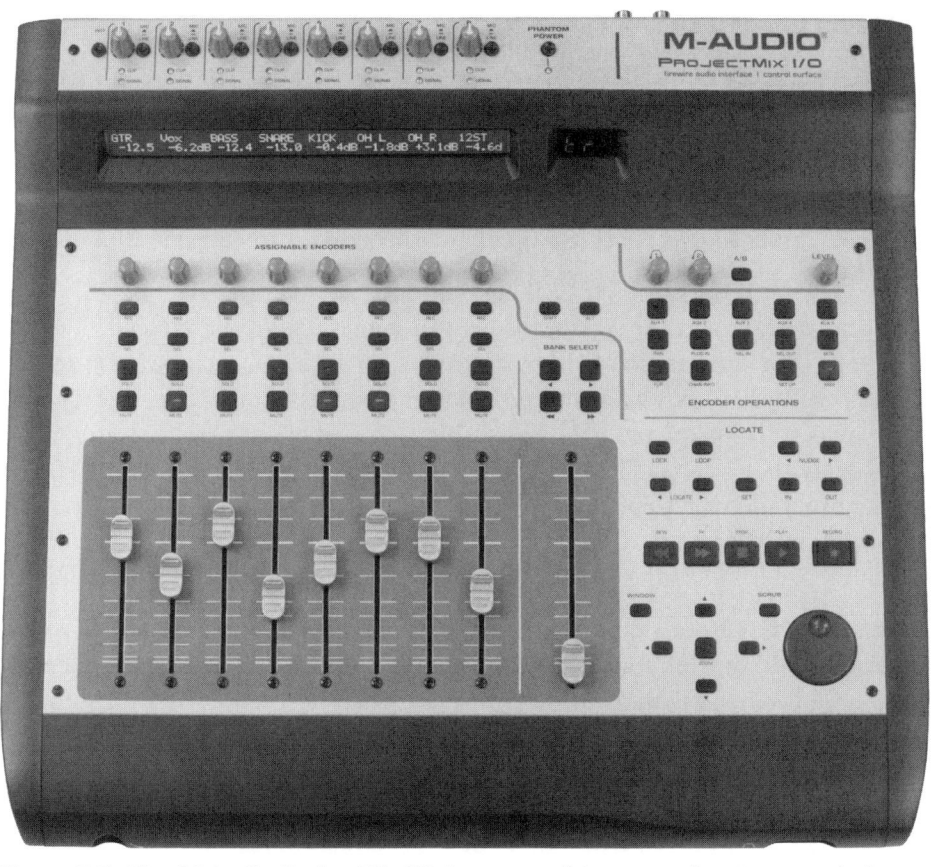

Figure 2.5 The M-Audio ProjectMix I/O has tons of inputs and outputs and gives you the ability to touch the controls of individual tracks instead of mouse clicking.

I will keep this section detailed to the most common types of interfaces used by amateur and professional musicians.

ASIO. I know by now you've heard me mention ASIO plenty of times, and it is for good reason. ASIO (*audio stream input output*) is a soundcard driver protocol for digital audio that was developed by Steinberg Media Technologies. Now, what does that mean to us? Better audio performance on a PC. Mac users, this will not apply to you, because your computer uses Core Audio and does not require ASIO. The main idea behind ASIO is to bypass Windows' internal mixer. Instead of the signal going from your device to the computer, then processing through multiple layers and going into the program, only to be run through the gauntlet again before making its way back to the device where you can actually hear it, ASIO bypasses the unnecessary layers. It allows the device to talk directly to the program and vice versa.

Is latency that bad, though? A good example is the "Row, Row, Row Your Boat" song that we all sang as children. "Row, row, row your boat, gently down the stream..." Then the next group repeats the line on top of the first group. So as the first group continues with "Merrily, merrily, merrily, merrily, life is but a dream," the second group begins its "Row, row, row...." The audio that you record is the first group singing, and the actual signal that plays back over your speakers is the second group when not using ASIO. I must admit that it is not as bad as an entire line of a song (usually), but the delay is there when using Windows generic soundcards. You want your sound to get to you quickly because when that happens, you have the perception that you are *in* the music rather than recording a vocal and then having to nudge it around to fit to the music or beat of the song you are working on.

So where is the line drawn with latency? Again, this sort of comes down to preference, but for the untrained ear, if your card can handle it without introducing pops and clicks, a good setting (in the Audio Settings menu, F10) is 512 samples, which introduces about 12ms of delay. At 1028 samples, the delay is still almost inaudible, but at 2048, the delay starts to be clearly heard because of the 47ms delay that occurs. There is latency for all programs because it creates the working buffer for the program, which is basically how it allows you to use it and make changes while updating information. Finding that happy balance between latency and how hard your computer works to minimize it will make your FL Studio experience much more worthwhile.

Outs and Ins. This has been discussed a bit, but I want to get into a few things you need to know when dealing with the ins and outs of your device. Starting in the playback (or output) department, it's important to find something that will suit your particular needs. So, will it be speakers or headphones? Will your neighbors hate you or love you? I would suggest both, because speakers give you a better spatial awareness when mixing and tend to sound closer to what the final product will play like on most systems. Headphones are great for mixing the subtleties in sound and nice for creation when you are trying to quietly put something together.

So with these in mind, it is good to know whether your device has these outputs. Take a look at the device you will be using. Typically, all devices will have a headphone out that you can plug a set of headphones into. Regardless of what type of headphone jack it is, there should be a connector that can make it work (unless you are using a USB headset, which is a different beast altogether and will not connect to a usual 1/4 inch or 1/8 inch jack).

The speakers are a great addition in your setup, provided you choose to use them. Many artists find the creation portion of music can work best with headphones, and incredible compositions can be made, but a final mix always needs to be tested on speakers. Your interface needs to work with your speakers, or you may find yourself needing to purchase more gear—which is a great excuse to go drool in the electronics store, but not necessary if you do a little research. Many interfaces will send out a line signal and require speakers that are self powered. Self-powered means that there is a power supply coming out of the back of one or both of the speakers, and this in turn plugs into an AC outlet on your wall, as shown in Figure 2.6. This will work fine with almost any interface, and at most you would need a converter just so the speakers can plug into your audio interface (in other words, a 1/4-inch adapter that converts into an RCA plug). Speakers that don't directly plug into the wall will require an amp to properly output sound.

Figure 2.6 You can see on the back of this speaker that it is self powered and has a port for its own cable that plugs directly into the wall.

Some interfaces have built-in power, but many meant for digital recording will only have non-powered outputs.

Now let's talk about the inputs and what you need to think about when considering signal going into your device. To begin with, what signal do you want to send into the computer for recording? Remember that unless you are recording live bands, most of the music created in FL Studio happens inside the computer, so all of that does not really come into play when considering inputs. What you need to consider are vocals, instruments, and other things that might be recorded. Vocal artists will need a microphone input, but there are many devices that can communicate with your interface (soundcard), such as keyboards with built-in sound or even a turntable for adding in scratch noises. Remember that a great deal of scratching can be emulated in FL Studio, but we'll get into that later in the plug-ins section.

Let's say that you are a singer/songwriter, aspiring hip-hop artist, or electronic music creator, and all you really need is a microphone input and an instrument input. This broadens the range of devices that you can use and, more importantly, afford! Many devices available have mic and instrument inputs that you can plug into and start working right away.

Things to be aware of when dealing with microphones include the following:

- Is it a condenser, dynamic, or ribbon mic?

- Does the mic require phantom power?

- What type of connection does the mic use?

- Does the mic have its own power supply?

These are all important because there is nothing worse than having everything set up, only to realize that your mic won't work with your device. Many USB devices do not supply phantom power, which is basically an electrical current that powers the mic and allows it to receive signal. Therefore, if you plug a condenser microphone into a device with no phantom power, it will not send signal into FL Studio. Remember that just because the mic cable fits, that doesn't mean it will always work. Pay close attention to what type of mic you need when looking to buy your interface based on the type of mic you want to use. I have received the best sound using condenser microphones, which do require phantom power.

Phantom Power Phantom power is used by condenser microphones and some DI (*direct input*) boxes and is a way of getting a DC voltage signal through the cable. The standard set that still operates today is 48V of power. This voltage signal charges two plates inside a condenser mic, and sound waves (such as singing or playing an instrument) that hit the plates create an electrical signal that can be sent to an interface for recording. It is important to know what mic you are using because a ribbon mic and even some dynamic mics can be severely damaged by running phantom power into them. Dynamic and ribbon mics suspend a coil or a metal ribbon in a magnetic field. Since movement of the coils or ribbons in these fields isn't activated using an electrical signal, phantom power is not necessary to use these mics.

If you're using a guitar, many devices implement their own built-in DI to allow you to simply plug in the guitar and play. This is important to note because the guitar is a high-impedance (Hi-Z) device, whereas line-level inputs are low impedance. The DI allows a high-impedance device to work properly with the unit and converts the sound to a low-impedance signal. Impedance is basically the amount of resistance to a signal that a device has. This resistance plays a part in the quality and sustained strength of the signal when it reaches its destination. It is useful to understand impedance because you might be plugging a high-impedance device into a low-impedance input, which can cause poor audio quality. A good friend and fantastic engineer, Preston Shepard, once told me this great analogy: The guitar signal is like water flowing through a 1-inch PVC pipe. The water is moving along very nicely with good force, and that would be high impedance. Connect the end of the 1-inch pipe so that the water flows into a 10-foot-tall pipeline (low-impedance device), and the water trickles through with no power. This is why when you plug a guitar directly into a line-level input, you get a weak, quiet, and often distorted sound. If the device says "instrument input," you are usually good to go with plugging your guitar in.

With keyboards and all other devices that send out a line-level signal, most devices will have an input for these to just plug in directly. These are the easy ones, and you can literally just plug and play.

MIDI Interfaces

What is a MIDI interface? It is a device that sends MIDI signal to the computer and allows for many different capabilities within FL Studio. I will dig a little deeper into what MIDI is in Chapter 5, "Recording and Using MIDI." Just know for now that MIDI is not audio, and audio signal will not travel over a MIDI cable. Most of the time you will see a MIDI interface in the form of a piano keyboard. Another familiar MIDI device is a drum pad device, where typically 16 touch-sensitive pads are arranged in a four-by-four setup. These are great because when set up properly, the harder you hit them, the louder the sound will be! Using a MIDI interface is a great way to add that "real" feeling to your music.

So is the MIDI interface required? Not at all, especially with FL Studio's Piano roll and humanizing abilities. There is even an option to play notes with your typing keyboard! I have found much more enjoyment and flexibility in FL Studio when using my keyboard or drum pads, especially when making music that uses virtual instruments. After some practice, you will find that a keyboard or drum pad at your side helps the creation and perfection processes of songwriting.

Preferences in FL Studio

Creating music can be seriously hamstrung when settings are wrong or disabled, so it is good to know how to set up your session and what the different portions of the Preferences menu do. I have found myself fumbling with different programs and unable to get my keyboard to play notes in the software because the menus were so spread apart and impossible to find. FL Studio makes it convenient for you to set up everything from a single window with side menus. You can access this window by pressing F10 on your typing keyboard. Although this tends to be the not-so-fun information, learning what each piece does can dramatically improve the speed with which you create and mix music!

Figure 2.7   The Trigger Finger is one example of a drum pad–style MIDI controller.

Figure 2.8   The Axiom series of keyboards is a piano-style MIDI controller with incorporated drum pad style.

MIDI Section

Figure 2.9 shows the tab where all of your devices that send or receive MIDI should be displayed. Here you can set up all of the MIDI routing and machine control you need. You'll

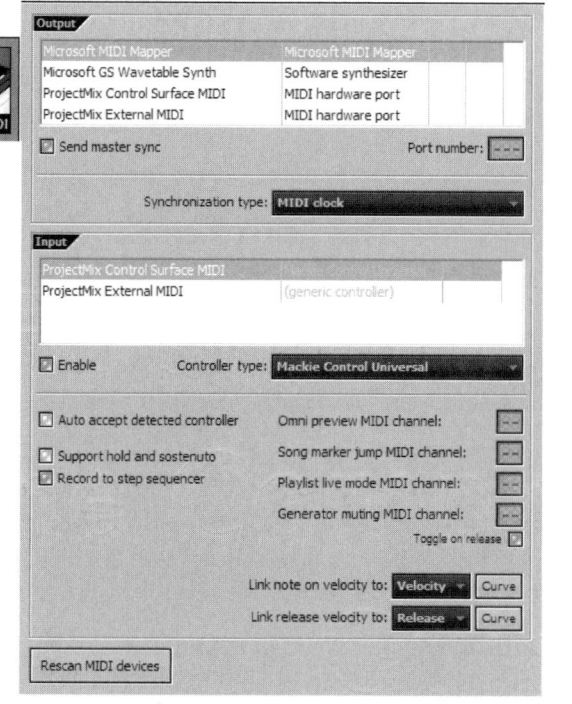

Figure 2.9 The Settings menu with MIDI selected.

find a better explanation of MIDI in Chapter 5, but for right now, you just need to know that this is the main station where MIDI gets passed around. At first glance you may see a large number of devices or none at all, depending upon your setup. Typically, if you have no MIDI devices hooked up, all you will see is Microsoft GS Wavetable Synth.

Output

The Output section of the MIDI settings (see Figure 2.10) is not as widely used as the Input section. Most of the time, someone will have a MIDI keyboard or drum pad that just needs to send in MIDI and turn it into sound using one of the plug-ins. This section covers those that need MIDI to speak to an external source. This would typically be used to make an external

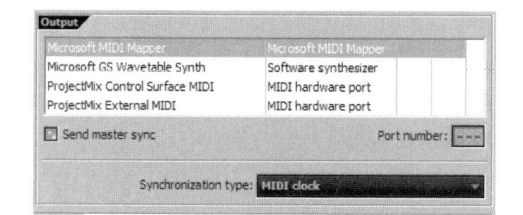

Figure 2.10 The Output section of the MIDI settings.

synth make noise, and that noise in turn can be played back into FL Studio. To set this up properly, just select your device from the Output menu and choose the port number on your device to which you want FL Studio to send data. The Send Master Sync button by default is not highlighted. This is if you want FL Studio to send a master sync signal to a MIDI device.

Note: For this to work, you need to navigate to Options > Enable MIDI Master Sync and make sure that it is checked!

The drop-down menu next to Synchronization Type is just for selecting what format of synchronization you want to use with your external device.

Input

The Input section is where you would set an external device to send MIDI into FL Studio. If you plan to play some music on a piano or drum pad that sends MIDI, this is your setup section! When your device is properly installed, plugged in, and—yes, I have to say it—turned on, it will appear in the Input window.

Within this section are an Enable button and a Controller Type drop-down menu, as shown in Figure 2.11. When you select your device, click Enable—this will tell FL Studio to start communicating with it. The Controller Type drop-down menu allows you to pick from a predefined list if there are more controls available on your device. If you see the device you are using, select it from the list, because this will ensure that the controls on your device closely match those in FL Studio. However, if it is a piano-style keyboard or drum pad, and you just want to control some virtual instruments, then the option Generic Controller will work fine.

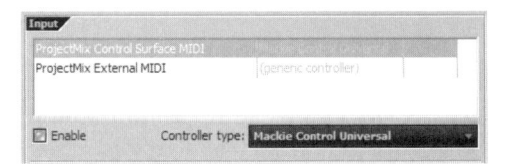

Figure 2.11 The Input section of the MIDI settings.

Controller and MIDI Channel Settings

This area contains some more advanced features that FL Studio has to offer and can be a great way to improve your workflow when you understand what they do (see Figure 2.12). When

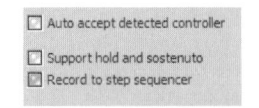

Figure 2.12 Miscellaneous options in the MIDI Settings window.

Auto Accept Detected Controller is enabled, it means that when you assign a control to a button, fader, or knob on your MIDI device, you will not be prompted to accept the change; it will map automatically. When using multiple MIDI controllers, it is best to leave this option disabled so assignments don't get incorrectly mapped. A great example of leaving this enabled is if your MIDI keyboard has faders and sliders, and it is the only device sending MIDI in, then you would leave Auto Accept Detected Controllers enabled so that you can quickly map faders on your keyboard to faders in FL Studio.

Support Hold and Sostenuto is an option that allows FL Studio to use foot-pedal messages to sustain notes played on a MIDI device. If you are using a foot pedal to add that extra layer of sound to your MIDI performance, then this option should be enabled. The last on/off button in the group is the Record to Stepsequencer option. This basically will record your performances directly into the Stepsequencer itself, rather than placing the notes on the Piano roll. Although you may find that you are able to work more quickly just using the Stepsequencer, this limits your flexibility, and I would just leave it disabled.

The next section (shown in Figure 2.13) is where your workflow can speed up immensely if you are using a MIDI keyboard. Omni Preview MIDI Channel allows keys on your MIDI keyboard to audition a channel from your Stepsequencer. Song Marker Jump MIDI Channel allows your keyboard to control where your song plays from based on markers that you place. Playlist Live Mode MIDI Channel will cause keys on your keyboard to audition patterns in the Playlist when you have Live mode selected. I will discuss Live mode alongside marker jumping and setup in Chapter 5. For now, just know that these settings cause your keyboard to perform speedy play-back and song navigation. Generator Muting MIDI Channel will make your keyboard keys mute channels in the Stepsequencer. You need to consult the manufacturer of your MIDI device to see how to set up MIDI channels. However, once you have done this, a great practical example would be to have these settings:

- Omni Preview: MIDI Channel 1

- Song Marker Jump: MIDI Channel 2

- Playlist Live Mode: MIDI Channel 3

- Generator Muting: MIDI Channel 4

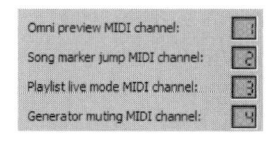

Figure 2.13 The MIDI control channel settings.

So with these settings in mind, suppose you have learned what each key does, or you might even have something taped to the keys or stickers to remind you of what each key will control. You will also need to know how to change MIDI channels on your MIDI device. If you are in the middle of a song, but you are getting writer's block, you can use these settings to speed up your creation. Suppose you have a pattern playing in the Stepsequencer that you like, but it is missing something. You have a few options of samples and tracks loaded into different channels in the Stepsequencer. With your keyboard sending MIDI out of Channel 1, you can play the pattern or section in the song that you want to add to and press keys on the keyboard to quickly listen to different options for adding to the music. Now if you need to hop over to a different part of the song, you can switch to Channel 2 on your MIDI keyboard and begin hopping over to different points in the song until you find the section that you want to work on. Now that you are in a different section, perhaps you want to layer some patterns on top of each other. With Live mode enabled and your keyboard sending out of MIDI Channel 3, now you can play different combinations of patterns that you have created in order to create something even fresher. However, suppose you get a new idea for a combination of channels from a pattern in the Stepsequencer, but it seems a little too busy, and something needs to go. With the keyboard sending out of Channel 4, now you can turn off channels quickly as the pattern loops and find which channels can be removed or muted.

Below these options is the Toggle on Release button (see Figure 2.14), which will tell FL Studio how you want buttons pressed on your MIDI controller to react with the virtual buttons and knobs inside the program. Basically, this means that buttons on your keyboard will act like on/ off switches in FL Studio (when Toggle on Release is disabled), forcing you to press once for on and again for off. Or, when the option is enabled, you press and hold for on, and as soon as you let go of the button, the switch will be off. One interesting use for this would be tapping a mute switch to create a manual stutter effect on a vocal. It's good to know where this switch is if you make a large number of manual changes to your sound.

Toggle on release ☑

Figure 2.14 The Toggle on Release button.

The final set of options (shown in Figure 2.15) contains the options for Link Note On Velocity To, Link Release Velocity To, and Rescan MIDI Devices. The Link Note On Velocity To option means that you are telling FL Studio how hard to play the notes that come in from your MIDI keyboard. When None is selected from the drop-down menu, all notes that come into FL Studio will be played at a constant velocity of 100. This can be useful if you are in need of droning notes that don't change volume, but typically the best option is leaving it on velocity, because this

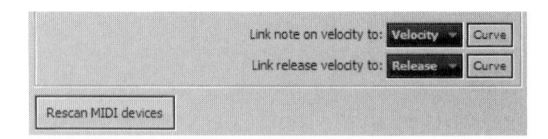

Figure 2.15 The Link Note On Velocity To, Link Release Velocity To, and Rescan MIDI Devices options.

means that however hard you play your keyboard is how hard the notes will register in FL Studio, with the MIDI scale running from 0 to 127. Mod X and Mod Y are options that can be selected when the velocity is controlled by a plug-in. Set the Mod X or Y curve on the plug-in and then select Mod X or Y from the menu, and the note velocity that is played on your keyboard will be dependent on the plug-in settings.

Link Release Velocity To refers to how fast or slow the velocity on a note will be released.

Velocity It's important to note that velocity is a value that determines the essential strength of the MIDI note. Although this is usually volume, velocity can also impact other factors, such as filter or overdrive effect. Many times, a note played at full velocity will sound very different that just the original note turned up in volume.

When the option is set to None, much like the Note On option, a fixed release velocity of 100 will be assigned to all incoming MIDI notes. Depending on the instrument that you are using, this could be beneficial if you needed the same feel on every instrument, but I suggest leaving this option on Release, because it will allow whatever you play on your MIDI keyboard to register in FL Studio exactly as you played it. The final option in the MIDI settings is Rescan MIDI Devices. Remember that if you opened up FL Studio before turning on your keyboard, usually it will not register the device until you click Rescan MIDI Devices. After doing this, the device should show up in the window. This button is also useful if the MIDI device randomly disappears, which I have seen when someone uses a loose USB cable.

Audio Section

This portion of the Settings menu can vary, depending on the interface and setup that you are using. This is the section that allows you to change and configure many options involving the device you are using to record and play back sound. You'll notice that in Figure 2.16, the Show ASIO Panel option allows you to bring up your interface's control panel. Most of the ASIO properties, including buffer and in/out routing, are set in the control panel of your interface. It is best to take a little time and figure out what each of the settings on your soundcard does, because this will help ensure that you have the proper settings all around. Regardless of how the control panel shows up on your computer screen (or in the Audio Settings window for some soundcards), the important thing to pay attention to is buffer. Sometimes it shows up as buffer size or buffer settings, but the idea is the same. This setting will tell your computer how much audio to load prior to playing in order to avoid skipping in the playback. This means that when you set a very low buffer (such as 128 samples or 256 samples), there is minimal audio preloaded, and things are played instantly. This is tied in with latency, which we discussed earlier (in the "Row, Row, Row Your Boat" analogy), and the lower you set the buffer, the lower the latency. So when you play a note on a MIDI keyboard, it records instantly and plays back instantly.

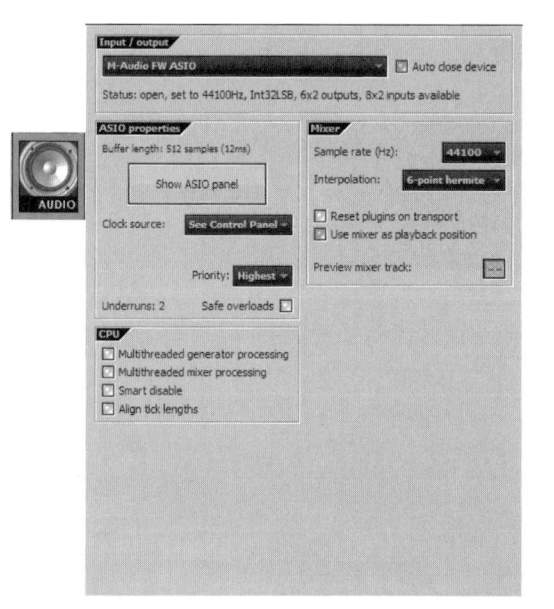

Figure 2.16 The Audio options settings.

So why not just place the buffer as low as it can go and make music? Because the computer you're using might not be able to handle the strain! It takes processing power to convert audio from the digital information inside FL Studio to the analog sound that we hear. It takes even more power when you record because the signal has to convert from analog to digital and then back to analog if you want to hear yourself while recording. If the computer can't make all the necessary conversions at the speed you want, it will start missing pieces of the conversion, and when it plays back, you will get pops and clicks in the audio or even total silence. If your computer can take the strain, I would insist on dropping the buffer to as low as 10ms so that everything runs in time and on point.

Buffer

- Low buffer = Fast audio response = Must have powerful computer

- High buffer = Latent (delayed) audio response = Better for slower computers

---

On the other end of things, a high buffer setting will allow audio to play with no audible pauses, but the response time will suffer. Imagine that you are recording your voice, and you have a high buffer set in the options. When you record the chorus and sing through the whole part, you will find that when played back, it doesn't match up perfectly because there was a delay in writing the music to the track. When the buffer is set to 2,048 samples, you will start to notice a delay because that amount of delay adds 47ms of delay to your sound. This means that it will take 47ms for you to hear a sound from the time a key is pressed on a MIDI keyboard to when it plays on your speakers or in your headphones. Also, if you set the buffer setting too high, then the computer will unnecessarily load too much audio into memory, and that can cause audio skipping as well. The best thing to do is to raise the buffer to a high setting, such as 2,048, and slowly lower the setting in increments until you hear audio skipping (if at all) and then raise it up one setting.

The common settings that you will see in the upper-left window of the audio settings are Priority and Safe Overloads (see Figure 2.17). Priority is similar to buffer because it affects how the computer will deal with the audio. When the Priority is highest, that means the computer will devote most of its attention to running the audio in the program. This is great to ensure no pops or clicks in the audio, but when you reach the maximum amount of CPU usage (the computer can't process information much faster), then you will see more freezing because the computer saves no processing power for the graphic portion of FL Studio, commonly called the GUI (*graphical user interface*). Lowering the priority will have the computer save room for other processes besides audio and prevent freezing. Again, this is one to test out, as a high Priority will give you better results.

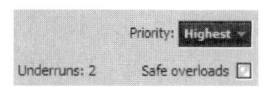

Figure 2.17   The common audio settings.

When activated, Safe Overloads acts in almost the same way and minimizes the chance for a lockup. When deactivated, it gives full attention to the audio. Underrun means that your sound-card is not keeping up with what you want FL Studio to play and is great for testing settings. If you have a high Underrun count, try changing settings to a lower buffer or spreading Priority around.

The Mixer tab, shown in Figure 2.18, houses some more audio options and begins with Sample Rate. The sample rate is the number of samples taken per second to properly reconstruct an analog signal in the digital realm. Noise, sound, and music that we hear are vibrations in the air, and we measure them in waves. For a computer to see these, a measurement is taken at different points of the waveform to re-create the waveform in digital form. Put simply, the computer needs to "draw" the sound for itself. The higher the sample rate, usually the more accurate the representation of the original sound you will get. If you are mixing a multitude of instruments and quality of sound is paramount, then using a high sample rate can be beneficial.

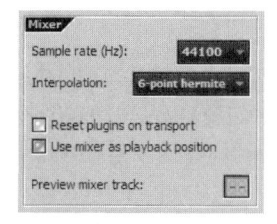

Figure 2.18   The Mixer tab of the Options menu.

I wouldn't bother going above 48,000, though, because most of the music that you will make still needs to be brought down to 44,100 so it can play on a CD.

Why 44,100 for a Sample Rate? Nyquist-Shannon Theorem! So why such a seemingly odd number for a sample rate as the standard for CDs to play? Well, the work of Harry Nyquist back in the early twentieth century paved the way for Claude E. Shannon to prove the theorem in 1949. They theorized that an analog signal can be perfectly replicated if it is twice the frequency of the highest frequency heard in the original sound. So this means that if you have a sound that resonates at 250 Hz, then it should be sampled at 500 samples per interval in order to reconstruct the waveform digitally. Rather than have a ton of sample rates floating around, they standardized CDs to run at 44.1k samples/interval. The reason for this is because humans hear roughly between 20 Hz and 20 kHz (20,000 Hz), so when the highest sample is doubled and given a little room, we get a 44,100 sample rate. This allows for a clean and error-free digital construction of the analog waveform.

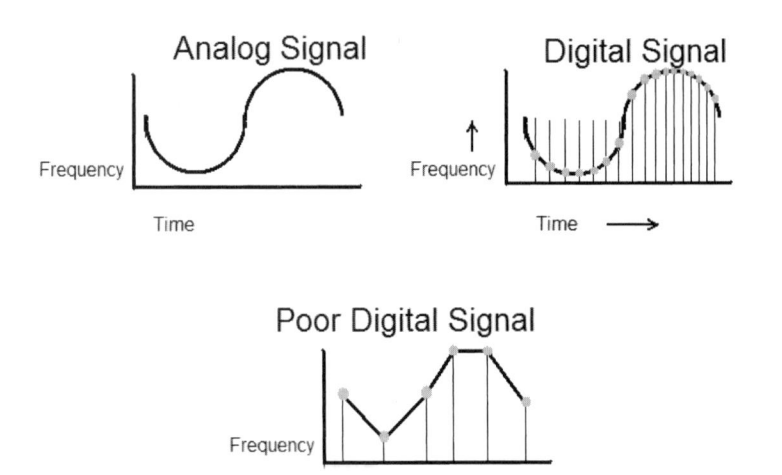

Figure 2.19 Here you can see how a properly sampled waveform looks in digital form and how, when poorly sampled, it draws an unclear picture of the waveform. When this happens, the audio sounds distorted or misses pieces of information in that sound and can even turn into silence!

Beneath Sample Rate is the option for changing your interpolation. For most PCs, you will find that the Linear setting works fine, but if you are in possession of a more powerful computer, try 6-Point Hermite, because this will produce higher-quality transpositions and pitch shifts when running the program. This means that when you stretch a sound to be higher pitched/speedier or compress it to be deeper sounding/slower, the resulting sound will not have artifacts (noises in the audio), whereas Linear can sometimes have high-pitched noises when a note is stretched to a great degree. The 64-512 Point Sinc settings are for extremely high-powered computers, for when a stretched sound must not have any unwanted sound. The problem is that the creators of FL Studio even mention that the 512 will most likely slow your computer to a crawl, if not freeze it completely! A good thing to know is that these controls are for real-time processing, as opposed to when you render your final mix, where the Interpolation controls are meant for the quality of the rendered audio, so this only affects how long it takes the song to turn into a playable MP3, Ogg, or WAV file.

It is important to know that these settings only affect notes that are transposed. Reset Plugins on Transport is an option that even suggests turning itself off when you hover over it with the mouse cursor. When this is checked, the plug-ins reset with the start and stop of a song, but this can cause pops in the audio when you're moving around quickly through a song. I would leave this particular option unchecked. Use Mixer as Playback Position is really only for when your Playlist song position cursor is jumping around or not doing what it is supposed to do. Preview Mixer Track allows you to set a different Mixer track aside from the master out (default) to hear audio previews from the Browser and metronome.

The final set of options, shown in Figure 2.20, help FL Studio perform better on the system that you have. Multithreaded Generator Processing and Multithreaded Mixer Processing both allow you to utilize a multi-core processor to its fullest by spreading out the processing over the different processors. Put simply, the work is spread out amongst the workers. Remember that this does not work when you have a single-processor computer. Smart Disable is one of the many awesome features that FL Studio offers. This turns off your plug-ins when they aren't being used and saves a good deal of CPU power. Even if you have a powerful computer, I see no reason to have this off, as I've noticed no problems when I've had it enabled. Align Tick Lengths can help third-party plug-ins run smoother.

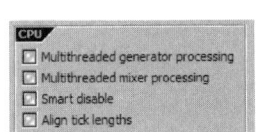

Figure 2.20 These toggle switches help your system run FL Studio better if available.

In the Settings menu shown in Figure 2.21, you can see a collection of general options. The first on the list, Associate Project Files with Application, is another in the family of questionable options. When you deselect this and try to double-click on a project when FL Studio is not open, Windows will ask you what program to use to open the project. When selected, Show Channel Activity Meters will show with light meters that there is signal coming into a channel in the Stepsequencer. Auto Name Channels will name the channels in the Stepsequencer based on the name of the audio clip or instrument you place in it. Auto Zip Empty Channels means that when you have unused channels with no data on them, they will be minimized. This is great if

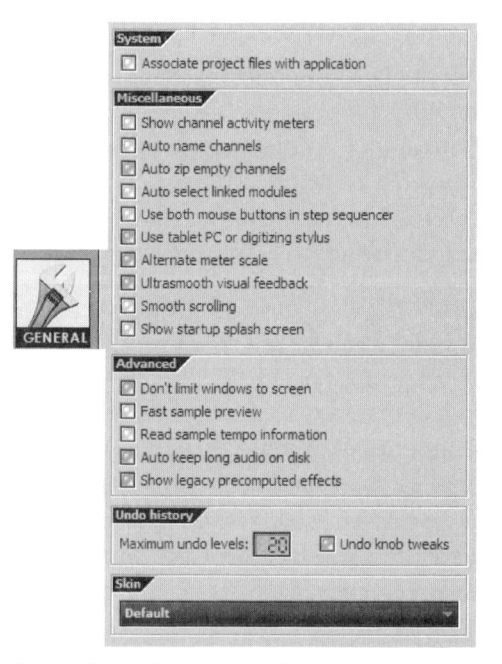

Figure 2.21 The General Settings options.

you have a smaller, single display screen and need a little more room to work. When enabled, Auto Select Linked Modules will make the plug-in selected highlight the particular track that it is using in the Mixer. If it is not selected, then you will be able to keep multiple windows open. Deselecting this option is great to see multiple effects running at once and easily navigate between settings. Use Both Mouse Buttons in Stepsequencer is great to have enabled because it allows you to left-click selections to make them disappear. This far surpasses the clumsiness of having to select an Erase tool and then go back to a Draw tool! Use Tablet PC or Digitizing Stylus should be selected when you are using a tablet PC. Alternate Meter Scale will change the peaks of your meters from –3 dB to –1.2 dB. Ultrasmooth Visual Feedback will improve the movement appearance of your song cursor, and on a similar thread, Smooth Scrolling works to improve the look of transitions when working in FL Studio.

In the advanced options, you'll find a few useful settings, including Don't Limit Windows to Screen. This is great when you have multiple computer monitor screens and would like to move windows around so that you can work effectively. Fast Sample Preview will play your selections from the Browser when previewing sounds or music instantly without using memory, but if the computer is unable to keep up with streaming that audio, you can get pops and clicks in the audio. Leave this enabled if you are not having trouble. Read Sample Tempo Information is for importing files that have been perfectly fit to match a tempo and that information is embedded in them. This is great for dragging and dropping samples into your project that don't need to be adjusted and automatically fit to the tempo of the song. Auto Keep Long Audio on Disk will force long pieces of music or sound to stream from disk instead of loading into RAM. This is handy when you have long pieces of music in a project, and you don't want to have to wait for the entire thing to load to open your project. Remember that this means if you select this and then jump into a project and hit Play, that long portion of audio may have not yet loaded. Show Legacy Precomputed Effects allows older projects with older effects to run in the new version of FL Studio.

As you may have guessed, this section leans toward helping FL Studio run better on your computer. The Maximum Undo Levels option is no exception, because it takes memory to remember what you have done in the project. Setting this higher will take up memory, but lowering it will reduce the number of times you can back up. Undo Knob Tweaks is the same idea, but now when you move faders or knobs on a plug-in, that is remembered *and* counted as one of your undo levels. The way I like to do it is to get to a certain point in the song where I am satisfied but not sure which way to go musically. At this point, I save the project under another name and continue working, so that if I get a different idea, I reopen the original and try a different musical path. The Skin setting will allow you to change the skins, but it can be a hassle when you are first learning the program. I would leave it on Default when you are first getting into the program.

The File section is a simple area that allows you to specify where certain files are located. In the upper section, you are able to select more folders that you want to appear in the Browser of FL Studio. This is nice when you have your samples, instruments, or loops on a different drive or hidden somewhere on your desktop, as you can see in Figure 2.22. The lower window is for telling FL Studio where you keep your VST plug-ins. If none of your plug-ins is showing up, this is a good place to check to make sure that FL Studio is looking in the right place! Just click the folder icon and point to the folder that contains the VST instruments, and everything should work fine.

At the bottom left of the Settings window, above the Bugs tab, is a button marked Project. Selecting this will bring up a final list of options available in this window. The first option is the Info button and allows you to alter information about the project, including title, genre, and author, and even offers a space to enter any pertinent information to the project. Underneath that is a place where you can include an online link to a website, and further down, the Show It on Opening option can be selected if you want this information to pop up when the project is opened. At the bottom of the list, there is information telling you when you started the project and, if you dare to look, how much time you have spent on it. The time spent can be reset by clicking the Reset Working Time button next to it.

The General tab of the project settings, shown in Figure 2.24, includes an option to place the data of your project in a specific folder, which is handy for keeping your own personal organizational style. The Time Signature section allows you to alter the meter of the song, so if you want that swing 3/4 sound, then this is where you would change it. Most songs are written in 4/4, but it is still a good idea to familiarize yourself with the feel of different time signatures. Timebase (PPQ) will tell FL Studio how precisely to measure when placing or editing audio. The

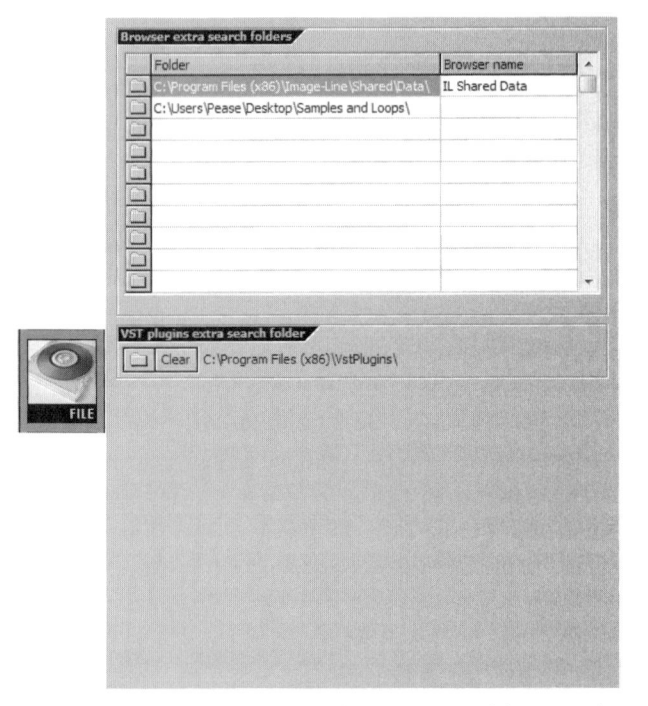

Figure 2.22   The Browser and Extra VST Folder Search settings.

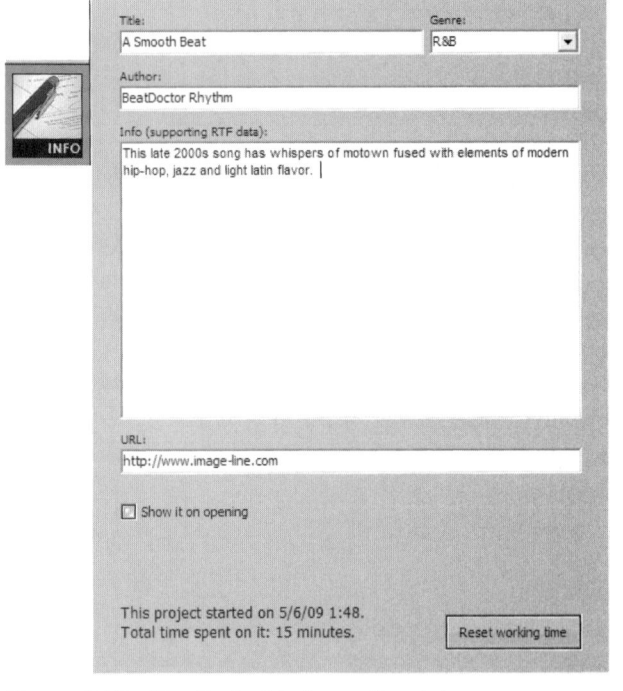

Figure 2.23   The Project Information tab.

Figure 2.24 The General Project settings.

default setting of 96 is good for almost any situation, and raising it will cause your computer to work harder and is only needed if you cannot place an audio clip or sound on the Playlist exactly where you want to. The Circular Panning Law option is something to test out, because this one comes down to endlessly debated preference. The basic idea is that with Circular Panning Law enabled, when you pan sound from left to right, the perceived volume remains the same, while when it is disabled, the sound gets louder when dead center, and the difference between center and panned hard right or hard left is much more noticeable.

Although some of these settings may seem a little foreign or oddly placed, the intention is to help you run FL Studio at its best. Taking the time to change and play with these settings will help you run projects with no glitches, but also give you a better understanding of what is going on behind the scenes, so to speak. In the next chapter, we'll look at the interface of FL Studio and go into what each menu does and why it can be helpful in producing great music with minimal effort.

3 FL Studio Menus and Interface

When I was first getting into music on the software side of things, I was paying my rent by DJing and serving tables. In both cases I had to use electronic equipment, and my success at that job was greatly influenced by my knowledge of how this equipment worked. As a server, the machine into which I entered orders was a fast-paced touch-screen machine that moved as quickly as I did. As a DJ, the equipment worked only as streamlined as I did, because if I just let it play, the next song would not mix itself in. In both cases I started with each piece of equipment at a novice level. However, the more I used each piece, the better I was able to enter food orders or freely mix in any request by the nearby dancing crowds.

This chapter is all about giving you the knowledge to successfully use the tools of the program. If you learn these tools and use them often, you will become faster and better able to create at your speed. The great thing about FL Studio's menus is that you can access your needed selection from many points, enabling you to work faster and choose what works best for you. In this section I will focus on what each piece of the interface does, how to access that menu, and why it would be helpful to your workflow and the creation process as a whole.

Menu Bar

The menu bar shown in Figure 3.1 is where most of the major functions occur and also where you can access settings and options. Some of these options are also available in different menus, which makes finding your desired selection easier when you're building a project. Some of these menus will seem familiar and can be reminiscent of other programs that you may have seen or used in the past. In my experience, understanding the menus in a program can greatly increase how quickly the ideas in your head drop into FL Studio. Imagine that you are just beginning a project, and the instruments you have chosen need to be grouped. Next, you need to copy the grouped patterns in order to make some adjustments in the copied version for a slightly differ-ent beat. This should be a fairly tall order, considering the time and work involved, but when every menu or quick key is familiar, you really can get those ideas out before they change or fade.

FILE EDIT CHANNELS VIEW OPTIONS TOOLS HELP

Figure 3.1 The menu bar.

File Menu

The File menu, shown in Figure 3.2, will be a common one if you have worked with most Windows programs and many Mac programs. It has most of the common functions for the overall project. New will open an empty project based on the template that you last used. For example, if you start with a hip-hop template, construct a song, and then decide to create a new one, when you choose New, that same hip-hop template will be used. Just below it, the New from Template option opens up a side menu containing templates that have effects, instruments, and routing all done for you (see Figure 3.3). Not every setting will be perfect when working on your own project, but the templates are great for achieving a good starting point. Take a moment to look through them to see what each one sets you up with, because you might find that the House template gives you the effects and settings that you are looking for in your hip-hop track and vice versa.

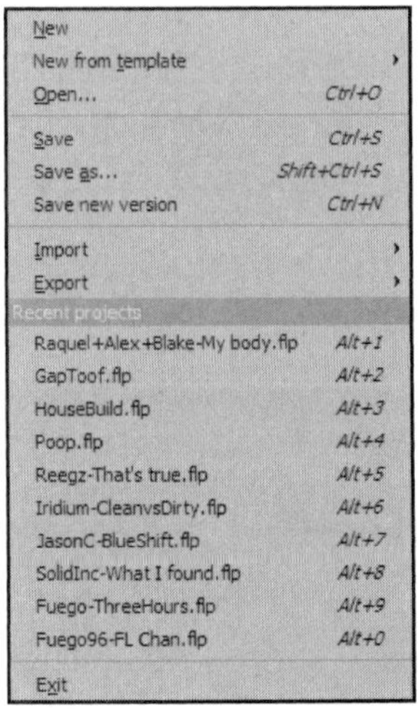

New	
New from template	▶
Open...	Ctrl+O
Save	Ctrl+S
Save as...	Shift+Ctrl+S
Save new version	Ctrl+N
Import	▶
Export	▶
Recent projects	
Raquel+Alex+Blake-My body.flp	Alt+1
GapToof.flp	Alt+2
HouseBuild.flp	Alt+3
Poop.flp	Alt+4
Reegz-That's true.flp	Alt+5
Iridium-CleanvsDirty.flp	Alt+6
JasonC-BlueShift.flp	Alt+7
SolidInc-What I found.flp	Alt+8
Fuego-ThreeHours.flp	Alt+9
Fuego96-FL Chan.flp	Alt+0
Exit	

Figure 3.2 The File menu.

The next option is to open a project, and when selected, it will prompt you to save the current project you are working on. The Explorer will open, and you will be able to navigate to where you saved your project and then open it up.

Save and Save As will both save the project. If you have already named the project, then selecting Save will just save the current project as is with the same name. If you choose Save before assigning a name to the project or you select Save As, then a window will pop up, allowing you to give

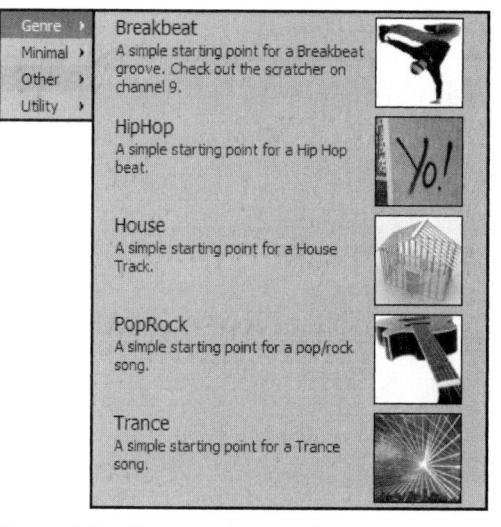

Figure 3.3   The template options.

the project a name. Save New Version essentially works the same as Save As, but it will save the project as the same name with a numerical value, so if it is the third time you have saved your HotBeat.flp project using the Save New Version option, it will be saved as HotBeat_3.flp. It is a good idea to save your projects with different names if you go in different directions with the music, but you don't want to trash your different versions. For example, if you make a hard house beat and want to try a breakbeat version that is choppier, save your project before changing anything, create the breakbeat version, and then choose Save As and rename it something easy to remember. Now you have a remix, and both versions can be edited separately. Aside from hard drive limitations, I always recommend saving large changes in a project as completely different projects to preserve what could be a masterpiece.

The Import option opens up to MIDI, where you can import MIDI data into your project, or you can import a beat to slice, which allows any WAV file that you have available to be sent into the project (see Figure 3.4). This works best with shorter audio files, because the longer ones have a tendency to act strangely and be cut up in odd places.

MIDI file...
Beat to slice...

Figure 3.4   The Import options.

The Export option contains all the choices you would need for sending your song out into the world (see Figure 3.5). We begin with Zipped Loop Package, which allows you to compress the file so that you can send it to a friend who has FL Studio so he can remix, master, or just listen. This option is also great for backing up your music, because it will contain all the audio files used in your project and settings necessary to play the project on a different computer with FL Studio. Just keep in mind that the plug-ins themselves will not be included in the file. Wave, MP3, and OGG are all for exporting your song so you can burn it on a CD or transfer it to your MP3 player.

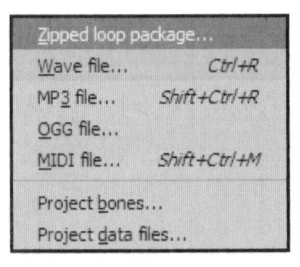

Figure 3.5 The Export options.

When you select the export as audio options (Wave, MP3, OGG), another window opens to reveal some saving options for your audio (see Figure 3.6). Under the Info area, make sure it says Song if you are trying to export your whole song! It will say Pattern if you are selecting a pattern to export, and these modes will switch with the overall selection of the project (in other words, if you are listening to it in Song or Pattern mode). Looping mode has to do with the audio

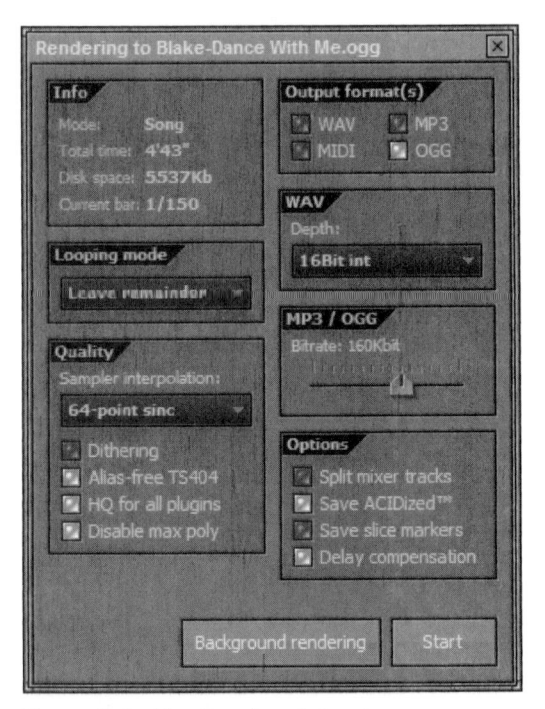

Figure 3.6 The Render dialog box.

samples that have audio effects that trail after the initial sound. With the default setting of Leave Remainder, the song will end when the effect is through producing sound. Cut Remainder will just end the song on the last bar without any effect trailing, so if there is a reverb, then that sound will die when the song stops. Wrap Remainder can be useful when you have a loop that trails or delays. The effect that happens after the loop itself will be placed on top of the next loop.

The Quality section (below Looping) will determine how good your audio sounds. No need to always wait for the 512-point export, because if you are just listening to a rough cut of a track, then Linear will be fine. However, if this is the final cut, I would use the highest for the final render.

Dithering is like adding noise to the music so that you don't notice any artifacts in the sound. FL defaults to leaving this off, so I would not select it unless you are finding odd quality with your exports, and it should only be used on the final render of your project. The last three I would leave selected, because Alias-Free TS404 prevents that plug-in from aliasing or creating strange noise, typically in the higher frequencies; HQ for All Plugins certifies that if the plug-in has that option (High-Quality), it will be used; and finally, Disable Max Poly tells the generators to ignore maximum polyphony settings for your channel. So if a piano is used and five keys are played, but the max amount of polyphony (notes that can be simultaneously played) is four, while the project is open, only four notes will play, but on that particular export, the fifth note will be heard.

Dither Dither has to do with the math behind drawing a waveform using points on a graph. When a sound is reproduced mathematically, there are points where audio is not drawn, because not every last piece of the sound can be perfectly drawn digitally (yet). So instead of having skips or awkward noise, dither breaks up the predictability of the noise in audio and spreads it across the frequency spectrum so that it ends up sounding similar to background hiss rather than a specific frequency that will grab your attention. A good way to think of dither is to take your hand with fingers spread and block your view to something in the room. Move your hand up and down, and you will see the rest of the image as your hand moves over it. So there is never any one point where you can see everything, but our awesome brains have the power to fill in the missing portions. This is similar to how dither fills in missing portions of audio using sound. As sound is added, the missing portions of the sound waves become white noise, so we don't notice that they are missing. Dithering is good in the final render when you reduce a song from 32- to 16-bit or compress it to an MP3.

The Output Format(s) section allows you to select how you want to export your project, and you will notice that the more selections you include, the larger the file size. This is because the file size is cumulative, based on your selections. The Depth selection will really only be changed when you are trying to put the export into a different software program for maximum sound quality. If you are trying to burn a CD or put the music on your phone or MP3 player, then use 16-bit. Bit rate very noticeably affects audible quality. Try exporting a 32-kilobit file, then a 320-kilobit one, and you should notice an impressive difference. This area is only affected when MP3 or OGG is selected as your export. A value of 160 kilobits will sound good for most situations involving the Internet or an MP3 player, but if you need quality, stick with WAV.

Split Mixer Tracks is great if you want each Mixer track in your project to become its own WAV file. This is awesome when you want someone to remix your project and you need to have individual pieces for them ready to go. Save ACIDized will add info to the WAV file for use with Sony Creative Software's ACID. Save Slice Markers places memory locations where notes are played, so a drum kit will be taken apart to individual sounds, and you will be able to use the individual slices. This is also great for the artist who wants to remix the beat but keep the same drum kit or even the same sounds! Delay Compensation is good for exporting full tracks, but if you are trying to create an exact start or end for your file, turn this off so you can get precise. Background Rendering is nice because it runs slower and allows you to do other things, but when it comes to audio, I say don't mess around. Render it at normal speed and go give your eyes a break from that computer screen!

The Export MIDI option is the section that you should be using when you're trying to capture MIDI data on a file. If you choose an audio format to export, you will ultimately have the option to export the MIDI as well, but stick with this way so you can separate the filenames and just call the MIDI data New Project MIDI or something to that effect. Exporting the project bones will take the settings and parameters you have selected for the project and save them but will not retain the actual sound files. Exporting the project data files will allow you to make or select a folder to drop all of the settings of your plug-ins and actual sound samples.

Below all this is a list of recent projects, which is one of my often-used selections. Much of the time I will find myself working on three projects at once, and this lets me hop between them without having to navigate to the proper folder.

Edit

The Edit section is fairly straightforward, but it is probably the most commonly used section in most music making (see Figure 3.7). Undo is the first option and will be used the most for

Undo playlist move clip	Ctrl+Z
Cut	Ctrl+X
Copy	Ctrl+C
Paste	Ctrl+V
Shift left	Shift+Left
Shift right	Shift+Right
Randomize...	Alt+R
Send to piano roll	Alt+P

Figure 3.7 The Edit menu.

nearly every musician. You will find it much easier to use Ctrl+Z than to navigate to this option every time, but either way this will go back one action that you have done. The amount that you can back up is determined by the settings you have, which were discussed in Chapter 2.

Cut, Copy, and Paste are familiar functions that can be used in many situations. In the Piano roll, you may have a group of notes that you like and want to copy for another section. This is where you would use Copy after selecting the desired notes. Then you can paste them in a different part of the song. Again, I find that using the quick keys for these (Copy: Ctrl+C, Cut: Ctrl+X, Paste: Ctrl+V) is much easier and will keep your workflow moving along.

Shift Left and Shift Right will move the notes in your Stepsequencer one space to the left or right. I love this feature, because when I am building a beat, sometimes the beat is perfect, but it's not starting at the right point. With the shift over, the beat created will just move one way or another, taking the last note to the beginning or vice versa.

Randomize will help with that writer's block by playing a random assortment of notes that can be manipulated from the resulting pop-up window (see Figure 3.8). Send to Piano Roll will take the notes that you plugged into the Stepsequencer and place them on the Piano roll. This lets you fine-tune the different notes and their velocity, pitch, and many other parameters. I'll deliver plenty of information on the Piano roll later in this chapter.

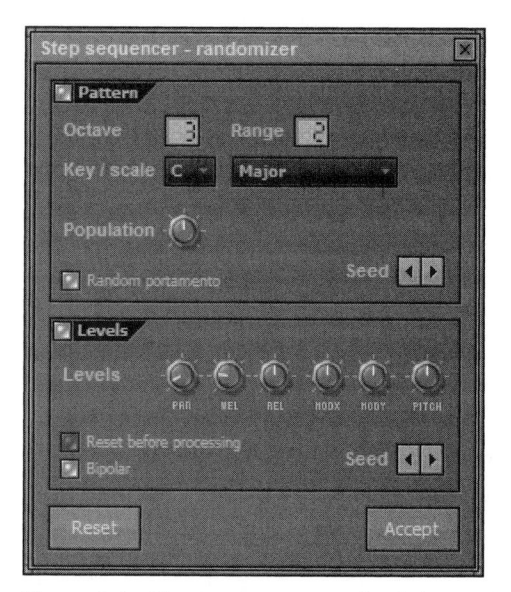

Figure 3.8 Here you can see all of the options available for the Randomize menu. Try getting something that sounds good to you and then send it to the Piano roll. There you can manipulate each note individually.

Channels

This area, shown in Figure 3.9, is great for adding, changing, and removing channels in your Stepsequencer. Add One will allow you to choose from a variety of options, including automation, audio clips, and even instruments. Beat makers, this is where you choose FPC to build your groove! We will get much more in depth into the different plug-ins and what they do later on in Chapter 6, "Instrument and Generator Plug-Ins." The remaining options will affect the channels that you have selected in the Stepsequencer, so pay attention when choosing these options, because even if you are working on the notes in the Piano roll of your bass and you have piano selected in the Stepsequencer, the piano is what will be affected by what you select in this menu. Clone Selected and Delete Selected do exactly as they say and can be useful when you have the perfect hook for a chorus, but you want to change a few things in the Piano roll for the ending of your song. Simply clone the channel containing the portion that you want to work with, and you will still have the original, but now you can mess around with the clone without affecting the original. Keep in mind that the notes do not get copied; only the instrument, routing, and settings do, so if you want the same notes, just copy them from the original Piano roll into the Piano roll of the cloned channel. Move Selected Up and Move Selected Down will move the channels around through the Stepsequencer.

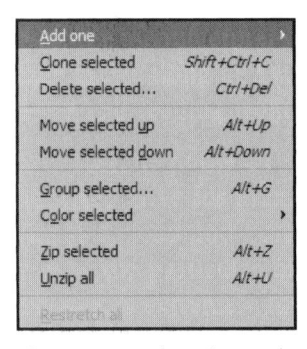

Figure 3.9 The Channel menu.

The last set of options is for all of you who like running a tight ship! I have found great headache relief in the form of organization during my years of using different programs. Especially with this program, where channels can become too numerous for even the largest computer monitor, Group Selected allows you to put different channels that have things in common in a group. If you have a hi-hat, kick drum, crash cymbal, and snare hit, you can select them all and group them. A prompt to name them will pop up, and you can name them anything you like, but in the interest of organization I suggest sticking with Drums.

Coloring your channels is next for those who find color coding things easier (or more pleasing to the eye). Gradient will create a flow between two colors based on the tracks selected. Keep in mind that if you select only one track and then select Gradient, all tracks will become selected, and once you change it, you cannot simply undo it. You have to actually go back through and re-color each track as you had it. If you like, you can even add icons to each track as you see fit, so your vocals can have a picture of a mic, and the drums can have a picture of a drum for easy identification.

Zipping the channels will just make them skinny and keep them in view but out of your way. You can click them anytime to bring them back to full size individually or unzip all of the channels. Restretch All allows you to re-stretch your audio when you have tempo changes and it is automated. If you stick to a solid beat without switching up, this will remain grayed out.

View

Hopefully, as you get better with using FL Studio, the menu shown in Figure 3.10 will not even be needed, because it contains the options for selecting the different windows that FL Studio has to offer. The first five can all be accessed using the F5 through F9 keys, and you will find that pressing these is much easier than going into this menu every time. Channel settings can be accessed here, but clicking on the desired channel will produce the same result and is much quicker.

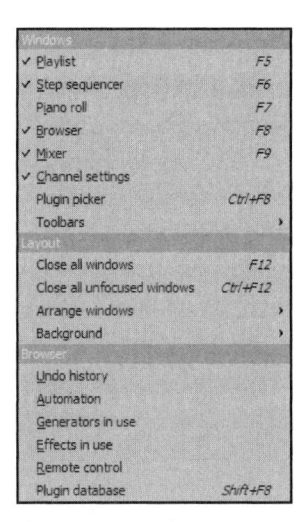

Figure 3.10 The View menu.

The Plugin Picker is a great way to choose a needed generator (instrument) or effect, and it is visually stunning! Try it by pressing Ctrl+F8. The Toolbars section will tell you which windows you should be able to see, including the unselected hint bar, which I find can be nice to have when learning the program because it will tell you what everything you hover over does, as well as tell you where your cursor is when hovering over the Playlist.

The Layout portion will affect how the windows look, including the background of the program. The first option should be placed into memory—F12. This will close all windows so you can open the ones that you want to work with. This is nice when there are effects and generators taking up all the space on your screen, and you need to clear the madness. If you are working on one thing and you want everything to close aside from that particular window, then press Ctrl+F12, and it will leave open the window that you have selected and get rid of all of the other clutter.

Arrange Windows gives you the option to place all of your windows back to the default setting (Shift+Ctrl+H) if you have moved windows so much that nothing looks familiar or Alternate, which simply places the windows in different positions. Outside Bottom Taskbar will make FL Studio sit beneath your Windows taskbar, and Save Current Arrangement will remember your window placement the next time you open FL Studio.

The Browser section of the View menu will open up the selected parameters in the Browser menu so you can view your undo history, the automation used, and even the effects and generators that you use.

Options

Figure 3.11 shows the Options menu, where you will find the setup for much of your project, and most of these were thoroughly discussed in Chapter 2. To quickly access these you can press F10, and while the option for pressing F11 is there, it is not necessary because F10 will open up the option to get to the same menu as pressing F11. The switches control whether each option is on or off. I will explain these switches a little further in the chapter, in the "Main Controls" section. Because these switches are on the main screen and they are easy to see, you will not typically use this menu.

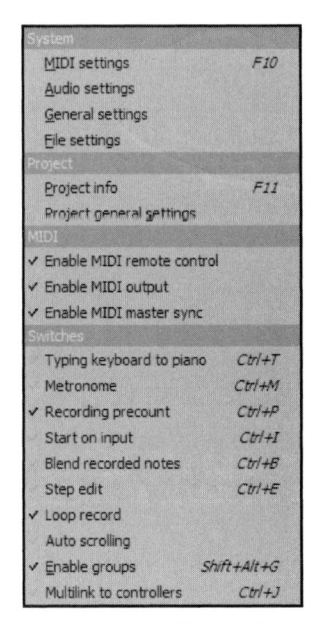

Figure 3.11 The Options menu.

Tools

This menu, shown in Figure 3.12, has an array of helpful options when working with your project. The first that shows up is Browser Smart Find. This is great for when you know part of a sound's name or an instrument that you can't quite spell. For example, if you were looking for a glockenspiel (specific bell) sound, you could just type "glock," and it will navigate through all the files in the Browser that have "glock" in the name. When the Smart Find is active, you can press F3 to cycle through the different items that appear in the Browser. F2 will reverse the direction of the found files in case you pass over the one you were looking for. One-Click Audio Recording will set you up to record into the Playlist or into the Edison recorder when you have Producer Edition or higher. We will look more closely at audio recording in Chapter 4, "Recording Audio."

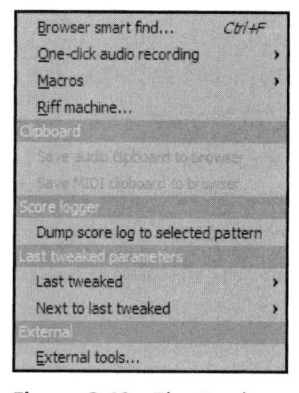

Figure 3.12 The Tools menu.

The Macros option (see Figure 3.13) branches out to reveal options for renaming the current pattern and jumping to the next empty pattern, but I think you will find the F2 shortcut for renaming is much quicker. As for jumping to the next pattern, if you are hovering over the pattern with the mouse, just use that, but if you have a ton of windows open, F4 will also jump to the next pattern in the Stepsequencer. Panic can come in handy more often than you think it would, as there are many effects and different clips that like to continue playing after

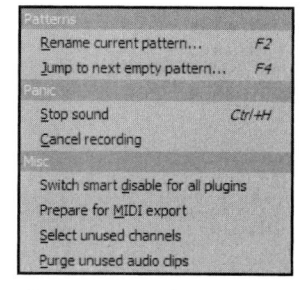

Figure 3.13 The Macros menu.

you press Stop. The Panic macro is Ctrl+H, and this will stop all audio, including clips that play past when you choose to press Stop. My take on this, though, is that if you are trying to stop it quickly, a macro is not the way to go. Luckily, pressing the Stop button twice does the same thing. The Cancel Recording option will stop and erase a recording while getting rid of the WAV file that is created as well. This is meant for when you have a bad recording that you know you don't want, but I would stay away from using this, because piecing together from different takes is a great way to remember different ways something can be sung or played.

Smart Disable for All Plugins is something that I recommend using regardless of your computer's power, because it turns off plug-ins when they are not in use. This will make everything run much more smoothly. There is also a global option for this in the Options section (F10), which we discussed earlier, and many plug-ins have their own Smart Disable option. Using the global Smart Disable either here in the Tools or in the Options (F10) menu will make everything more responsive, but be aware that issues can arise when using third-party plug-ins, so turn this off if you experience problems.

Prepare for MIDI Export will turn all your channels into MIDI out channels. This is a great, speedy way to have MIDI out ready to go, *but* it will turn *all* of your channels into MIDI out and get rid of the channels that you may not want to change. I don't recommend using this option unless you are familiar with MIDI and that is specifically what you are trying to do with your project. Select Unused Channels can be useful when you want to clean up your project. You can select this, and any channels that do not contain notes will be removed. So when the project is at a good point, and you think you are ready to put it on a CD or send it to a mastering studio, you can clean up the look of the project with this option. Purge Unused Audio Clips works in the same fashion, and any audio clips that are not being used in the project will be removed.

The Riff Machine (Alt+E when inside the Piano roll) is the jackhammer that breaks writer's block! This awesome little option will give you something new every time (see Figure 3.14). When it opens, the Riff Machine comes to the front, and just behind it is the Piano roll for the notes created. Upon opening, the Riff Machine will start playing a random series of notes from a randomly selected instrument. This is definitely something to explore and utilize, because you can even specify the key of music and the range of notes. In exploring this option for myself, I put together a short house beat using the notes arranged by the Riff Machine. The only thing I did differently was change the instrument that the channel was using, and I got the sound that I didn't even know I was looking for.

The first thing you see when opening the Riff Machine is Step 1. Ultimately, you could use all eight steps for fine-tuning the exact sound you are looking for without even using the Piano roll! The first step deals with the actual progression of notes as the section goes from start to stop. Remember that if there is no variation in the parameters you select from any of the steps, then there will be no change when turning the knobs for those parameters, because they deal with variation. So if the notes are only dead center with no panning, then when you move the knob for panning variation, nothing will happen because there is no left/right to vary from.

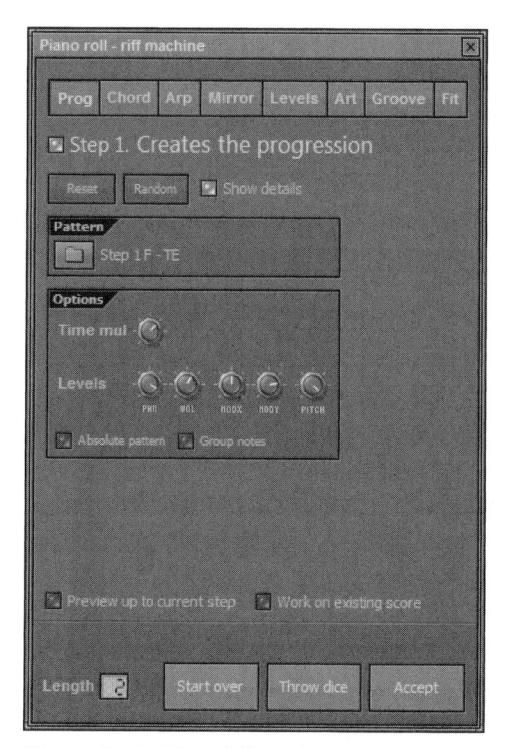

Figure 3.14   The Riff Machine.

Step 2 deals with turning single notes into chords that play in the Piano roll. This step worked for me when I started with a new Piano roll open and drew a few single notes inside. Then I opened the Riff Machine with the quick key command Alt+E and chose the options Work on Existing Score (located at the bottom of the Riff Machine window) and Preview Up to Current Step so that no other steps were affecting the notes I made. As you go deeper into other steps, different parts of the Riff Machine will change your note placement on the Piano roll.

The third step is the Arpeggiator function and is where you get your stabby-sounding synth leads. This option takes the notes, cuts them up to your liking, and then quantizes them to the grid that you've set up for that particular Piano roll. By default, the grid will be the same as your global settings for your project, and this will be fine. Remember that if there is no grid set and it is on None, then the Riff Machine won't know where to put the notes. This section can be great for turning long, boring notes into chopped-up notes that can add great rhythm to a song.

The fourth step will just take the notes you have and mirror them vertically or horizontally. When some notes that you have laid down are close but not quite there in the Riff Machine, try flipping them!

The fifth step is what will make those notes sound like they were played by a professional keyboard player. Most of us are not robots (although I have doubts about some of my elementary teachers), and we play notes with slight variations in velocity, which in this case will translate to volume. With this step you can add variation to the notes to make them hit slightly harder or softer and produce a range of velocity. The panning is great for giving the synth that "all over the room" sound. Articulation refers to note length and is the sixth step in the Riff Machine. This goes hand in hand with Step 5, because while the strength with which notes are hit and left/right panning will humanize a performance, so will how long a note is played. This option will vary each note length slightly, so that each one is not ending at the exact same time.

The seventh step has to do with how close to the grid the notes stay. Again, this will give that realistic sound to it, because the notes will not play perfectly on each grid value; they will bump slightly over, depending on your settings.

The final step in the Riff Machine is the Fit option and will tell the notes where they are allowed to play. This is helpful when you have an artist playing in a specific key and he needs notes confined to that key. You can also choose starting and ending points for how high and how low you want the range of notes playing to be contained in. So if you only want notes to go from C3 to F#4, then just select that range on the keyboard. If you want a specific scale played, then select that scale from the drop-down menu next to the Key option, where you can choose what key you want the notes to be played in.

Help

As the name would suggest, this is the menu where you can find helpful information about FL Studio and its affiliates (see Figure 3.15). The first area is the Contents section, and in my opinion, it should be one of the most used windows for you when learning or even mastering the program. There are so many capabilities in FL Studio, and this is a great way to pinpoint what you need to find. I never access the Help Contents this way, though, because the quick key (F1) is easy to remember and has a feature that many applications do not—the Help menu opens to the section of FL Studio that you have open. For example, if you are making notes on the Piano

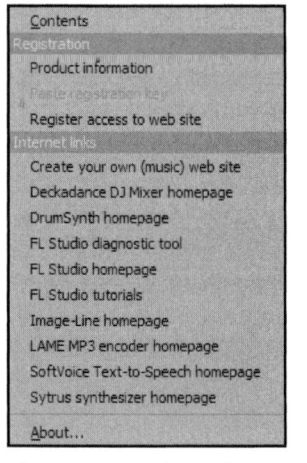

Figure 3.15 The Help menu.

roll, and you're wondering how to edit something in that window, press F1 while the Piano roll is selected, and the Help menu will automatically open to the Piano roll section! Image-Line's Scott Fisher did a fantastic job on the FL Studio manual, and using the built-in manual, you can search keywords and browse an index of topics related to the manual.

Under the Contents option in the Help menu are your registration options for activating your copy of FL Studio. Here you can paste a key if you have a boxed version or access the Internet to activate a demo version of the software.

The Internet Links section is loaded with plenty of helpful links that can answer questions regarding MP3 encoding and different generators and plug-ins and will even point you to online video tutorials.

Main Controls

Figure 3.16 shows the main panel that you will see without the need to travel through menu lists. All of these buttons or switches can be accessed right away, and when they are open, they can be viewed anytime as long as there are no plug-ins or other windows blocking them. This is similar to your car's speedometer, tachometer, and oil levels, because in both cases, the dials let you know what is happening with your car/project. We will take an in-depth look at what each knob does so that you have a full understanding of the knobs' functionality and how they can be used to successfully make music. It is important to note that most of these windows can be moved around to your liking, but we will focus on the default placement so that it is easier to find the sections I reference.

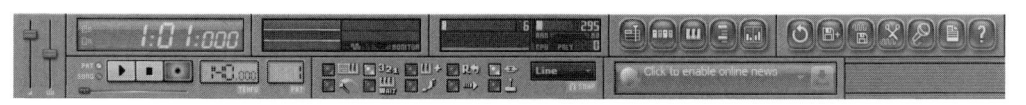

Figure 3.16 In the driver's seat with the main controls of FL Studio.

The first things that will catch your eye are the two buttons that cannot be selected or adjusted (see Figure 3.17). The top one is MIDI/Audio Sync Beat and will change color when FL Studio is sending master sync data (located in the MIDI settings of the Options menu, F10), depending on what is happening in the song. This can act like a visual metronome and will blink green at every beat and blink blue at every start of a bar. The problem is that it can also waste CPU power, so unless you are utilizing the Send Master Sync option, it should be disabled, and you will not see the colors change with the tempo of the project.

Figure 3.17 The master controls.

Just underneath is the MIDI Input Activity indicator that will tell you when MIDI information is being received by FL Studio *and* will tell you if that MIDI information is connected to anything. If you are playing notes on a keyboard, and an instrument is being triggered by the MIDI keyboard in FL Studio, then you will get a red blink every time you hit a key on the keyboard. On the other hand, if you have a MIDI keyboard that has some slider controls, and you have not mapped those to anything, the light will still blink, but it will blink green, letting you know that the program is getting your MIDI information, but you haven't assigned that slider to anything. We'll talk more about MIDI and assigning sliders in Chapter 5, "Recording and Using MIDI."

To the right of these two light indicators are sliders for the master volume and master pitch of the song. These are global, meaning that everything is affected when you move these sliders. The volume control will quickly adjust the overall volume of your project, but the volume adjustments should be made with the Mixer (F9). The master pitch will bend everything up or down in pitch so it will sound lower or higher, depending on which way you move the slider. The advantage to this is that the speed does not change, so if your song is slightly out of tune in general or with another project that you need it to be tuned to, you can gradually pitch it to match. Remember that this slider affects everything in your project, so if you are looking to change the pitch of just one channel or track, you should not use this control.

Moving along to the right of the master sliders, we come to the transport and time display (see Figure 3.18). The options available in these windows will be among the most common that you will find yourself using in FL Studio. The time display will show you the position of your cursor in the Stepsequencer or the Playlist. The buttons inside the time display on the left of where the numbers are allow you to switch between a bar/beat view, where each number will tick with the beat, a step display that shows each step from the Stepsequencer, or a simple time display that will show you in minutes and seconds where you are in the song. These modes can be toggled by clicking the buttons themselves or simply by clicking the numbers in the time display. Personally, with all of the advantages this program has, I would leave it in the bar/beat display or the step display so the numbers run with the song's tempo. I would only use the time display if I were planning to score a film or writing music that has no specific tempo to adhere to. This will *not* change the tempo or any other settings of your song, so viewing it in minutes/seconds will not affect how the song sounds, but it can make it more difficult to work with.

Figure 3.18 The transport and time display.

The transport panel lies below the time display and will control many aspects of your project. The Pattern (Pat) and Song buttons are the heart and soul of FL Studio and what really make it stand out as a recording application. These are the switches that will alternate playback of your project between using the Stepsequencer pattern that you have selected in the Stepsequencer

(Pat) and the sounds put together in the Playlist (Song). The quick key for this is the L key and will alternate between the two when pressed. This is a fantastic way to jump between what you have in your Playlist and something new you may be putting together in the Stepsequencer. Play and Stop are next to that and are very self explanatory, but it is good to remember that pressing Stop twice will stop all music, and pressing Play again after the song is playing will pause the music. While the spacebar is frequently used for stop and start, if you want the music to pause, the quick key is Ctrl+spacebar. The Record button is a little different, and when you click on it, you will see a new set of options unless you disable the pop-up by choosing Don't Ask This in the Future.

The menu that comes up from clicking (see Figure 3.19) will allow you to record audio into Edison, into the Playlist, only the automation and score, or everything, or it will show you a window that will give you a little extra help. Keep in mind that you can set a recording filter (what you want to record) by right-clicking on the Record button. However, I recommend using left-click so that you don't accidentally set a filter incorrectly, record only automation, and miss that perfect vocal take.

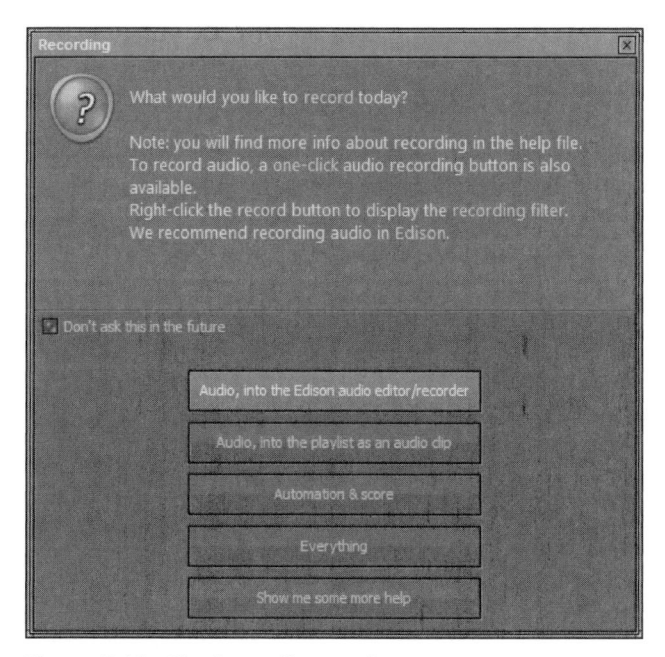

Figure 3.19 The Recording options.

Recording into Edison basically means that you are saving the audio into a plug-in and are able to manipulate it within Edison itself. Recording into the Playlist will drop your audio directly into the Playlist for you, and you can edit and adjust it there. Recording automation and score will allow you to record the notes played either on a MIDI keyboard or on your typing keyboard and any automation changes, such as panning or volume. This is great for when you have a vocal take that you want to freehand move around from left to right, and you set the recording to automation and score. Then you will only be recording the panning changes on the vocal. We will look more closely at recording audio in Chapter 4 and recording score and automation in Chapter 5.

Just beneath the Play and Stop buttons is the Song Position button. Although small, this is a great way to quickly navigate through your session. This is useful for those of us who have too much equipment on the computer desk, and we have allocated a space for the mouse that is far too small. This button can quickly get you anywhere in the song regardless of its length, and you won't have to lift the mouse five times just to get the song position marker all the way to one part of the song.

The Tempo field lies just to the right of the Record button and will tell you the master tempo on which your song is based. Typing in a tempo *can* change the tempo of everything in your song, but it can also be a headache waiting to happen. Typically, you will want to set the tempo early on and stick with it. If you only have a beat that you made using the Piano roll and sequencer, and you have not yet recorded audio, however, you will be able to change this tempo number, and everything will automatically change with it.

Audio will not automatically stretch with the song unless Stretch Audio is selected (not the default setting), so that great guitar part you recorded will not initially fit with the rest of the song. Fear not! There are ways around this, and you can stretch the audio to fit, which we will get into later in the recording chapters. For now, just know that a good idea is to set a tempo and stick with it. The final area is the pattern selector and allows you to navigate to different patterns in both the Stepsequencer and the Playlist.

In Figure 3.20, you can see the peak and monitor meters in action, and their job is to give you a visual image of the music that is playing. The monitor on the left will give you a basic idea of how the music is responding at different frequencies when in Spectrum mode, so when the bass is heavy, the left side will be jumping. The other option for the monitor is Oscilloscope, which acts in the same way but instead creates waves on one or two lines to represent the frequency response. Although there is an actual button to change between these two modes and off, you can avoid buying the glasses you didn't know you needed (due to the miniscule size of the buttons) and just click the monitor itself, and it will go through the different modes.

Figure 3.20 The output monitor panel.

To the right is the peak meter, and you can use your mouse to roll over the jumping meter (going left to right) and see how close to zero it is at. If the peak meter is hitting the far right and turning the line after it yellow with a red top, that means the music is clipping. Clipping is bad in the digital world because it flattens the waveform and makes the sound distorted (see Figure 3.21). If you see this, then you need to turn down some volume levels. When the song is peaking at −5 to −3 dB (in FL Studio) at its loudest, you should have no unintentional distortion.

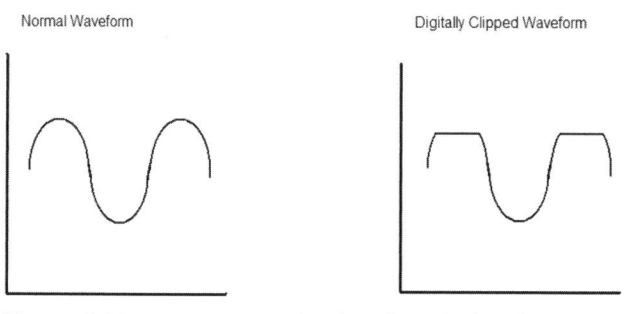

Normal Waveform   Digitally Clipped Waveform

Figure 3.21 You can see in the digital clip that the waveform flattens, and to us it sounds like distortion.

The memory usage area shown in Figure 3.22 is great for those who need to keep an eye on how hard their computer is working to run FL Studio. If you set up everything properly, and your computer is up to speed, then this section may not interest you, and you can easily remove it. (Right-clicking in an empty area where the toolbars are located will give you the option to choose what you would like displayed.) However, it is nice to have for reference when you have a project working that is using a large number of audio clips. When these clips add up, they start using FL Studio's available memory, so if you have a large number of takes that make a drum track, you can consolidate the audio clips into one stereo mix to free up some memory. If you find that your computer is struggling and using too much CPU power, Smart Disable Plugins can help, but you could always render the sound coming from the generator into a stereo track— then turning off the plug-in will free up CPU. Keep in mind that doing this adds more audio tracks to the project and will affect your memory usage.

Figure 3.22 The memory and CPU meters.

Many of the shortcuts in this section are there for your convenience if you happen to forget the quick keys, and some have extra features aside from single quick key actions. I will deal with both because the first half of the shortcuts have quick keys assigned to them that I suggest learning and using. From left to right, the shortcut panel buttons will open or focus on the Playlist, Stepsequencer, Piano roll, Browser, and Mixer (see Figure 3.23). These are fairly easy to remember because the quick keys are (in respective order) F5 through F9 to access the same windows.

Figure 3.23 The shortcut panel.

The second half of the shortcuts menu has some familiar and not-so-familiar options. Undo is the first option and will only undo the last action you did. Say, for example, you erase a piece of audio and then change a note in the Piano roll. If you press Ctrl+Z twice, the note you changed in the Piano roll will go back to its original position, so clicking Undo a third time will only place the note back to where you didn't want it and leave the piece of audio removed. By pressing Ctrl+Alt+Z, you will keep going backwards through your actions, rather than toggling between your latest changes. You can also access this Undo option from the Edit menu. You can go into the undo history using the Browser, too, for a quick overall look that allows you to undo to a certain point with one click.

Next to the Undo option is the Save As button, which will give you the option to name the project. This button also acts as a trainer, and it will train you to save your projects because it flashes every five minutes until 10 minutes have gone by without a save, and then it will flash every 30 seconds. Some may find this annoying at first, but if you get used to saving your project after every recording, you will not notice the flash. Personally, I find it far more frustrating to get a perfect take or an awesome random pattern from the Riff Machine, only to have the computer crash and lose everything up to the last save point (gulp—if there was one!).

Continuing to the right is the Render as Audio File button, which will open the dialog box, allowing you to save your project in many formats.

The next button on the extended shortcut list is very useful and has a few interesting abilities. The Open Audio Editor button, when clicked, will simply open Edison, allowing you to manipulate your audio recordings as needed. It is good to know that the program that opens can be changed using the External Tools dialog box (Tools > External Tools), where you can set the path to the program that you want to open with the Open Audio Editor button or even the program you want to open when FL Studio opens. When you right-click this button, it will open a new instance of Edison for when you have multiple audio recordings that need to be adjusted. A great feature of this button is if you have an audio clip that you would like to adjust specifically, then you can simply drag it over this button, and Edison will open up with the audio clip already loaded!

To the right is another way to record with one button, and if you find yourself in this menu a great deal, then you might find it useful, but using the Record button to record tends to be the most intuitive way to go about things, in my humble opinion.

The next shortcut opens up the project info, where you can change the name and details of your project. The final button opens the Help menu.

We are always told to not push the shiny red button, but in this case it will allow you to change many things having to do with recording in your project (see Figure 3.24). We will start with the top row, going left to right, and then finish with the bottom row, also moving left to right. The first option is one of my favorites, and I am surprised that many more recording software programs do not adopt this function—Typing Keyboard to Piano Keyboard (Ctrl+T); see Figure 3.25. This is

Figure 3.24 The recording panel.

Figure 3.25 The Typing Keyboard to Piano Keyboard layout.

a great option for those of us who do not have a MIDI keyboard handy or are traveling and come up with an idea on the road. When this is selected, your typing keyboard will play notes that can be recorded onto the Piano roll. They will register note pitch and note length, but volume will not change, because most typing keyboards are not pressure sensitive. When you right-click this option, you can set the base octave that you would like your keys to play, and the layout can change between piano and Janko. Unless you own a Janko keyboard, you will leave this on piano.

Next to Typing Keyboard to Piano Keyboard is the Count-In option (Ctrl+P), which will click a designated amount of times before recording begins. This is essential when tracks are perfectly on beat, and you need to get that groove and tempo going in your head before you start recording. Right-clicking this button will allow you to set how many bars you want to click off before recording begins.

Blend Recorded Notes is the next option and will cause newly recorded notes to blend with the ones that are already there, so when you almost have a beat that you are working on and you want to add each part individually, this is a good way to do it.

The next option works in conjunction with blend notes because this button will allow looping of a segment. I am not a good piano player, but I am good enough to play each hand in different recordings. With loop enabled and blend notes, you can play the chords with your left hand and then allow the pattern to loop, and when it comes back around, you can layer the extra notes in to make a full sound, as though a professional pianist is playing.

As we discussed earlier, you can group notes and clips together by using the quick key Alt+G when patterns or notes are selected. Note and Clip Grouping (Shift+Alt+G) is a global command that will turn the groupings on or off. This is handy when you have a group of notes on which you need to lower the volume, but then you want to change the panning of one note in the group and don't want to affect the rest of the notes in that group.

The final button on the top row is the Global Snap selector, and this drop-down menu gives you options for setting how you want your clips and MIDI data to be placed in the project. When you have Main selected in the Piano roll, Playlist, and event editor, then the selection made in the Global Snap selector will dictate where the notes are placed on the grid when moved around. For example, if you have an audio clip on your Playlist, and the Global Snap selector is set to 1/2 beat, then you can only move that audio clip every 1/2 beat, and you cannot move it in between. This is nice when you just need to drop a drum beat into the Playlist, and you don't want to mess around trying to make sure that you have it exactly on the bar that you want it. Aside from None, Line, and Cell, the selection you make here will also affect the MIDI notes that you play in the Piano roll. If you do not have perfect beat or timing, you can have FL Studio do the work of perfectly hitting those beats by setting the Global Snap, and the notes will automatically fall into place!

The metronome (Ctrl+M) starts off the bottom row and is paramount to the beat makers out there who like to stay on beat but still stay in the tempo. You can change the sound of the metronome by right-clicking the toggle switch (again, the shiny red button) and choosing between hi-hat, tick, and beep. The Wait for Input button (Ctrl+I) will cause FL Studio to pause recording or playing until a note is received from your MIDI keyboard or a key is pressed when Typing Keyboard to Piano Keyboard is active. This is nice when you want to have FL Studio start recording and can be a nice setup to have a quick remote Play button for when you are listening back, but I think it is best to use this for recording, if necessary, and otherwise leave it off.

The Step Recording toggle switch (Ctrl+E) allows you to play at your own speed and will only enter notes into the Piano roll as quickly as you play them. This is great for slowly going through a portion of a song and getting the exact notes that you want without having to wait for the song to loop back to the position you are at. With this option selected, pressing Record is not necessary when adding notes in the Piano roll. Next to this option is the Auto-Scroll, which will keep the scroll bar viewable on your computer screen as the song plays. I find that it is useful to try both and see which option suits you best, because this one comes down to preference and what makes you work faster and more efficiently.

The final button is the Multi-Link Controllers button and will allow you to control multiple parameters of automation, such as panning and volume. It will be further discussed in Chapter 5.

The online section, shown in Figure 3.26, is the news feed and download center for FL Studio. The first button works like a news ticker at the top of your screen to display new products and their availability, and the lighter button to the right opens the online downloader. A web window will open up only when you click on the online window, and the online section itself will not activate until you first click it. This is a great way to get more instruments, plug-ins, and updates and visit websites that have useful tools for your music making. When you are working and have made a few projects, your instruments can get stale or lifeless because you have overplayed them to yourself. Many programs lack the ability to instantly update their catalog, as FL

Studio can do. I have found many times when making a new track that listening to something fresh and unheard can spark creativity even if I decide not to use it in the final mix.

Figure 3.26   The online section prior to activation.

Playlist

When creating music inside FL Studio, there are many steps that go into creating your tracks. The Playlist is where you place the different parts of your music and arrange them how you would like the song to sound when played from beginning to end (see Figure 3.27). As you build your song and find parts that you like, you will begin placing the patterns in the pattern block section (lower half) or dropping clips into the clip tracks (upper half). To make life easier,

Figure 3.27   A song using only the clip section (upper area) of the Playlist.

it is best to stick with using the upper section because you can see what is going on inside the patterns when you use pattern clips. Clips in the Playlist can consist of events, MIDI notes, audio, and even automation. Within these sections you can completely rearrange a song and save it as a new version, and while other programs can provide obstacles to efficiently changing what you want, FL Studio provides tools to help you get those changes made as quickly as you think of them.

By default, the clip tracks will be laid out on top, and the pattern blocks will be on the bottom. The upper section will consist of many different clips, all the way down to no clips if you are building everything in the Stepsequencer. When recording audio tracks, the sound can be routed to any of the 99 Mixer tracks, which we will discuss in Chapter 4. For now, just know that your audio clips that show up as waveforms will be placed here, and recording to the master track is not a good idea even though it can be done.

Automation can be controlled here, so if you would like a left-to-right pan, you can manually set it here with automation clips. I will discuss more on what automation is and how it is used in Chapter 5. MIDI notes can be dropped in here, and when you have a series of MIDI notes you like, by placing them on the Playlist as MIDI notes you keep them open to editing and are never stuck with what you made. The notes you place in here can also control events, such as changing the pages of the Notebook plug-in or causing the graphic characters in the Fruity Dance plug-in to perform certain dance moves.

The lower section is for placing pattern blocks that are created in the Stepsequencer. A good way to picture this is to consider two different drum beats that are made with the same tempo in two different patterns. Imagine that Pattern 1 is a light drum beat that plays in the beginning of a song, and Pattern 2 is a heavy drum beat that follows the intro and plays through the rest of the song. Blocks are drawn on the first pattern track so that the light drum beat plays for a few bars. Then on the second pattern track in the pattern blocks area, blocks are drawn after Pattern 1 in the timeline so that after the light drum beat plays, the heavy drum beat will follow. The pattern blocks don't contain any visual information, they just tell FL Studio which individual patterns to play when in Song mode.

Now that you have a general overview of the Playlist, let's take a closer look at what each of the menus (see Figure 3.28) can do for your music making. As you read over these options, remember that this section is just telling the song which part to play at what time.

Playlist Options

The first branch that comes off the Playlist options is the Edit section; it contains familiar shortcuts that are used in many programs (see Figure 3.29). The first four may be burned into your memory from programs such as Microsoft Word, and if they aren't, I strongly suggest you learn them. These are based on the selection that you have made in the Playlist, and the four options will cut (remove from the Playlist, but you can paste it anywhere without copying), copy, paste, and delete (remove from the Playlist without being able to paste the selection anywhere) any clip

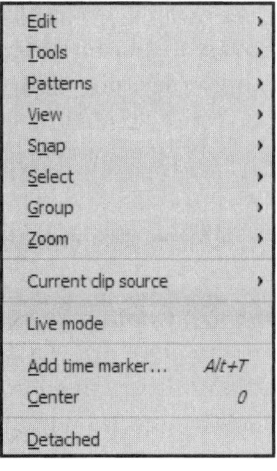

Figure 3.28 The Playlist options.

or pattern block. Regardless of which option (delete or cut) you choose to use, you can always undo a delete and get your clip back. Delete All will clear everything off the Playlist, but I would suggest saving the current version and renaming unless you want to completely scrap what you have.

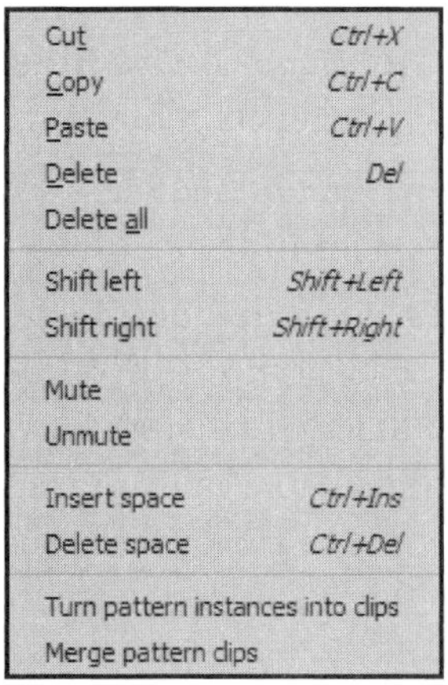

Cut	Ctrl+X
Copy	Ctrl+C
Paste	Ctrl+V
Delete	Del
Delete all	
Shift left	Shift+Left
Shift right	Shift+Right
Mute	
Unmute	
Insert space	Ctrl+Ins
Delete space	Ctrl+Del
Turn pattern instances into clips	
Merge pattern clips	

Figure 3.29 The Edit section of the Playlist options.

The Shift Left and Shift Right options will move the selection the respective ways an amount based on your Snap settings. This means that if your Snap settings are at 1/2 beat, then when you select Shift Right, the selection will slide to the right 1/2 a beat. This is nice when you need to bump a selection a certain amount and can come in handy for small moves, such as 1/32 beats.

Mute and Unmute will prevent audio clips from playing completely, so even if there are effects on a sound, the effects will not play as well. Insert Space (Ctrl+Insert) can be used for making room to add in extra parts or a break in the song. Where you start your selection is where the space will begin, and where the selection ends is where the rest of the song will be moved to. Delete Space (Ctrl+Delete) will cut out a section and push the beginning of the selection to the end of the selection while erasing everything in between. This is fantastic for when you have added too many bars in a song, and you need to erase that extra bar without affecting the rest of your song. By selecting that bar and choosing Delete Space, the bar will go away, there will be no space, and the song will play perfectly through unless you cut off audio—then usually it will create a popping sound.

The Turn Pattern Instances into Clips option will take any pattern block placement and drop it onto the Playlist. Although this can be useful when you want the typical look of a project, where you can see the MIDI notes and audio clips rather than arbitrary blocks, it is not necessary, and an entire project can be built in the Stepsequencer and arranged in the pattern blocks. Merge Pattern Clips will take all of the selected pattern blocks and combine them into one track in the clip track section. When this is done, they act as a collective, and you cannot individually edit the notes without opening the Piano roll.

The Tools menu has Quick Quantize, which sits alone with no other options (see Figure 3.30). This will snap your patterns to the Snap selection you make.

Figure 3.30 Quick Quantize.

The Patterns menu will open up a series of options (see Figure 3.31) that will allow you to manipulate the pattern tracks in the pattern block section, which in turn causes the pattern clips in the Clips section of the Playlist to adhere to the settings. (For example, renaming a pattern track in the pattern block area will rename the clip of the same pattern in the Clips section of the Playlist.) The first is Rename (F2) and should be easy to remember because it is one of the F keys. You can change the pattern name, which I highly recommend because it will help you to stay organized. The option to change the color will also come up, and you can choose from a wide array of shades and hues.

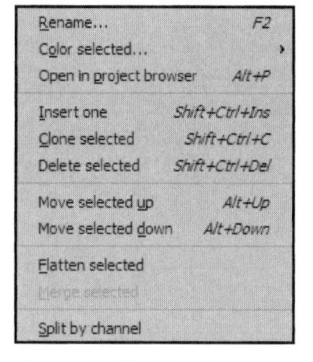

Figure 3.31 The Patterns menu from the Playlist options.

Color Selected will offer two choices, and Gradient will cause the color to blend from one color to the next across the tracks you select. This is nice when you have a drum section that you want to visually stand out, and you select those patterns and choose a red and then a blue so that for just that section, the color will blend from red to blue across those tracks. Random takes the color organization out of the picture and simply livens up the appearance of your patterns by assigning random colors to the selected patterns.

Open in Project Browser (Alt+P) is a great way to navigate and disable any part of your project. If you want to quickly turn off a pattern, sound, or effect, it will show up in the Browser, and clicking on the name will allow you to disable it. Right-clicking the name will bring up another set of options where you can quickly bring up the Piano roll or parameter changes (panning, volume, envelopes, and so on). This is a valuable navigation tool, and familiarizing yourself with it will help you to move quickly through the parts of your song and make rapid changes.

Insert One places an empty pattern before the one you select, while Clone Selected will copy all of the tweaks you have made to a pattern but will not place any blocks in the pattern block window. Use this when you have the perfect pattern, but you want to change one parameter for a different break and then place that block in the section where you want the beat to change (see Figure 3.32).

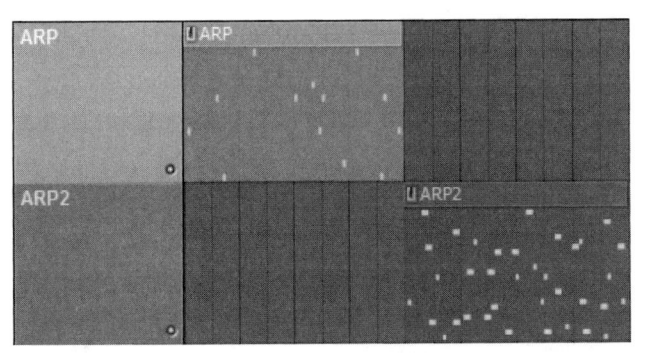

Figure 3.32 Here you can see a cloned pattern with altered notes that is placed after the original to create a different sound.

Delete Selected will remove the selected pattern from the pattern block window. It's good to know that this cannot be undone, so use caution when deleting patterns.

Move Selected Up will bump the selected pattern(s) up, and Move Selected Down will move them down one space in the pattern block window. Flatten Selected can be used to give your project a clean look and prevent moving of single pattern blocks. When selected, if there are a few blocks in the pattern, they will be consolidated into one block.

Merge Selected will merge two or more patterns into one, and Split by Channel will take the pattern and expand it to include each in-use channel from the Stepsequencer and branch it out in the pattern list. When you use Split by Channel, you can place a specific kick groove in a different part of the song or remove just the hi-hats during a specific section, where you would have to otherwise copy the pattern and make an entirely new one because the original was all of the sounds in one pattern. See Figure 3.33.

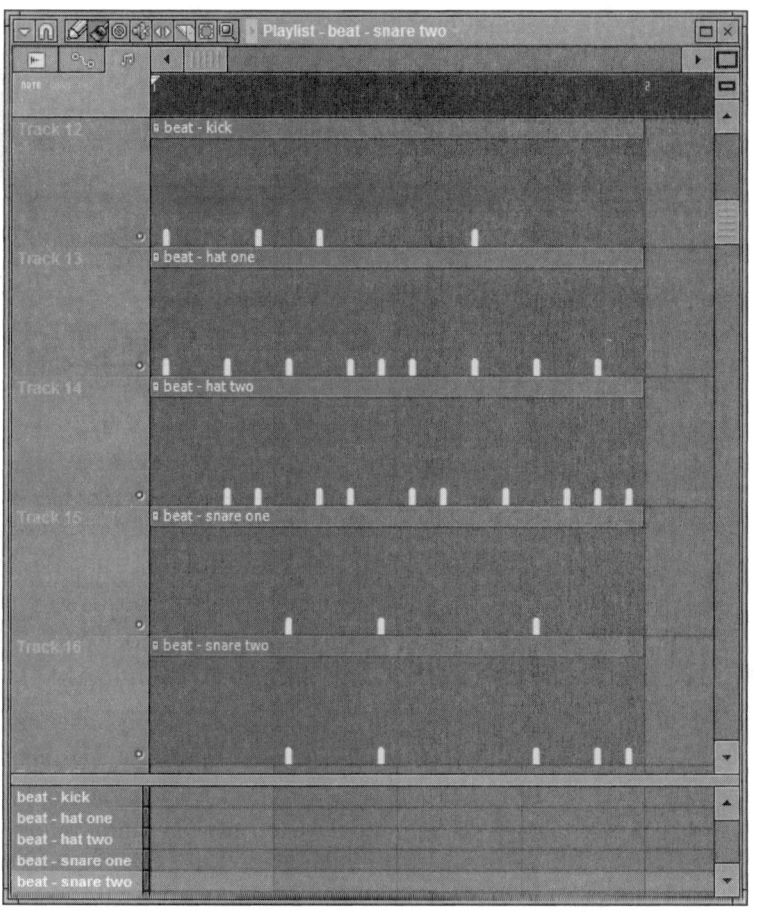

Figure 3.33 A drum beat that has been split by channel, allowing you to place individual sounds in the clips section.

The View menu adjusts the look of the Playlist and will not affect your project musically (see Figure 3.34). This section will come down to personal preference and what helps you best work on your projects. The first option will bring up a window allowing you to change the background grid color. Invert Grid will flip the background grid lines to their opposite color, so if your lines were black, they will turn white. Alternate Grid will make the lines more pronounced, so if the background grid lines are set to black, the grid lines will thicken. Again, this will come down to not just what is easier to use, but in some cases what is easier to see. The view option for behind the clips can be modified to be transparent, be opaque so that no grid lines can be seen behind clips, or have a glass appearance.

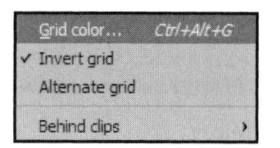

Figure 3.34 The View options in the Playlist.

By now you have heard me mention Snap settings more than once, and Figure 3.35 shows the menu where you can adjust how closely to the beat you can move clips and pattern blocks. Remember that the settings here are for the Playlist, and unless they are set to Main, they will not automatically adhere to the global settings of your project. The best way to avoid running into this is to leave everything on Main and only adjust the global settings. The smaller the number you choose, the more potential places you can place clips and pattern blocks. If you need to move a drum beat over 1/4 beat and have the Snap setting at one beat, you will not be able to put the drum beat where you need it, because it will pass over the 1/4 beat and skip to the next full beat. When the Snap setting is at None, you can freely move the blocks and clips without any grid to adhere to. When setting the Snap setting to a full bar, you will be able to quickly move parts around without fear that they may not be at the right place.

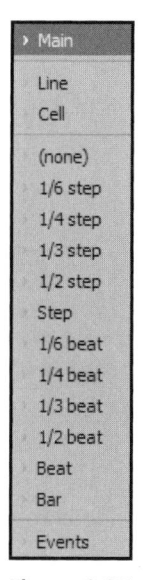

Figure 3.35 The Snap settings menu in the Playlist.

The Select menu provides some ways to select different parts of your project (see Figure 3.36). Deselect (Ctrl+D) will drop the selection that you have and leave you with no selection. Select All (Ctrl+A) will highlight everything in the Playlist. This becomes very useful when you want to turn your project into a stereo track to put on a CD, and you need to select everything for printing to audio (turning all tracks into one audio track).

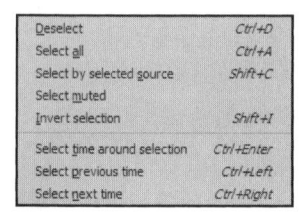

Figure 3.36 The Select menu in the Playlist.

Select by Selected Source means that when you have a clip selected and you choose this option, all associated pattern blocks and clips will also become highlighted. Select Muted will select any channels that have been muted, which can be useful when you want to hear everything, including tracks that you may have turned off, because after selecting them all, you can choose Unmute from the Edit menu.

At first, it took me a minute to figure out the purpose of Invert Selection, but then I reached the point where I wanted to export two halves of a song. After exporting the first half, rather than using the mouse, I used Invert Selection (Shift+I), and it selected everything that I had not selected.

Select Time around Selection (Ctrl+Enter) will place the timeline marker around the selection, so if you have a vocal that lasts 2 1/2 bars, the timeline selection will be for those 2 1/2 bars. This can be great for looping an entire song without having to drag a ton of menus, because all you hit is Ctrl+A to select everything and then Ctrl+Enter to cause the timeline to be highlighted from the project beginning to the end.

Select Previous Time (Ctrl+Left Arrow) and Select Next Time (Ctrl+Right Arrow) are favorite quick key combos of mine for when I am editing and jumping around a project. If you are trying to listen to your song piece by piece, you can select an area on the timeline—say, four bars, for example—and when you choose Select Next Time or use the quick key, the timeline will automatically select the next four bars, and playback will start there.

Group (Shift+G) and Ungroup (Alt+G) will create or remove a grouping based on your selection (see Figure 3.37). When you create a group in the Playlist, hovering over it will cause the group to have a different hue and color than the rest of the clips or blocks, making it easily identifiable. When clips or blocks are grouped, choosing one of the clips or blocks will highlight all in the group automatically. This can be helpful when you're trying to keep an eye on a section or adjust all pattern blocks at once.

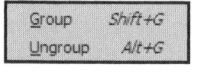

Figure 3.37 Group and Ungroup.

The zoom options are used fairly often by nearly everyone, and it is a good idea to know these quick keys (see Figure 3.38). The numbers used are the ones on the QWERTY keyboard and *not*

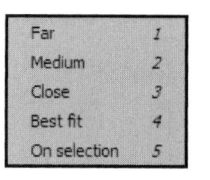

Figure 3.38 Zoom options in the Playlist.

the numerical keypad. The farthest zoom out is 1, while a medium view is 2, and the close view can be chosen by pressing 3. Pressing 4 will fill the window with as much of the project as the track count will allow, and pressing 5 will zoom into a selection made in the timeline. A useful combination of these quick keys is to find a section that you want to work on, such as a vocal, and then select the vocal, press Ctrl+Enter to highlight the duration of the vocal in the timeline, and then press 5. This is a two-key combo that can immediately zoom you into the area that you wish to work with.

Another option for getting a bird's-eye view of all your clips is to mouse over Current Clip Source in the Playlist options list, and it will bring up the entire project collection of clips. Below that option is the Live mode toggle, where you can switch between Regular mode and Live mode, which can be used to audition clips on the fly. I will discuss Live mode further in Chapter 5. Add Timeline Marker (Alt+T) will bring up a small window that allows you to name a marker to place on the timeline. These are great ways to identify breaks in your project or even general song structure, such as chorus, verse, bridge, and so on. They can also be used to jump around the song when in Live mode, which, again, I will further explain in Chapter 5. Center (0 on the QWERTY keypad) will adjust your screen so that the position marker is in the middle of your screen. This is helpful when you have auto scrolling turned off in the recording panel, and you want the screen to jump to the point in time where the timeline is. The final option will detach the Playlist and allow you to move it offscreen and onto another monitor if one is available.

Playlist Quick Buttons

In Figure 3.39, I included the Snap button in the picture, which will bring up a menu (refer to Figure 3.35) to select the Snap setting for the Playlist grid. Aside from that button, the rest are mapped to quick keys, and when Typing Keyboard to Piano Keyboard is not selected, then you will be able to press single keys to change the tool you are using in the Playlist. If you need to play instruments with your typing keyboard, press the Shift button with the tool command keys (for example, Shift+P to draw).

Figure 3.39 Playlist quick buttons.

The Draw tool (P) will allow you to place single clips and patterns in the Playlist, and when you click the selection, it will move with the mouse until you release it. The Paint tool (B) is similar in that it places clips and pattern blocks, but as you move the mouse, it places duplicates of your selections as you move horizontally across the grid. Use this tool when you have a beat that you need to repeat for a few bars without worry that a duplicate will be out of place.

Delete (D) will remove any pattern block, clip, or group when it is selected with this tool. Mute (T) is great for toggling the playback of a single clip, so when you need a part or multiple parts muted, hold the left mouse button and drag over what you need to turn off. To unmute, just select the muted part or drag over a muted selection, and it will play and no longer be grayed out.

The Slip tool (S) is for changing the length of clips and pattern blocks, and when selected inside a clip, it will move the clip as far left as you drag the mouse, while leaving the clip shell in its original location. The Slice tool (C) will cut the visual of your clip so you can take out unwanted sound or single out a section in the audio. The tool will split a clip into two pieces, and the size of the pieces will depend on where you make a slice. If you make a slice straight down, then that is where the clip will be cut, and if you make a diagonal line with the tool, the clip will be cut between the upper and lower cutting points of your clip. Right-clicking a selection with the Slice tool will remove the smaller of the two pieces when a selection is sliced into two pieces. I don't recommend cutting the pattern blocks, because they create a new pattern block track and can create confusion and a general mess in the project.

The Select tool (E) will allow you to select single clips, a rectangular area that will include all clips or pattern blocks in it, and multiple selections by adding the Shift key. Zoom (Z) is incredibly useful for visually navigating your project in the Playlist (see Figure 3.40). When using the Zoom tool, you will be able to highlight a rectangular area that, after you release the mouse, will fill the Playlist with your selection.

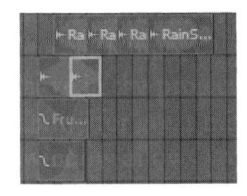

Figure 3.40 The Zoom tool with Shift held down, about to select an area on which to zoom.

The makers of FL Studio created a program that is meant to have options so you can tailor how you use the program to suit your needs. However, I believe that an efficient way of using these tools is to focus on switching between them as little as possible. I suggest using Draw (P) and Paint (B) primarily and holding Ctrl, which will shift the tool into the Selector tool until Ctrl is released. This prevents toggling tools with keystrokes, and usually after selecting something, you don't want to select something different. If you need to make multiple selections, hold Shift+Ctrl while dragging or selecting, and you can make selections that are not next to each other. The idea is that after making a selection, you can move it around even when the Draw or Paint tool is selected and draw in other patterns quickly.

Zooming can be achieved by using the shortcuts 1 through 5 on your QWERTY keyboard and pressing Shift+Z for a quick zoom into a clip. Slicing is located near all of the keys I prefer to use, and pressing C will allow a quick slice of your clip. This use of the tools may not work for you, but I have found that it saves me time when editing and creating.

In Figure 3.41, Play/Pause and Playlist selection are the buttons located to the right of the tools. Pressing Ctrl+spacebar will play/pause the song in Song mode or a pattern in Pattern mode and is a faster alternative to moving the mouse up to this button, but this button will always trigger Song mode automatically. The Playlist selection, when clicked, will produce a drop-down list that allows you to select a clip that you can place in the Playlist.

Figure 3.41   The song Play button and clip selector.

Focus Clips Tabs

Beneath the tools are your clip focus selections, where options will change based on which type of clip you choose to focus on. Right-clicking on any of the focus clip tabs will bring up the list of that type of clip so you can immediately click in the Playlist and drop that clip in. The audio clip focus is first and, when selected, will display the options Zero-Cross and Stretch, as shown in Figure 3.42. The Zero-Cross option means that when you slice or change the length of an audio clip, the break between clips or the clip end will happen at the point where the waveform is at the zero point (see Figure 3.43). Although this option is not perfect and sometimes will still cause pops in the audio, the purpose is to prevent those pops by separating the sound where there is minimal noise.

Figure 3.42   The clip focus tabs with audio focused.

Stretch will compress or expand the audio clip to fit any resizing you do. This means that when stretch is highlighted and the Channel Settings Time Stretching option is set to Resample, the audio clip will play faster when shortened and play slower when lengthened. This is great for remixing a song and getting it to fit the tempo you want, rather than the one at which the clip was recorded.

The automation focus clips tab brings up Step and Slide as options (see Figure 3.44). Step is a useful feature when Step-Editing mode (Ctrl+E) is turned on. We discussed earlier that step

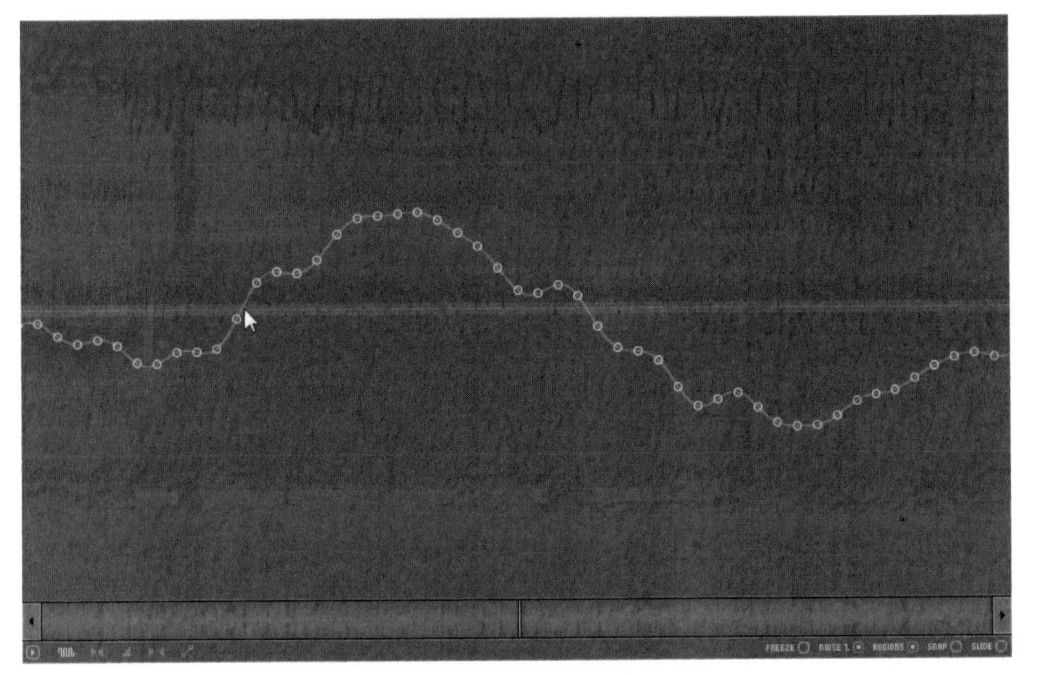

Figure 3.43   In this image, the mouse pointer is pointing at the zero-crossing point of a waveform.

editing means you can slowly edit along piece by piece, but in automation clips the mouse can be dragged across the clip to draw a freehand curve for the selected parameter (see Figure 3.45). This means that if you have a sound being controlled by an automation clip—let's say volume— you can draw the volume change right over the automation clip. The number of points used to draw the curve depends on your Snap settings. When you hold Shift and draw, the space between points can only be straight lines running horizontally or vertically, which will create literal visual steps on the curve (see Figure 3.46). The Slide option will allow other curve points to retain their relative distance horizontally when moving curve points. When it is disabled, only the curve point you select will move.

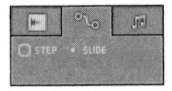

Figure 3.44   The clip focus tabs with automation focused.

The pattern clips focus refers to a visual representation of the blocks that you place in the pattern block tracks (see Figure 3.47). The options for these clips will affect the colors for the patterns when they are placed on the clip tracks. The Note option will cause the clips to be the same color as the main pattern that the clip is from. Chan will use the parent channel's color, and Pat will use the parent pattern's color. I enjoy coloring them individually, which can easily be done by right-clicking a pattern and choosing Rename and then clicking the color box next to the name.

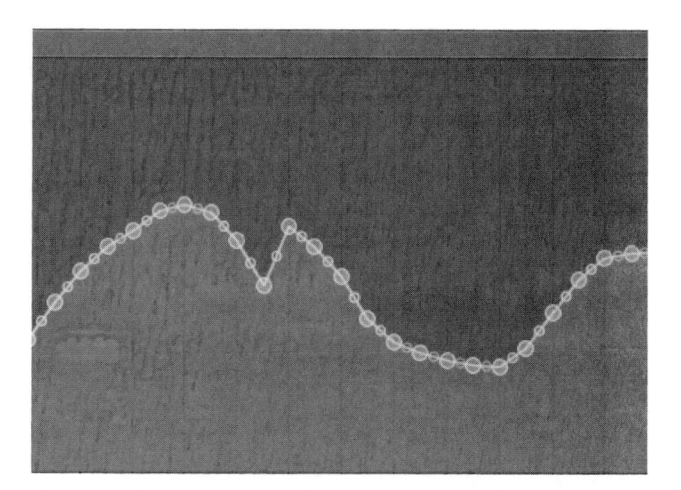

Figure 3.45 An automation curve drawn freehand with step editing active and Step selected in the automation tab.

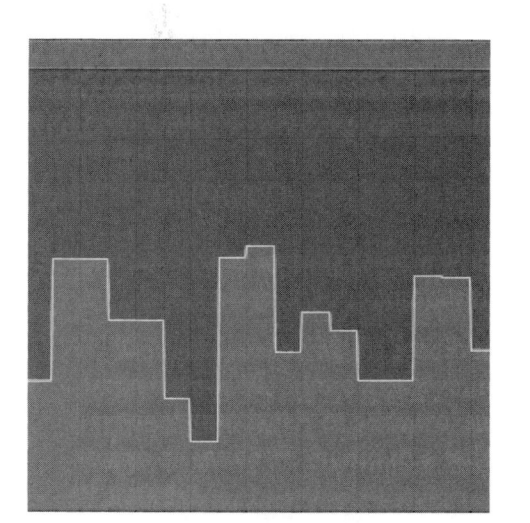

Figure 3.46 An automation curve drawn with Shift held down to ensure straight vertical and horizontal lines.

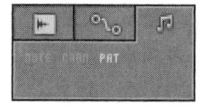

Figure 3.47 The clip focus tabs with pattern clips focused.

Playlist Navigation and Extra Options

In Figure 3.48 you see the Playlist with many clips and no pattern blocks, because where there would normally be pattern blocks, there are pattern clips for easier editing. On the sides are the usual scroll and zoom functions, but I find myself only using the top scroll button, because when you right-click this button, you can drag the mouse in all directions, and the Playlist view will move in all directions with the mouse. With zoom, use the 1 through 5 shortcuts, and for horizontal zoom, hold Alt and use the scroll wheel to zoom in and out.

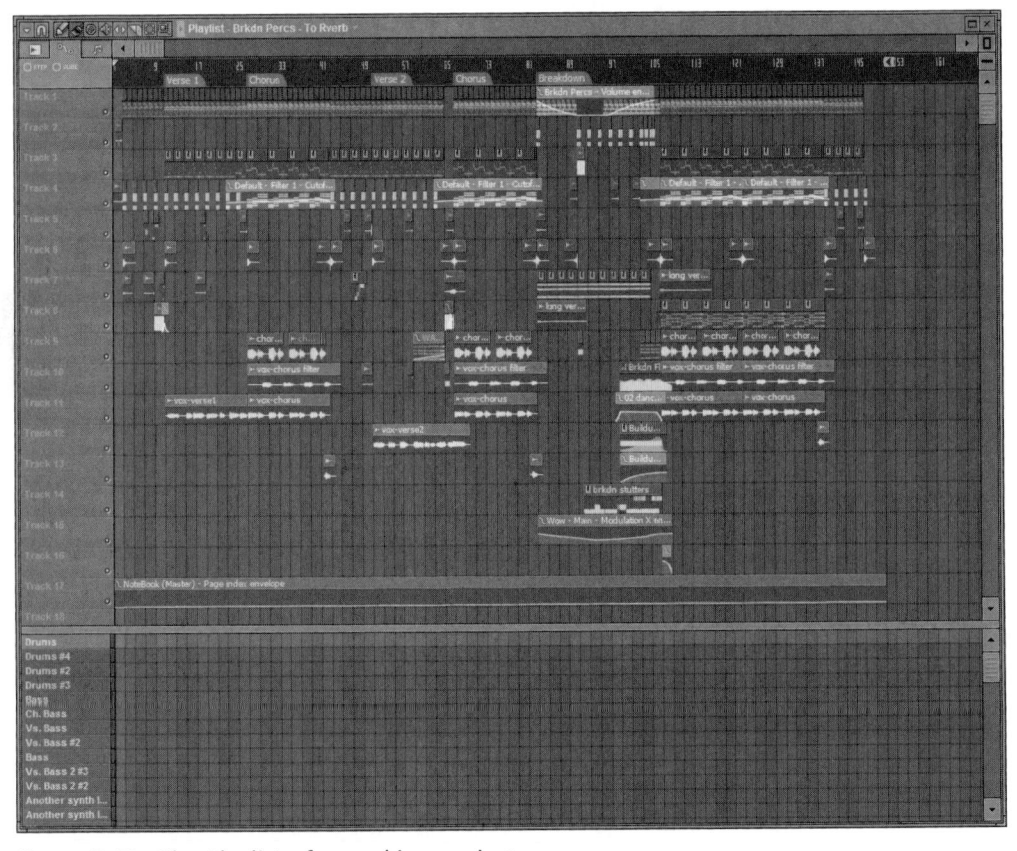

Figure 3.48　The Playlist of a working project.

Every clip placed in the clip tracks will have its own menu that can be accessed by clicking in the top-left corner of each clip. Some of the options will not be available for every clip type, but the ones that are there will behave the same across the three clip types. Preview will play the clip, and you can press Stop to halt the sound. Select Source Channel will allow you to replace a clip with one that you select from the list. When using the Paint tool, you can place a clip down regardless of what clip it is and select a different one from this list and then paint it however many times you wish, making adding sections incredibly easy. Be careful with this option, because if you have more than one clip selected, it will change *all* of those clips to that selection!

Edit Pattern will open the Piano roll, allowing you to tweak notes, and Channel Settings will open the settings for that particular channel. So if you open the channel settings for an instrument, you will be able to change the sound and any other parameter available for that instrument.

Rename will allow you to rename the clip so that you can easily see what version or sound you are working with, so you don't get confused when there are four versions of bass in the Playlist. Make Unique will create a copy of a pattern that you can freely edit without affecting the original. Pay special attention to this because if you make a change to a clip, when you paint that clip, the changed version will be the one that is painted. Select All Similar Clips will highlight all of the clips that are the same as the selected one and can help with editing multiple clips at once.

The Select Region option will bring up any existing regions to select from the side menu so that if your sample has defined regions or markers, such as when it is dragged out of Edison, you can automatically select one, and the clip will collapse to the selected region. This is great for using a series of vocals when you have set markers that identify where the chorus, verse, and other sections are located in the sample, because you can add the whole sample and quickly select a region, such as the chorus, to place in the Playlist. Chop will open another menu (see Figure 3.49), allowing you to slice your audio based on the selection you make in the submenu. This is great for getting pieces of audio to rearrange for creating a new beat, adding emphasis to different parts, or even giving vocals a manual stutter effect—although there is a plug-in that will do it for you, and I will show you how in Chapter 6.

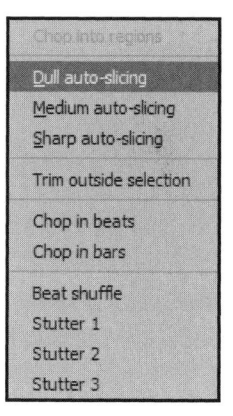

Figure 3.49 The Chop menu options.

Edit Sample is a quick way to load an audio clip into Edison. Detect Tempo will figure out the tempo of a clip and allow you to set FL Studio to that tempo, which works well when you don't want to stretch a sample and the project is based around that sample. Fit to Tempo will do the opposite and stretch the sample to the tempo that is already set in FL Studio.

The Automate option will allow you to create volume and panning automation for the audio clip, and if two audio tracks are next to each other, there will be an option to crossfade the two as well. This option is the fastest for getting two audio clips to seamlessly play without sound immediately dropping out or starting.

We have gone over the functionality of the options that show up when clicking the pattern block tracks and contain movement and renaming options.

Channel Window (and Stepsequencer)

The creation of the Stepsequencer set FL Studio apart from other recording software and drew people in to the original versions when it was known as FruityLoops. At first glance, many will just see buttons in rows that will play sound if they are highlighted when the scrolling light goes past the buttons. The key is to not see a Stepsequencer, but rather to see a window containing channels of individual parts of your song (see Figure 3.50). There are many ways to make sound in the channels, but for now, imagine that every different event (something that makes sound or alters it) is placed horizontally in channels.

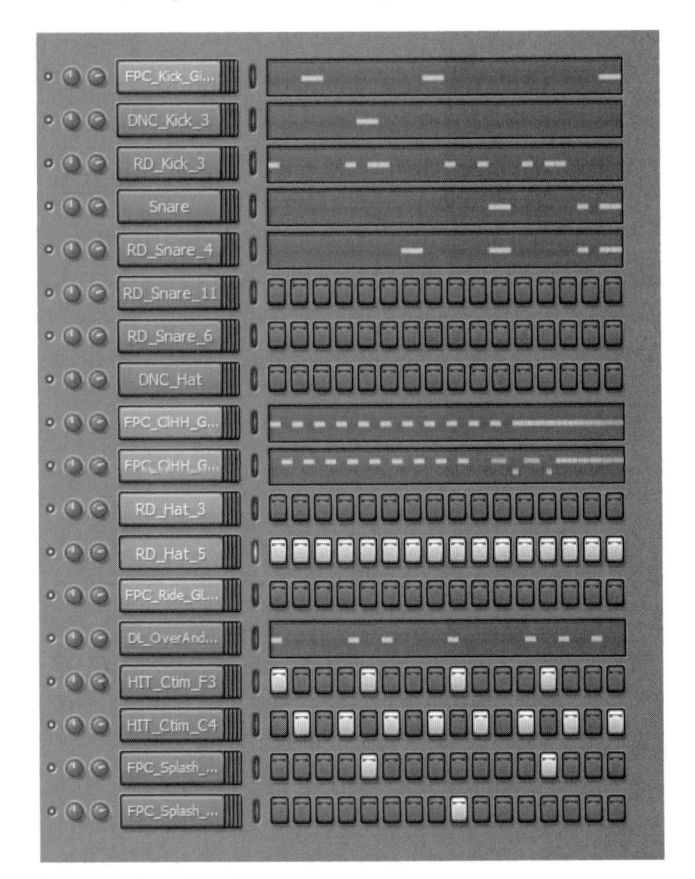

Figure 3.50 The Stepsequencer.

In this section we will look at the Channel window in two uses—basic and complex. In basic, we will look at the Stepsequencer and only highlight steps (each button). Most FL Studio users will use the steps to quickly make a repeatable drum beat or play a one-shot sound effect, such as a cowbell…and as world-famous producer Bruce Dickinson notes, "You're gonna want that cowbell on your track." The complex side of the Stepsequencer will allow a much wider range of options when building a project. As you become more familiar with FL Studio, this will be the road of choice, because the ideas you have are not always single note.

First we will look at the basic side of the Stepsequencer. In Figure 3.51, you can see that as the orange light scrolls across the bottom of the Stepsequencer, the kick, clap, hat, and sub kick will be triggered when passing a highlighted step and will play that sound. This is a quick way to create a beat that will be accurate and can be changed instantly. The steps can be activated or deactivated by left-clicking, while right-clicking will make the space blank. After the audio is loaded in the channel, highlighting the steps is all that needs to be done to trigger sound when in Pattern mode. We will look at loading sounds in the next section; however, right now I want to give you an overview of the basic features to understand what the Channel window can do.

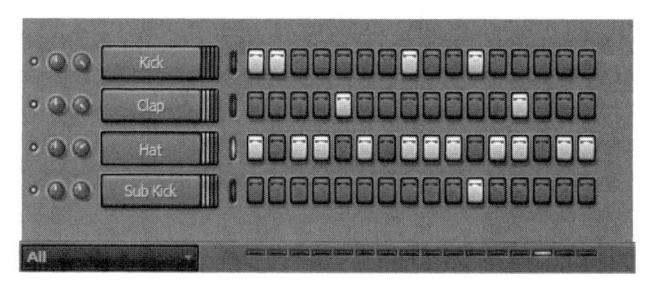

Figure 3.51 A drum beat set to a tempo of 98 beats per minute with 40 percent swing.

Basic Stepsequencer Menu

The first section at the top of the Channel window has a series of global options designed to affect all the channels (see Figure 3.52). The first changeable option is the box that by default will have two lines in it. This tells FL Studio how many beats you want in the pattern. This means that if you raise it up to 16, you will get 16 beats per bar (64 steps) to enter in single sound events for that pattern in Pattern mode, but when the pattern is placed in the Playlist as a clip, it can cover more than one bar when played in Song mode. This can be helpful with creating drums that have a few changes in them and would not sound correct repeating every four beats.

Figure 3.52 The Channel window settings.

Next to that is the Repeat Stepsequencer toggle switch, which will play an important role in your music making using steps and is necessary when certain parts in a pattern play longer than the number of steps assigned to the channels. For example, if you have recorded some piano for a pattern, and it runs for eight bars, but the drum beat on the same pattern plays only four bars, the drums will stop playing after the first four bars, and the piano will continue playing the remaining four bars with no drums. By selecting this switch, the highlighted steps will repeat and play the full eight bars. We will discuss patterns that play longer than the number of steps a little later in "The Deeper Side of the Channel Window" section, but it is good to know the purpose of this option.

The Play button for the pattern is located next to the Repeat Stepsequencer button, but the spacebar works just fine for playing a pattern and is much quicker. Even if you are in Song mode and press Play on this button, it will automatically place you back into Pattern mode.

To the immediate right of the Play button is the pattern selector, which, when clicked, will bring up a menu (see Figure 3.53) that allows you to navigate to different patterns and name each one that has data in it (otherwise it won't show up in the list). I strongly suggest naming your patterns, because when you start building projects that contain 30 or more patterns, finding anything becomes impossible. There are some other familiar options we have already seen in the Playlist that apply in this menu as well. Keep in mind that the submenu containing options such as Delete, Clone, and Move Up only applies to the channel that you have highlighted to the left of the options.

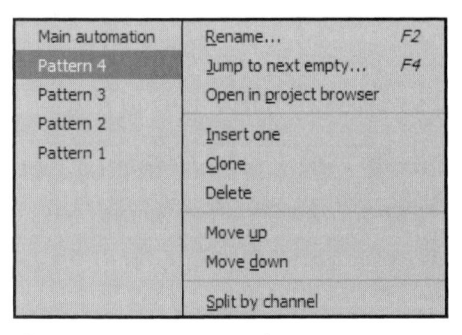

Figure 3.53 Pattern selector.

Moving farther along the top menu brings you to the Swing setting. This will add a swing feel to the highlighted buttons as they trigger sound, but it will not affect anything else. Be careful when using this option, because it will affect all patterns in the Stepsequencer, so if you only want one section to have swing to it, then add swing in the Piano roll.

The next button will bring up a graph editor window that will allow you to change the pan, velocity, release, filter cutoff (mod x), resonance (mod y), pitch, and shift of the selected channel. In Figure 3.54, I have adjusted the velocity of the hi-hat channel to give it a more realistic sound of someone playing it. Keep in mind that if you have multiple channels selected, changing these parameters will affect all channels selected. You don't want everything to accidentally pan left in the song! The pitch option can be used to alter notes but is based on a percentage of pitch change, not actual notes, so stick with the keyboard editor for those changes.

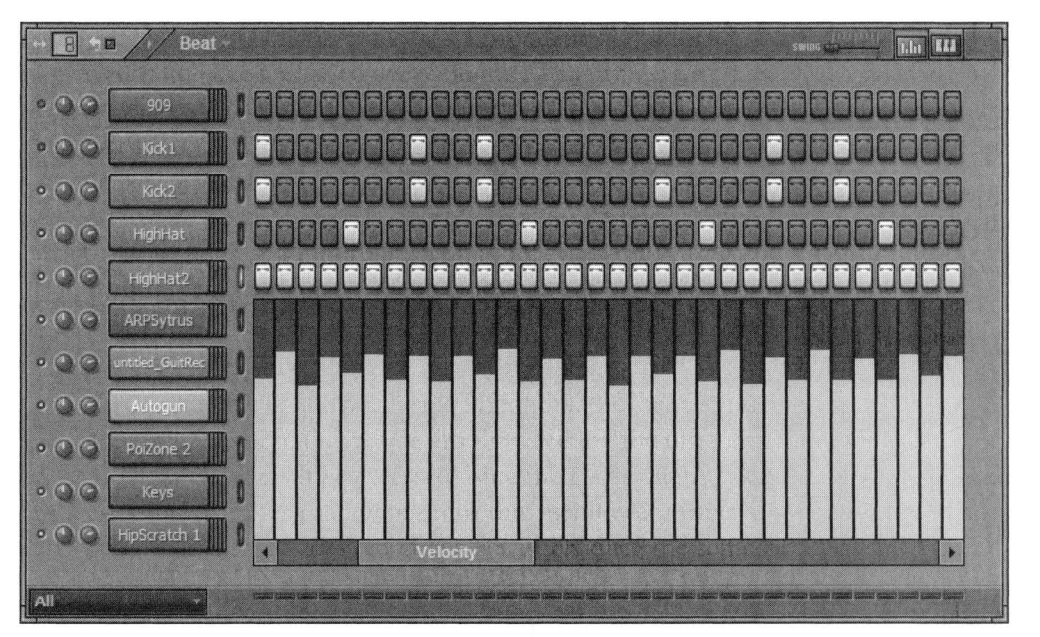

Figure 3.54 The graph editor.

The final button in the Channel window menu is the keyboard editor, and this option allows you to change notes. Suppose you have a piano loaded into the Stepsequencer, and it only needs to play once a beat, but you want to change the notes to create a melody. Opening this window will give you a mini piano with orange marks on it that represent the steps. The light notes are unused steps, and the dark notes are where a sound is being triggered. Moving the note up or down will change the pitch a semitone up or down but still will only play a single note.

At the top of the piano is an option to create a slide so the note slides into the next rather than just changing, but it is important to know that only native FL Studio instruments can do this, so those third-party plug-ins will not support the slide notes.

I did want to mention the drop-down menu in the bottom-left corner of the Channel window because this is your channel groups selector. For the incredibly tidy musician, this will navigate through groups that you have chosen and named for quick access. To really make this helpful, you would want to create a group of channels by highlighting them when All is selected from the Group menu drop-down and then naming that group something appropriate, such as Horns if everything selected is your horn section. This will allow you to choose Horns from this menu so you can easily edit in the Channel window without having the Channel window be crowded.

The Deeper Side of the Channel Window

When I refer to the complex side of the Channel window, I am referencing the use of more than highlighted steps in the sequencer. Anything can be recorded into a pattern and then placed on the Playlist. I wanted to start by explaining the Playlist so that you would see where patterns and sound go, and then break it down to the individual channels of a pattern in the Channel window. Adding a new channel was discussed earlier and can be done by going into the Channels menu at the top left of FL Studio. An alternative that I suggest over using the Channels menu to add a channel is dragging directly from the Browser. This can be easier for navigating through the available sounds, instruments, effects, and presets, but we will look more closely at Browser use in the "Project Browser" section of this chapter. However you add a channel, any sound at any length can be recorded into the Stepsequencer. When you record an instrument into the Piano roll—for example, a piano solo—there will be a visual representation of where the notes lie on the Piano roll instead of the steps (see Figure 3.55).

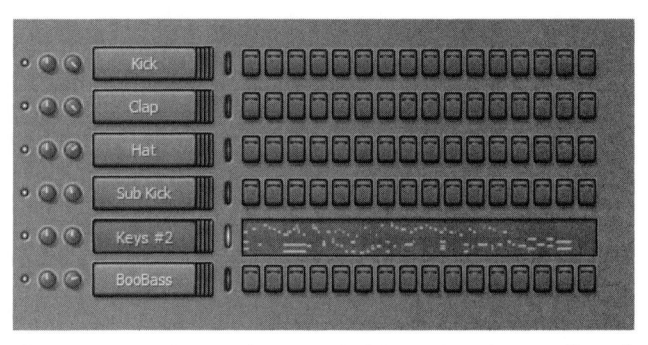

Figure 3.55 Piano solo recorded into the Piano roll and displayed in the Channel window.

To further tweak individual channel sounds in the Channel window, you can use the Channel Settings menu that will pop up when you left-click on a channel button. If an instrument is loaded into the channel you select, the instrument UI will usually pop up if it has one, but the Channel Settings menu (see Figure 3.56) will still be available. The options will appear different, depending upon what you have loaded into the channel, so if you select a channel containing an audio sample, then you will be given the options shown in Figure 3.56. At the top-left corner of all Channel Settings windows is a menu that will allow you to save the channel state. This can make your life easier because as you create settings that sound flawless, you can save them and apply them to different sounds and even different projects!

Some menus will have the option for Assign Free Mixer Track, and that will assign the sample to the first available track in the Mixer so you can add effects and automation. The audio sample has a menu where you can reload the sample, rename it, open the audio in Edison, detect the tempo (which is not very effective on longer audio samples with no beat), bring up the Properties window, and change into spectrum view or multichannel waveform view. For quick access, right-click the visual of the audio when the sample (SMP) tab is selected (see Figure 3.57).

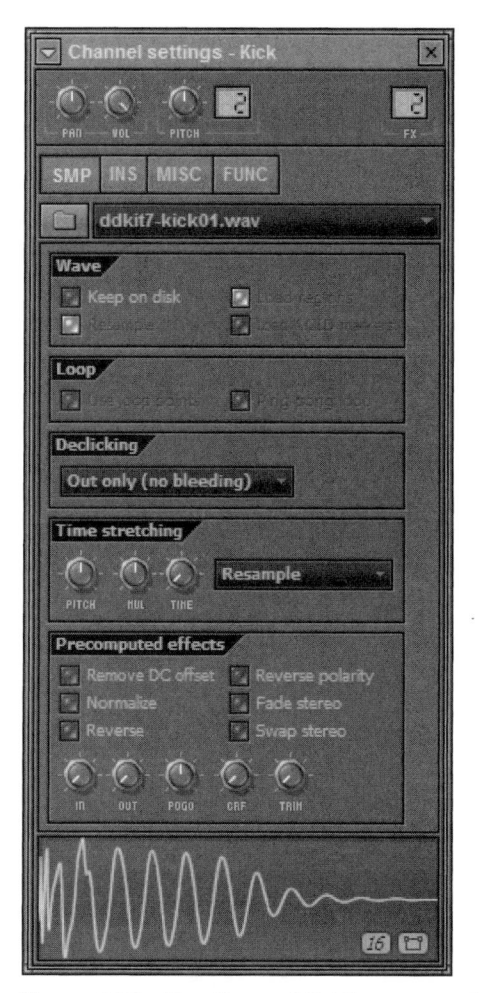

Figure 3.56 The Channel Settings menu for an audio sample.

Figure 3.57 Right-clicking for the sample menu.

The upper section in audio samples will have a channel pan, volume, pitch adjuster, and a box (marked FX) that will take the audio sample and send it to one of the Mixer tracks (see Figure 3.58). Instruments will have no routing and will display "–" because they are sent through the master track; however, you are able to assign each one to different tracks in the Mixer. Rather than use any of the available volume faders in the Channel Settings menu, it is best to assign channels to Mixer tracks and then stick with the Mixer for your channel volume adjustments. This prevents having to search for a turned-down volume knob when the Mixer track to which the channel is linked is set to full volume.

Figure 3.58 Channel Settings global controls.

When the SMP tab is selected in the Channel Settings menu, the first option available is a folder icon that, when clicked, will allow browsing of samples (with favorites) and loading of presets that you had previously created (see Figure 3.59). The Wave portion (see Figure 3.60) gives you the option of Keep on Disk, which will stream more of the audio from disk instead of loading it into RAM while remaining inside the 2-GB (3-GB with extended memory used) limit; this will load sounds faster but can actually hinder performance in the form of pops and clicks in the audio. Resample will raise the quality of the sample but take more disk space because it will create a larger file. Sometimes samples have data in them that determines loop points in a sample, and the Load Regions option will display them. Load ACID Markers will place ACID markers on the sample and is very similar to Determine Loops Points.

Figure 3.59 The folder icon opens an explorer allowing you to navigate to your compatible file of choice while the title displays the name of the loaded sample.

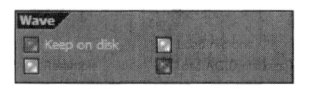

Figure 3.60 The Wave options of the SMP tab.

The Loop section, shown in Figure 3.61, is only available for samples with loop points in them, because the first option will allow you to set a loop point so the sound plays only between the

Figure 3.61 Loop options of the Channel Settings menu.

loop points, and the second option will create an audible ping-pong effect where the loop is reversed and placed on the end of the original sample.

Declicking (see Figure 3.62) provides a drop-down menu to help with samples that do not start or stop on the zero crossing without changing the length of the sample. The No Bleeding options provide a fade-out, Transient (Bleeding) will add a longer fade, while the Generic and Smooth options will insert a fade-in and fade-out. Remember that these are only for the displayed sample and available when that sample has loop points.

Figure 3.62   The Declicking section of the Channel Settings menu.

The Time Stretching feature (see Figure 3.63) can be useful for quickly changing the pitch of a sample without affecting the length it plays (Pitch), the amount to stretch the length based on a multiple of the sample (Mul—for example, two times the sample length or four times the sample length), or stretch the length based on beat or time increments (Time). The drop-down list next to these dials will allow you to set a stretching method based on the type of sample you are using. Try out these different options, because the subtle difference may be exactly what you are looking for.

Figure 3.63   Time Stretching options in the Channel Settings menu.

The Precomputed Effects section, shown in Figure 3.64, helps with altering the sample in many different ways. In these options you can remove the DC offset, normalize the sample (which raises the volume to a "normal" level when it is too low), reverse the sample, reverse the polarity of the sample (which literally flips the waveform upside down), fade stereo (which will apply a fade to the sample that can be controlled by the in/out knobs), and swap the stereo (which will switch the left and right sides of the audio sample if it is stereo).

Figure 3.64   Precomputed Effects section of the Channel Settings menu.

DC Offset DC offset in the analog world is the offset of volts in an amp input or output, while in the digital world, the offset can be caused by the analog-to-digital conversion of an interface. In either world, the voltage difference is either positive or negative, so removing the DC offset in digital applications such as FL Studio involves the program reading the voltage offset, then applying the opposite voltage so that the value reaches zero. (For example, a +1.2 voltage offset can be fixed by applying −1.2 voltage offset to the sound, giving you zero and removing the offset.) DC offset can lower the headroom of a sample and even your entire project, so cancelling the voltage offset amount can greatly increase the dynamic range. In FL Studio, a simple toggle switch will turn on DC offset for immediate cancellation of any voltage offset in the signal.

The pitch-bend knob (Pogo) will allow you to add pitch bend to the sample, and the CRF knob will crossfade your samples, which can produce cleaner loops. The final (Trim) knob works like a gate on the sample, and adjusting it will tell FL Studio at what volume it should close the gate and stop playing the sample. By setting the gate continually higher, the point where sound stops playing gets louder, which can be useful with live recordings that have a long tail of ambient room noise on the end.

The Instruments tab (Ins) incorporates LFOs and ADSR envelopes, discussed further in the "What Is an LFO?" section of Chapter 6 and the "What Is an ADSR Envelope?" sidebar following this paragraph. The Miscellaneous (Misc) and Function (Func) tabs both involve generators and will be discussed in Chapter 6. The main thing to understand is that these settings will affect the sample itself in some way and are good tools for manipulating how you would like something to sound.

What Is an ADSR Envelope? ADSR stands for Attack, Decay, Sustain, and Release. The settings of each will change how the envelope affects the signal. While an ADSR envelope can affect nearly any parameter, it is commonly used to affect sounds. You will see an ADSR envelope option on many of the generators because of the way it affects the signal. For this example, we will discuss the effect an ADSR envelope has on sound. The attack portion of the envelope is how long a note takes to get to the maximum level, so a long attack would be a sound that gradually increases in volume and doesn't start off strong. The decay portion of the envelope is how long it will take the note to go from maximum level to a sustained level, so this encompasses the highest level (volume in this case) of the note to where it stops dropping in volume while the note is held down. The sustain amount represents the level that the note plays after it finishes the decay portion of the envelope. The release is how long a note will play after being released until the level (again, volume in this case) reaches zero. This means that a

long release will cause the sound to play long after you stop triggering a sound, like the
release of a key on a MIDI keyboard.

Now that we have a good understanding of where the patterns are arranged and where the
sound is coming from, let's take a look at where that sound is built—the Piano roll.

The Piano Roll

The Piano roll is a great feature that some DAWs (*digital audio workstations*) or recording software programs seem to neglect. While they tout their audio recording capability, when it comes
to MIDI recording and sound manipulation, they can sometimes fall short. Modern artists have
not just the desire but the need for a tool that reliably captures their music and lets them edit and
manipulate it to their heart's content. That is what the Piano roll is all about (see Figure 3.65).

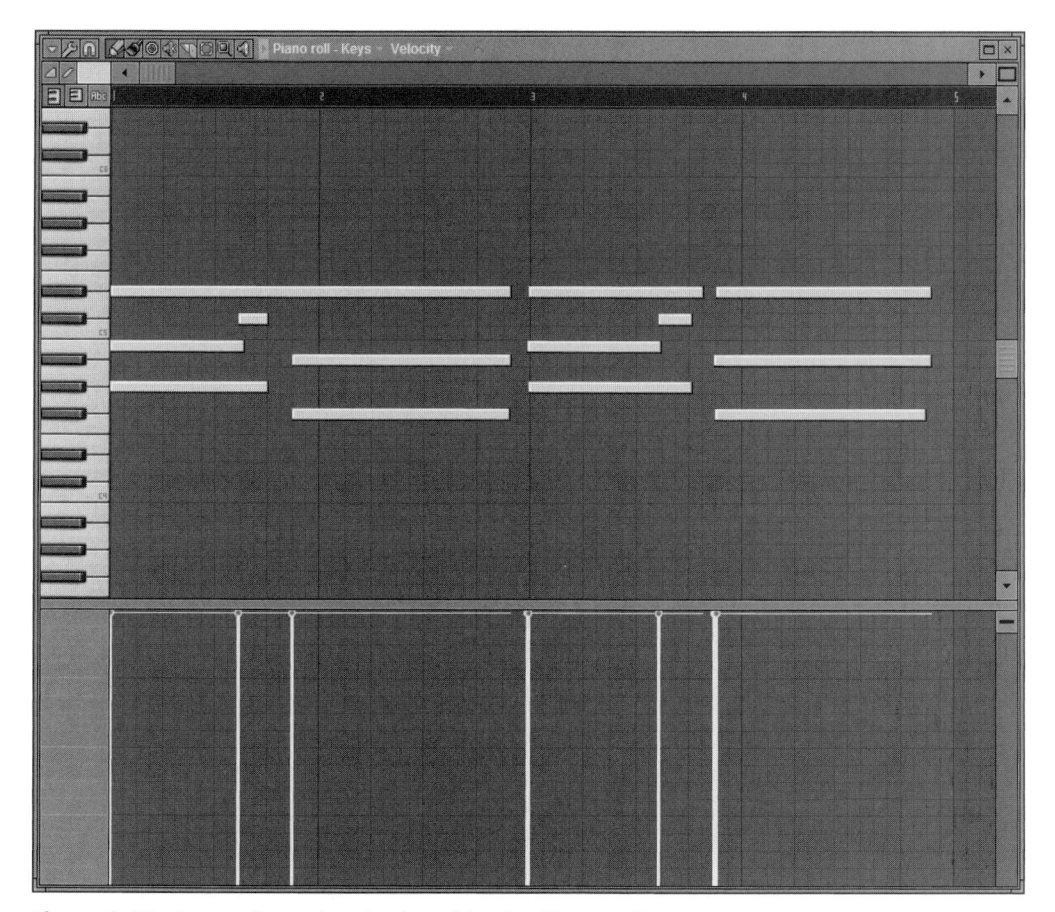

Figure 3.65 Some piano chords played in the Piano roll.

The Piano roll takes its name from an earlier music-reproduction technology—an actual roll of paper with holes in it. The roll would be loaded into a player piano and scrolled past a pneumatic switching mechanism. The holes would trigger the mechanism to play the correct notes. While originally a mechanical and slightly cumbersome technology, the Piano roll concept provides a useful visual metaphor for modern MIDI sequencers and editors.

While the old Piano roll had a set value (that is, once the holes were created in the paper, they could not be altered), today's tools are much more dynamic and flexible. Not only can the notes themselves be moved, chopped, re-pitched, and stretched, the instruments can be changed and manipulated. The Piano roll is basically a grid with an X-axis (left to right) and a Y-axis (up and down), where the X-axis represents time (the composition starts on the left and ends on the right) and the Y-axis represents the pitch of the notes to be played (the higher the note is placed on the Y-axis, the higher the note's pitch will be). Sometimes multiple instruments will be represented within one Piano roll, and the note's position on the Y-axis will determine which instrument is played—for example, A#3 might represent a drum kick, while C3 would be a snare hit. We'll talk more about note manipulation later in this section, but right now let's take a closer look at the Piano roll itself.

The first thing you notice when opening the Piano roll is the keyboard running down its left-hand side (see Figure 3.66). Although this can represent percussive instruments, it's best to think of it as a typical piano keyboard, with lower-pitched notes at the bottom and higher-pitched

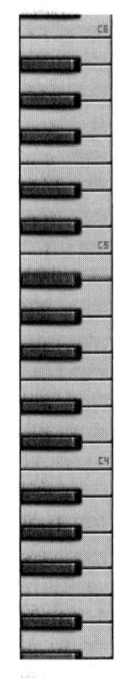

Figure 3.66   The graphic representation of a keyboard in the Piano roll.

notes at the top. Notes that you place on the grid will trigger notes on the virtual keyboard to the left, and you can actually see the animation of the keys responding to these notes.

Below the grid where the notes are placed is the event editor, where you can alter many parameters of the event, such as panning, velocity, and cutoff frequency. I use the term *event* in reference to the blocks placed on the Piano roll because all blocks do not always represent pitched notes; they sometimes represent notes slides or single instrument sounds, which we will discuss later in this chapter, in the "Note Color and Portamento" section. Similar to the Piano roll grid, the event editor's horizontal axis represents time, but the function of the vertical axis can vary based on which event parameter you have chosen to control. Figure 3.67 shows the event editor in action, where the highest position on the vertical axis is panning the event to the right, and the lowest position on the vertical axis is panning the event to the left. The tails appearing after notes represent the length of the note, which makes it easier to identify tightly grouped notes.

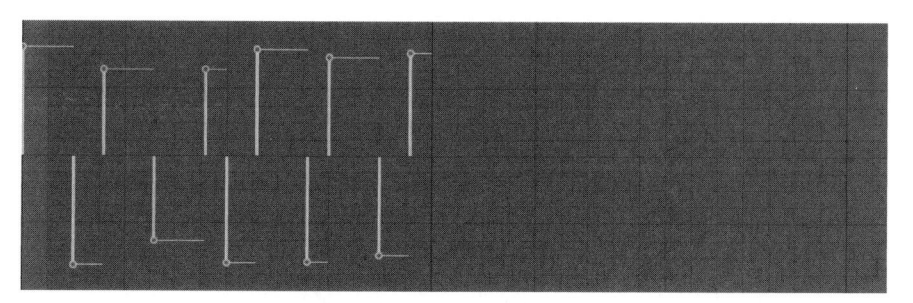

Figure 3.67   Panning using the event editor.

> **Note:** A quick way to access these adjustments is to right-click the empty area to the left of the event editor.

The Piano Roll Menus

The Piano roll has a serious set of menus that allow maximum manipulation and creativity for your generators and samples. It is important to go through these and understand what they do, because the Piano roll is the core of music making in FL Studio, and as I mentioned before, when you know where to find an option, the ideas pour onto your musical canvas without effort. We will start by looking at the corner button of the Piano roll, where you will find the greatest number of options (see Figure 3.68).

File

Many times when creating a groove in the Piano roll, I imagine the melody in a different song or as the basis of a new project altogether. A great idea can get lost if you like it, but it doesn't fit the song, and the notes are changed…it's gone. Open Score and Save Score As address this

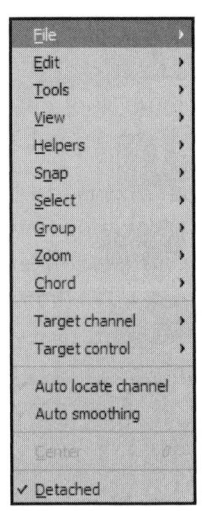

Figure 3.68 The main Piano roll menu.

problem by allowing you to save the current Piano roll by itself and then open it in another project (see Figure 3.69). If you have a MIDI file that you need to bring into the project, Import MIDI File will bring up a dialog box that allows you to choose the tracks and channels you wish to import. The Import MIDI dialog box will also give you the option to combine new incoming MIDI with the MIDI notes already on the Piano roll by selecting Blend with Existing Data. I suggest leaving Realign Events highlighted, because it will place your incoming MIDI at the start of the Piano roll. Only turn this off when you need the MIDI to begin at a certain point in the Piano roll. Export as MIDI File will turn that current Piano roll into a MIDI file, and if you need to paste MIDI data from any sequencer, choose Paste from MIDI Clipboard.

Figure 3.69 The File menu in the Piano roll.

Edit

The Edit menu, shown in Figure 3.70, begins with the familiar edit functions we typically see; however, the key is to remember that this menu is for the notes (blocks on the Piano roll) and their parameters (velocity, panning, modulation, pitch, and note release). Transpose moves selected notes vertically, while Shift moves notes horizontally on the Piano roll, and the Discard Lengths option (Shift+D) will cut all of your notes to the minimum grid setting, which by default will be set to Main. If you need shorter notes, change the Snap setting for that Piano roll before selecting Discard Lengths. Change Color (Alt+C) will change the selected note(s) to the color that is displayed in the upper-left corner of the Piano roll beneath the Snap to Grid button, and if no note is selected, it will affect all notes. If you have the default green selected, highlight a note that is green and then select Change Color—nothing will happen because the note is changed into the same color.

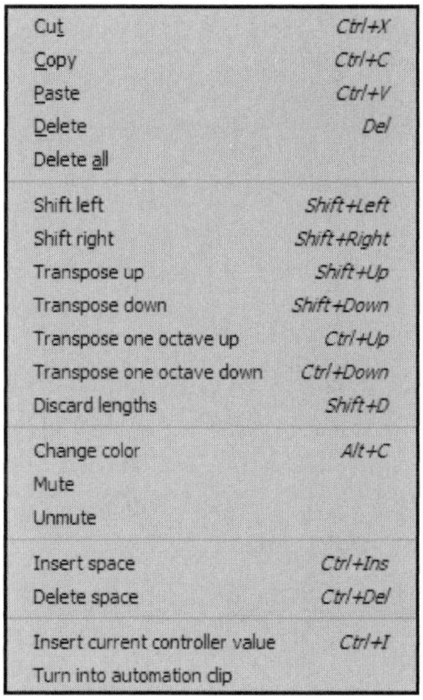

Cut	Ctrl+X
Copy	Ctrl+C
Paste	Ctrl+V
Delete	Del
Delete all	
Shift left	Shift+Left
Shift right	Shift+Right
Transpose up	Shift+Up
Transpose down	Shift+Down
Transpose one octave up	Ctrl+Up
Transpose one octave down	Ctrl+Down
Discard lengths	Shift+D
Change color	Alt+C
Mute	
Unmute	
Insert space	Ctrl+Ins
Delete space	Ctrl+Del
Insert current controller value	Ctrl+I
Turn into automation clip	

Figure 3.70 The Edit menu in the Piano roll.

We are familiar with Mute and Unmute, but Insert Space may not be as common of a function and will literally create a space between points (notes). The distance created will be the timeline selection, and the notes involved will be the highlighted ones. As you can see in Figure 3.72, the notes have had space inserted between them (whereas there is no space between them in Figure 3.71). The space inserted pushes the notes to the right, leaving the notes prior to the selection in place.

Delete Space, on the other hand, will delete notes in the selection and bring the notes that are to the right of the selection over to the left to match up with the start point of the timeline insertion. Insert Current Controller Value will allow you to paste automation data, as shown in the difference between Figure 3.73 and Figure 3.74, where the current parameter value (panning) in Figure 3.73 was pasted to the beginning of the selection in Figure 3.74. This only happens when a parameter is changed (such as turning the Pan knob to the left) and you want to paste that setting to the event editor in the Piano roll. This will only work with selections that are event editable, such as panning, volume, and pitch. Turn into Automation Clip will create a clip that you can place on the Playlist.

Figure 3.71 Notes prior to inserting space.

Tools

The Tools menu of the Piano roll (see Figure 3.75) gives you instruments for designing and altering your sound. Many of the options here allow you to break free of writer's block and create chords with no prior musical knowledge!

The first option that comes up in the Tools menu is the Riff Machine, which we discussed earlier, followed by Quick Legato, which will perform a short version of Articulate (see Figure 3.76). Articulate is great for changing up note length to create a more human sound to the notes played.

Quick Quantize (Ctrl+Q) will snap your selected notes to the positions closest to the current Snap setting. When open, the Quantize window (Alt+Q) (see Figure 3.77) will allow a wider range of options for aligning your notes.

Quick Chop (Ctrl+U) will cut selected notes on the Piano roll into pieces based on your Snap settings, which can be great if long notes are not creating the sound you want. Select them and

Figure 3.72 Notice that the notes maintain their distance relative to each other horizontally, and both have moved the amount of the timeline selection.

chop away to see what you can come up with! Similar to the previous tools, the full Chop window (see Figure 3.78) will open to reveal more options specifying how you want to cut the notes.

The Arpeggiator (see Figure 3.79) is similar to Chop but will allow you to specify a range of notation and can even stretch or compress the selected area.

Strum (see Figure 3.80) is an ingenious tool that can vary the note start point and velocity to create a real strumming sound. When a guitarist plays a chord, the strings do not play at the exact same time, and this tool replicates that. Combining this tool with chord placement of notes when using a guitar generator can yield some impressively realistic results.

Flam (see Figure 3.81) adds a short note that is just before the selected notes in the Piano roll to create a quick double-hit similar to two drum sticks hitting a snare one after the other. The Claw Machine (see Figure 3.82) can turn an otherwise simple beat into a complex or abstract groove that may be exactly what you are looking for.

The Limiter (see Figure 3.83) will keep the notes within certain pitch boundaries (for example, C#3–D5) set in the Limit options window. Flip is a quick option when you just want to flip the notes on the Piano roll horizontally or vertically. Randomize (see Figure 3.84) will bring up options to scatter your notes based on the settings you plug in.

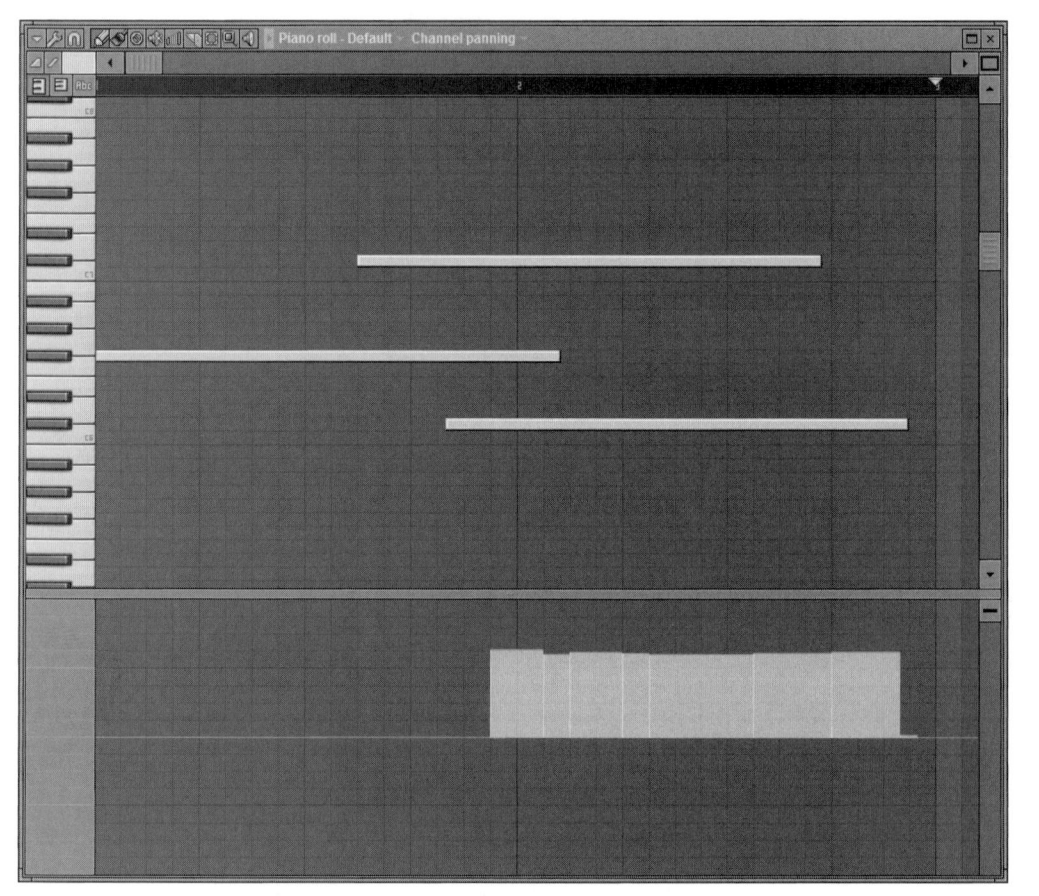

Figure 3.73 Panning automation for a portion of the notes.

The Scale Levels option will bring up a window allowing you to change the amplitude of your note. This can come in handy when a generator changes sound or response, much like the tone of a piano key differs when pressed firmly versus softly. If the sound you want is not there, try opening this option and adjusting the knobs for more tension on the notes or where the note is played loudest.

The LFO window (see Figure 3.85) will only open when you are working with the event editor (the area beneath the notes in the Piano roll), and the visual wave drawn will affect the parameter chosen. In Figure 3.85, the panning climbs to the right then slopes to the left. By altering the speed, the panning will happen more quickly and can bring needed life to a song.

View

The View options, shown in Figure 3.86, are fairly simple, and as you might guess, they only affect the appearance of the Piano roll. Grid Color will change the background color of the

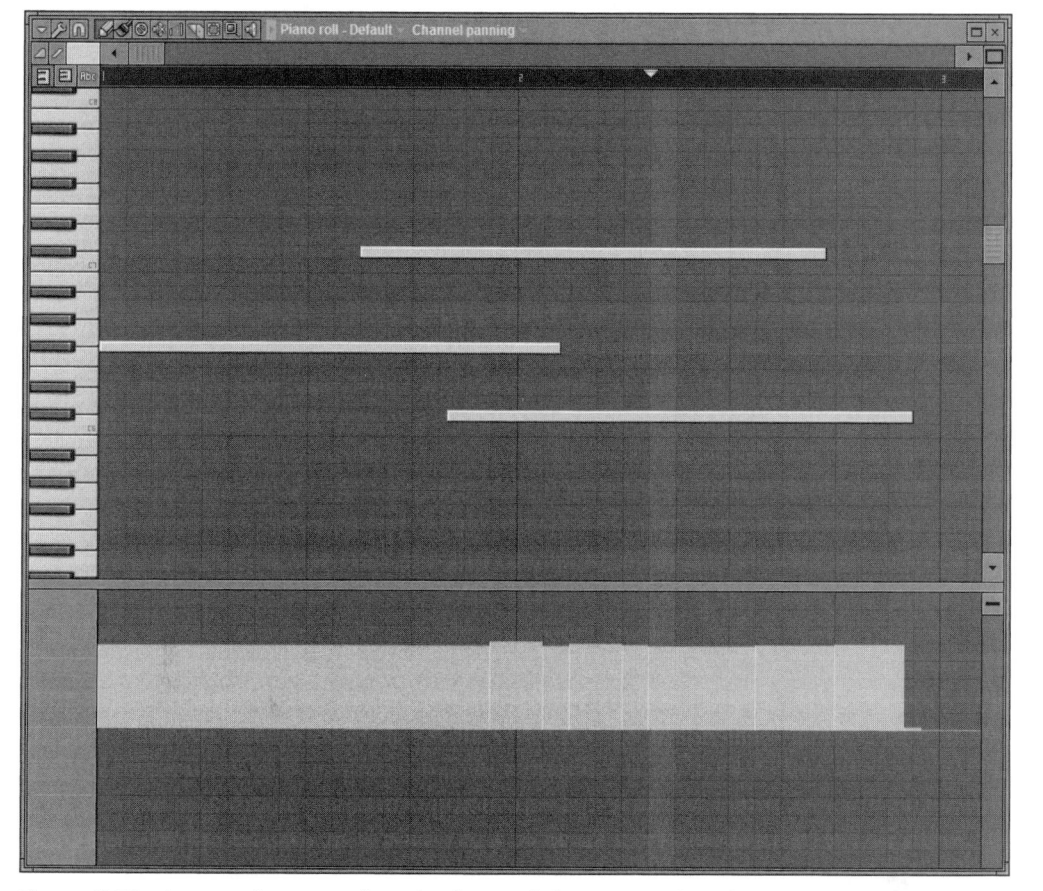

Figure 3.74 Automation pasted at the front of the event editor based on the timeline selection.

Piano roll, but there is no quick undo, and you will need to select the default color again to get it back, so use caution. Invert Grid, as discussed before, will reverse dark lines and light lines on the grid, and the Swap Panels option will place the Piano roll notes below the event editor window.

Helpers

View Note Helpers, shown in Figure 3.87, has been very useful to me when I am placing note by note because I am unable to play the notes that I am thinking of live. In many programs you must first move the mouse and watch what note it is on to tell you where you are about to place a note. With note helpers turned on, the grid will turn light gray for the ivory piano keys and dark gray for the ebony keys all the way across the grid.

Detect Scale will determine the scale notes you have selected (or the entire Piano roll, if nothing is selected), but a few notes must be placed for this to take effect. The View Length in Note

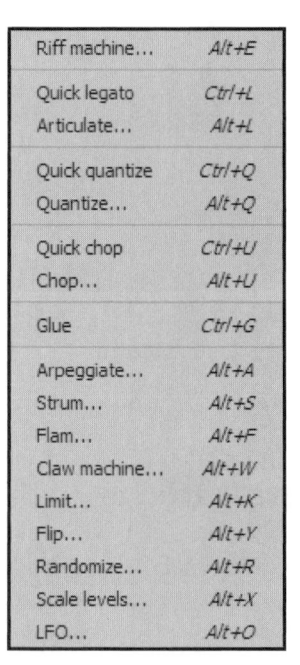

Riff machine...	*Alt+E*
Quick legato	*Ctrl+L*
Articulate...	*Alt+L*
Quick quantize	*Ctrl+Q*
Quantize...	*Alt+Q*
Quick chop	*Ctrl+U*
Chop...	*Alt+U*
Glue	*Ctrl+G*
Arpeggiate...	*Alt+A*
Strum...	*Alt+S*
Flam...	*Alt+F*
Claw machine...	*Alt+W*
Limit...	*Alt+K*
Flip...	*Alt+Y*
Randomize...	*Alt+R*
Scale levels...	*Alt+X*
LFO...	*Alt+O*

Figure 3.75 The Tools menu in the Piano roll.

Figure 3.76 You can see the Articulation dialog box, where, from the Option drop-down, you can select from Legato, Portato, and Staccato. This runs from long notes (legato) to short notes (staccato), and the lengths are affected by the Multiply knob, while the Variation knob controls differences of length.

Properties option means that the length of the note will be shown in the event editor. This helps you get an overview of which notes are automated where, because rather than stacked dots, the lines show which note is at each point in the event editor (see Figure 3.88).

Ghost Channels will bring up the Piano rolls of all other channels in the selected pattern and display them in a translucent color for reference. You can't edit these ghost channels; instead, they are there to show you a visual representation of where other channels are playing in the

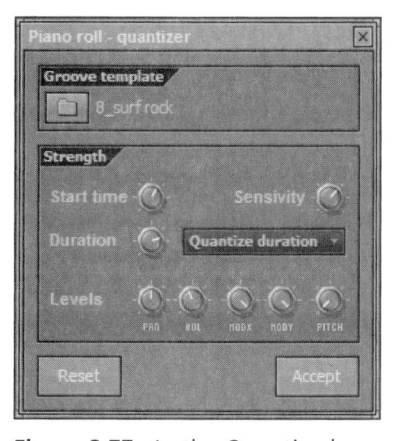

Figure 3.77 In the Quantize box, you can specify start times, note duration, and end times when performing quantization. The folder icon will allow you to import preset quantization settings.

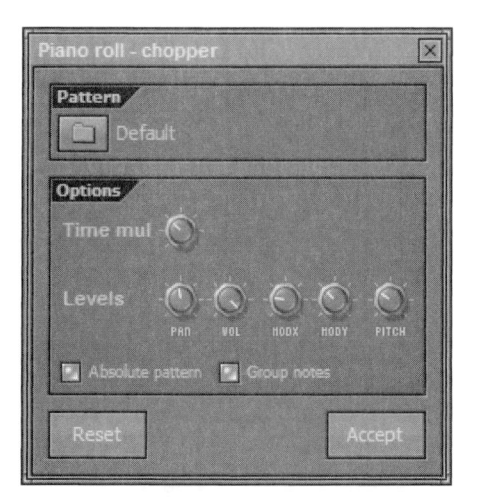

Figure 3.78 The Chopper can have presets loaded from the icon or manually set using the knobs. Absolute Pattern means that the notes will be cut on the grid, but when turned off, it will cause notes to chop based on their own starting points.

Piano roll. Let's say you have two channels using the Piano roll in a pattern. One is a hi-hat, and the other is a kick drum sound, and you want to spice up the timing of your hi-hat. If you have it in your head that you want to have hi-hat notes immediately before and after the drum kick sound, it helps to actually see where the drum kicks are happening rather than using trial and error to move the hi-hat notes around. By selecting ghost channels, these kick notes appear in the Piano roll of the hi-hat. This works in reverse, too, so the hi-hat notes will appear in the drum kick Piano roll.

Figure 3.79 The Arpeggiator gives you options for creating a melody based on certain patterns, note range, and individual note length. Try turning the Gate knob to create notes that stop playing more abruptly.

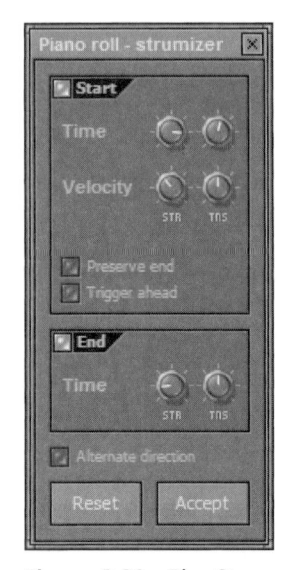

Figure 3.80 The Strum option will allow you to manipulate when the note starts to play, along with how strong that note is played.

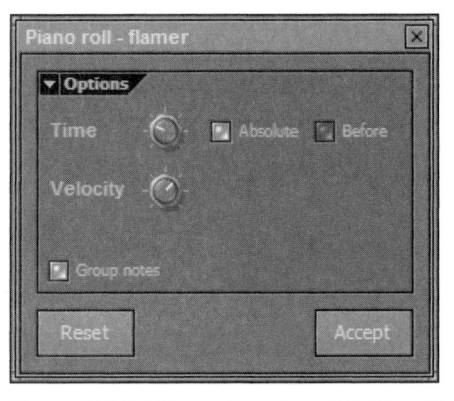

Figure 3.81 The notes placed before the selected notes with the Flam tool are great for creating a snare drum flam.

Figure 3.82 The Claw Machine gives you options for taking out notes when a beat needs to be changed up or may be too busy. Period will determine the period of time that the Claw Machine will perform changes, and Trash Every will determine how often notes are dropped within the chosen period.

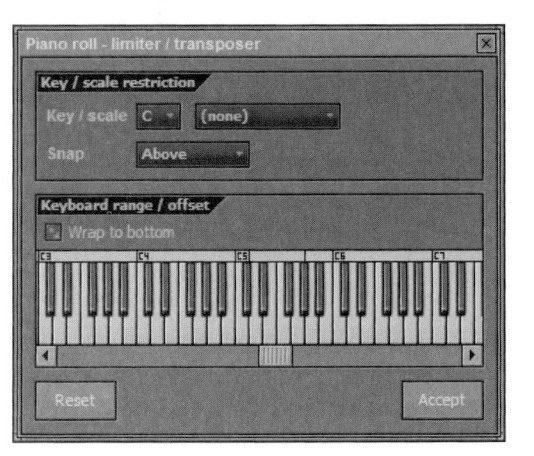

Figure 3.83 Limit keeps the notes in a certain range and can also keep them within a certain key. This can be excellent for keeping your melodies sounding good without fear of sour notes.

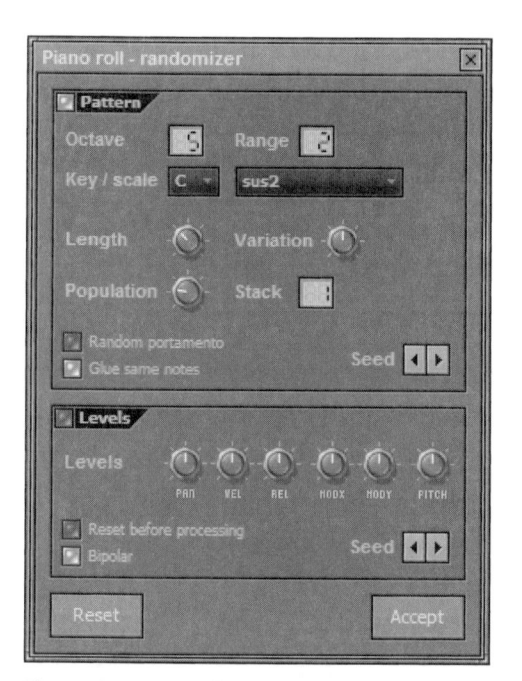

Figure 3.84 Randomize can contain a certain note scale and range, but it goes beyond that by allowing you to increase the number of notes in a section as well as randomize automation parameters, such as volume and panning.

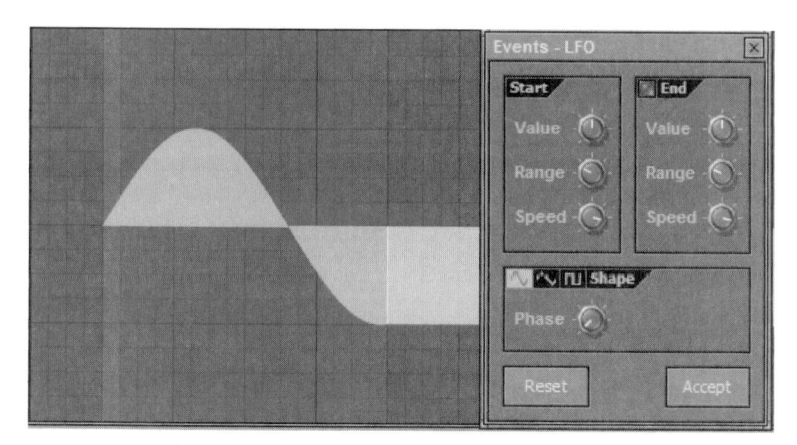

Figure 3.85 The LFO window can be a great aid in getting automation to line up just right.

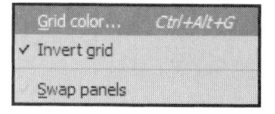

Figure 3.86 The Piano roll View options.

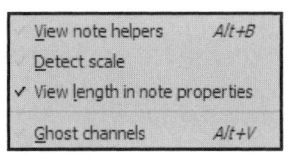

Figure 3.87 The Piano roll Helpers section.

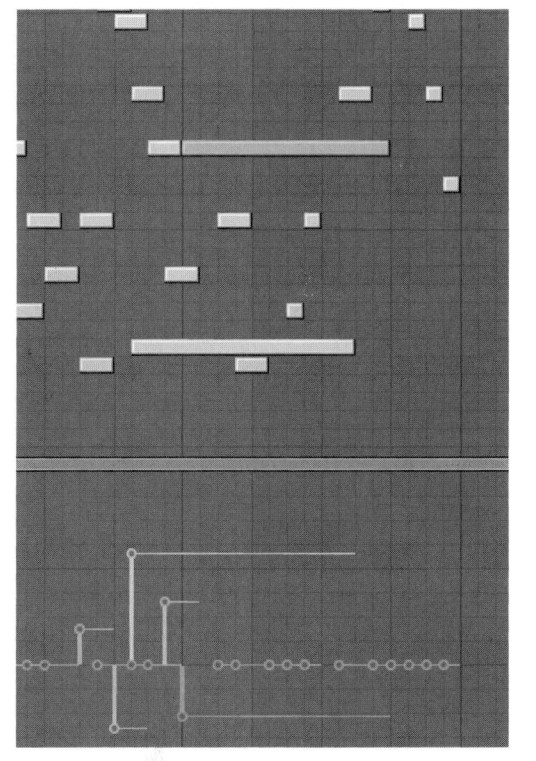

Figure 3.88 With View Length in Note Properties checked, you are able to see the tails of the notes in the lower event editor.

Additional Options

Moving farther along down the Piano roll Main menu (refer to Figure 3.68), we have already gone over Snap settings, but it is good to take note that these are the Snap settings specifically for the Piano roll unless Main is selected (default). The selection options are familiar, and great quick keys to keep in mind are Ctrl+Enter for Select Time around Selection, which will automatically place a timeline selection around the notes you have selected. This is useful for looping a section to hear it quickly and to go through multiple sections using the same time spacing (moving the timeline but keeping the length of the timeline selection), use the quick keys Ctrl+Right Arrow or Ctrl+Left Arrow to move the timeline in those directions. Group allows you to group specific notes that you select, but it will only be active if global grouping is selected in the recording panel.

The zoom options operate on the same 1 through 5 sequence, and I find myself using 5 the most because it zooms right in to what I am working on. The Chord option will bring up a list of chords that you can draw or paint directly into the Piano roll and is a valuable tool for getting your notation on point. The Target Channel option will allow you to scroll through channels available for Piano roll editing, and Target Control will allow you to scroll through the event editor options, but I suggest selecting the drop-down from the top of the Piano roll and right-clicking the empty area next to the event editor for quicker access.

The Auto Locate option will bring up the first Piano roll with data when navigating through patterns, which is great when you have a ton of channels and the Piano roll you are looking for is located 40 channels down. Auto-Smoothing will take your drawn automation and smooth it out when you release the mouse button from drawing if it was drawn with straight lines.

Center (0 on your QWERTY keyboard) is a great way to create your own scrolling when Auto-Scroll is not turned on. Every time you tap 0, the screen will center on the timeline marker, so as your song plays, you can view a part, let the timeline marker scroll offscreen, and then jump to where it is with one keystroke. Detached is for those of us working with more than one monitor and will allow the Piano roll to be placed on another window and not confine it to the single monitor space.

Piano Roll Tools

Although the tools in the Piano roll appear similar to those in the Playlist, they are slightly different because of the tool options available (see Figure 3.89). The first option is another place to conveniently change the Snap setting of the grid. Draw (P), Paint (B), Delete (D), Mute (T), Cut (C), Select (E), and Zoom to Selection (Z) are all familiar options, but in the Piano roll a Scrub tool (Y) is added for precision playback. They all operate in the same way and apply to the notes in the Piano roll. The Scrub feature can be used to hear a short part over and over without having to wait for playback or mess with the timeline selection. With this tool selected, you can click and drag your mouse over a section of the Playlist to play your project at any speed forward or backward for critical mixing.

Figure 3.89 The Piano roll tools.

Note Color and Portamento

The Slide (S) feature in the Piano roll allows easy pitch bend manipulation of notes when using FL Studio's instrument plug-ins (see Figure 3.90). The generator playing the sound must be able to slide notes in order for this to work. The way that you get notes to slide is to first choose a note and place it on the Piano roll and then place a slide note of the same color above or below that note. The note as a whole (slides included) will play the length of the original note, and the slide note will only affect where the original note slides to and how quickly that note slides.

Figure 3.90   Slide, portamento, and note coloring.

In Figure 3.91, the middle note is the original note, while the notes above and below are both slide notes. There is only one sound that plays, but as it does, it quickly bends up from the first slide note and continues playing at that pitched-up note until it reaches the bend down note, where it will slowly bend to the drawn slide note. To bend back to the original note, a slide note must be placed on the same note position (vertically) as the original note, and it will bend back to the original.

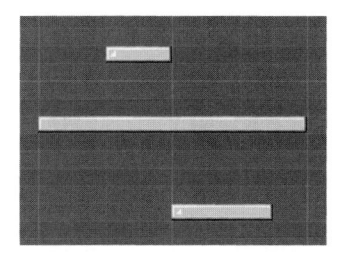

Figure 3.91   A single note that slides up and then down.

The Portamento button will cause a short slide from a note prior to where the portamento event is set and will only work with generators that are included with FL Studio, not with third-party VST instruments. The color palette offers 16 colors for the notes to be drawn in, and each color represents a MIDI channel associated with the inserted plug-in. This is great for getting different instruments within a plug-in to play, but keep in mind that this MIDI signal stops at the plug-in, so if you want to send MIDI out to an external device, you need to use the MIDI out plug-in. The color will affect the behavior of the notes as well, such as in Figure 3.92, where I have the same

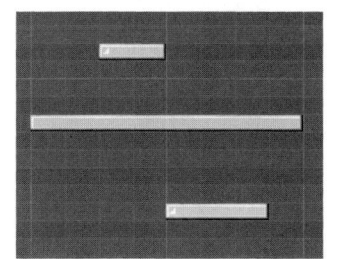

Figure 3.92   A single note that slides up but is unaffected by the slide down note that is a different color.

single note with two slides but have colored only the first slide the same as the single note. In this example, the note will bend up and stay there and will not be affected by the slide down note because it is a different color. This is necessary when you only want certain notes to slide, as opposed to every note parallel to the slide note.

The Piano roll is easily the most versatile music-making tool in FL Studio, and I believe that most of your creating will be done in this window when using virtual instruments. Always remember that the options you choose from this window will only affect your Piano roll notes and their parameters. This is where even the tone deaf can use the help of Chord and Identify Scale options to create sonically pleasing music. The event editor is where specific parameters can be altered quickly to create volume fluctuation and traveling sound that darts from left to right. However, what if you don't want to create volume changes, but you want to set volume levels and add effects? That is where the Mixer comes in and will typically be your last stop in the music-making process before exporting a project to audio.

Mixer

Now that I have given you a look at where sound is created and where it is arranged, we need to focus on where it all goes. You have built channels into patterns, and now the audio clips and pattern clips are properly placed where you want them on the Playlist, but it's time to get some levels set and effects running. This is the control center where all of your audio, after it is generated, will run through on its way out to the soundcard. The purpose of this section is to inform you of what the Mixer can do, and later we will get into specifics of how the plug-ins work.

The Mixer (see Figure 3.93) gets its name from the function that it performs, because within the Mixer is where all of the different sounds (multiple tracks of audio) are mixed together to become a song (a single stereo output). FL Studio's Mixer blows past nearly every home recording

Figure 3.93 The FL Studio Mixer.

software program in available tracks, allowing use of up to 99 insert, 4 send, 1 selected, and 1 master track! Keep in mind that you will only be able to run 105 tracks if your computer can handle it, and if there are effects on the tracks, most computers cannot handle such a workload. Regardless of track count, keep in mind that use of the Mixer is a linking game, and routing your sound properly is key to quickly navigating the program while using it efficiently.

Mixer Menu

The Mixer menu, as shown in Figure 3.94, houses options for moving tracks, changing audio, and most importantly linking the Mixer tracks to channels!

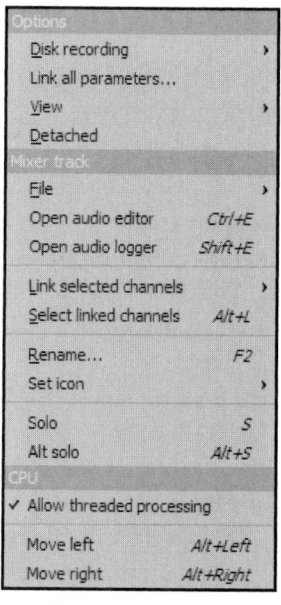

Figure 3.94 The Mixer menu.

Initial Mixer Options

The upper corner of the Mixer, much like every window in FL Studio, has a menu with many helpful options. The first set involves Disk Recording options, and Render to Wave File will convert all tracks that are ready to record into a WAV file. Don't worry; we will go in depth into audio and MIDI recording in upcoming chapters. It is debatable whether Auto-Unarm is useful, and it comes down to personal preference. On one hand, when you are finished recording, there is no risk of recording onto multiple tracks, erasing takes, or encountering any number of errors, but the argument would be for those of us who like doing multiple takes and don't want to re-arm every time.

Auto-Create Audio Clips will place your recordings into the Playlist automatically when in Song mode, which gives you an instant visual of the audio. In Pattern mode it will create the audio clip channel. Latency Compensation tells FL Studio to adjust the latency created by the plug-ins before playing out of the master output. 32-Bit Float Recording means that recordings will be saved as 32-bit, which is a higher quality, but remember that CDs only run at 16-bit, and MP3 files are even lower quality, so it is not always necessary to operate at this bit depth. You really only need to select 32-bit when your soundcard is recording at 24-bit (if it has that ability); otherwise, you can leave 32-bit unchecked.

Latency Compensation (Delay Compensation) When audio runs through cables in the normal world, there is no delay because it is just an electrical signal that fires through the cable. In the digital world (our computers), the audio is nothing more than numbers that represent information. The conversion from this mass of numbers into something you can hear takes time to process in your soundcard. The longer this conversion takes, the longer it takes for the sound to reach you. This can be distracting when you are trying to record and monitor your input, because it causes an echo effect and can place the recording out of sync with the song. Delay compensation looks at the input delay being caused and speeds up the audio (or slows the rest of the song down, however you see it) in order to make it fit properly in time with all other sounds in FL Studio. You will commonly see delay compensation when referencing plug-ins, but in FL Studio, you will typically not have to worry about this, depending on the soundcard that you are using. In both cases, the soundcard can still cause latency, and clips may need to be nudged in the Playlist.

Link All Parameters is essentially a master list of software parameters that can be linked to a hardware controller. When you choose this option, you will be able to select from a list that you can follow up by moving a hardware controller, such as the slider on a MIDI keyboard. So if you choose Master Volume and move the slider, every time you move that slider during the open project, the master volume will move with it. A notable feature of this selection is that it will automatically jump to the next parameter on the master list after a hardware controller is moved. This makes mapping a large number of parameters to your MIDI controller much easier.

The View menu only contains toggle switches and again will not affect anything other than the appearance of the Mixer. The Big Mixer option will place a large version of the selected track's level meter in between the effects and the tracks themselves. Another way of getting the visual readout is to insert the WaveCandy's plug-in on the selected track for a large choice of visual metering options. Names at Bottom will move the track names below the level meters and volume controls, while the Tracks on Right Side option switches the tracks and effects list positions.

Mixer Track
This portion of the menu pertains specifically to selected Mixer tracks and begins by allowing you to save and open Mixer track states, which are like snapshots of all the settings your Mixer

track has. This snapshot saves as a file and, when opened (even in a different project), FL Studio will read the settings and instantly replicate them on the new Mixer track. If you find yourself working with audio such as dialogue-only interviews that need the same treatment (effects, compression, and so on) every time, save your settings and re-import them, then add or subtract to taste rather than always building from scratch.

Browse States will place Mixer track states in the project Browser, which is by default on the left. Open Audio Editor will bring up Edison for that audio clip, while Open Audio Logger will open an instance of Edison that will record the outgoing audio from that track.

Link Selected Channels will take the channels that you have highlighted in the Channel window and send their audio output through the track you have selected. This makes routing fast and easy when compared to manually having to go in through a long list of menus just to get the signal flowing properly. Here you choose channels, then choose the track, then link them, and the audio from the channel(s) will play through that track. A great new feature in FL9 is the ability to drop an instrument preset that automatically links to the channel. For example, drag an instrument preset such as Ogun Bass 2 and place it on an empty Mixer track. The channel created for the instrument will automatically link to the selected Mixer track, and the plug-in will pop up with the selected preset. This feature can greatly improve your workflow, and I highly suggest taking advantage of it. By far the quickest way to assign channels to tracks, though, is to select the channels you want to link to tracks and then choose Link Selected Channels > Starting from This Track. This will separate each channel onto its own track that is automatically named.

Rename (F2) in the Mixer is the same as with other windows and will change the name and color of the selected track. Set Icon will allow you to assign a graphic to the selected track and can help you quickly find a track, especially when there are 50 tracks running, and you have run out of differing colors.

While you are familiar with Solo (S), Alt-Solo (Alt+S) makes finding routing for solos unnecessary. If you have a vocal that is going through a send and possibly an EQ, when you only solo the vocal (provided it is not also going through the master track), you will not hear anything because the sends do not solo as well. Alt-Solo includes the audio of tracks routed to and from the selected track so that the sends (if there are any) do not get left out. I recommend using this unless you are trying to hear a dry sample (audio with no effects).

Allow Threaded Processing will spread out the workload of the Mixer, including the plug-ins being used, across multiple computer processors, provided there is more than one in the computer.

Mixer Interface

The Mixer is laid out with 99 stereo tracks (100 including the master track) that can be linked to the channels in the Channel window and four send tracks that can receive signal from a track or channel and run that signal through effects on its way to the master output. This shoots way past many programs that only allow 32 or 64 tracks, because if the available outputs are 64, then in many programs that means you get 64 mono tracks or 32 stereo tracks. FL Studio Mixer tracks are all stereo, so you should have no shortage of space! The four sends are not limiting, because any one of the 99 Mixer tracks can act like a send. Let's start by taking a look at a single track (see Figure 3.95).

Figure 3.95   A single Mixer track.

Although projects can differ in routing and setup, a good general way to look at these tracks is as individual or groups of audio. That audio is triggered in or routed to these tracks before going through the main output, which is what we hear through our speakers. You can right-click the top of each track for the Mixer track options that we discussed earlier.

Traveling downward, you see the track number, icon, and name, where all aside from the track number can be edited through the Track menu. The moving meter lines are graphic representations of the volume, which can be tracked in decibels (dB) by hovering your mouse over the big meter display of the selected track. The tiny green light below each track meter is basically an on/off switch when left-clicking and a solo switch when right-clicking. A speedy way to toggle Alt-Solo and Solo is to toggle between Alt+right-clicking and just right-clicking the green button.

The single knob is the master panning of that track, and the fader running up and down beneath it is the volume fader. This design closely relates to those big consoles in a professional studio, and the effects processors are off to the side. Beneath the track volume is the send or sidechain switch. Left-clicking the switch creates a send or makes a send active, and right-clicking the switch allows you to choose between a send and a sidechain signal.

The FX switch is versatile, because left-clicking it will disable or enable effects on the track (if there are effects inserted), and right-clicking will bring up or close all effect windows. This is the best way to navigate through what can quickly become piles of plug-ins.

The final button is a Record Arm switch, which means any audio going through the track will be recorded to your computer.

The next section of the Mixer we will take a look at will give us an idea of where plug-ins are inserted and how audio is routed with our hardware inputs and outputs. The top portion is a drop-down of your available inputs, and when record-arming a track, you will be prompted to select one. This is where you would choose Input 2 if you had a mic plugged into the second input on your soundcard.

Below the input selection are eight slots to insert a plug-in (see Figure 3.96), each with a tab that gives you options for these plug-ins. The first option is the immense list that FL Studio has to offer, including any third-party plug-ins that you may have loaded and a few additional options for saving and recalling plug-in settings. These will be addressed in the plug-in section of Chapter 6. For now, remember that this is where they are inserted to have effect on the audio coming through the tracks.

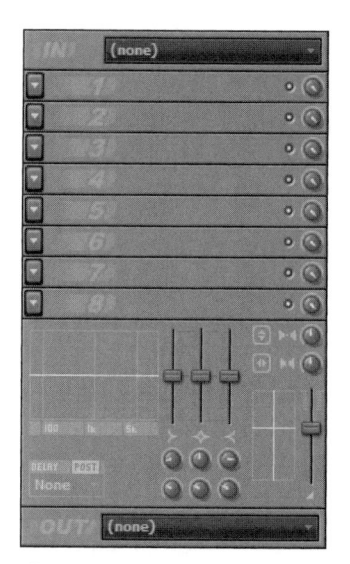

Figure 3.96 The I/O, effects racks, and general controls of the Mixer.

Below the plug-ins is a parametric EQ (see Figure 3.97) that is useful for small changes, but I recommend sticking to a plug-in for maximum tweaking ability. You can manually adjust your curve in the section on the right or use the knobs below the graph to set your values. In the upper-right section are two toggle switches and two rotary knobs. When activated, the switch with the vertical arrows will flip the phase of the incoming signal for when a waveform is out of phase and creating poor audio quality. The switch with the vertical arrows will make the left output of the track play out of the right and vice versa.

The upper rotary knob will increase stereo separation of the audio when turned counterclockwise when the incoming signal has stereo information, so this knob will have no effect on a

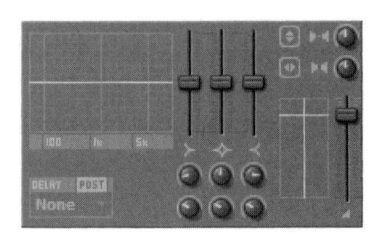

Figure 3.97 General Mixer track controls.

mono vocal recording. The knob will also bring audio into the middle until it is completely mono when turned clockwise. The last rotary knob is basically another send knob and will control the send level of an active send track. This can be convenient, but I find staying with the sends in the main Mixer track strips affords me more flexibility and makes getting used to the routing even easier.

The lower-right portion of this section is a master volume and pan that I do not recommend using because using the volume and pan knobs on the main strips prevents having to go through each individual track to change the settings. If you know the specific delay that a plug-in is causing in any value (beats, bars, samples, and so on), then you can choose the option in the lower-left corner and enter the value. This is really only necessary when a plug-in is slowing down audio and causing it to be out of sync with the project tempo.

The final section is the output to your soundcard, and by default the master will be set to your Analog 1 and 2 outputs (left and right stereo outputs). You really only need to change these around when you want to send certain tracks to different outputs. Different tracks going to different outputs can help you tailor a mix for artists when they don't want to hear the whole song. Many bass players I have worked with prefer only drums, so you can duplicate the drum track and send one to the main mix that you are listening to while sending the duplicate to a different output that is going to the bass player's headphones. This is only one creative way of output routing, and your imagination is the only limit to what you can do.

The song may be arranged nicely and have great breaks and hooks, but if it is not mixed properly, it will still sound like a garage demo. Taking the time to understand the Mixer and being able to fully utilize it is paramount to your success when dropping a final copy of your music. One key feature of the Mixer is being able to link nearly any software controller (knob or fader in FL Studio) to a hardware controller (MIDI controller or keyboard with faders). Linking the volume controls gives you that hands-on feeling when working on the final cut of your project and allows you to listen and move faders rather than search for a track, point and click, then try to find another track. With the knobs or faders linked, you can immediately juggle multiple parameters, such as volume, and make everything sit nicely in the mix. To get this pleasant "sitting in the mix" sound, taking time to EQ sounds where unneeded frequencies are removed and using compression to give your projects more volume will be key effects used for getting a quality final product.

Project Browser

The project Browser is for easy location of presets, audio samples, and projects (see Figure 3.98). FL Studio has made it easy on you by allowing drag and drop so that you can drop presets on a generator or place audio samples directly on the Playlist. You can also access any project, including the ones you have created, premade projects, and even tutorial projects (which I highly recommend).

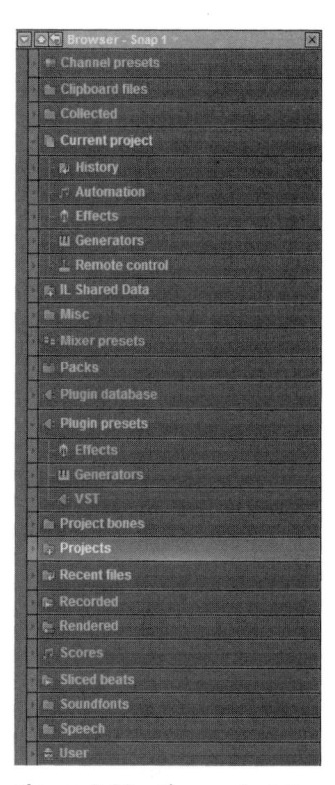

Figure 3.98 The project Browser.

We have discussed many different ways of bringing up sounds and presets in the Browser using shortcuts in menus of other windows so that we can get a bird's-eye view of all clips and presets related to our selection, but I have not yet explained how to fully navigate the Browser.

The Browser menu, shown in Figure 3.99, can be accessed by clicking the upper-left corner of the Browser window and begins with a set of familiar options. While we have discussed the Find options in the Browser and how to use Smart Find, some quick keys to take note of are F2 and F3, as they will jump one result back and one result forward, respectively, through the current search.

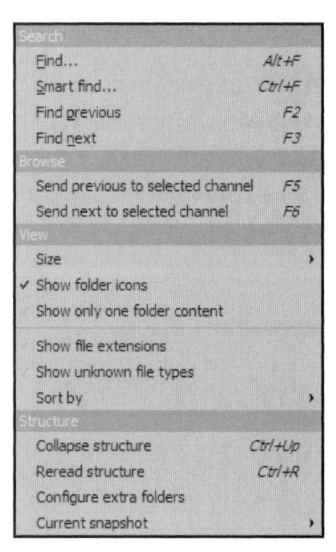

Figure 3.99   The Project Browser menu.

The View portion of the Browser menu is the most important part, because how you set up the appearance will determine how effective you are at finding files you need. The first option will allow you to change the Browser font to your liking (and vision) and display icons next to the folders in the Browser. Show Only One Folder Content is very helpful for not allowing the Browser to get too cluttered, because it will only allow the opening of one folder at a time. Show File Extensions will add the file type, such as .wav or .ogg, to the name in the Browser, and Show Unknown File Types allows files to display in the Browser that FL Studio would not normally recognize.

The Browser allows you to sort by group, but if you know part of the name of your desired file, stay with the Smart Find option.

Structure still relates to the view, and Collapse Structure is a quick way to view all the parent menus quickly. Reread Structure will display any files that were made while you had FL Studio running, so if you downloaded a plug-in preset or an audio file and it is not showing up, try choosing this option.

Configure Extra Folders will allow you to make a directory leading to files that you want to use in FL Studio, but which are outside of the typical FL Studio file locations. I found this handy when working with projects that someone had on a hard drive, where I pointed FL to them, and all the needed files showed up in a folder in the Browser.

Browser snapshots are an easy way to recall a certain look of the Browser when you find yourself using effects from similar folders often. To save a snapshot, select the snapshot number that you want FL Studio to remember and then open the Browser to the folder you want. Now when you press that number with the Browser focused, the Browser will automatically open the folders that you set. The Plugin Picker has been discussed, and like the other files in the Browser, each plug-in can be dragged and dropped to its desired location.

The important detail to keep in mind with the Browser is mainly its appearance, because it is how you use it (if at all) that can create success or headache. As I have professed, knowing where things are (or at least how and where to look for them) can be the difference between the exact sound you want and a mediocre beat that doesn't stand out. The drag-and-drop ability of the Browser is more powerful than many users take advantage of, and I suggest taking a little time to explore all of the options we have discussed. Now that we have laid out the entire interface of FL Studio, including features and how to use them, it's time to put this knowledge into action. In the next chapter, we will look at recording audio into the program and weigh the benefits and pitfalls of the different recording options available.

4 Recording Audio

Vocals, guitar, piano, drums, bass, and a wide array of instruments require recording into FL Studio. There are ways to emulate these sounds, which we will look at in the next chapter, but for now, it's time to focus on the real stuff. With audio recordings, there are no second chances or fixes once it is recorded, right? Wrong! Even recorded audio can be manipulated to fit a tempo or pitch, and with the powerful tools available from FL Studio, these tasks are easy to perform. Mammoth programs, such as Pro Tools, have time-stretching plug-ins, but that one plug-in can cost *four times* as much as FL Studio with everything included! Seriously, let that sink in a moment.

In this age of technology, wizards crunching numbers in a computer lab have been able to give us the tools for making music that no longer require a black American Express card to purchase what is needed. Many recording programs out there will give you the ability to record anything you like, but they lack in editing abilities, while others are limitless but, as previously mentioned, can simply cost too much money. FL Studio allows you to record, has the editing capabilities, and is at a price that will not devastate your funds. In this chapter we will explore recording audio into FL Studio and the many ways that we can easily manipulate the sound to our liking. We'll start off with a little explanation of how to set things up, then demonstrate a few recording examples, and finally look at the creative ways we can edit our recordings.

What Is Needed to Record?

This chapter focuses on recording audio and not MIDI, so the virtual instruments and generators will be discussed in the following chapter. Here we'll take a look at recording vocals and real instruments, which is quickly becoming the only tangible medium remaining in much of music today. I love live bands, but much of the music that you hear in commercials and on the radio is nothing more than music created from scratch in a program with a live singer placed in the mix. The main things that we need are obvious—computer, interface (soundcard), mic, and something to record (vocals, guitar, and so on), but there are a few things to be aware of when getting set up. It is my goal to give you the necessary information for recording audio so you never get stuck wondering what to do next or why something isn't recording.

The Many Faces of FL Studio

As you might have noticed, there are a few versions of FL Studio available, and each comes with progressively more features. The key is choosing what you want to do with FL Studio and which (if any) limitations you are able to live with. In my opinion, because of the low cost of the entire program even at the highest level, I recommend getting the best that you can afford. You might not *think* you need a tool or a feature, only to find out down the road that it is exactly what you need. You can always upgrade, but learning the tools available right away will allow you to work quickly with no future roadblocks.

FL Studio Versions Available

- FL Studio Express

- FL Studio Fruity Edition

- FL Studio Producer Edition

- FL Studio Signature Bundle (Formerly XXL edition)

We could take a look at what everything can do, but that is the purpose of this entire book, so for now I will focus on the limitations of each version and provide a few examples of how it might affect you when choosing a purchase.

The Express version has no Piano roll and cannot record, but it is great if you only want to create loops and simple music riffs that you play live. The Express version also will not allow you to run FL Studio inside of another application, such as Pro Tools, so if you want to send audio into another program, you will have to export the WAV file of your project and then import it into the other software program. In this version you are also unable to have automation events for patterns, so if you want to affect everything in a pattern, you would have to individually change each channel parameter.

The Fruity edition is starting to look more like the FL Studio that we all know and love, but it still lacks the ability to record audio. In the Fruity edition, you have use of the Piano roll to make sounds and play instruments. These two versions will allow you to basically make beats, but the moment you want to record vocals or a real instrument, you will see just how incomplete these versions are.

The Producer edition is the standard FL Studio structure and contains everything you will need to record audio and make music. This is the version that I will be basing this entire book on and the minimal version you will want to be using. The Producer edition allows recording with Edison, so you will finally be able to lay down that vocal track you've had written down.

The Signature bundle is the most-for-your-money purchase because you get the Producer edition with hundreds of dollars worth of plug-ins added to the package. The added tools give you a larger arsenal for creating and editing sound in your projects and in my opinion is worth every penny. From a musician and an engineer's perspective, I suggest the Producer edition as your minimum purchase because you will find that the inability to record audio can greatly hinder your music making.

Interface Inputs

So after that can-and-cannot section, let's jump back into the audio recording aspect by taking a look at the interface we will be using. Sadly, I am unable to describe setup for every device made—that would be a painfully long book. So, I'll give you an overview of what you need to focus on.

When you are recording, you need inputs on your interface so that the sound can pass into FL Studio and be digitally recorded. If you will be recording vocals, then you're going to need a mic input of some sort on the interface. If you are recording an instrument that has a line output, then you can also use a mic, but you will usually get a cleaner sound by using a line input on you interface.

When you open the Mixer (F9), you can see the available inputs from the drop-down menu next to the word IN (see Figure 4.1). Each insert track has its own individual IN menu, allowing you to select as many inputs as your interface physically has. Most of us will only need one input so that we can record vocals or a bass riff, but if you want to record drums or a symphony with multiple parts to be mixed, then your interface will need more inputs. Consequently, you will need more mics and cables, too, although for me, getting more gear is a happy day.

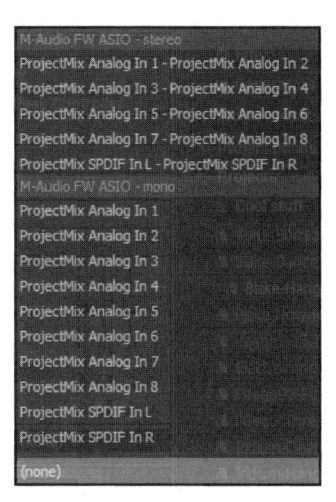

Figure 4.1   The input list for an M-Audio project mix.

On the other end of capability, if you are trying to use a USB microphone that uses the onboard soundcard of your computer, and you do not have an interface, you will witness a few draw-backs that are common to any recording software program that uses ASIO. Using ASIO4ALL will allow you to record with a simple USB mic or one that plugs into your computer's sound-card and causes FL Studio to think that you are using ASIO. There are certain onboard soundcards that can cause latency when trying to monitor recording, so if this is necessary for you, consider upgrading to an interface that uses ASIO. So now the fun part: Let's actually look at recording audio and your options for doing so.

Recording with Audio Clips in the Playlist

This way of recording tends to be the most familiar to those of us who have seen or used other recording software programs. This is a great way to quickly get some audio laid out on your Playlist when you don't need any editing. If you find that you need to make some changes to the audio, you can always load the audio into Edison, which we will discuss in the next section. Think of this method as shooting first and asking questions later, because what you record will drop directly onto the Playlist as an audio clip (see Figure 4.2). Initially, this fell into my comfort zone because the recording is in view and will play back in the song with no routing or adjusting. For singer/songwriters and full bands, this is a great way to get everything to show up as a collective grouping. From single- to multiple-clip recording, the setup and preparation are key to getting your recording done right.

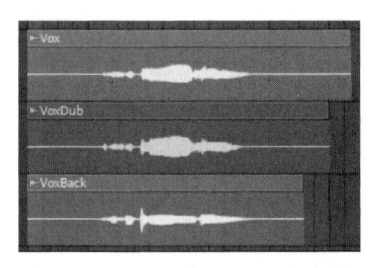

Figure 4.2 Audio recorded directly to the Playlist.

Multi-Microphone

When a musician who is new to FL Studio's architecture first glances at the Mixer and Playlist combo, he or she might see a few options for routing that are similar to other programs, but the way you can link tracks is much more expedient and dynamic. Take a look at Figure 4.3, and you will see that I have set up eight tracks for recording drums.

The first thing I did was name and color them by hitting F2 and going through them. I find it very helpful to name your tracks prior to recording so that you can quickly and easily find the audio you need. A quick way to scroll through the tracks is to select the Mixer (F9) and then hover over the tracks and roll the mouse wheel. At the bottom of these tracks is where I record-armed the track and saved the name of each file as the track is named. For example, when I record-arm a track (click the disk-shaped icon at the bottom of the track), a window opens to name and save the audio that is about to be recorded. If I am arming the kick track, I name the file Live Kick so I know that it is the live kick drum. This seems basic, but forgetting to name tracks and recordings can quickly slow down your creation process when you get stuck trying to find a certain audio clip.

Figure 4.3 Eight tracks set to record.

In Figure 4.3 I have the Crash track selected (which you can tell by the little arrow at the top of the track), and I have the input set to my fourth analog input. Each named track has one of the eight inputs assigned to it, and these inputs can be found at the top right of the Mixer (see Figure 4.4). When you record-arm a track and do not have an input set, you will automatically be prompted to choose an input from a drop-down list, where you can select from stereo inputs at the top or mono inputs at the bottom. This is where many people run into problems with their interfaces, because when you select a stereo input for a mic input that is plugged into, for example, Input 1, it will only play back out of Channel 1. This causes you to hear your vocal recording in one speaker or one side of the headphones, because the recording is a combination of Input 1 (left speaker) and Input 2 (right speaker). By selecting Mono, you are taking that single input and playing it through both the left and the right speakers.

Figure 4.4 Input of a Mixer track.

So now that we have all of our inputs selected, we'll click the Record button and choose to record onto the Playlist. Keep in mind that there is a recording filter on the actual Record button, so make sure that audio is selected by right-clicking the Record button to see the filter. With the metronome turned on (Ctrl+M), we get our one-bar count-in (which can be changed to two bars by right-clicking the Countdown before Recording button) and have our drummer play a section. The results will show up in order (see Figure 4.5) and play back together as though it was a single microphone, but now you have control of each piece of the drum set, which makes mixing

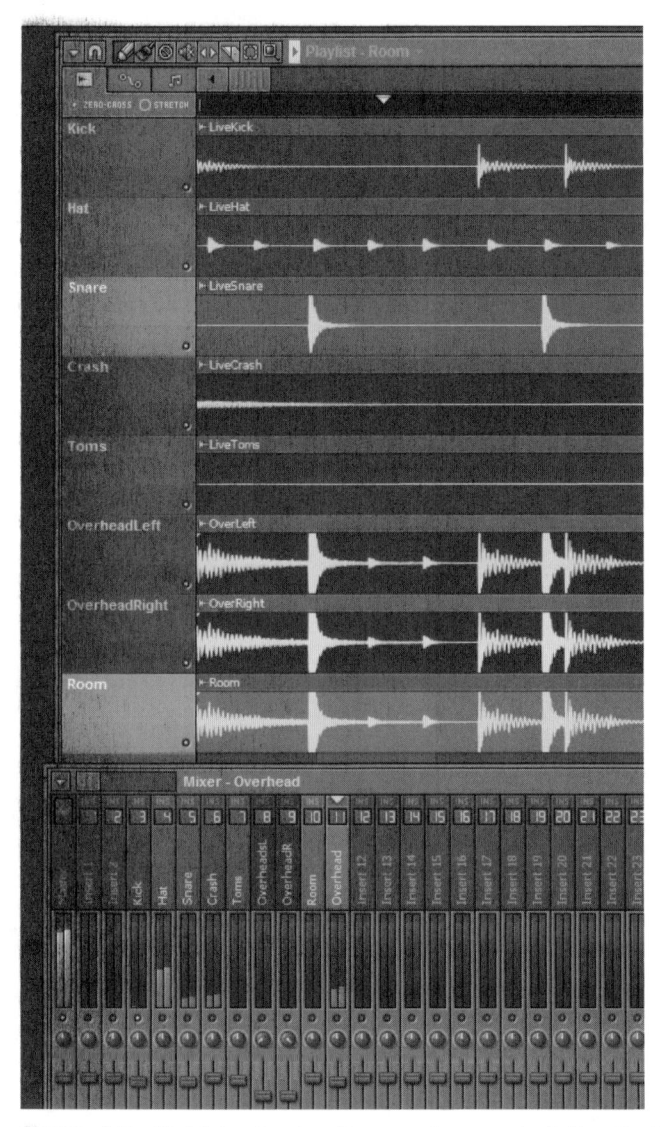

Figure 4.5 Eight tracks simultaneously recorded directly to the Playlist.

much easier. Recorded audio will not show up in the Playlist until you press Stop, but if it still does not show up, make sure that you have Auto Create Audio Clip selected (Mixer Main menu > Disk Recording > Auto Create Audio Clip).

Link your channels to your Mixer if you have not yet done this, so that each fader in the Mixer will control different parts of your mix. With the channel selected in the Channel window, right-click on the Mixer track that you want to link to that audio clip, as shown in Figure 4.6.

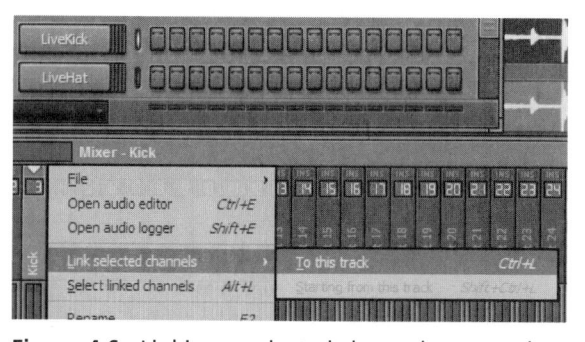

Figure 4.6 Linking a selected channel to a track.

Single Microphone

So what if you only have one mic, and you want to do a few recordings in this fashion? Not a problem at all! Again, record-arm a track and select your input. Usually it will be Input 1, but be certain that is where your mic is connected to the interface. Now click Record onto the Playlist and record the audio that you would like. The recording will begin where you have placed your play position marker and end where you choose, or it will record to the point where your selection stops. So if you have an area highlighted in red, the recording will stop once the play position marker reaches the end of the selection. This can be problematic if you are recording a vocal that goes beyond your selection, because it can get cut off (see Figure 4.7). My recommendation is to not bother with highlighting sections until you are ready to start mixing and editing—this way, it will record as long as you like. Some artists I have worked with came up with great vocal fills after they would sing a part, and if I was still recording, I could take that fill and place it in the mix as with the example of Figure 4.8, where the third vocal was a later portion of the first take.

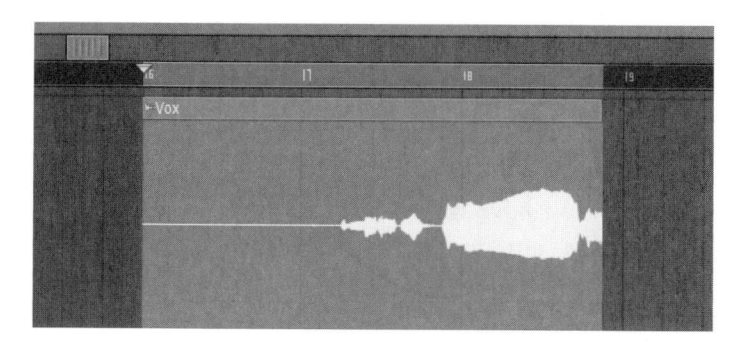

Figure 4.7 Selecting an area to record can cut off the end of your vocal if it goes beyond the selection.

One thing that should be mentioned is your recording levels and what constitutes a good level. The idea of recording is to record the sound loud enough so your preamp volume is not in the sound, but quiet enough to prevent distortion. In the tests that I ran with my soundcard, the input levels in FL Studio accurately matched those in the software control panel of my

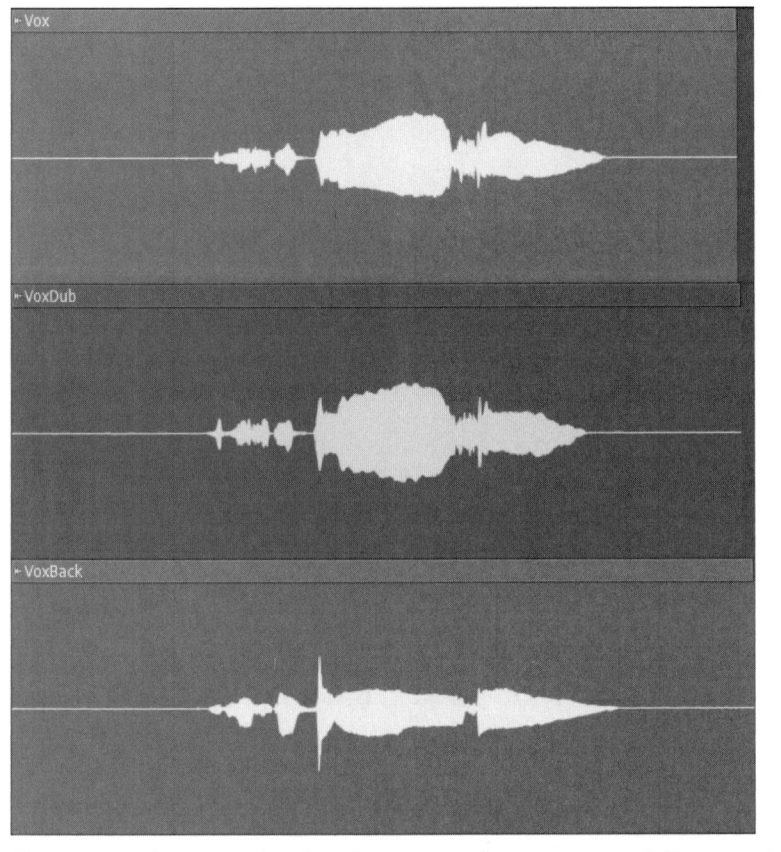

Figure 4.8 Three vocals taken from one take to create a fuller sound.

soundcard, so I could set levels using just my preamp without having to adjust for error of software. I found that recording between –20 dB and –10 dB gives me a clean recording with no distortion. By watching the meters in FL Studio, I saw that there were peaks between –14 dB and –8 dB, and this gave me clean recordings. There is no real golden rule, but a good start is recording loud enough so there is no preamp hiss and quiet enough to prevent distortion.

Here is the important thing to remember: If you have multiple tracks with the same input selected, and they are armed, you will record the same thing onto different tracks. This isn't a huge deal, but your projects can quickly become cluttered with unnecessary channels and audio clips, so pay attention to your armed tracks. Once your audio has been recorded, remember to link the channels to the Mixer tracks. Keep in mind that this can be done later, but it is best to keep organized as you work and will make tweaking your song very easy.

So your question may be, is this the fastest way to record? Well, in a sense yes, but the clips are not immediately as flexible as recording into Edison, so in the long run you could potentially be slowed down a step if you have major editing to do on your audio. In my opinion, if you are recording multiple inputs all at once, Playlist is the way to go. FL creators swear by recording into Edison, and I have to agree that the features for solo recording, such as auto-inserted loop-point markers, can make your experience smoother than the Playlist options, but even the creators wouldn't argue that eight Edisons opened up just for drums alone can clog up your project visually and productively. I use the Playlist record for many of my recordings. Especially when you have those pitch-perfect vocalists who do not need auto-tune (I was not blessed with this ability), drop that vocal on the Playlist, link to the Mixer, and move on. For loop recording, such as getting that perfect guitar solo or vocal line, try out Edison, but Playlist recording will lie in the comfort zone of those familiar with other recording programs and is my personal choice.

Recording Audio Clips into Edison

I mentioned multiple recordings in the Playlist, but for single, one-shot recordings, Edison is the tool to use (see Figure 4.9). It is great for those who require the ultimate in control for editing, stretching, and looping smaller recordings. It is important to know that your computer uses RAM to hold audio in the Edison window, so the more instances of Edison you have open, the greater the strain on your system. Try to imagine that the Edison is a place to hold your short recordings that you can edit individually. The Edison will tell the audio when to play and automatically place it at the point of the song you recorded, but you can also drag the audio itself out of the Edison and onto the Playlist.

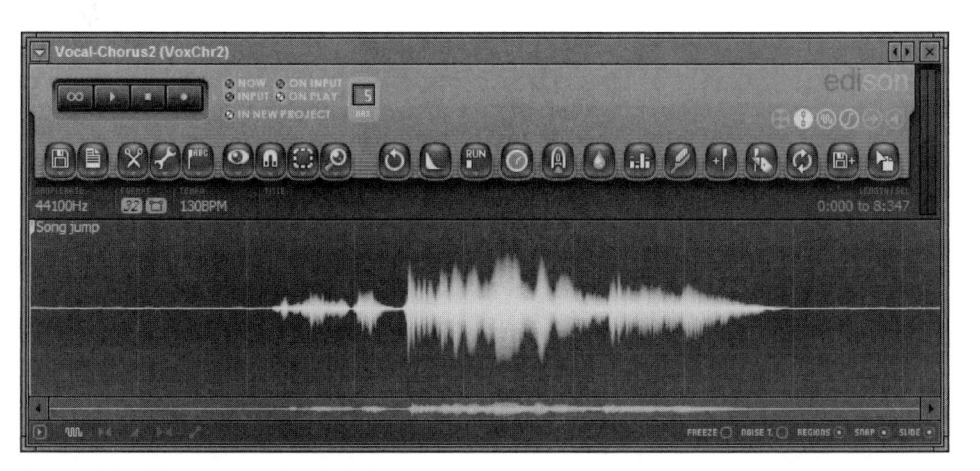

Figure 4.9 The one and only Edison.

Let's take a few minutes to get a general overview of the features available in Edison.

Transport

The Edison transport (see Figure 4.10) is a simple and familiar set of buttons that is very similar to most transports in recording software. The first selection will loop the playback within the

Figure 4.10 Edison transport controls.

Edison; this is great for quickly listening to a portion of audio that you are working on to make sure it is just right. The Play button is self explanatory, but keep in mind that this Play button will only control playback of the audio contained in that instance of Edison.

There are no surprises with the Stop button, and the Record button next to it will cause recording to begin when you press Play on the main transport of FL Studio. What I like about this is that you can just hit Record, and the incoming audio will be put into RAM. Again, this is for clips under 10 minutes, so avoid Edison for long passages, such as recording an entire jam session that is a couple hours long, because it will use a large amount of your computer's memory.

Recording Options

The toggle switches shown in Figure 4.11 allow you to adjust how Edison reacts when recording audio. Now means that the moment you press Record in Edison, it will start recording. This can be problematic because it will not automatically line up with the song when you try to drag the audio onto the Playlist.

Figure 4.11 Edison recording options.

On Input will cause recording to begin when Edison receives an audio signal, such as a voice or an instrument. To adjust how loud you want a signal to be for recording to start, drag your mouse over the level meter in Edison, and you will notice a green bar spanning the waveform window growing larger or smaller. The audio that stays below this level will not be recorded. When you have a bit of room noise, such as a loud computer, traffic outside, fans, and so on, then use this option so you don't capture two minutes of your computer humming, but bear in mind that if that noise will be there regardless, sometimes it can come in handy with Edison's noise reduction feature.

Input works in the same way, but rather than a continuous recording, the recording will stop when Edison receives silence. See Figure 4.12.

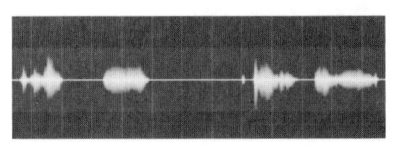

Figure 4.12 This image shows the sensitivity of the On Input and Input options that you see when dragging the mouse over the level meter. With this setting, the audio already recorded would have not made it into the Edison because the signal is below the threshold.

On Play is my option of choice because this means that recording will start when you press Play on the master transport. This ensures that your recording will line up with where you started recording, and it makes dragging the audio file over to the Playlist an easy task.

The In New Project option will essentially record over your last take in that instance of Edison, and the Max section allows you to set the maximum time that Edison will record before looping back around and recording over past recordings (in that instance).

Menu Bar

The menu bar of Edison, as shown in Figure 4.13, is the control center for the plug-in. This is where you will find the options that make editing audio a breeze.

Figure 4.13   Edison menu bar.

File

Many of these options will be familiar to you by now, so I will stick to broad definitions unless clarification is needed. The first button (File) has a series of options beginning with New, and this will open a new Edison window. Load Sample will allow you to bring in a file from anywhere on your computer, so if you have vocals that were recorded elsewhere, and you have them saved on another hard drive or even a flash drive, you can access them here.

Save Sample will allow you to save the sample as you have it inside Edison. Once you have the recording that you want, you can save it and then place it on the Playlist and close Edison so you can save on computer memory or keep it stored for a completely different project. If you have an awesome part that doesn't seem to fit the song you are working on, you can save it, and the best part is that you can record any sound that goes through FL Studio.

The Export Regions option allows you to save portions of the sample inside Edison, and if there are markers set (which is automatic when loop recording), then the sample will automatically be split into different files based on the marker positions, and the files will be saved in relation to the marker names. So if you have three parts in a single Edison instance that you like, just set the markers, select the region, and export it, and all three parts will be saved separately.

Export Display will take a picture of the instance waveform and turn it into a JPEG image with information on the waveform in the image. The Settings option will open a dialog box that first has a drop-down allowing you to tell Edison what to play when you are using a MIDI keyboard for control.

Note Preview will play the entire Edison sample, Slice Preview will play slices of the audio, and Auto will decide whether to play the whole thing or slices, based on the note range and whether you have slices in that instance of Edison.

The Settings selection opens up a dialog box with options for setting your keyboard to play note previews or slices of audio. In this section you can also set Slave Playback to Host options, such as Ignore Host Selection, which will allow you to select an area in the Playlist for Edison to base its playback timing on. This means that if you have a selection in an Edison recording that takes three seconds to start making sound (there is silence or no vocals at the beginning), then that selection in Edison will take three seconds to play from the beginning of the area you selected in the Playlist instead of playing immediately or from the beginning of the Playlist. Ignore Own Selection will cause a selection that you make in Edison to tell the Playlist when and where to play. Going back to the main File menu, the final list is the 10 projects that you opened most recently, including any demos or tutorials.

Format

The Edit Properties selection will open up the Sample Properties window, where you can adjust the information of the file, format, and tempo and set root notes for your sample so that plug-ins will have a root note to work with. The resolution can be changed from 16- to 32-bit floating, which is the standard format that FL Studio will use, but it takes up more space, and 16-bit is CD quality. The final option is great for making a mono signal into a stereo signal or vice versa. For example, if you want your mic recording (mono signal) to have a doubled signal, choose Stereo, and Edison will double the recording and place one on the left channel and one on the right channel.

Edit

The Edit section houses options that I won't go into, but I will touch on the ones that are not repeats of items discussed already. The Undo Using Mix options will bring up a list that shows the last changes made, and you can go back to a certain point based on your selection. Disable Undo for Large Samples will come in handy when (even though I suggested against it) you are using large samples, so that FL doesn't use memory on remembering changes that you made. This will prevent you from undoing any changes, though, so be warned!

The Paste options are great for cutting up your audio and moving it around. Paste Insert will take your copied selection or region and insert it where you make your selection, so everything underneath will be moved farther down the timeline. This is great for repeating a vocal or adding in a verse when you forgot to sing a part—not that you would ever do that, right?

Paste Mix options will allow you to apply envelope changes or EQ changes anywhere on the sample. Paste Stretch will open a window allowing you to make time-stretching adjustments to the sample about to be pasted. The Paste Replace (Drum) option will open a window allowing you to determine the decay of drum hits. This is useful when you have a drum sample with audio that cuts off on the end of it. Opening this tool has FL Studio redraw the decay into the sound so that cutoff sound is no longer present.

Trim will cut out everything outside of the selection you have in Edison. Click-Free (Smooth) Editing, which is on by default, will try to make sure there are no pops or clicks in the audio when different edits are made, such as cutting a sample in the middle of the audio.

Tools

I wanted to include an image of the Tools menu due to the number of options located in this section—and as you can see in Figure 4.14, there is plenty to choose from. Cancel All Envelopes

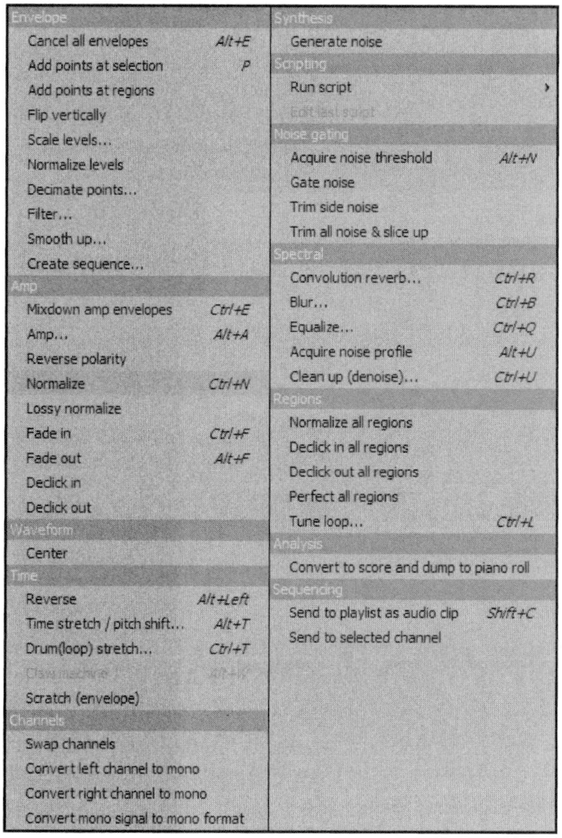

Figure 4.14 Edison's Tools menu.

is a quick way to trash your automation settings, so if you are unhappy with the way you wrote some volume changes, this option will clear them all out so you can start over.

Add Points at Selection will place control points that you can use to adjust your envelope settings to the beginning, middle, and end of the region you have selected. Add Points at Regions is similar, but it will add points at the region boundary. While you can always draw them in, this feature will allow you to quickly make a selection and have the points written in, so if you want a certain section to be, for example, lower in volume, use this option.

Flip Vertically will allow you to try out the reverse of the settings you made, so if you want a pan to start on the left instead of the right but pan at the same rate, use this switch. Scale Levels and Normalize Levels will bring up a dialog box allowing you to affect the envelope setting that you currently have.

The last option available in the Envelope section (Create Sequence) will open up a window that allows you to adjust the envelope to react to steps similar to the Stepsequencer (see Figure 4.15).

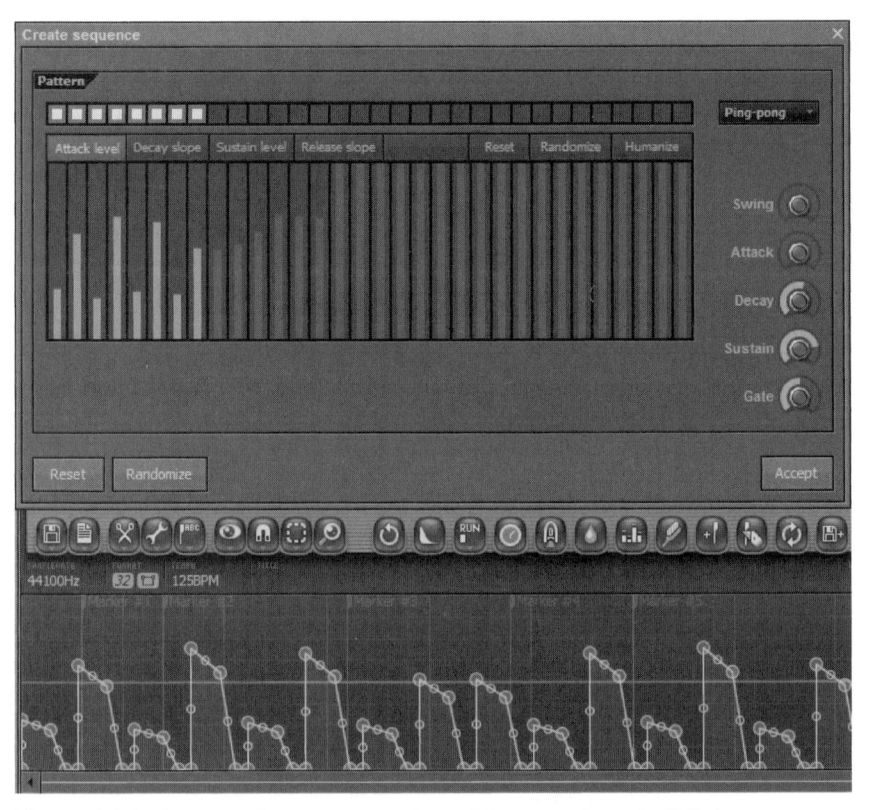

Figure 4.15 A created sequence and resulting envelope in Edison.

This is a great option for quickly inserting a pan into a sample without having to draw every point.

The Amp section begins with Mixdown Amp Envelopes, which will take your envelope settings and apply them to the sample permanently (although you can still undo). The Amp option opens a window allowing you to make changes to a stereo sample and adjust separation and channel volume.

Reverse Polarity will flip the waveform upside down and invert the phase. Normalize and Lossy Normalize will boost your sample so that the loudest part of the audio is brought up to 100 percent of the maximum level and all audio is adjusted based on the amount that the loudest part is brought up.

Fades can be applied like any sample, and Declick will remove any clicks at the beginning of a sample, which can be useful for dealing with loops. Center will remove any DC offset, as discussed in Chapter 3.

The Time options will allow you to do the stretching that is needed to fit the audio in with the rest of your song. The stretching will be familiar, aside from the Claw Machine option. We have discussed the Claw Machine, but the important thing to note in the Edison is that beat markers must be set or a tempo must be recognized in the sample for this option to even be selectable. Adding beat markers will be discussed when we cover the Regions portion of the menu bar.

The Scratch feature allows you to use an envelope to "scratch" your audio similar to a DJ with records. Left to right represents time, while up and down represents the point where the sample will play. So for the sample to play normally, you need a line going diagonally upward from the bottom-left corner to the top-right corner. Drawing an upside-down V will produce a scratch sound, but as you will see in Chapter 6, "Instrument and Generator Plug-Ins," Wave Traveller will be a much simpler option. The Channels section will allow you to make changes based on the left and right channels of the audio, and Synthesis will produce a white noise either in the region that is selected or throughout the entire Edison window if there is no selection.

The Scripting option allows you to write your own code for changes to the audio, but it is outside the scope of this book to delve into code and scripting. For those champions of coding, you can use Pascal and Visual Basic to write your scripts. The Noise Gating section will allow you to tell the audio in Edison when to play based on how loud or quiet it is. Remember that to set a threshold, just click and drag over the level meter so that you can see a green bar appear over the audio. Trim Side Noise will automatically cut out any audio that is below the threshold you set, and Trim All Noise & Slice Up will cut out audio falling below the threshold you set and create regions based on the leftover audio pieces. So if you record three words spoken apart from each other, such as "hit," "that," and "beat," selecting this option will separate those words into three regions that you can instantly place anywhere that accepts audio in FL Studio.

The Spectral section houses options for opening convolution reverb, blur, equalize, and denoise tools, and each will open in its own window upon selection. The Regions list has familiar options aside from the Tune Loop selection, which will open a dialog box that lets you adjust loop settings when you are creating a loop out of the audio loaded into Edison.

Analysis allows you to convert the audio to score and dump it to the Piano roll, which is great for being able to "play" the pieces of sound on your MIDI keyboard or place them randomly in the Piano roll. This option is amazing because it will slice the loaded sample, figure out the pitch of each slice, and then map it to the Piano roll automatically! The Sequencing option will allow you to place the audio on the Playlist, but the Drag button is much easier and requires less menu navigation, in my opinion.

Regions

The Regions options (see Figure 4.16) will allow you to make changes to any regions you create in Edison. Think of the regions as parts of the audio that you decide will be different sections. So if you have a vocal recording that has a verse and a chorus in it, you can select the verse as one region and make the chorus another.

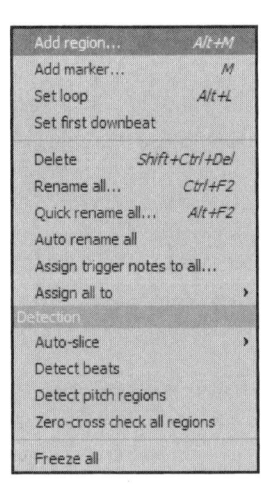

Figure 4.16 The Regions options.

These options are great for breaking up your vocals for easy identification of parts when your recording is a little longer. The first option will add region markers at the beginning and end of an area that you select (see Figure 4.17), and the Add Marker option will just add a marker at the start of the section. Add a marker to define a point in time in the audio, such as a break, and use the region marker to define a section of audio. Set Loop will make your selected region loop on playback.

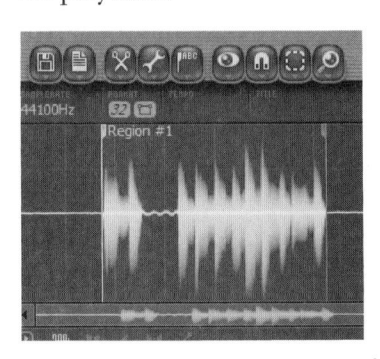

Figure 4.17 Adding a region when an area is selected in Edison.

The next option (Set First Downbeat) is great for creating an essential tempo map of your audio. This means you will tell FL Studio where your downbeats in the audio should be. This helps your audio fit perfectly with the rest of your music and has it automatically lock to the tempo of your current project if there is no tempo information in the recorded audio (which there usually isn't). I use this for vocalists who can't seem to stay on beat but are still able to sing. Setting downbeat markers keeps their vocals right on point with the rest of the song because the audio adjusts itself to the project tempo when placed on the Playlist. Use the set downbeat marker and move it accordingly, and if the grid in Edison needs to be adjusted, you can Right-Shift+Right-Ctrl+click (and hold) on the grid in Edison and drag until the grid is lined up.

A great way to use Right-Shift+Right-Ctrl is to hold the keys down and then simply click to set a downbeat marker instantly! Using this combo will speed up the process of matching your audio to the tempo as well as perfect playback that is slightly out of time. After holding the combo and placing a downbeat marker, you can let go of the keys, move the downbeat marker to the proper spot, then press the key combo again and align the grid to the audio.

The Assign options allow you to play the regions that you create in Edison on a MIDI controller or keyboard. This is awesome for being able to play a vocal part that you want broken up or that you want to repeat quickly.

The Auto-Slice section will take your audio and slice it into regions based on the selection you make from the Auto-Slice menu. Dull auto-slicing just means that only a few regions will be created, Medium will give you a few more regions to work with, and Sharp means that you will have many region slices to work with. Remember that any can be erased, and you can always add regions if you are not happy with the auto-slice results.

The different grid slicing options will slice the audio, depending on which grid line size you select, and the audio itself will have no effect on the slice that is made.

Detect Beats will try to determine the downbeat and tempo by itself and will draw markers accordingly (see Figure 4.18). If the beat or groove is more ambient, FL Studio will have a tough time trying to figure out the beat, but you can add markers as needed. In Figure 4.18, I have imported a groove that I made by dragging it into Edison from the Browser and selecting Detect Beats. Now when I drag it into the Playlist, it is already matched with the tempo that I have set for my project. This is great for bringing in beats that you liked but didn't think fit the song you were working on, which is why I suggest saving everything! You might run out of space, but that is what extra hard drives are used for, and many that have a terabyte of space are very affordable.

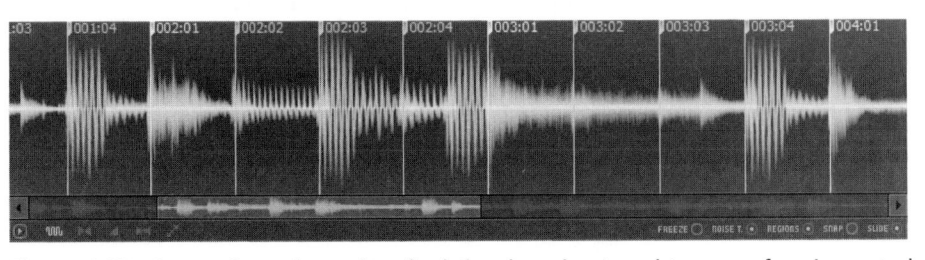

Figure 4.18 Detect Beats is used to find the downbeat and tempo of an imported audio file.

Detect Pitch Regions is a fantastic tool for monophonic sounds that will separate your audio into regions based on melody. Vocals can get tricky when the vocalist is wavy, has vibrato in the voice, or is simply off key, but instruments playing single notes work great for this. Detect Pitch Regions basically finds the notes in the audio and separates each into its own region. The regions are mapped to your MIDI controller so that pressing the keys will play the regions. The Assign to All option allows you to choose to map the regions to your whole keyboard, white notes only, black notes only, or none, where the keyboard does not play the regions.

If you are getting pops and clicks in your audio at slice points, you can select Zero-Cross Check All Regions. This moves region markers to a point where the audio is silent to prevent any problems. Freeze All will prevent you from making any mistakes by turning off editing abilities of regions.

View

The View section, shown in Figure 4.19, will help you select the appearance that you want to represent your audio and how precise your spectrum view will display. Spectrum will change your default view into a spectrum view where left to right is still time, but up and down represent the frequency that is playing, and volume is represented by the color of the spectrum.

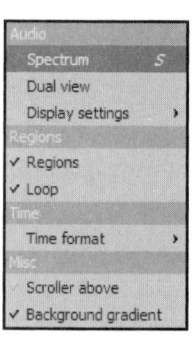

Figure 4.19   The View menu has options that allow you to manipulate Edison's display.

Dual View will show both waveform and spectrum views together. The Display Settings options (see Figure 4.20) begin with Fancy mode, which will make the waveform smoother in appearance (see Figure 4.21). The Waveform Channels will affect the waveform appearance, with Mono combining the waveforms into one summed waveform and Multichannel having both left and right on top of each other (see Figure 4.22).

The left and right channels are actually different colors—the left side is drawn on top of the right side, and you can see the difference by selecting Left to display the left side and Right to display the right side. However, remember that if they are the same signal on both sides, you will not see a difference. The left and right coloring is only apparent when the left and right are different (even slightly).

Spectrum Resolution will allow you to raise and lower the definition of frequencies in Spectrum mode. Natural Scale will make more room for the lower end of frequencies when working in Spectrum mode, so if you are using the Spectrum mode for analysis on a bass recording, select this option. Natural Weighting will change the spectrum view to better represent how we hear frequencies, so that those shrill mid-highs will be brighter and easier to spot in Spectrum mode.

The quality settings affect the look and response of the graphics in Edison, and the higher you go, the more computer power you will need.

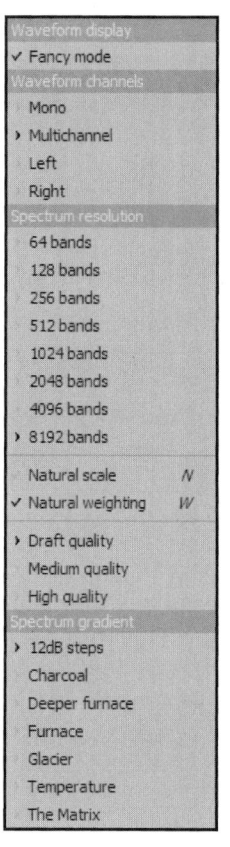

Figure 4.20   Edison's Display Settings options.

The final selection from the Display Settings is the Spectrum Gradient, and each option will affect the colors of the spectrum. This one will be entirely up to your preference, and if you are using spectrum view, I suggest trying these out until you find one you like.

The Regions section contains toggle switches that will turn off either the region markers or the loop markers. This will not prevent a selected section from looping, but it will get those pesky markers out of view without removing them.

Time Format will allow you to see the position of your selected region in samples, min:sec, bar: beat, or auto-mode, which will decide for you. The Misc options will allow you to place the scroll bar above or below the audio in Edison. And by selecting Background Gradient, there will be a 3D effect placed on the background of the sample window.

Snap

The Snap settings are for telling your envelope points and region markers what to align with. When I say "envelope points," I am referring to the points drawn on an envelope where they change their parameters—for example, where the volume starts to go up. Snap to Grid will make

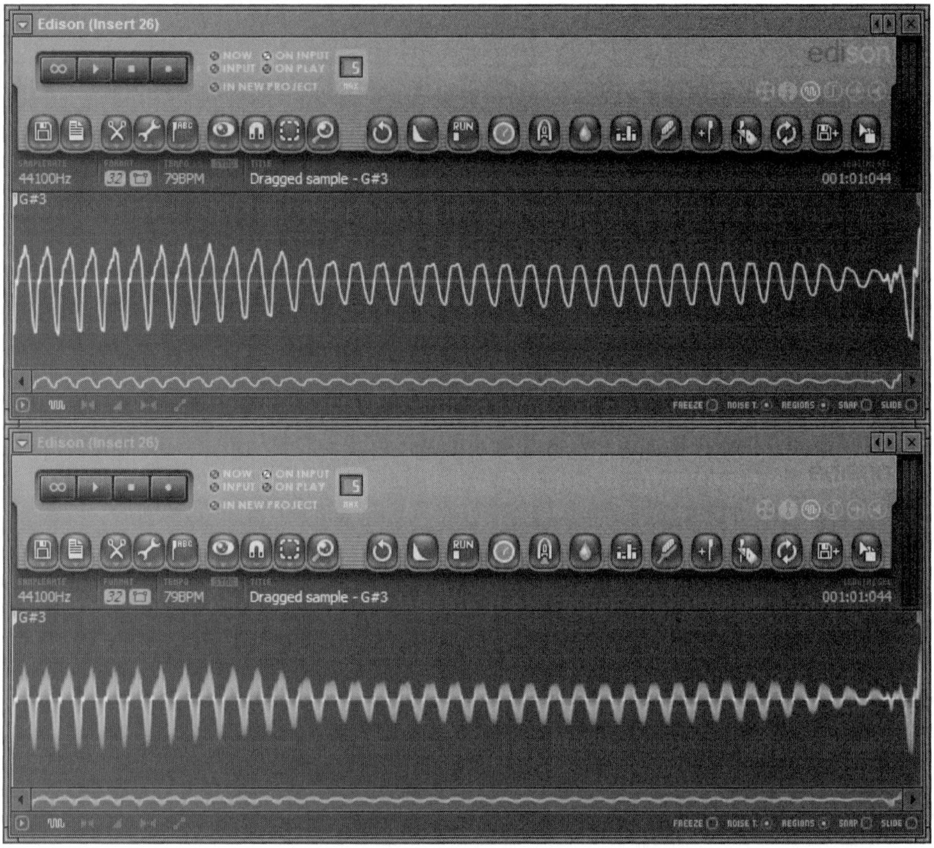

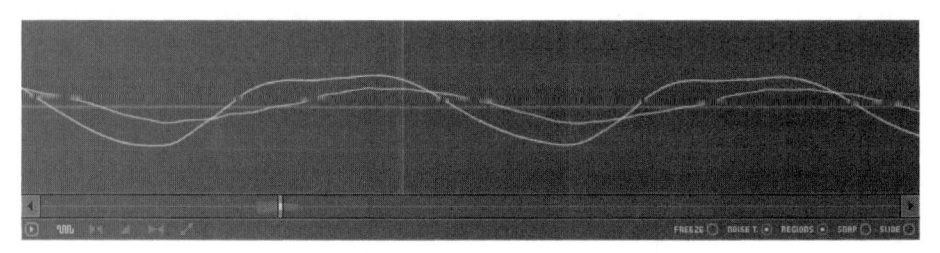

Figure 4.21 These two identical sounds show the difference between using Fancy mode (lower instance Edison) and turning it off (upper instance of Edison).

Figure 4.22 With Multichannel view selected in Edison, the color may be difficult to see in this image; however, the blue-colored line representing the left channel and the pink-colored line representing the right channel are easy to discern in the program.

those points stay on the grid in the background of Edison, and Snap to Regions will keep the points linked to the regions you create.

The Samples option will cause the envelope to snap to samples, which is very precise and the way to go if you are planning on some heavy automation. Snap to Zero-Crossing is effective when you want changes in automation to happen where audio is absent so that there are no clicks and pops in your audio. Snap to Pitch will cause the envelope points to snap to positions in the audio where pitch changes are detected. If you are finding that your automation points are not lying where you want them, try experimenting with these different options.

The Selection and Zoom options are fairly self explanatory, but it is good to note that the up arrow will deselect your current selection, and Ctrl+A (when Edison is selected) will zoom in on the region that you have selected.

Sample Editing Buttons

The collection of buttons shown in Figure 4.23 will be useful when you are performing direct changes to your audio and will allow you to individually manipulate each region. The Undo button works similarly to the main Undo button, but this one will only undo your undo that you just did when pressed twice. To go back further, right-click the Undo button, and the last 10 changes will be shown so that you can go back to a certain point.

Figure 4.23 Sample Edit buttons.

The Fade-Out button will create a fade-out of your selected region when left-clicked, and when right-clicked, it will remove any clicks that are happening in the audio by adjusting the region to a zero-crossing.

The Script tool will allow you to run scripts that are written in Pascal or Virtual Basic, but again is outside the scope of this book. Any tools you need for audio manipulation can be found within FL Studio without using scripts.

Time Stretch will allow you to independently adjust the time and pitch of your audio so that you can get that desired speed or sound if you do not want it to snap to the grid. Here you can slow down your voice to make it deeper or speed it up to create a new vocal that has a different rhythm from the rest of the audio.

The Convolution Reverb option will open a dialog box that allows you to place reverb on a sample, but I suggest using the reverb plug-ins for adding reverb, because if you drag the audio onto the Playlist and end up not liking the reverb or thinking it is too heavy, you will have to start over with the original sample.

The Blur tool allows you to take your sample and smooth it out if you don't like how harsh it is coming in or playing. The EQ tool will open a dialog box that allows you to create an EQ envelope for your audio, which is useful for quickly removing unwanted frequencies.

The Clean Up button will open a dialog box that allows you to remove clicks or random noise in your sample as well as adjust the frequency that plays in the sample. One example would be if a bass line is too thick and overpowering—you can open this tool and raise the frequency limit where you are hearing the most trouble. At first it seems a little backwards, because raising the bar will make the sound quieter, but think of it as a limiter that suppresses the sound.

The Add Marker button will add a simple marker at the beginning of your selected region when left-clicked, and if you right-click the button, it will add a region marker that surrounds your selection. Auto-Slice will slice up the region you have selected, so if you want the whole audio sample sliced, press the up arrow to deselect any selections and choose Auto-Slice.

The Loop Tuner will allow you to fine-tune any loops that you have made by adjusting any pops and clicks, the volume of the loop, and any crossfades that need to be applied to the loop. If you have a selection that you want to make a loop, just right-click this button, and the selection will be made into a loop automatically.

My favorite tool available in Edison is the Final button, which is a drag option. This allows you to drag the entire sample (when nothing is selected) or a specific part into any part of FL Studio that will take it. I usually use this to drag my sample onto the Playlist, but your imagination is the limit, because the sample can be dragged into any plug-in that will accept it. By far, the fastest way to place an audio selection onto the Playlist is by pressing Shift+C when Edison is selected.

Extra Controls

The set of buttons shown in Figure 4.24 performs different tasks for working with Edison, beginning with the Scrub tool. By clicking and dragging, you can play the audio forward or backward by moving the mouse left or right.

Figure 4.24   The special controls of Edison.

The second button is the Slave Transport button, which will cause Edison to play when Play is pressed on the main FL Studio transport, but I find that this can be a nuisance when you're trying to listen to different parts of a project, and I typically leave this option off, but keep in mind that it can be useful for auditioning different takes and loop recording.

Click-Free Editing will place a quick fade-in and fade-out on your selected regions to prevent pops and clicks and is the fastest way to do this without navigating through menus. Disable Auto-Scrolling prevents the view of your sample from moving when the play position marker goes outside of the viewable area. Mute Input is great when you need to quickly mute the mic that you are recording with to prevent hearing any room noise or outside sound when working with your audio sample.

Sample and Envelope Selectors

The first button you see in Figure 4.25 is a menu button that will allow you access to all of the buttons that we discussed earlier. It's nice when you are not familiar with the graphic buttons, but you know the name of the menu you are looking for.

Figure 4.25 The Main Menu, Edit Sample, and Envelope Selector buttons.

The next button is the Edit Sample button, which will bring your waveform (or spectrum view) back into the Edison main window when looking at an envelope.

The next four buttons refer to the different envelopes available, including pan, volume, stereo separation, and an all-purpose envelope button that can be linked to any effects placed on the audio sample. As an example, open up the EQ setting, pull down the low frequency, and then accept the changes. Now select the All-Purpose Envelope button and have the horizontal line of the envelope start at the bottom and then come all the way to the top and then back to the bottom (like a V shape). Now select Paste Special Envelope, and the audio will be affected by the low-frequency removal when the line is above zero and will return to normal sound when the right side of the V shape is back down at zero. This is a great way to remove bass from a section of audio, and if you are comfortable doing it this way, then it can be very quick. But fear not, because there are simpler ways to do this when we get into automation in the next chapter.

The final set of selections in Edison, shown in Figure 4.26, consists of toggle switches that affect the way Edison will react to attempted changes and any selections. The Freeze option will prevent any changes to the audio; this is good for when you just need to listen to parts and have the itchy trigger finger that accidentally hits a quick key without noticing. You will also see the envelope better because this option will visually remove control points that can accumulate across the image of the envelope.

Figure 4.26 The miscellaneous feature switches in Edison.

The Noise Threshold button will show or hide the noise threshold (green bar) that we discussed earlier. The Step Editing mode will allow you to click and drag the mouse over your envelopes and will draw points every step that it changes. This is a great way to get very defined envelopes.

The Snap button will turn on/off Snap editing and allow you to either freely make changes or confine your changes to a Snap setting, as discussed earlier. The Slide button is important to note, because if you notice, when you move an envelope point or region, the remaining ones move with it. By selecting Slide, only the regions and points you move will move. I usually keep this one turned on so that I don't have to worry about adjusting more than one point if I choose to move one point in the sample.

The Breakdown

Now that you have an in-depth understanding of Edison and all of its functions, the big question is "Should I use this?" In my opinion, yes and no. For short vocal passages, Edison is great, and the editing abilities are superb. Imagine that you have a vocal sample you want to record, but it is not getting there on the first take. With In New Project selected, you can quickly dump the previous version until you get the take just right or keep all of the takes and Edison will automatically split them into regions, allowing you to quickly shuffle through parts you like or dislike. Many will find use for the Beat Detect feature because it will take an audio sample and find the beat, and when you place it on the Playlist, it will automatically be matched to the project tempo without you having to do any stretching or use any plug-ins. Basically, Edison will allow you to perfect your audio before even placing it on the Playlist and prides itself on its loop recording abilities.

When I say no to Edison, I am referring to long audio passages that span well over 10 minutes. (Remember that multiple takes can use too much space as well.) Even the most robust of computers can fall prey to memory shortage when too much of the RAM is used on Edison. Aside from sample length, I also say no to using effects inside Edison, because there are many more options that are limitless when trying to add EQ or reverb to your audio. I suggest using Edison to adjust timing and placement of your audio rather than how it sounds. Recording onto the Playlist will ensure that the audio is placed properly, and regardless of the length, once it is recorded, it is using a minimal amount of memory compared to Edison. The Playlist has the stretching options needed, but if you are recording direct with your project playing, then there should be no need to adjust your timing (usually). If you are recording multiple instruments, just record to the Playlist, because handling tons of instances of Edison is nothing short of ridiculous and time consuming.

Recording Surroundings

Your recording quality will be limited by a number of factors, and your surroundings play a vital role in the end result. It is important to be aware of everything around you when you need to get that perfect recording, and be sure to use your headphones for double-checking your recordings for quality. This can be especially important with vocals, because many noises can creep into your recording without any notice, and if your vocalist has gone home, then you will need to bring him or her back in and spend more time and money re-recording what should have been a great series of takes in the first place. The key is to make sure everything is properly set up and ready to record. Although this book is not devoted to recording and the theory involved, it is good to have a brief overview of what you should monitor.

Clean Power

Many things can cause problems when recording audio, and one of them is the power source. I have helped many people building studios who would get random buzzing sounds and static in their audio even when they recorded inputs that were turned all the way down. One instance was from someone using a power outlet that was on the other side of the wall from his main entertainment center, and another was a gentleman who had power coming directly in from a huge electrical line. In both cases the trouble was solved by adding a power conditioner to plug into the wall.

This is not to say that these are the only causes for this problem, because there are many more that purchasing a power conditioner will fix. So is it magic beans or not? Well, if you don't have any noticeable problems, then it might not be worth the purchase, but if you use old electrical lines, then it may be worth considering. My house was built quite some time ago, and the lines are not pristine, so prior to buying a power conditioner, I would get a slight hiss in my recordings. When music is playing in a project, all the sounds hide amongst many others sonically, but when I solo a recording, the disparity between pre- and post-purchase makes it worth every penny.

Acoustics

This is a big part of how mixes that you make in your studio will sound the same on a radio, a stereo, and, although it is compressed, even an MP3 player. A big problem many people have is that when they create their perfect mix in the studio, it comes out lacking power everywhere else they play it. Acoustics and speakers play a vital role in being able to hear what your end result will be.

Again, I must stress that this is a brief mention of why this knowledge helps, and deeper insight can be found in the many books that address studio setup and acoustics.

The speakers you use should have flat response and not boost the low and high frequencies to properly hear what the mix will sound like when put it on a CD or an MP3 player. When you are sitting, the speakers should be an equal distance from your head sideways, but the distance toward you will depend on the size of them. You want the best part of the audio to surround your head. Many monitor speakers that you purchase will have a guide for setting this up, too.

Now you have perfect placement, but sometimes you can get a finished product that still doesn't match what you mixed. This is from early reflections causing cancellations in your hearing. When two identical waveforms hit each other, you can get cancellation or phasing problems where one waveform is playing immediately after another. The problem occurs when a waveform bounces off of a surface and returns to your sweet spot too quickly. To avoid this, there are many ways to tune your studio professionally, and these tips and tricks can be found in the literature available. (There are tons!) For the home studio, something as simple as a heavy rug or comforter can stop these bouncing waveforms when placed a few inches off of a flat wall. The hot spots are the walls to your left and right where your speakers are, above your head, the floor, and your rear walls. There are more intricate explanations if you are interested in perfecting a studio, and I highly recommend searching deeper into this topic, because it helped me adjust the problems I was having with my mixes.

The last thing I want to point out is your computer. Having this in the same room as you are recording is not ideal, but it can be done. Many computers seem quiet until you open a music project and it starts putting in some work. The blaring fan can be heard in every recording and can end up affecting your overall project because when you have a few vocals going at once, that fan hum is boosted in volume for every recording playing. You can try to EQ out the fan, but many times it will adversely affect your vocals and give them a flat sound. Moving the fan behind a comforter or into another room is a frugal yet effective solution, but if you can afford it, they make boxes that quiet computers down to very low decibels. Beware of overheating your computer, but a proper enclosure for the computer can make a big difference when you record in your studio or room.

At this point, you have learned all you need to know about recording audio in FL Studio and the setups that can improve your overall finished product. In the next chapter, we will look at recording MIDI and the different ways you can easily manipulate the sound that is triggered. We will look at what MIDI is and how it is used so that you have a better understanding of what is going on behind the scenes, and then we will get into different devices that work with MIDI. There will be a detailed explanation of automation and how it can be used to control different parts of MIDI as well as audio, and then we'll finish off with a look at Live mode.

5 Recording and Using MIDI

U pon hearing the word *MIDI*, many people think of cheesy sounds from a synthesizer or simply don't know what it is. MIDI stands for *musical instrument digital interface*, and although it comes out of the early '80s, it is widely used today even in places you might not consider. Many cell phones that are in use today have some sort of MIDI sequencer built into them to play ringtones. In this chapter we will explore the history of MIDI and look at a few examples of using it in FL Studio. We will also look at how MIDI information can control different parameters of nearly every knob in FL Studio. And I'll explain Live mode and its use with a MIDI controller to play different parts of your music. This will allow you to come up with entirely new creations live and on the fly!

MIDI

MIDI was created in an effort to simplify the massive amounts of incompatible synthesizers that were available in the '70s. If you wanted to play multiple instruments, you needed multiple keyboards because you would be unable to run signal through all of your music emulators. Keyboards would trigger the sound of one synthesizer, but then that device might not work if connected to a different synth. Your home studio was a mess of keyboards and tangled wires that you constantly had to change.

MIDI fixed this by creating a protocol, or common language, that all of these synths could read, allowing you to interconnect devices and trigger them at different times using one keyboard. Musicians were able to bring more virtual instruments into their music, which ended up running rampant in '80s songs. Virtual instruments have greatly increased in quality, and many that are used today are indistinguishable from the real thing. The virtual pianos available today have replaced the need for a real piano, and they even have different controls that imitate how hard keys are played based on the MIDI information received by your computer.

The Devices

It is important to know first and foremost that MIDI is *not* sound, and MIDI alone will make no sound. This is why a MIDI controller or keyboard will not have an audio output—because there is no sound to play! There are piano keyboards that have built-in sounds and only have audio output, but we will focus on MIDI keyboards (including keyboards with built-in sounds that send MIDI) in this chapter. A great way to think of MIDI is to compare it to your computer typing keyboard. If you turn on the Typing Keyboard to Piano Keyboard feature, you can play instruments inside FL Studio using the bottom two rows of letters, but you can't plug that keyboard into a speaker and expect it to make sound. Both keyboards in this example send data only, and MIDI is just a form of data, so rest assured that neither will make sound if plugged directly into a speaker.

Another way of thinking of MIDI is to compare your MIDI keyboard to a symphony conductor. The conductor plays no instruments directly but guides the performance of the musicians in the orchestra. The musicians playing their instruments are like the software instruments in FL Studio because they can play sounds, but they need to know when to play. MIDI information tells these sounds when and how to play rather than making the sound itself. In most cases MIDI is used in conjunction with a piano-style keyboard that will usually have a pitch bend and modulation wheel on it, but devices that use MIDI are nearly limitless and are constantly being reinvented. I once helped an engineer set up a MIDI laser harp that sent MIDI signals based on whether the laser lights were blocked by the fingers. Aside from playing like a harp, it was a little overkill as far as inventions are concerned, but it was very interesting to see in use. There are even entire MIDI controllers premapped to control all the parameters of DJ software, but for FL Studio I will focus on two MIDI controller types—the piano-style keyboard and the MPC-style beat pads.

Piano-Style Keyboards

Piano-style controllers will suit almost every music style when the keys are pressure sensitive. This means that the harder you play, the louder the instrument will be. There are variations where notes that are firmly pressed will cause the sound to change, but usually the volume is affected. Keep in mind that the keyboard only sends information and not actual sound, but the software responds to the way the MIDI keyboard is played. Those that make beats will miss out on the touch-sensitive pads that seem to have become a staple in beat making unless their keyboard comes with them (see Figure 5.1).

Figure 5.1 The M-Audio Axiom 61 is a piano-style MIDI controller.

The keyboard can vary from a basic range of keys with no additional controls to ones like you see in Figure 5.1. They will sometimes have even more knobs available. The knobs and faders on your keyboard can be mapped to almost anything in FL Studio. You can create your own virtual mixing board using the faders on your keyboard alone!

The size of the keyboard only matters if you actually play the piano—then you might want a larger one for playing live. But the smaller ones will work for every musician because the keyboard can send different octaves of notes. For example, you could play the lower part of a piano riff and then come back, raise the octaves on your keyboard, and play the higher part, creating a full keyboard sound.

I find that having a larger keyboard does help when auditioning sounds so that you can hear a few different octaves, because the sound you are looking for may not sound right a few octaves up, but when cycling through hundreds of presets, it can be missed when only a couple of octaves are available for immediate playback. You can always press Up Octave on the keyboard, but trust me, once you start searching deep into your instruments, you will move quickly through different sounds looking for the right one. The MIDI keyboard is the utility instrument and can represent almost any virtual instrument you can throw at it.

Drum Pad Controllers

The drum pad controllers like the Trigger Finger (see Figure 5.2) can be found among many artists out there who fancy themselves as beatmakers. They are specifically desirable to these

Figure 5.2 The Trigger Finger is a controller with 16 touch-sensitive pads.

types of musicians because the touch-sensitive pads are larger than keys on a keyboard and give you plenty of room to strike the pads.

A great advantage to these pads is also that they are durable, so hitting them with moderate force over and over won't wear them out. I know that keyboards are supposed to be designed the same way, but I have seen many MIDI keyboards come in for repair because the piece that reacts to the keys being pressed breaks, and then the entire range of keys needs to be replaced. Although it does happen, I have never seen pads that came in for repair due to overuse.

The Trigger Finger is a MIDI controller, so there are no internal sounds, and it is only sending MIDI signal, much like the keyboard. The knobs and faders can be mapped to most parameters in FL Studio, similar to the keyboard as well. The big difference is that it is designed for making beats, and even the FPC (a drum instrument plug-in) has 16 pads that are similarly mapped like the Trigger Finger.

So which should you purchase? If you can afford it, I would say both, but remember that the Axiom (refer to Figure 5.1) has both keys *and* touch-sensitive pads, so buying another device is not necessary. If you can find a combo like this, make that your purchase.

If price is an issue, you have not yet purchased any gear, and you are just beginning in the music field, I would stick with a piano-style keyboard that is velocity sensitive (the keys register how hard you play them). You can make drum beats on a keyboard, and you get the same velocity-sensitive touch when playing a beat, but it will take some getting used to when playing on the slim keys.

Another reason is flexibility with different instruments. You can use the Trigger Finger to play chords of a piano, but they have to be mapped, and this can be a pain even when you know what you're doing. The same holds true when using any synth, and you will find the drums pads limiting. Regardless of the instrument you choose (or find a great deal on), in the next section I will show you how to specifically set up each type and get it to work in FL Studio.

Setting Up Your MIDI Devices

We will begin by looking at two different setups for MIDI controllers, starting with the Axiom keyboard and then moving to the Trigger Finger. Both setups will be very similar, but we will open an instance of two different instruments to display where they are effective. If you are only using one or the other, then you can skip to that section or read both for a complete understanding of setting up the devices, because you might add gear as your studio builds.

Setting Up a Piano-Style Keyboard

The first thing to be aware of when using a MIDI controller is whether your device requires a driver to properly be recognized by your computer. Many MIDI keyboards will need a manufacturer driver on any system aside from Vista 64-bit and any Mac operating system. The drivers for your MIDI keyboard can usually be found at manufacturer's website unless none are required. In my case, I am running Vista 64-bit, so MIDI controllers are for the most part plug and play, meaning that when I plug it in, Windows will assign drivers for it, and everything will work.

So, you take out the Axiom and connect it to the computer through USB, which will give the keyboard its power and send MIDI signal to and from the computer. The Axiom is powered by the USB, so no additional power supply is needed, but keep in mind that some USB ports do not supply enough power for some devices, and an external power supply must be used.

Windows will install the driver automatically on a Vista 64 operating system, and then you are ready to open FL Studio. Press F10 to open to your MIDI options, and under the Input section, you will see your keyboard. Highlight it and make sure Enable is selected (see Figure 5.3). For the Controller Type drop-down menu, Generic Controller is fine. This option will work for almost every controller, but if you see the name of your device in this drop-down menu, go ahead and select it.

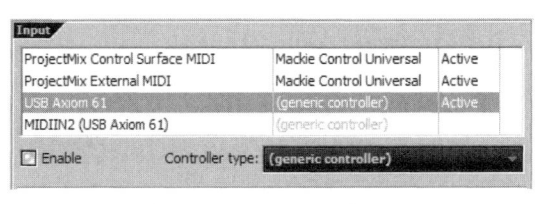

Figure 5.3 The MIDI Input section.

Now you can close the menu and press F6 to display your Channel window. Go up to Channels from the main menu bar of FL Studio and choose Channels > Add One > FL Keys. The output of FL Keys is routed to the main output in the Mixer, so upon opening FL Keys, you will be able to play and hear piano. If you are not hearing any sound, you may need to reset the keyboard or contact technical support for assistance. At this point you can play and hear piano sounds and play with the settings in FL Keys to hear different sounds triggered from your MIDI keyboard.

Setting Up a Drum Pad Controller

For this example, we will be plugging a Trigger Finger into the computer and using the FPC to create drums. Much like the keyboard, certain operating systems may require a driver in order to run the Trigger Finger properly, so any needed drivers should be downloaded and installed prior to opening FL Studio. In my case, Vista 64 allows the Trigger Finger to be plugged in and start working immediately. For complete assurance that your device will work, you can browse the list of supported devices in the Controller Type drop-down menu and base your purchase off of that. This means that your device will be premapped to FL Studio and ready to work immediately!

With drum pads, it is easy to forget that you were messing around with settings to make different notes or trigger different instruments, so I recommend doing a factory reset on your keyboard to begin. This causes all of the information sent by the Trigger Finger to be its default values.

Plug in the controller and open FL Studio. Go to the Options menu (F10), make sure you are on the MIDI tab, then highlight the Trigger Finger. Make sure Enable is selected and the Controller Type drop-down menu says Generic Controller, as shown in Figure 5.4. If you are using a device that shows up by name in the list, then select that, but Generic Controller will work for most MIDI controllers.

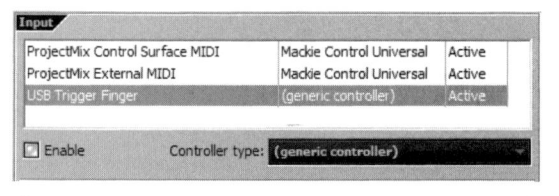

Figure 5.4   The Trigger Finger showing up in the MIDI Input section.

In this example, I will use a different method to get to the instrument. Start by making sure that the Channel window (F6) is visible, then press Ctrl+F8. This will open the Plugin Picker, allowing you to choose your instrument from a graphical list. At the bottom of the graphics are categories that will narrow your search. Hover over the Drum option, and only a few will remain, with the first being the FPC. Click and drag (keep holding the mouse button down until you get the instrument to the Channel window) the FPC over to the Channel window and insert it into an empty channel. The FPC will pop up, and at first glance it bears a striking resemblance to the Trigger Finger itself.

The reason why I had you do a reset on the Trigger Finger is because the pads will not line up perfectly with the drum pad pattern of the FPC. This way, when you run into this problem, you will know what to do. Start by using the mouse and selecting the lower-left pad (Pad 1) of the FPC. The sound will play once, and the hint bar at the top of the screen will tell you the pad number and the note that is playing. After pressing the note with the mouse, the actual note will display in the top-left portion of the FPC (see Figure 5.5).

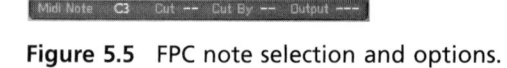

Figure 5.5   FPC note selection and options.

Select the note itself—in this case, C3—and a menu will open (see Figure 5.6) with a long list of available note options. Choose Learn and press the lower-left drum pad (Pad 1) on the Trigger Finger. Now the first pads on both are mapped to each other, so when you press that pad on the Trigger Finger, the linked pad on the FPC will light up and play the sound that is loaded. To map the rest, follow the same order of mouse-clicking the pad on the FPC, choosing Learn, and then pressing the corresponding pad on the Trigger Finger.

Keep in mind that switching drum kits can change the settings you have linked with the FPC. A better option would be to change the notes that the pads of the Trigger Finger are sending into

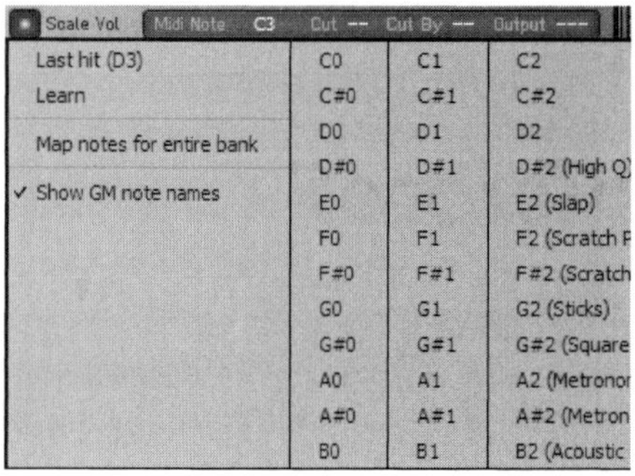

Figure 5.6 FPC MIDI note selection list.

the program so that the pads are always matched to the FPC. To do this, you need to individually change the notes on your Trigger Finger.

Although this is not a tutorial on the Trigger Finger, sometimes companies can leave you lacking proper documentation and feeling slightly in the dark. Every controller will be different, but for the Trigger Finger, press the pad that you want to adjust and then press the Save & Exit and Exit buttons together to enter Edit mode. The lights above the buttons will flash; now turn the C1/ Note/Min knob until you reach the note that is needed to play the correct pad in the FPC. Press the Save & Exit button twice, and the note is stored.

Keep in mind that sometimes the notes do not read correctly or are slightly off, so you will have to do a little reasoning when properly mapping. For example, if the Trigger Finger says it is sending C#3 (which looks like C.3 on the LED display), FL Studio may read it as a C#5. If this is the case and you need FL to read a C#3, then drop the Trigger Finger note down two octaves to C#1 so that FL Studio reads it as a C#3 (the note you wanted).

Again, remember that this example of mapping is specific to the Trigger Finger and will not always apply to every controller. For specific note mapping, you will want to read the manual of your device regarding how to do this. If the documentation is not there, then checking forums and searching online tutorials will usually guide you to an answer.

Using the Piano Roll with MIDI

We have learned about the features of the Piano roll and the different tools that we have for manipulating sound, but we haven't looked at any real examples. Throughout this section, we will look at building a few riffs and some examples of how to change notes and their properties. Producer and songwriter Josquin de Pres once told me "Sure you know what everything does, but can you use it?" At first, this seemed like a redundant question, but the more I thought about it, I realized that his point was, "Can you use all this stuff properly and efficiently?"

The more I worked with artists and other engineers, the more I saw that knowing how to perform tasks in recording software prevents you from getting stuck when creating. I'm not talking about writer's block, because that is when you are just at a loss for ideas. The problem is when you have the ideas and you can't make them happen due to fumbling around through menus. Trust me; losing an idea to ignorance when you know exactly how you want it to sound is very frustrating. Preventing this is solved by acquiring the knowledge, and in the next few sections we will look at actually using the Piano roll with a few instruments.

The Instrument

The Piano roll is the grid that houses MIDI notes and triggers the instrument you have selected, so first off, let's choose that instrument! Open up FL Keys and then right-click the channel and choose Piano Roll (see Figure 5.7). This will open the Piano roll option, allowing you to play, record, and draw notes on the grid. Remember that even without a MIDI keyboard, you can still follow along using your typing keyboard (when Typing Keyboard to Piano Keyboard is selected, or press Crtl+T to toggle it on and off). The typing keyboard will be basically the same as a MIDI keyboard, but it will not have velocity control (usually volume), so the notes will all play at the same volume.

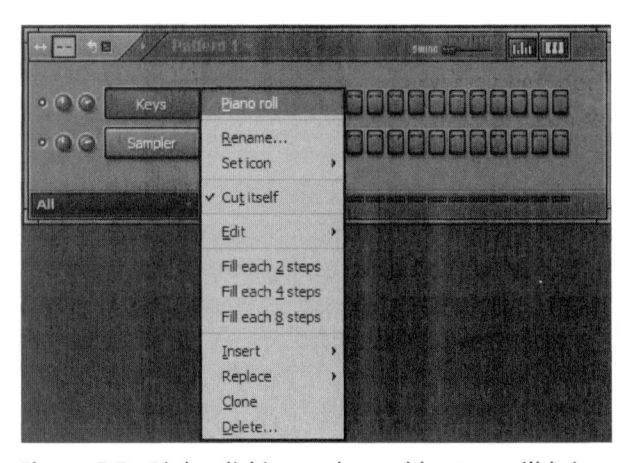

Figure 5.7 Right-clicking a channel button will bring up its options.

Before getting into recording and editing of MIDI, take a moment to link your instrument channels to Mixer tracks, so that you don't have to do it later. You can always delete unused channels or mute any that you don't want playing, but setting it up beforehand gives you the ability to quickly silence a single instrument. With the FL Keys channel selected in the Channel window, press F9 to bring up the Mixer. Right-click on an empty Mixer track and choose Link Selected Channels > To This Track (or use the quick key Ctrl+L). After selecting this option (see Figure 5.8), you will see the Mixer track change to Keys because of FL Studio's auto-naming feature (see Figure 5.9), and now the volume and muting can be controlled with the single track. Without doing this, all the channels will run through the main Mixer channel, and it will be frustrating trying to solo individual sounds when mixing unless you use the Mute and Solo switches located on each channel. Now we are ready to start making some sound using MIDI!

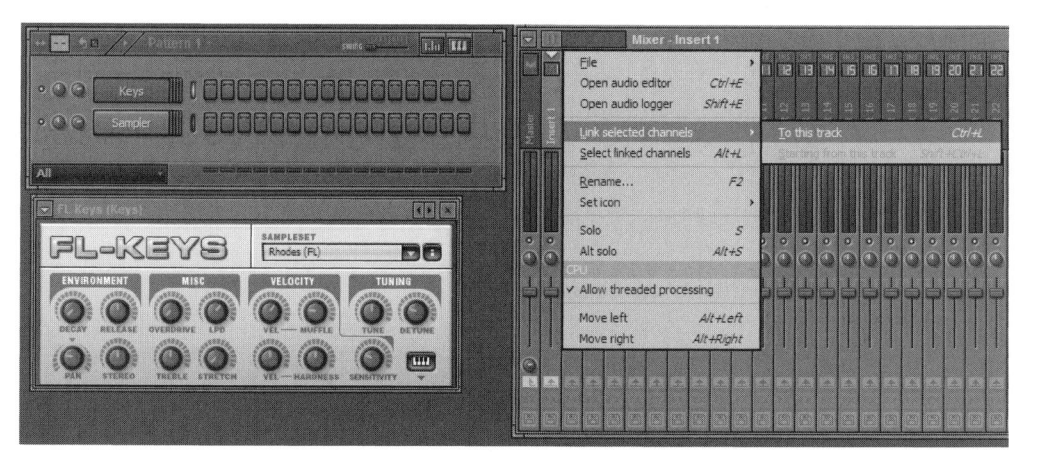

Figure 5.8 Linking a Mixer track to a selected channel.

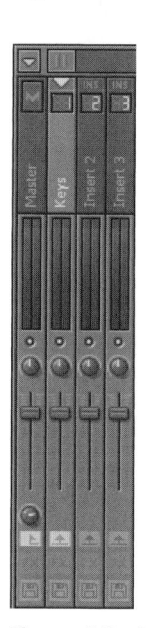

Figure 5.9 The Mixer track, auto-named to reflect the name of the channel to which it is linked.

Recording in the Piano Roll

Let's start by making a recording that plays for two bars using our FL Keys channel. Before doing anything, make sure that you are in Pattern mode, not Song mode. For this example, you don't need a complicated piece; just play a few notes over the two bars.

Begin by toggling the metronome on or pressing Ctrl+M so that you are able to keep your recording on beat. We also want Countdown before Recording turned on (Ctrl+P), and by default it will give you a one-bar lead-in. This gets you prepared to stay with the beat, because most of the time it can be difficult to stay on beat when starting immediate recording with the music.

When you go to record, you will hear four clicks, and then recording will begin. For this example, lower the tempo to 110 by clicking on the tempo indicator in the main transport (see Figure 5.10) and dragging downward until you get to 110. Make sure that you click the big numbers, because the small number will lower and raise the tempo in small increments.

Figure 5.10 The tempo indicator in the main transport.

These different actions may have made the Piano roll disappear; just reopen it by pressing F7. Now right-click the Record button in the main transport and make sure that Automation and Score are selected. Pressing the Record button will cause it to turn orange, and pressing the spacebar will start the count-in metronome. If the Recording Options dialog box pops up, select Automation and Score and then press the spacebar. See if you can get four notes to sound decent over these two bars. After playing these, if you find that you have played a little past the two bars (see Figure 5.11), you will see that the pattern goes to the next bar before repeating. Because you only need two bars of piano, use the Slice tool (C) to cut off the end of the last note (see Figure 5.12) and then delete it by right-clicking the end piece.

Figure 5.11 Notes recorded into the Piano roll using FL Keys.

Remember that for right-clicking to delete the note, you need to use the Draw (P), Paint (B), or Slip tool (S), and remember that Typing Keyboard to Piano Keyboard must be disabled for these shortcuts to work. I'm going to take a guess and assume that there are a few of you out there

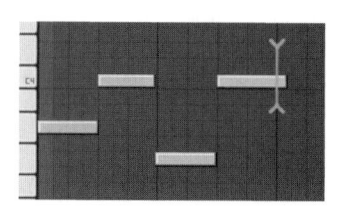

Figure 5.12   Slicing the end of a note that goes beyond the desired two bars.

who don't want to play notes, but who still want to create them. For those of you to whom this applies, just use the Pencil tool (P) to draw four lines on the Piano roll that sound good over the two bars. Or, if you are feeling a quick burst of creativity, try turning on the Typing Keyboard to Piano Keyboard function with step editing (Ctrl+E) turned on.

Now, whether recorded or played, we have MIDI notes on the Piano roll that are triggering sound from FL Keys, and that sound is routed to its own track in the Mixer. At this point, if you wish, you can turn off the metronome so that you are only hearing the piano.

First, we'll make a new channel with the same instrument so we can play a different part on top of the first recording. The fastest way to do this is to right-click the FL Keys channel in the Channel window and choose Clone (see Figure 5.13). This will create another FL Keys channel with the same settings as the previous one, but it will not contain the Piano roll information.

Figure 5.13   Cloning a channel.

First, change the pattern number to 2 by making sure the Channel window is highlighted (F6) and then pressing the right arrow on your keyboard. Again, get in the habit of quickly linking everything first! In this case, you can link the second channel of FL Keys to the same Mixer track, because you will probably want the same effects on the keys so that they sound like one person playing one part.

Now you have the same instrument on two different channels, so you can tweak different parameters and they don't affect each other, but both still go to the Mixer where the same effects will be applied. In this mode, though, the first pattern that you made will not automatically play because now you are listening to the second pattern, which has no Piano roll notes. To fix this, select the first pattern by highlighting the Channel window (F6) and then press the left arrow key to go back to Pattern 1.

Now you can see the original piano recording notes in the Channel window. With the Channel window (F6) focused, press the up arrow to make sure that the first FL Keys channel is highlighted, then press Ctrl+C. Now press the right arrow so you are on the second pattern and press Ctrl+V to paste the notes into the new Piano roll. You can also change patterns by clicking the pattern indicator in the main transport (see Figure 5.14) and dragging the mouse up or down. You can also select specific notes in a Piano roll by Ctrl-clicking and dragging (see Figure 5.15) over the ones you want and then pressing Ctrl+C to copy them. Then you can paste the notes into different channels and patterns. Remember to keep the Channel window in focus; otherwise, your copy and paste quick keys could be working elsewhere in your project.

Figure 5.14   The pattern indicator in the main transport.

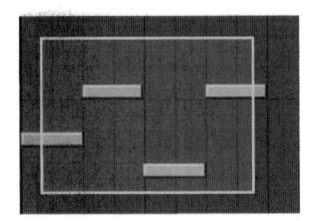

Figure 5.15   Holding Ctrl while dragging allows you to select multiple notes.

When you have more than one channel active in a pattern, you can use the Target Channel drop down inside the Piano roll to navigate through the different Piano rolls of a pattern. To try this out, right-click on the second FL Keys channel (still in the second pattern) and select Piano Roll. Click at the top of the Piano roll where it says Keys #2 and select Keys (see Figure 5.16). This is a speedy way to cycle through different active channels in one pattern.

Using the same Target Channel drop-down, let's change the Piano roll back to the second FL Keys channel so we can record on top of our original notes that we copied into the Piano roll of the original FL Keys channel (see Figure 5.17). I want to point out here that the original recorded notes are still in the Piano roll of the first FL Keys channel in Pattern 1. I am taking you through these menus to better understand navigating them, and after you record a second part, you can delete the original notes in the first FL Keys Piano roll. This gives you two patterns that work well together that you can separately place in the Playlist.

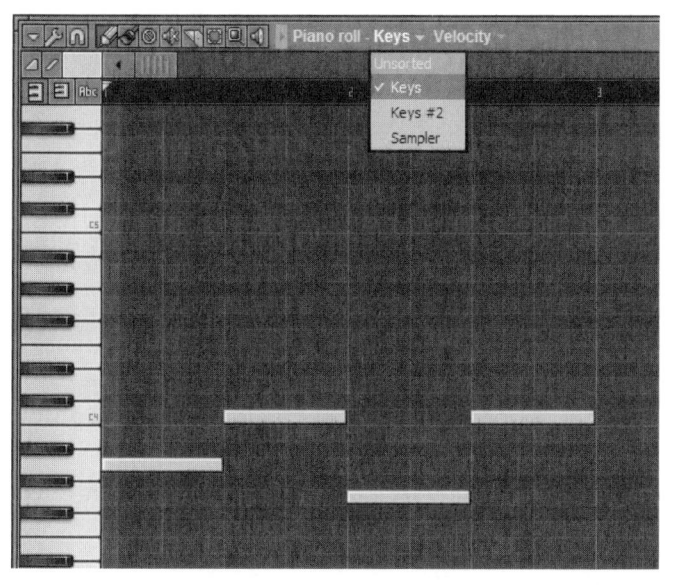

Figure 5.16 Navigating through different Piano rolls within the same patterns.

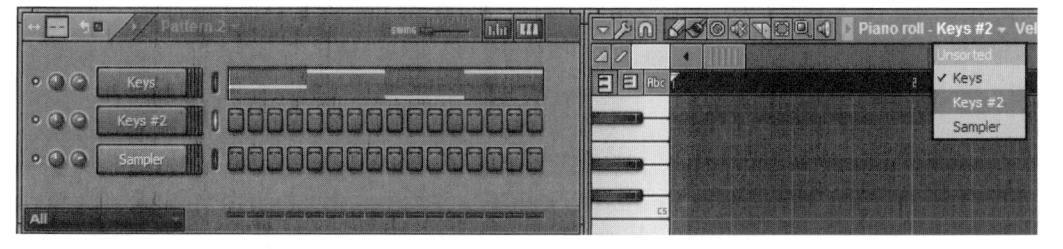

Figure 5.17 Selecting the Piano roll for the second FL Keys channel.

Press Record, select Automation and Score, press the spacebar, and record a new piece that is four bars this time. Wait! The first channel didn't keep playing after the first two bars (see Figure 5.18). No problem! First, undo the "recorded stuff," as FL Studio puts it, by pressing Ctrl+Z. Now open the first FL Keys Piano roll so you have your first four notes visible. Highlight them (Ctrl-click and drag) and then, while in Pencil mode (P), hold Shift and click and drag any note to duplicate all selected notes for dragging to the next bar. Now you have four bars of the music to work with (see Figure 5.19).

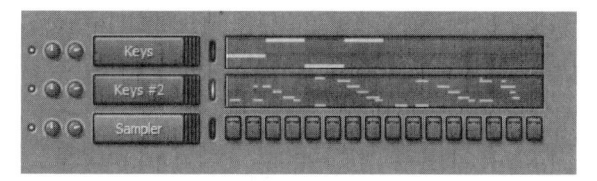

Figure 5.18 Recording on the first channel.

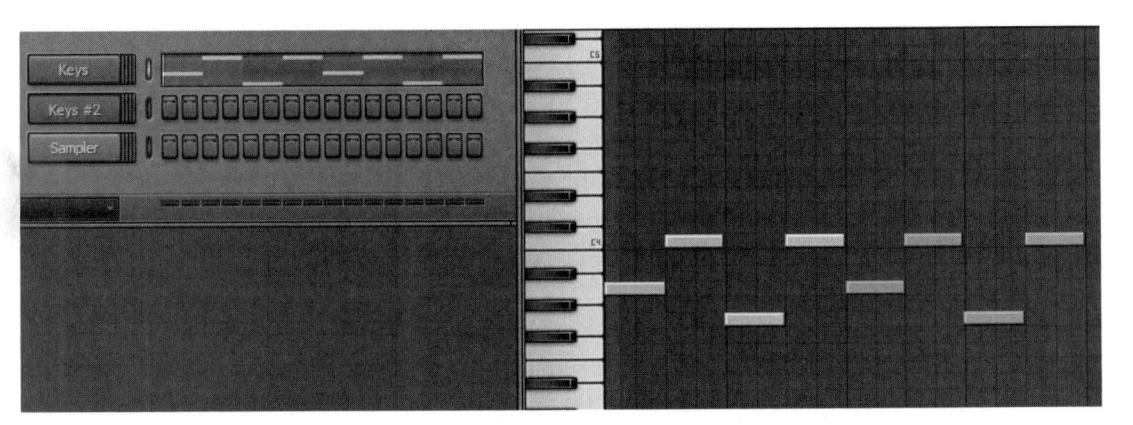

Figure 5.19 Copying notes in the Piano roll.

Change the Piano roll back to Keys #2, and you are ready to record more notes into this new channel using the same method as your first recording. After you get the recording you want, you can delete the notes from the first Keys channel in the second pattern, and now you have two different patterns that play with each other and can be dropped on the Playlist.

Now we have taken a detailed look at recording MIDI and getting notes on the piano to make sound, as well as routing the sound that the MIDI notes create. There are many tools available with the Piano roll, and they were discussed in the "Piano Roll" section of Chapter 3, but the purpose of this section was to give you a look at building in the Piano roll with MIDI notes. These notes can represent any instrument and even individual sounds, which will usually display by name when the Name option is chosen from the Piano roll, but the concept is still the same. This is how you begin building your music using live MIDI recording and drawn notes. Even with drums, the same process will work, but sometimes if the sound samples are just right, then you can use the Stepsequencer to just play the notes as one-shot instances. MIDI information is not used only in the Piano roll to create music; it is also used to control nearly every knob and fader in FL Studio, which we will look at in the next section.

More Uses for MIDI

While we have dealt with MIDI as notes that are sent to the computer, we did not look at the other abilities of MIDI. Because MIDI is nothing more than information, it can be interpreted any way that FL Studio wants to. The examples that we will look at are creating automation using MIDI and how nearly everything can link to your keyboard or mouse movements. Then we'll look at using the MIDI keyboard to control Live mode for creating new grooves and loops.

What Is Automation? The basic idea of automation is all around us and is used in many facets of life. The idea behind automation is to take out the manual part of an action and replace it with something that automatically performs the task. Outside the realm of digital recording, we see automation in many factories that produce computers, cars, and appliances, because they use robots to automatically build different parts instead of having people manually build them. Prior to automation, audio engineers would have to manually change the volume of different tracks while recording final sound levels of a song. If they made a mistake, it could get costly because the tape they used to record with was being wasted on takes to get the volume to change at the right time. Similar to robots requiring programming prior to performing their tasks, knobs and faders need to be told what to do and how to react. For example, setting pan automation, where a sound in FL Studio is heard in the left output and gradually sweeps over to the right output, removes the need for manually grabbing the Pan knob and turning it while you are recording.

Controlling Knobs and Faders

So with a little better understanding of what automation is, now we can look at the different ways to control knobs and faders using your keyboard or mouse. To have change occur, the changes need to be entered into FL Studio so it can repeat these changes at the correct point in your song. It is important to know that not all knobs will react in the same way, and the quickest way to tell what can be done with them is to hover over the knob that you want to automate and look at the hint bar. When you see a red dot (see Figure 5.20) in the hint bar when hovering over a knob or fader, that control can be automated. The automation can be recorded, and you are able to open up the event editor for additional modification. If you see a red MIDI-port image (see Figure 5.20), then the control can be linked to an external source, such as a MIDI keyboard. Most of the time you will see both images when hovering over controls of native FL Studio plug-ins.

Figure 5.20   The image on the left (red MIDI port) indicates an automatable control, while the image on the right (red dot) means that the control can be linked to an external source.

Single-Link Automation

We will continue with our two takes of piano and focus on creating automation for the volume controls, so that you can see how powerful these tools are for altering your music. For this example, I will assume that you have two different patterns that you can place in the Playlist, so go ahead and place two instances of Pattern 1 and one instance of Pattern 2 across the Playlist (see Figure 5.21).

The first example we will look at will be linking an external controller to the volume control and setting up an automation recording. Start by deciding which knob you want to use on your MIDI keyboard. Right-click the channel volume of your first piano take and then select Link to Controller (see Figure 5.22).

The resulting box that pops up (see Figure 5.23) will allow you to remove any conflicts, so if there was an accidental link, it will be removed (as well as many other options). But for this example, just move a fader on your MIDI keyboard, and the dialog box will disappear, and the fader on your MIDI keyboard will now be linked to the Keys channel volume control.

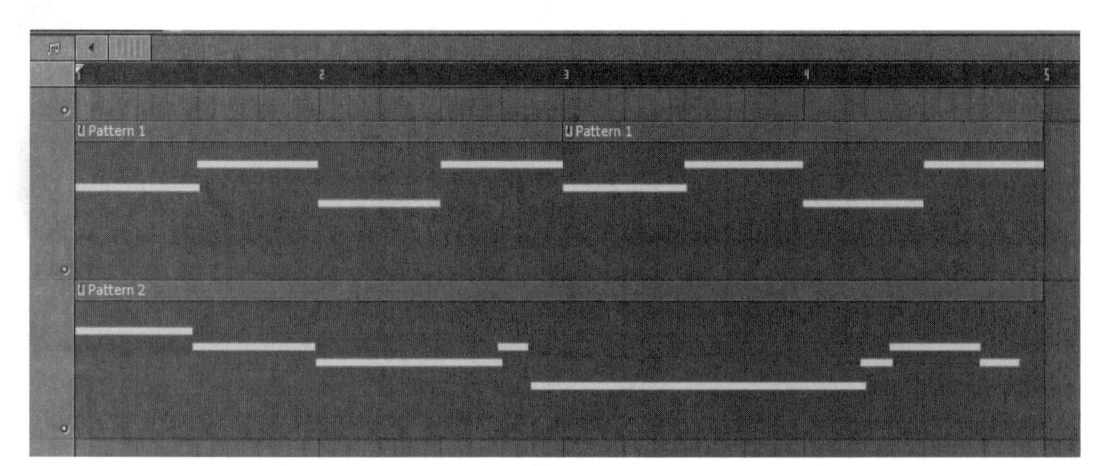

Figure 5.21 Dropping pattern clips into the Playlist.

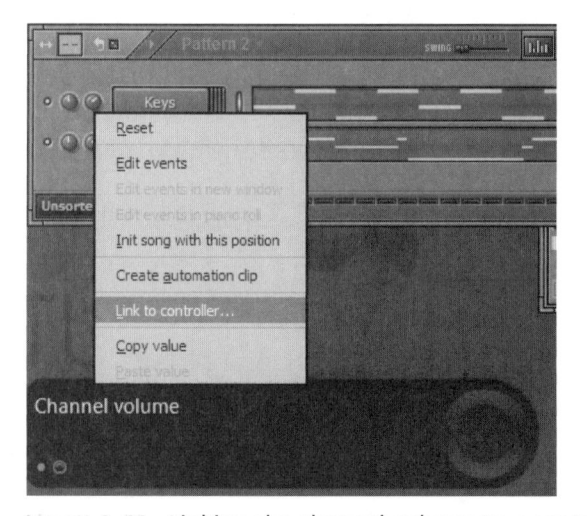

Figure 5.22 Linking the channel volume to a controller.

Now right-click on the Record button and make sure that only Automation is selected (see Figure 5.24). This will make sure that you don't record over any notes accidentally. Note that if the Recording dialog box pops up and you select Automation and Score, you will have to right-click the Record button again to deselect Score. Turn on your metronome and press R to start recording. You will hear the count-in, and then FL Studio will start recording the moves that you make with your MIDI keyboard fader. Try gradually increasing the volume starting at zero and press Stop when you reach the highest point in volume that you want. Turn off recording by clicking the Record button. Turn off the metronome, and now you have created volume automation!

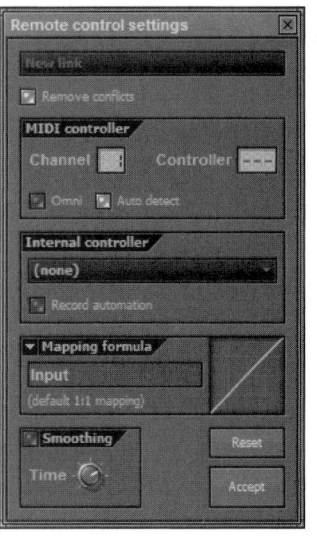

Figure 5.23 The Remote Control settings.

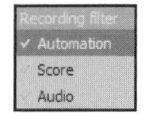

Figure 5.24 Recording automation only.

This automation can then be edited precisely by right-clicking the volume control that you just automated and selecting Edit Events (see Figure 5.25). A new window will open, giving you a visual representation of your automation in which the horizontal axis is time and the vertical axis is knob position (see Figure 5.26).

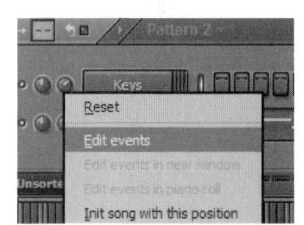

Figure 5.25 Selecting Edit Events from an automatable parameter.

In this window you can do slight adjustments or complete reworkings of the automation that was recorded. Most of the tools will be familiar, but I want to mention the LFO option from the Tools menu (see Figure 5.27). This will create a pattern and will affect the changes of your automation, much like an LFO affects audio. Rather than the audio's waveform being affected, though, only the volume will change, based on the curves drawn on the graph (see Figure 5.28).

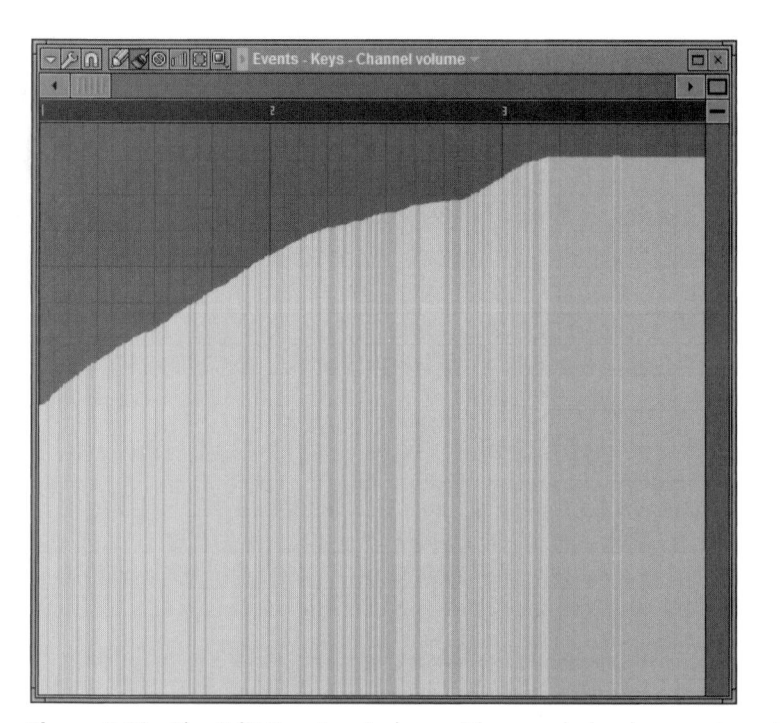

Figure 5.26   The Edit Events window with recorded volume automation.

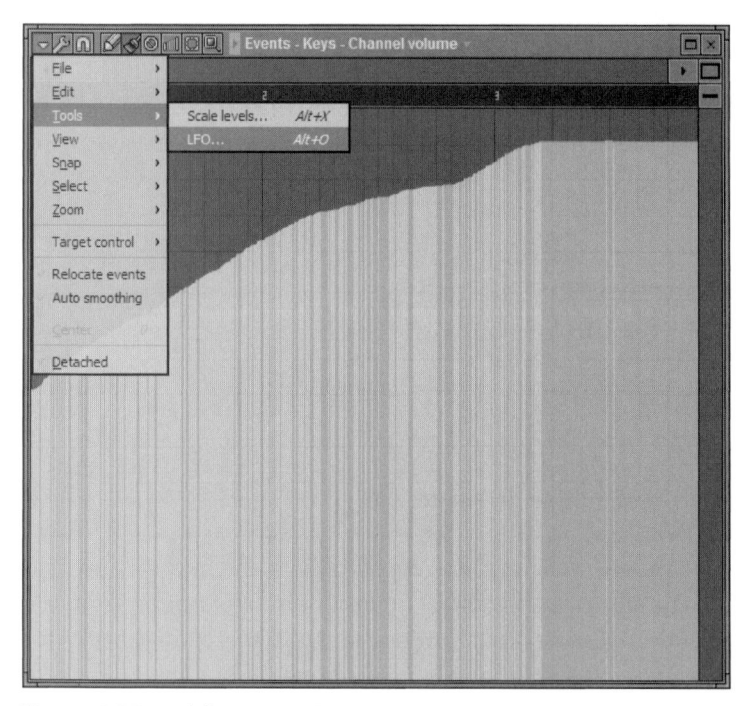

Figure 5.27   Adding an LFO to an event.

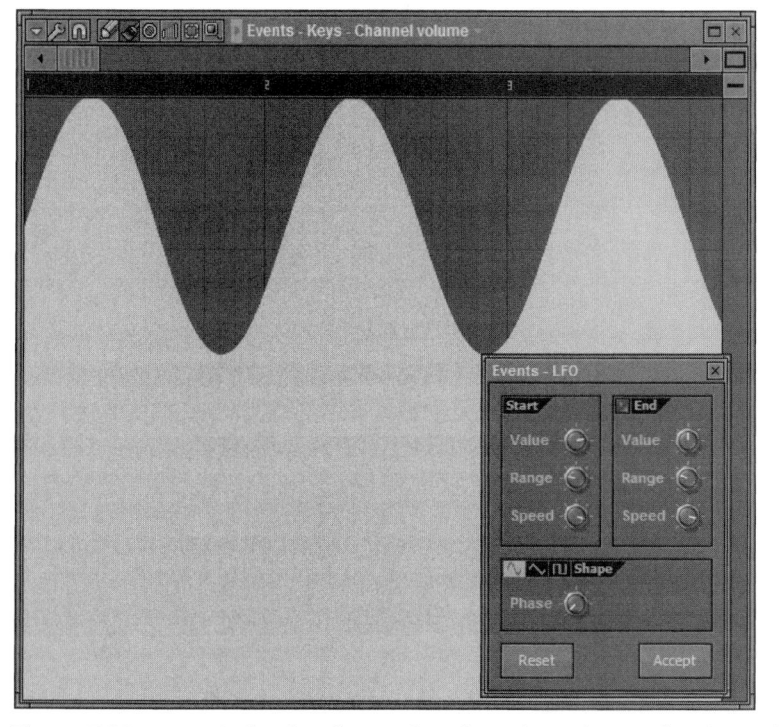

Figure 5.28 An LFO that has been placed on the volume of a channel.

Another option is using your mouse to record the automation. To perform this, select Record Automation and move the control in the software (like the Volume knob we just controlled) using your mouse. Then turn off the recording, and you can still edit the automation by right-clicking the control in the software that you automated and selecting Edit Events. Initially the action is manual, but remember that this is just programming the automation so that it will re-create your volume changes every time the music plays back.

My personal favorite for creating automation is using the automation clips. These are placed into the Playlist, similar to audio and pattern clips, but rather than play audio or use MIDI to trigger sound, they tell FL Studio where the knob that you are automating should be positioned at that point in the song. This is a very effective way to always be able to access your automation quickly and visually see it without navigating multiple windows.

I want to mention that you can use your live automation recordings and turn them into automation clips by opening the Edit Events window and selecting Edit > Turn into Automation Clip from the main menu (see Figure 5.29). In this example, though, we will start from scratch and automate panning of a track using a new automation clip.

Begin by right-clicking the channel panning of either of your piano takes and choosing Create Automation Clip (see Figure 5.30). When you do this, press F5 to open your Playlist, and you will see the automation clip inserted into the first empty track (see Figure 5.31). The line running along the

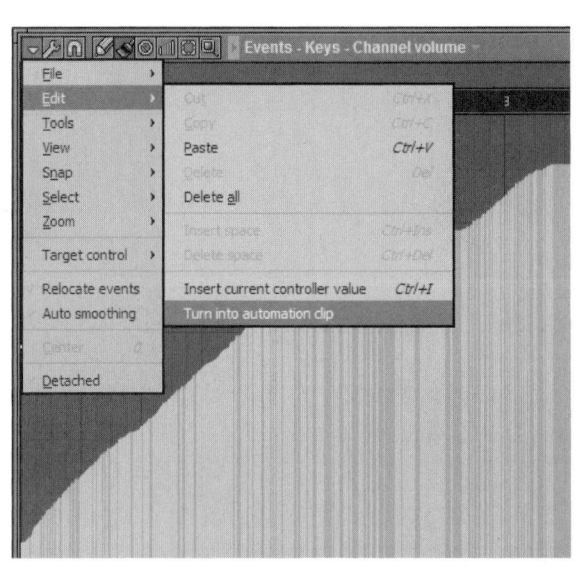

Figure 5.29   Changing a live automation recording into an automation clip to place on the Playlist.

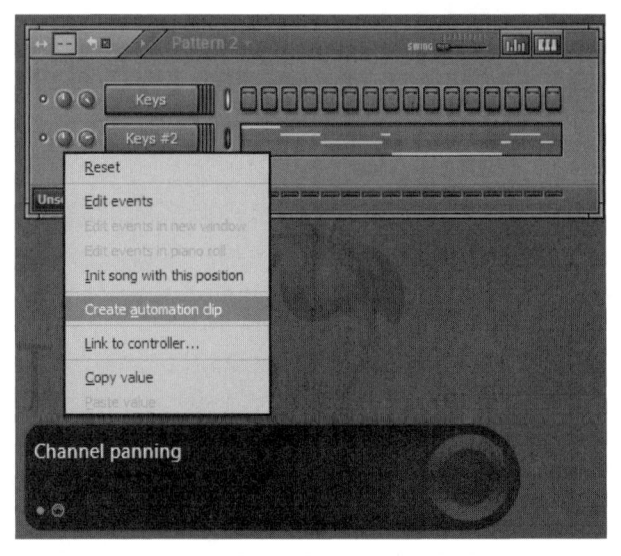

Figure 5.30   Creating an automation clip.

automation clip represents the panning, where dragging the line up to the top will be panning the sound to the right, and dragging the line all the way down will be panning the sound to the left.

Try making the line start at the top and go to the bottom over the length of the clip (see Figure 5.32). The Pencil tool is best, and left-clicking will add points on the line, while right-clicking will remove them. You will notice that the piano sound starts in the right output and gradually moves to the left output as the clip plays.

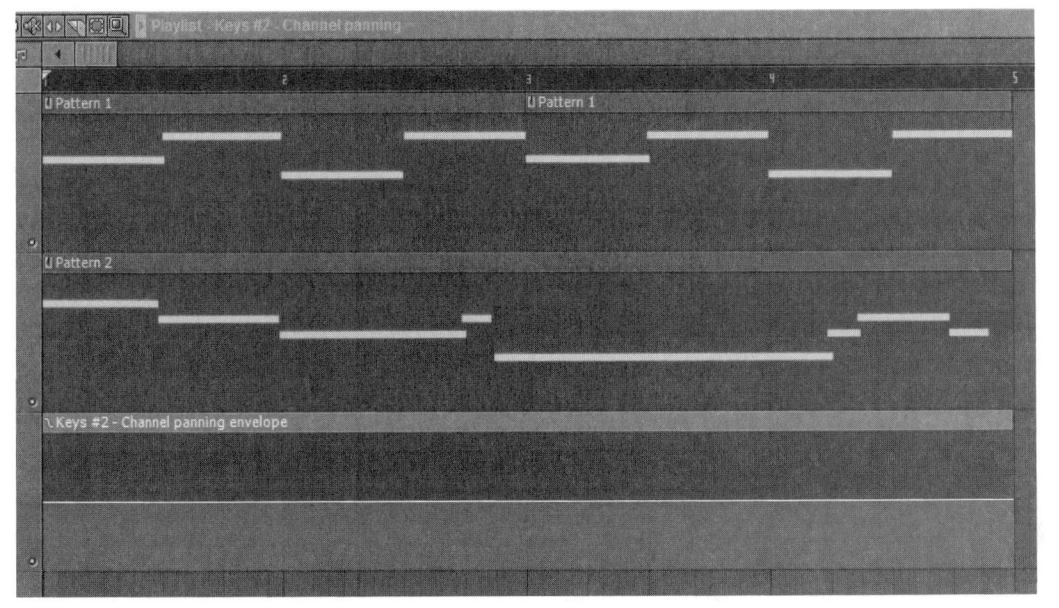

Figure 5.31 A panning automation clip dropped into the Playlist.

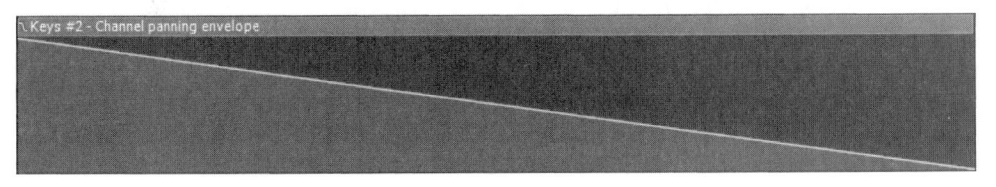

Figure 5.32 An automation clip that causes channel panning to go from right to left.

Volume and panning were the two automatable controls that helped me grasp the concept of automation and how it works. Now that you have a good idea of what you can do using MIDI with automation as well as creating your own clips that you manually draw, remember that any automatable knob can perform these tasks. The key is experimenting with different parameters, such as filters or cutoffs, so that you understand how easy it is to make changes to your sound that you like and keep those changes happening. With a strong foundation of understanding, we will look at linking multiple controllers for automation purposes.

Multi-Link Controls

This option is great for setting up multiple links with your MIDI keyboard, because it allows you to create multiple links between your keyboard and the software with one selection. From the recording panel, select Multi-Link to Controllers and make sure that the box next to the graphic (see Figure 5.33) is bright orange (toggled on).

Figure 5.33 The Multi-Link to Controllers toggle switch.

Before making any changes, it is good to understand what this button will be doing. It will read every change that you make (to any automatable parameter, such as panning or volume) in FL Studio and remember them all in sequential order. Then, as you move knobs or faders on your MIDI keyboard, they will sequentially control each knob that was moved in the software.

So if you want to control the volume of one track and then the volume and panning of a different track, select Multi-Link to Controllers and then move the first track's volume. (The amount you move the knob doesn't matter because you only need FL Studio to see which knob you want to control.) Then move the second track's volume, and finally move the Pan knob for the second track. Now these will map to your keyboard in order, so in this example, the first fader on your MIDI keyboard that you move will be mapped to the volume of the first track, the second fader will be mapped to the volume of the second track, and moving the third fader will map to the panning of the second track. After moving the third fader, you can turn off the Multi-Link to Controllers button, and your mapping is finished! This is an example of temporary linking, where the links will work for the duration of the session and then stop when you close it.

If you find that you are using a particular fader on your MIDI controller to control the same plug-in or parameter, such as a master volume control, you can set a global link. These types of links will hold even in new sessions, so if you link a fader to control the panning of a plug-in, the next time you open that plug-in, your fader will still control the panning. To set it, adjust the parameter that you want to control, then right-click the Multi-Link to Controllers toggle switch, choose Override Generic Links, then move the fader on your controller to which you want to link the parameter.

It is important to know that temporary links will supersede global links, so even if you have a fader linked to the master volume control globally, if you temporarily link the same fader to a panning control, that fader will control the panning for the session and then revert back to the master volume control when you close your session.

This can be done for as many faders and knobs as your MIDI controller has, multiplied by 16, because each mapping can be different for the available 16 MIDI channels. You will need to consult the manufacturer of your keyboard for how to send different MIDI channels, but for now just know that you will have enough controls to move any fader you would want to automate. My favorite use for the Multi-Link feature is to select all of my volume controls in the Mixer and then link them to each knob on the keyboard. This was much faster than manually entering in each one, and it gave me hands-on individual track control similar to professional boards with just a MIDI keyboard!

To finish this section, I want to mention two alternative ways of using linking in FL Studio. When you're using external plug-ins, sometimes they will not have the easy right-click option that allows you to link the control to a MIDI keyboard fader. In these cases, you can move the knob that you want to link and then go to Tools > Last Tweaked > Link to Controller (see Figure 5.34). Lastly, move a knob on your MIDI controller or keyboard so it links with the

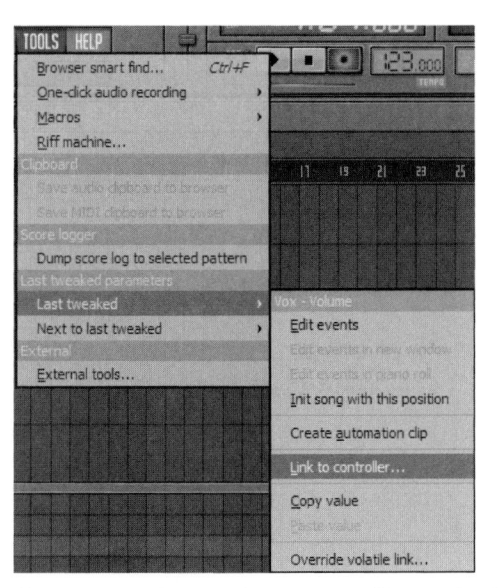

Figure 5.34 Connecting a controller to the last tweaked option.

software knob. Now that volume control you couldn't right-click can be manually controlled. The same knob can be turned into an automation clip by instead moving the knob in the software instrument and then selecting Tools > Last Tweaked > Create Automation Clip.

The other way of using linking that I want to mention is the use of volatile links. This can be especially useful for anyone who owns a MIDI keyboard that only has a pitch bend and modulation wheel. What this setting will do is link any automatable software knob to a single fader or knob on your keyboard, and when you move a different software knob, that new knob will be controlled by the same hardware knob on your keyboard and will remove the previous link.

The reason this is great for those with only a modulation wheel on their MIDI keyboard is because when you select the modulation wheel to be the volatile link, it will remap to whatever you change in FL Studio. For example, move a knob in the software and go to Tools > Last Tweaked > Override Volatile Link (see Figure 5.35) and then move your modulation wheel on the MIDI keyboard. Now move the volume of one track using the mouse and then move the mod wheel, and you can see that it now controls the volume. Now use the mouse to change the panning of a track and move the mod wheel. This time the mod wheel controls the panning, but it doesn't control the volume anymore. This behavior will repeat until you choose the Override option again and press Reset and then Accept. This will remove your mod wheel from the linking process (see Figure 5.36).

Up to this point, we have explored the many uses of MIDI in our software and how it works within it. You now know a decent amount about what automation is, how it can work with MIDI, and ways to link controllers to your hardware, so getting volume control for a track should be no problem. The final section in this chapter will look at how FL Studio reads

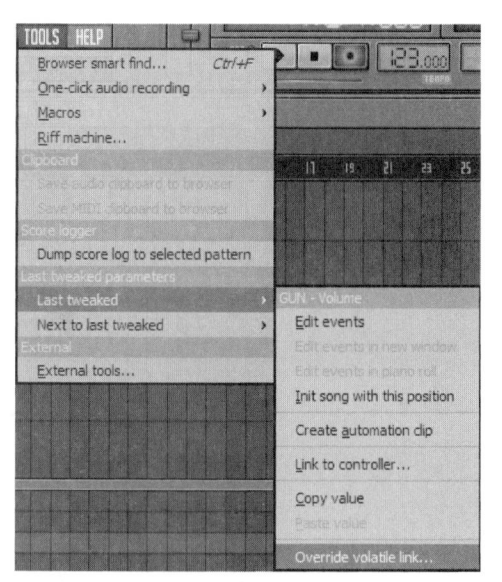

Figure 5.35 Using the Override Volatile Link option.

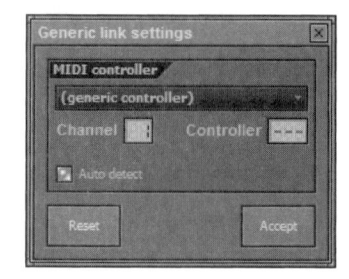

Figure 5.36 A freshly reset volatile link.

MIDI information to play different pieces of music on the fly and how you can create and record your own live performances.

Live Mode and Marker Jumping

There are two main ways to create music live using FL Studio and play it back in different parts. The first option we can utilize is Live mode, and we begin by looking at the different ways in which Live mode triggers sound.

When Live mode is engaged, you can have your patterns play in a continuous loop or as a one-shot, where it plays the length of the pattern and stops. In Figure 5.37, you can see that both Poizone and the Nature pattern are set to play one time for the length of the loop and then stop playing, while Bass will continue to loop. To toggle patterns to be one-shot versus continuous loop, right-click them, and to activate them (turn the loop or one-shot on or off), left-click them so that any highlighted ones will play and those not highlighted will not.

Figure 5.37 Patterns in the Playlist with Live mode engaged.

To use this well with your MIDI keyboard, you can leave all your patterns set to loop because you can make them one-shot by turning them off after triggering them to start playing. The MIDI keyboard will be mapped to the patterns automatically beginning with the middle C on your keyboard, and as you get higher on the keyboard, the keys will trigger higher-number patterns. The only thing to be aware of for setup is on the MIDI Options (F10) menu, where you set the Playlist Live Mode MIDI Channel (see Figure 5.38). In my example, I have set my keyboard to use Live mode on MIDI Channel 3. This means that for the keyboard to control Live mode, I need to set my MIDI keyboard to play on MIDI Channel 3.

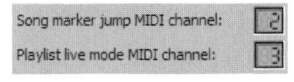

Figure 5.38 Setting the Playlist Live mode MIDI channel.

A key thing to remember is that having other clips in the Playlist can mess you up, so clearing them all out is the best way to alleviate this. Make sure you save your project under a different name before starting Live mode, and add Live to the title so you don't wonder where all of your clips went when you open it. Then delete all the information on your Playlist in the upper and lower regions.

Also make sure that you are in Song mode when using Live mode so that you are able to continuously change up your sounds or let them run as long as you'd like. Selecting a pattern to loop will do nothing when the song position marker isn't moving, so make sure you hit Play before starting in with Live mode. When you hit Play, if no patterns are highlighted to play, then you will hear nothing until you highlight one, and it will play based on your current grid settings. In other words, if you have your grid set to a bar, then the pattern will begin at the start of the next bar, and any other patterns that are highlighted to play will wait until the next bar to play. I suggest you don't turn off the grid settings, because it is very easy to get the beats and sounds completely out of sync.

The last thing I want to mention about Live mode is that if your patterns start off of the first bar and do not trigger right away, typically you will run into problems with everything sounding out of sync, so Live mode works best when the patterns are crisp and right on beat.

If you have an entire project set up in your Playlist, and each section has a marker indicating the different parts of the song, then you can use your MIDI keyboard to jump around to these different sections. In the project that I have created in Figure 5.39, you can see that there are

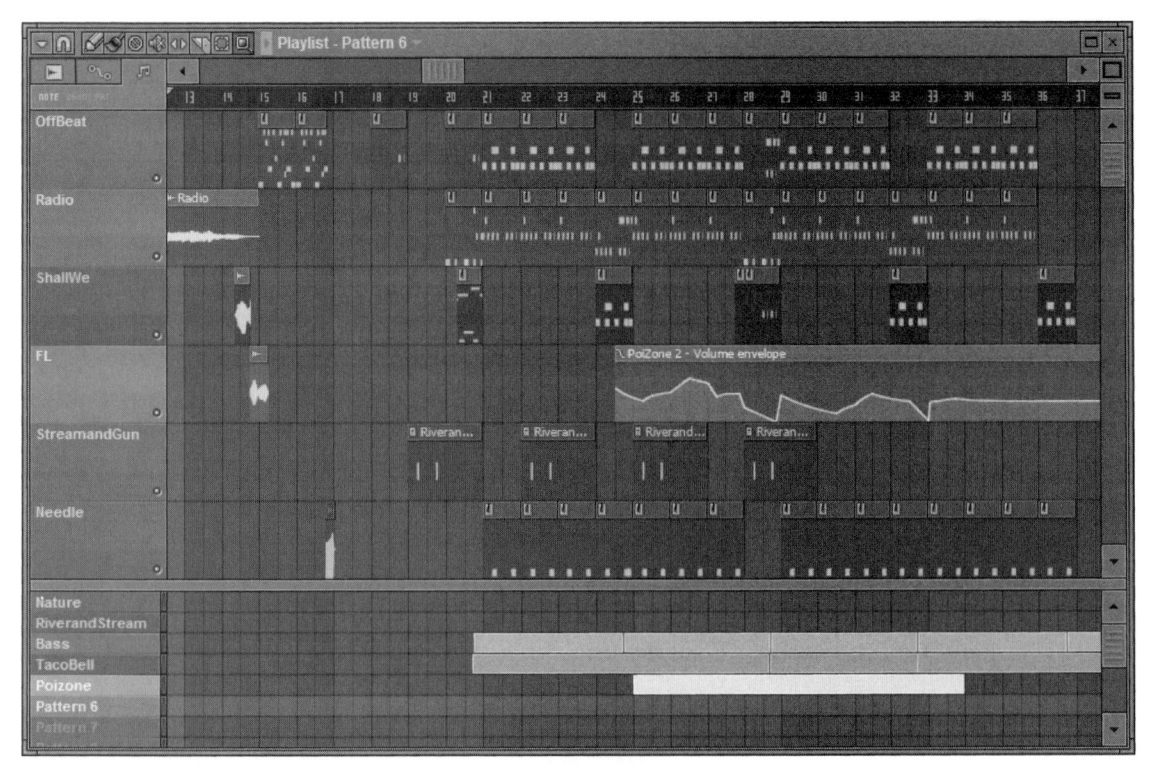

Figure 5.39 A working project in FL Studio without markers.

multiple parts with an intro, different breaks, and instruments. Unlike Live mode, marker jump-ing will play portions of the song that you have already created rather than single patterns. You can spread out your patterns and sounds across the Playlist and make markers for each one to jump to, but it will only play that section, so it is best to just place markers in different spots of a song you have already made.

For this example we will assume that I have placed all of my markers at different points in my song, such as the intro, the breaks, and the main beat (see Figure 5.40). With this finished, I am ready to start using my keyboard to jump to different spots. Remember that you need to assign a MIDI channel to the marker jumping in the Options menu (F10). In this example I have my MIDI keyboard controlling marker jumping on MIDI Channel 2.

Although you can use the MIDI keyboard to control the marker placement, I find that it is easier to just insert the markers manually, rather than taking the time to memorize what key places markers or removes them. The white keys will sequentially jump the song position marker to the marker to which the keyboard is mapped (see Figure 5.41), and as in Live mode, you must press Play on the main transport to make any sound play.

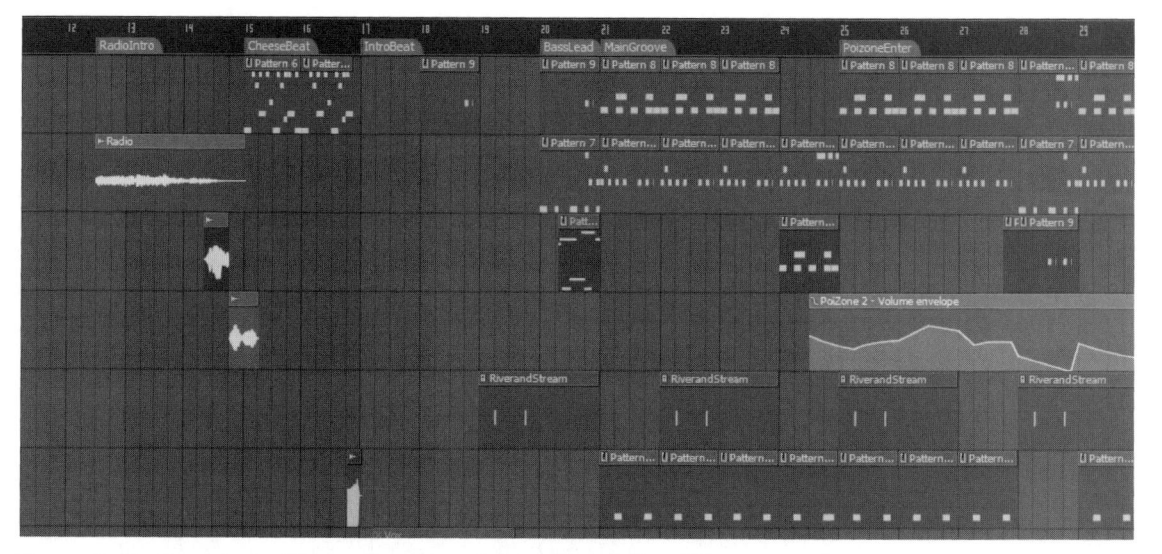

Figure 5.40 A project with markers placed throughout the different sections.

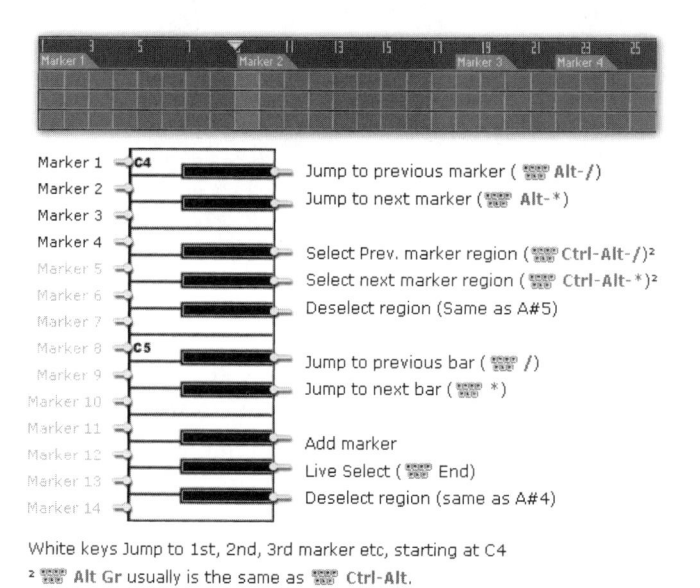

White keys Jump to 1st, 2nd, 3rd marker etc, starting at C4
² ⌨ Alt Gr usually is the same as ⌨ Ctrl-Alt.

Figure 5.41 An explanation of marker jumping commands from the online FL Help file.

With your markers set and the song position jumping around from keys pressed on your keyboard, you can record your live performance! In the Mixer, select an empty track and insert Edison into the main Mixer channel (the one farthest to the left). Select Now for when to begin recording in Edison and press Record in Edison. Edison will pick up any sound that goes through the main Mixer, so everything you play will be recorded and captured in Edison. This is a great way to audition different parts of a song or to manually create a new version of your project (see Figure 5.42).

Figure 5.42   A live performance using marker jumping recorded into Edison.

So we have looked at pretty much all things MIDI that will be used in FL Studio, and I have given you many examples of how to use it. We discussed automation, which at times may have seemed a tad repetitive, but only for you to fully understand how amazing of a leap automation in digital music is for technology. Now that you have a strong understanding of how to use MIDI and create notes and changes in the Piano roll, in the next chapter we will take a deeper look at the included instrument plug-ins and generators. It is my hope that you will be able to combine your knowledge from this chapter with the upcoming plug-in chapter so that you never get stuck again when trying to create a sound. We will look more closely at the settings of each plug-in and how they can be used to change sounds within the plug-in, as well as sounds affected by the plug-in.

Instrument and Generator Plug-Ins

Not too long ago, if you wanted drums in your music, you would have to pay someone to play the part, and then it would take hours of cutting actual recording tape to get the sound right when the drummer wasn't as on tempo as you wanted. Solo artists were usually nothing more than a guy with a guitar. When armed with FL Studio, though, a guy with a guitar and FL Studio becomes an entire band with post-production abilities. The bass, drums, synths, violins, pianos, and a ton of other instruments can be emulated or "faked" to give your music that complete sound. Even guitar strumming can be mimicked, and full chords can be played.

This chapter takes a look at the incredible world of software instruments and generators and how they can be used. We will take a look at each instrument and generator that comes included with FL Studio and look at some examples of using them. By the end of this chapter, you will have nearly all the information you need to make music in FL Studio and, most importantly, where to find that sound you are looking for. To begin this chapter, we take a look at the plug-ins you can install into FL Studio and how to install plug-ins that are not native to the program.

What Formats Can We Use?

There are a decent number of formats that plug-ins can run as, and FL Studio will accept most of the ones you will find. To begin, VST/VST2, or *Virtual Studio Technology*, was a standard developed by Steinberg (creators of Cubase) so that third-party plug-ins can be recognized in recording software. Most of the plug-ins you will find either support or run in this format, and FL Studio will recognize most, if not all, of these. Remember that developers make mistakes, too, so if something doesn't run properly, it is not likely FL Studio causing the trouble. FL Studio's plug-ins conform strictly to the VST specification, and there are times when third-party plug-ins don't stick to the standard, which can cause a wide range of issues.

DirectX plug-ins are a standard developed by Windows that will work in FL Studio, provided that you have installed DirectX Media. This download can be found on the Microsoft website. DirectX 2 plug-ins require DirectX Media as well, but these will use the Fruity Wrapper plug-in to run. Buzz effects are also supported, but they use FL's Buzz Effects adapter plug-in in order to work properly.

Supported Formats Here is the list of supported plug-in formats for FL Studio:

- VST
- VST2
- DirectX
- DirectX 2
- Buzz Effects
- FL Studio native plug-ins

Installing Non-Native Plug-Ins

This section is for helping you install that plug-in that you love, but FL Studio hasn't seen yet. In this example I will be installing iZotope's Ozone 4, which is an amazing mastering suite and has tons of features, such as EQs, multi-band compressors, limiters, and many others, along with a great selection of presets.

First, you will have to install the program, and there are too many plug-ins available to go through that part. It is good to know that it is best to keep the third-party plug-ins out of the FL Studio installation directory. Assuming you have installed the program, we will start by pointing FL Studio to where you keep your plug-ins. Many times, when they are VST plug-ins, they will be stored in C:\Program Files\Steinberg\VST Plug-Ins. My computer is running a dual-boot system, and the directory happens to be Program Files (x86)\VstPlugins. As you can see in Figure 6.1, I have selected the VstPlugins folder to be my extra VST search folder in the

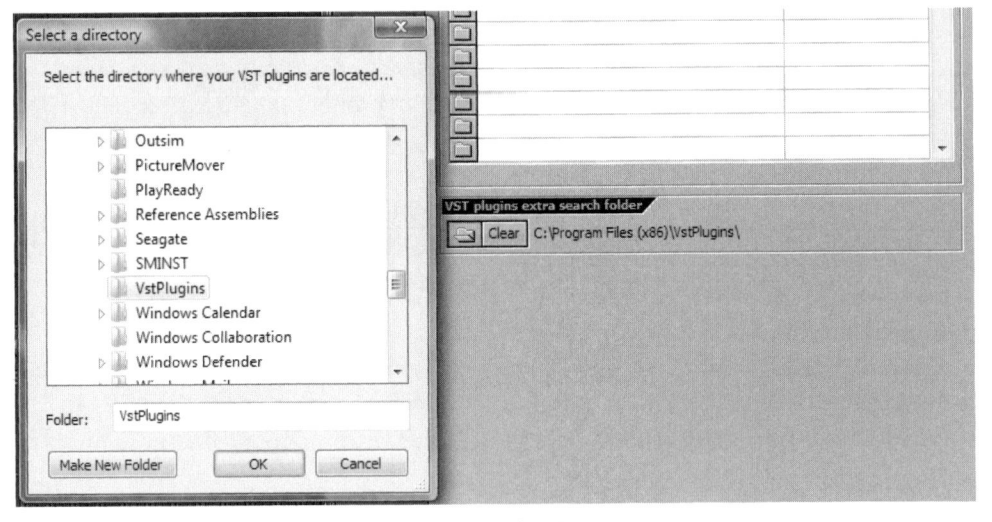

Figure 6.1 Directing FL Studio to extra VST plug-ins.

Options menu (F10), under the File tab. All the FL plug-ins will be in FL Studio's own folder, but for the other plug-ins residing in a different folder, this is where you tell FL Studio to look for them.

Now navigate to Channels > More, and upon selecting More, a list of all your plug-ins will show up. If you have recently installed your plug-ins or changed the extra search directory, then you will want to select Refresh at the bottom of the list. As you can see in Figure 6.2, Ozone 4 still isn't showing up, but after clicking Refresh and choosing Fast Scan, Ozone 4 will show up with the rest of the plug-ins (see Figure 6.3). After selecting the box next to Ozone 4, it shows up in the main plug-in list and opens upon selection (see Figure 6.4).

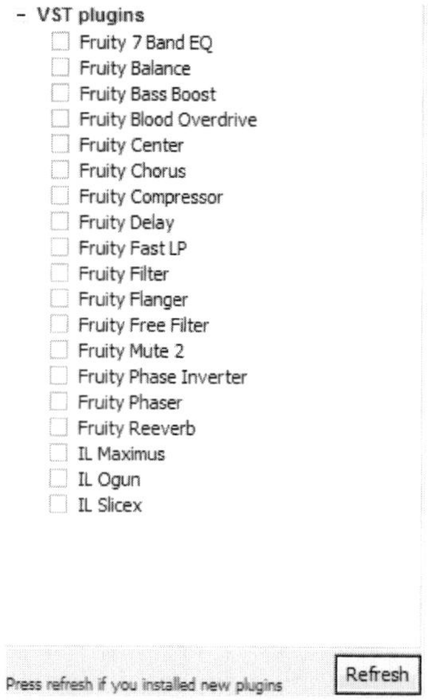

- VST plugins
  - [ ] Fruity 7 Band EQ
  - [ ] Fruity Balance
  - [ ] Fruity Bass Boost
  - [ ] Fruity Blood Overdrive
  - [ ] Fruity Center
  - [ ] Fruity Chorus
  - [ ] Fruity Compressor
  - [ ] Fruity Delay
  - [ ] Fruity Fast LP
  - [ ] Fruity Filter
  - [ ] Fruity Flanger
  - [ ] Fruity Free Filter
  - [ ] Fruity Mute 2
  - [ ] Fruity Phase Inverter
  - [ ] Fruity Phaser
  - [ ] Fruity Reeverb
  - [ ] IL Maximus
  - [ ] IL Ogun
  - [ ] IL Slicex

Press refresh if you installed new plugins   [Refresh]

Figure 6.2   The available plug-ins after selecting More from the Channels menu.

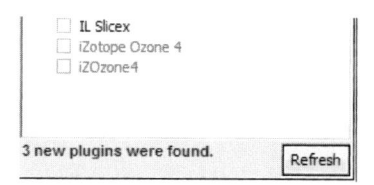

- [ ] IL Slicex
- [ ] iZotope Ozone 4
- [ ] iZOzone4

3 new plugins were found.   [Refresh]

Figure 6.3   Getting Ozone 4 to show up after installing it.

Included FL Instruments and Generators

Now that we have had a chance to look at installing plug-ins that FL Studio didn't come with, it's time to dig deep into the included plug-ins of FL Studio. These are the bread and butter of your digital sound-making. Many can affect sound that you record into FL as well, but most will

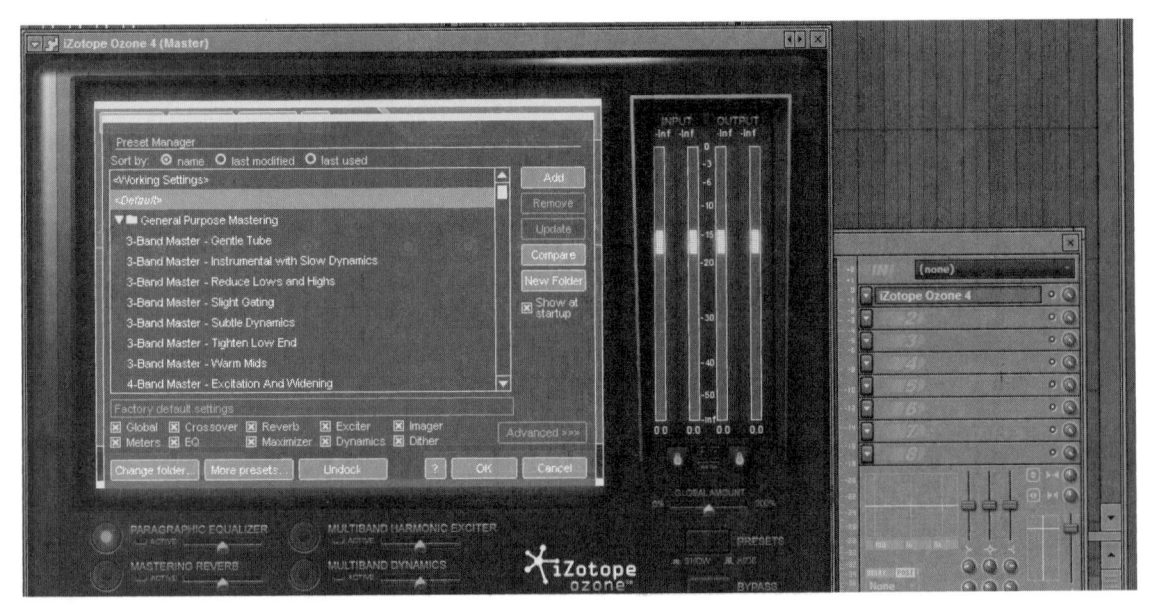

Figure 6.4   Opening Ozone 4 after FL Studio recognizes it.

be generators that produce sound for you to add to your projects. There is really no way to discuss all of the presets in these plug-ins, because as you will find with plug-ins such as Autogun, there are more than four billion presets to choose from, and your exploration will end up being key in finding sounds that you like or that would fit in your project.

3xOsc

3xOsc, shown in Figure 6.5, is a great oscillator tool for creating tons of different sounds that you can use as a quiet pad (a layer of sound in the background) or a stabbing arpeggiator that puts more rhythm in your music. The settings for the oscillators are the same, and the first set of boxes allows you to choose the shape of the oscillation.

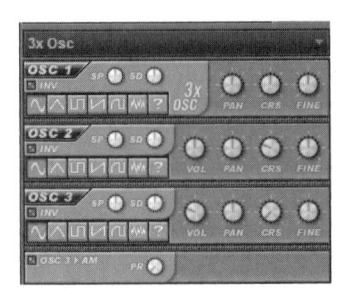

Figure 6.5   3xOsc.

Changing up these shapes alone will give you a plethora of options to work with. The Invert Toggle switch will flip the phase of that particular oscillator, so if you are looking at a digital drawing of the waveform, it will be turned upside down, which can help with creating a stereo effect if the sound is giving off too much of a mono feeling.

The SP (Stereo Phase) knob will basically allow you to move the oscillating wave forward or backward in time. This feature is great for widening the sound of your 3x Osc instrument and giving it more depth. The SD (Stereo Detune) knob can essentially do the same thing, but you will notice that the tones between the left and right channels become out of tune the more you adjust them. Feel free to experiment with this, but I have found more success in changing the stereo phase when looking for an interesting sound.

The CRS (Course) and Fine tuning knobs will tune the entire oscillator rather than cause the left and right to become out of tune with each other, and I have found this useful when working with remixes that are slightly out of tune. Adjusting this will allow you to hit those in-between tones without affecting the entire channel. Just remember that you made changes so you don't wonder why your instrument is out of tune when you try to play it.

The last two selections include a toggle switch (OSC 3 > AM) that allows you to cause the third oscillator to be amplitude modulation for the first two oscillators, as well as a Stereo Phase Randomness (PR) knob that will allow you to add varying degrees of randomness to the stereo phase of all oscillators. This plug-in will be reminiscent of early synths and will have a very classic sound to it. Many of us may have noticed that these types of sounds are really starting to creep back into modern music. The easiest way to find the presets is to go to your Browser—at the top is the Channel Presets menu. Open this, and directly underneath will be all of the presets for the 3xOsc to peruse. I highly suggest trolling these sounds, because although many of them seem simple, it is these simple sounds that combine with many others to create awesome arrangements in your projects.

There are a few complicated concepts inside this plug-in, but its relative simplicity is a good introduction to synthesis and hearing how it works. It is very difficult to explain different oscillator shapes without actually hearing them.

Autogun

Autogun, shown in Figure 6.6, is simply amazing due to the quality of sound and the mind-boggling number of presets. This plug-in allows for maximum creativity because of the variance in sounds available, which are based on the Ogun synthesis engine. The number crunchers at Image-Line did the math, and for you to sit down and go through each preset, at one preset per second, 24 hours a day, every single day, it would take more than 136 years. So in this case, you really don't have to worry too much about someone using the same sound as you with this instrument. The interface is very simple and easy to use because it is just left and right buttons to scroll through presets. Or, you can roll the dice with a random number entry by choosing Enter Preset Number from the Options menu. The large dial in the middle will control the plug-in volume, and the yellow lights located beneath it are known as the "magic" level. This control will add a fullness with stereo enhancement to your sound.

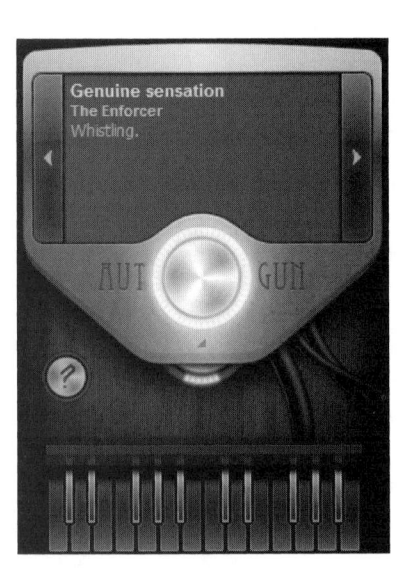

Figure 6.6 Autogun.

BeepMap

BeepMap, shown in Figure 6.7, is an interesting plug-in that basically uses images to create sound. The sound that is created is based on colors in the picture, where red color in the image will control the wave playback on the left side, green will be on the right, and yellow will be a mixture of left and right.

Figure 6.7 BeepMap.

This can be a little daunting to wrap your head around when first explained, but just know that the different colors you see are all responsible for affecting the sound you hear. The vertical height of the colors will represent the frequency of the produced sound (sine wave), and two factors affect the frequency range (how high or low the note will play). The first is the Frequency knob, which will affect the range of the entire image height, and the second is the Use Blue option, which will determine the frequency range of each pixel in the image.

The Length knob will allow you to change how long a note plays based on each pixel in the image, while the Open option will bring up a list of literal pictures to import. Remember that these pictures act like presets for the sound, so loading a picture into this plug-in will determine the sound that you hear when playing notes.

Grainy will give your sound a grittier feel to it, and the Loop button will cause your sound to play until you release the key that you are using to trigger the sound. Widen will create a larger left/right separation for your sound, but keep in mind that this will not be noticeable with all sounds.

BooBass

The BooBass plug-in, shown in Figure 6.8, is a very basic plug-in that gives you a nice emulated bass sound. The idea of this plug-in is to sound like a real bass, and the controls that come with it are relatively simple. The different knobs affect the frequency based on which one you move. The Bass knob will adjust the frequency in the lower end, which you will find very useful for softening up bass lines that are playing a little too heavy in the lower region. The Mid and Treble knobs will affect mid and high frequency ranges, respectively. Getting your bass to sound right here will help you avoid too much EQ work on it later. This plug-in is very user friendly, and getting the sound you want is as simple as turning the knobs.

Figure 6.8   BooBass.

Chrome

Chrome, shown in Figure 6.9, is a fun way to trigger visualization effects for your project. There are many ways to use this, but making music is not one of them. Think of this as an image generator that "plays" different images from notes on the Piano roll or a MIDI keyboard.

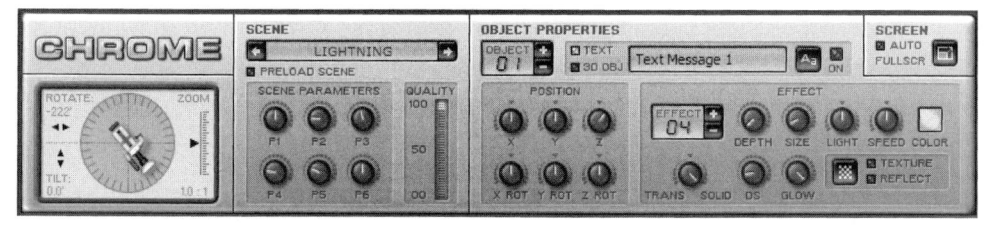

Figure 6.9   Chrome.

The first thing to note is that in most cases, you will need to run the Graphics Tester. This is very quick to do and prevents systems that shouldn't run Chrome from actually using the plug-in by testing the capabilities of your graphics card. To locate the Graphics Tester, navigate to Start > Programs > Image-Line > FL Studio > Advanced > Graphics Tester and double-click the Graphics Tester icon. If you are unable to find the Graphics Tester, you can run a quick search using your Start menu (see Figure 6.10).

Figure 6.10   Searching for the Graphics Tester on Vista.

Chrome can be treated like an instrument that plays a spectrum of color rather than a range of frequency. As you go up and down the Piano roll, the colors will change like a spectrum (violet, blue, green, yellow, orange, red). You can see that in Figure 6.11, I have written in some notes on the Piano roll of Chrome to trigger fireworks, and each key as you go up or down will be a different color. Left to right in the Piano roll will still operate as a function of time, and the grid will be based on your Snap settings.

When first looking at Chrome, the dial on the left will control the rotation, tilt, and zoom of the image, and these controls can be mapped to your MIDI keyboard for controlling the image by hand. (Right-click, choose Link to Controller, and then move a MIDI keyboard fader or knob.) The Scene button will allow you to open a different scene (the adjustable image), or you can click the left and right arrows to toggle through the different options.

Figure 6.11 Getting creative with Chrome.

Each scene will vary slightly in how the Scene Parameter knobs will affect the image, but when you mouse over the knob, the description will be displayed in the hint bar. If your computer is suffering (or worse, freezing up on you) when using Chrome, try lowering the Quality bar, because this will increase the performance of the plug-in by lowering the demand on the graphics card.

The Object Properties section (see Figure 6.12) will allow you to place an object or text over the scene and control the look and movement. To select a 3D object from FL Studio's files, highlight the 3D Object box and click the button to the right of where it says No Object. If you want text as the object that sits on top of the image, then highlight Text, and you can type in any text you wish and change the font by clicking the button to the right of the text entry area.

Figure 6.12 Object Properties section.

To the left, the Auto FullScr (full screen) button will cause the Chrome plug-in to take up the entire screen of your monitor when you press Play in the transport. The knobs and selections below the object and text selections will allow you to manipulate the size, depth, transparency, glow effect, shadowing, and rate that it moves. The upper Position knobs will move the object on the selected axis (X,Y,Z), and the lower Position knobs will move the rotation of each axis.

To add texture to your object, you can highlight Texture and then use the button next to the toggle switch to open a list of choices. This is a great tool to send visualization out, especially in a live performance setting, where you are using your MIDI keyboard to change effects and trigger colors. While you are playing your live set, you could have your performance name flashing randomly or even exactly when you need it to, using your MIDI keyboard (see Figure 6.13).

Figure 6.13 Using a text object with lightning being triggered from a MIDI keyboard.

FL Keys

Looking for a great piano sound? Look no further than FL Keys (see Figure 6.14), and the best part is that this is not a demo! There is software out there that will cost you more than FL Studio itself, and you won't be able to hear the difference when a little reverb is applied.

Figure 6.14   FL Keys.

There are three initial settings by default: Piano, Rhodes, and Roto-Organ. Many of the knobs will be familiar to you by now, but it is important to take note of a few to fully understand this plug-in's abilities. Under the Misc section, the Stretch knob will determine how much the sound is pitched based on the note pressed above C#5. You can adjust the high notes by –50 to +50 cents so that those higher notes will bend down or up slightly. (One hundred cents represents a semitone.)

The Hardness knob will affect the level of overall brightness of your notes, and the Sensitivity knob will control how FL Keys reacts to different note velocities. So if you want the keys to play at a constant velocity, then turn this knob completely to the left, and no matter how firmly or softly you press a key with your MIDI keyboard, the notes will stay at the same volume.

The Detune knob will allow you to add a random detuning to your piano keys, and this can add a realistic sound to your performances, because many pianos played might have a few notes slightly out of tune here and there. The more detuning that you add, though, the more that your notes will be all over the place in pitch.

FL Slayer

FL Slayer is a great guitar emulator and will allow you to create full chords of clean or distorted guitar for your projects (see Figure 6.15). This is great for soloing with a keyboard or plugging in chords to play for that gritty effect. This effect is designed to re-create a guitar with effects and will not affect incoming signal, so it can't be used as an effects board for your real guitar.

The Mode drop-down list will affect how FL Slayer responds to MIDI notes in the Piano roll or notes played on your MIDI keyboard. None will cause Slayer to play like a normal synth, and AutoChords will create guitar-style chords based on the notes that are played. PowerChords is a setting that will produce a familiar three-string playback that is usually used with heavily

Figure 6.15 FL Slayer.

distorted guitar. It is great for getting that rock sound. Strumming will play chords strummed out and is great for clean chord playing. Solo Fixed will allow you to add a slide sound so that as you change notes, they will slide up and down to each other, and Solo Dynamic will essentially do the same thing, but the amount of glide will be dependent upon the distance between the notes played. For example, two notes next to each other will quickly slide, while notes an entire octave apart will take longer to slide between.

The Speed wheel will control the speed that the virtual guitar is strummed and will give the playback a real sound to it, rather than six notes played on top of each other. The Hold switch next to this, when turned on, will allow the notes to continue playing (like the strings of a guitar continuously vibrating), but beware, because this can get irritating if you want the note to stop and it just keeps playing.

The String and Coils selections will allow you to choose what the guitar should sound like based on the strings it is using and the pickups. The Pitch Bend option will allow you to choose between a fine and a coarse pitch bend by toggling the Glissando button. Linking the Pitch Bend knob to a fader on your MIDI keyboard allows you to get that wicked bending sound that real guitarists achieve, and you can even create an automation clip to get the bend perfected!

The extra knobs on the guitar picture itself will all affect the different noises that a guitar would naturally make. Experiment with adding and subtracting these to create your ideal guitar sound.

The Amp and Cabinet selections will allow you to add an amplifier sound to your guitar and mimic that sound playing through a stack of speakers. So rather than set up a complicated chain of effects, speakers, and a mic to record the sound, everything you need is right here!

Drive will determine the amount of distortion for the guitar, Presence will affect the brightness of the guitar, and Feedback will simulate literal feedback from an amp.

The MFX-90 is like a built-in effects board that you can set to respond either prior to the amp or after. Effects beginning with AMP will affect the sound before going to the amp, while MST effects will affect the sound coming out of the amp.

There is a great collection of guitar effects that you will find with many guitar effects processors, and it will be well worth your time to familiarize yourself with how each effect will affect your sound. Place some notes in the Piano roll and scroll through these settings so that the next time you are looking for a stereo sweeping sound (DubDelay) or tremolo, you will know where it is and how to use it.

The Parameter knobs will control different aspects of the effect that you select. This plug-in is very versatile and great for those of us who have great guitar parts in our heads, but who have never picked up a guitar. I have played the guitar for roughly two decades now, and using this plug-in is still an option to me for ripping solos that I still can't play.

FPC (Fruity Pad Controller)

This is the plug-in to create beats with (see Figure 6.16)! Any sample can be used, so you can use it to trigger sound effects or even play entire songs, but pretty much everyone using the FPC will be using it to make the backbone of their projects. If you are only planning on triggering sounds that are perfectly on beat and that are not played live, then I suggest using the Stepsequencer to make your beats, because it will prove to be much easier.

Figure 6.16 The FPC.

One way to place the sounds your hear in the FPC into the Stepsequencer is to middle-click (center mouse button/scroll wheel) the sound in the FPC, and an instance of Edison will open. Then use the Drag tool to place it in the Stepsequencer (see Figures 6.17 and 6.18).

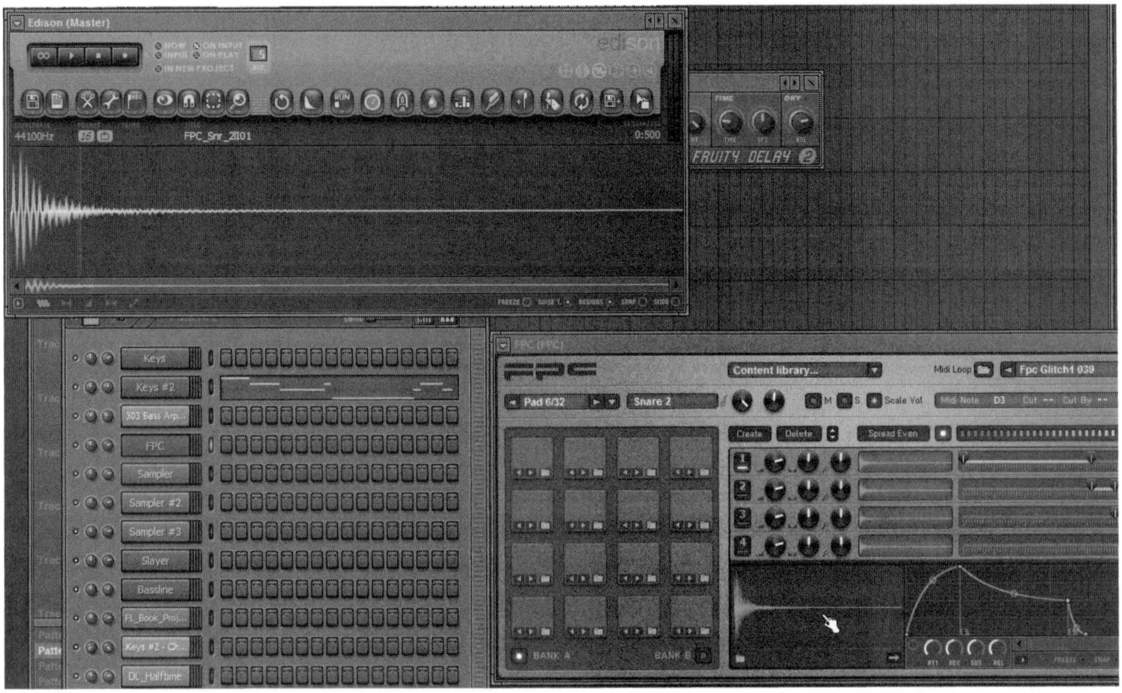

Figure 6.17   Middle-clicking the sample to open an instance of Edison.

Figure 6.18   Using Edison's Drag tool to place the sample in an empty channel.

Now you have the samples placed in the Channel window and can start sequencing a beat using the step entry (see Figure 6.19).

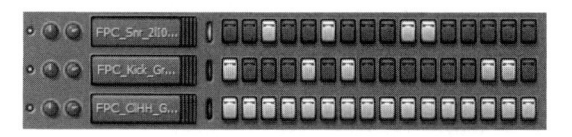

Figure 6.19 Using the Stepsequencer to create a beat using the newly placed samples.

The important thing to remember is that Edison will be sitting on your master track, and this will limit you with respect to editing specific tracks. To get around this, after linking the channels in the Channel window (F6) to individual tracks in the Mixer (F9), simply remove the instance of Edison in the master track, and the samples will still play based on the step sequencing.

Now that we have looked at a way to use the sounds in FPC, let's take a look at the FPC itself and triggering the sounds inside the plug-in. The first drop-down menu that you will see is the Content Library. This allows you to download more drum sounds from Image-Line. They will be a mix of free sounds and sounds you can purchase. For this example, we will look at installing one of the free drum kits, so that you can learn how to add sounds using this online feature. Remember that you need to be connected to the Internet to use this feature.

Begin by clicking the Content Library button, and the Image-Line Content Library window will open with options for downloading (see Figure 6.20). Under the Online section, navigate to the HipHop section and select the HipScratch 2 (Free) option (see Figure 6.21) and then click the Download button at the bottom of the Content Library window.

The Download Manager will open and detail the progress of your download (see Figure 6.22). When it is finished, navigate to the sample you just downloaded in the Content Library under Downloaded > HipHop > HipScratch 2 and select the Download button again (see Figure 6.23). When you choose the Download button after making a selection from your downloaded section, as opposed to the online section, it actually loads the samples into the FPC rather than downloading again. Now when you click the pads of the FPC, the loaded samples will be from the HipScratch kit that you downloaded.

The buttons to the left of the Content Library will allow you to enter in preset patterns that are placed in the Piano roll. This is great for getting you started with making a beat, and you can easily adjust any note or the timing of any note like you would with any information that is in the Piano roll. Remember that this will not change the sounds that are played; it will only affect the pattern. (Remember our discussion on MIDI?)

These presets tell the FPC when to play the notes rather than the content (the note sound that plays). There is a multitude of presets available, and you can access them through the MIDI File button or by scrolling through the presets using the left and right arrows. If you are not fantastic

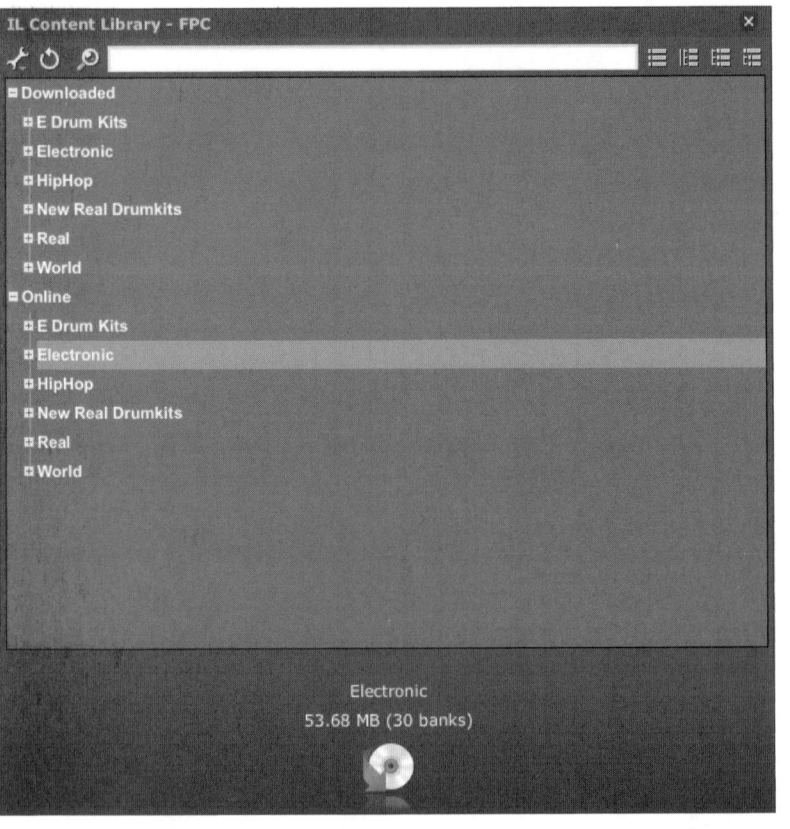

Figure 6.20 The Content Library.

at making beats, you are out of ideas, or you really just need a filler beat for having a more natural metronome, this is where you select a pattern to play.

In Figure 6.24, you can see that I selected Hiphop 08 from the preset list and how it automatically placed MIDI notes on the Piano roll. The best part is that because you are using MIDI, the sounds will conform to the tempo that you already have set for your song regardless of the pattern. I recommend using a pattern with no other information on it, because if you have another channel that goes longer than the set pattern length, the beat will stop and not play again until the pattern has finished playing (see Figure 6.25).

At this point we have looked at using the pads and adjusting the MIDI notes in our recording MIDI chapter, but we didn't look at the FPC's ability to edit the actual sound. This is great for quickly tweaking parts of your sample to get the sound just right. The important thing to understand about Figure 6.26 is that this menu will look the same when clicking on different pads, but each one will be unique to each sound.

The volume, solo, and mute controls will be familiar to you and will individually control each pad as it is selected. The note settings were discussed in the "Setting Up a Drum Pad Controller"

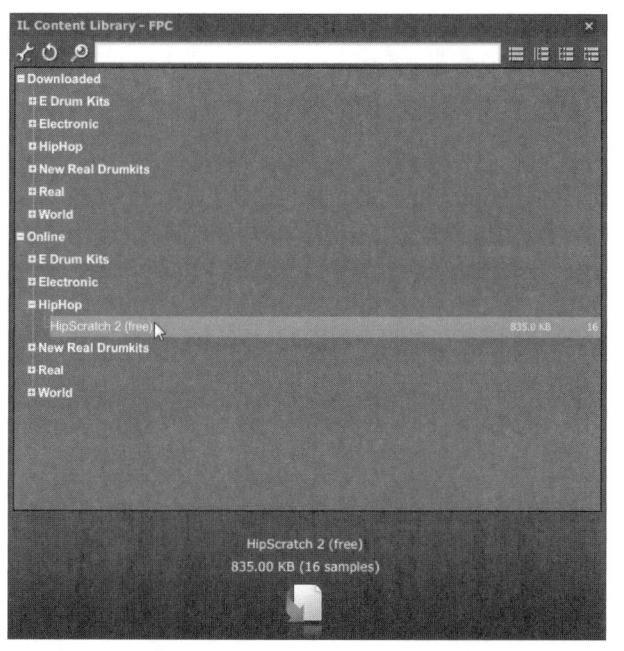

Figure 6.21   Navigating to the downloadable sample.

Figure 6.22   The Download Manager.

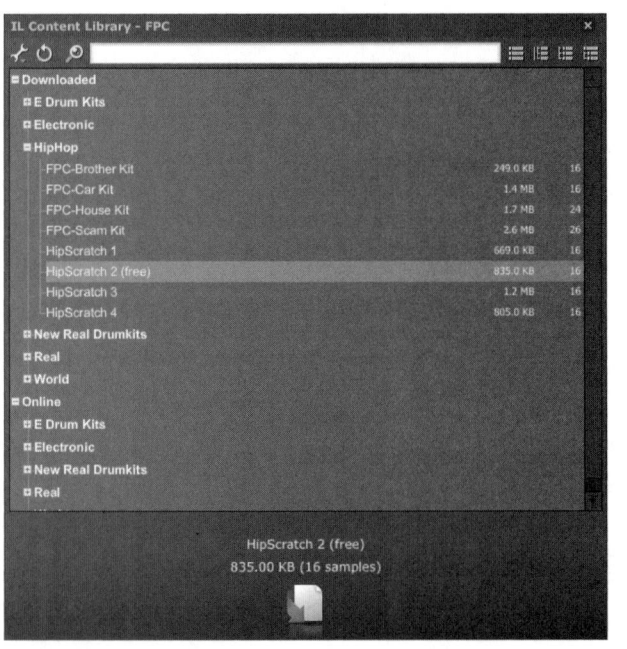

Figure 6.23 The Content Library.

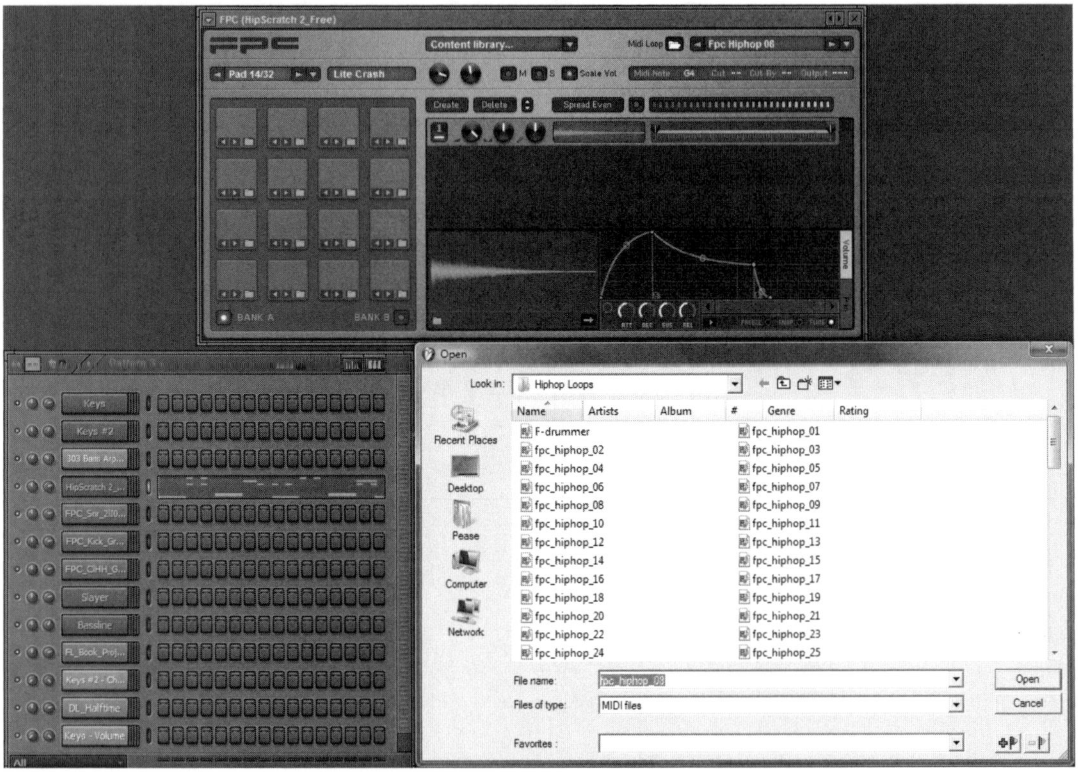

Figure 6.24 Inserting a MIDI pattern into the Piano roll using the FPC presets.

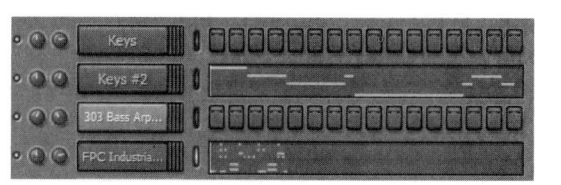

Figure 6.25   MIDI inserted into the Piano roll when another channel plays longer than the pattern length setting.

Figure 6.26   The individual pad properties.

section in Chapter 5, but it is important to know that the Cut and Cut By settings are used like sampler channel settings. So if you need one pad to stop the sound of another, this is where you would set it. A great example is when you have an open hi-hat and a closed hi-hat sound. When the closed hi-hat strikes, if the open hi-hat continues playing, it will sound wrong. You want the closed sound to "cut" the open hi-hat and stop it from playing so it sounds like a drummer actually playing live.

To do this, you would set the open hi-hat to be cut by (for example) 3 and then have the closed hi-hat cut 3. This can be used for any sample, and any sound can stop any other sound from playing.

The last option is an Output setting that allows you to route individual sounds to different outputs on the Mixer. The number output that you choose will be relative to the FPC placement, so if you have the FPC on Mixer Track 4, and the output for a particular pad is set to 3, the sound will play on Mixer Track 7.

The FPC has a Layer section (see Figure 6.27) that allows you to create variances in your sounds based on velocity, or how hard you play a note. To better explain this, we will take a single sample and turn it into a panned sample that, when played softly, will play on the left, and when played hard, will play on the right.

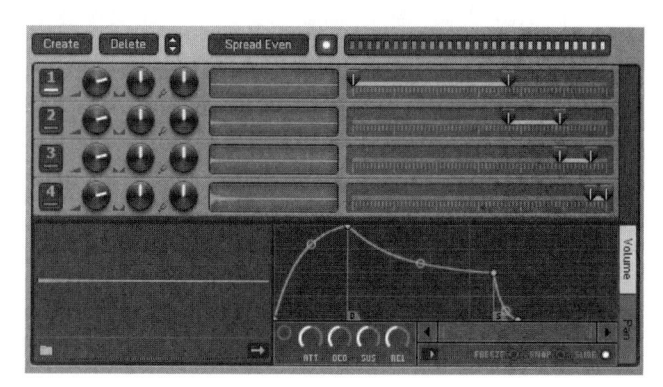

Figure 6.27   The Layer portion of the FPC.

Start by selecting any pad on the FPC so that it plays a sound, and make sure that there is only one layer visible after playing it (see Figure 6.28). Now select Create, and another layer will be added. This will be an empty layer, so nothing will play at first. We need to bring in the same sample (in this example), and the quickest way to locate it is to right-click the sample in the first layer and choose Show in Browser (see Figure 6.29).

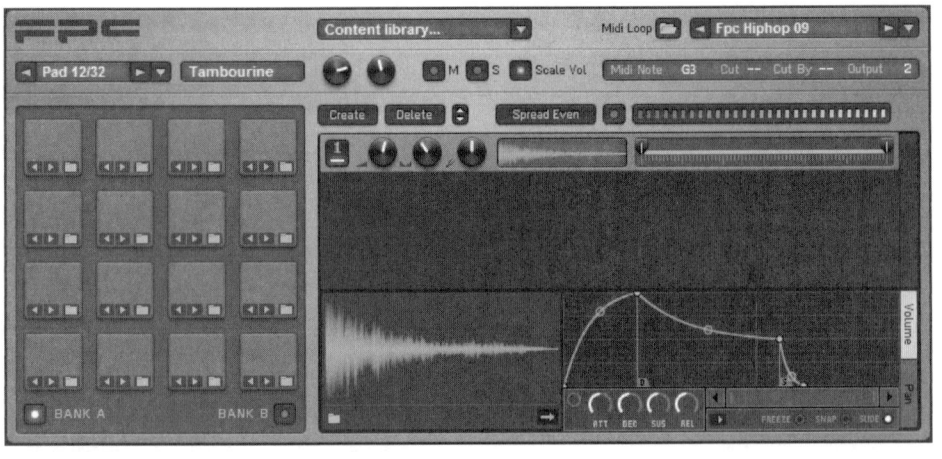

Figure 6.28 A single layer in the FPC.

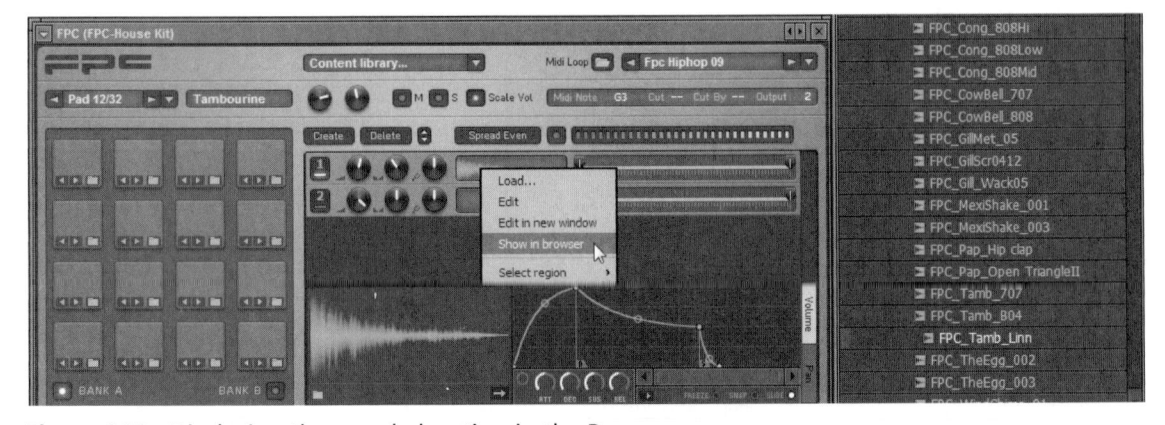

Figure 6.29 Displaying the sample location in the Browser.

Now drag the sample from the Browser into the empty layer (see Figure 6.30). For this example we will select Spread Even, so that the first layer is notes that are played softly and the second layer is notes that are played loudly. Keep in mind that you can change the range on either sample, and Spread Even will evenly divide the velocity response among any number of layers that are added.

Figure 6.30 Dropping a sample into an empty layer.

Now pan the first layer to the left and pan the second layer to the right. What you have done is told FL Studio that when this note is pressed, if it is pressed softly, then Layer 1 will play, but if it is pressed firmly, then Layer 2 will play. Because we adjusted the panning, if you play softly, the sample will play in your left ear, and when played firmly, it will play in your right ear.

Below this section is a typical ADSR envelope to adjust your layers individually. It will react in the same way based on the layer that is active.

This is a good amount to take in, so when beginning with layers, know that each layer will only play based on the velocity range that you set, and volume can be controlled by the layer settings, but velocity will not always be volume. For example, if you set Layer 1 to respond to low velocity but raise the volume, and Layer 2 responds to high velocity but the layer volume is dropped, when you play firmly, the sample will play quietly. Most would never use it this way, but it is just to illustrate how unrestrained your abilities are when using layers.

Rather than point out each feature in the Layer section, I wanted to take you through an example of using it so that you can see it in action rather than just reading about what buttons do, because this plug-in is one of the most powerful digital drum controllers available today. The flexibility of adding layers adds to the already powerful feature set that allows quick adjustments and velocity-based sound tweaking. With the layers, you can even add different samples so that the same key plays different sounds, depending upon how hard that key is pressed!

Practice with this plug-in, and so you don't fear affecting a project you may already be working on, open a new project and just play with the FPC for a bit. Add layers and different sounds to different pads while trying to adjust each one in a different way. Trust me; once you create a drum beat and it sounds exactly like it did in your head, you'll be glad you took the time to experiment.

Fruit Kick

Although the FPC is a hard act to follow, the Fruit Kick (see Figure 6.31) is outstanding for creating a custom kick sound. This plug-in works best when used with the Stepsequencer, in my opinion, because you can still link the channel to its own Mixer track for effects, but the sound will be one shot when the Stepsequencer is used.

Figure 6.31   Fruit Kick.

This is the simple method, but also know that you can find the pitch of your kick drum and match it to the song using the Piano roll. The drum will still be the same general sound based on the changes that you make to the available knobs, but as you move up and down the Piano roll, the pitch will change. The knobs are fairly simple, and there are presets in the Browser (Plugin Presets > Generators > Fruit Kick), but this is one of the easier plug-ins to experiment with, because there is no loading involved if you don't use a preset.

Max and Min will both act like frequency filters, but Max will determine the lowest frequency, while Min will determine the highest frequency that is played. Dec will tell the kick sound how fast to play through the frequency range set by your Max and Min knobs, while A. Dec will determine how long the kick sound will linger.

Click and Distortion (Dist) will both add to the kick sound's character by adding a click to the start (through phase offset) or distorting the sound by forcing the waveform to clip. Try the extremes of each, and you will be surprised by how many familiar kick drum sounds can be replicated with this simple little interface.

Fruity Dance

The Fruity Dance plug-in (see Figure 6.32) allows you to control an animated character that will dance based on notes played in the Piano roll or live on your MIDI keyboard. This generator is fairly straightforward, and opening the Piano roll will allow you determine when the character will perform certain dance moves.

The Show and Hide Piano roll notes allow you to display and hide the character based on when the MIDI notes play in the Show and Hide rows. In Figure 6.33, I have drawn in a back-and-forth pattern where the character will appear and disappear every beat using the Show/Hide rows, but you can see that the dance move MIDI note still plays. Even if the animated character is hidden, she is still performing dance moves in the background.

The big drop-down is a menu that displays all of the available dance moves, but this is for sticking with one dance move for the entirety of your project. If you want to change it up even a little bit, I suggest using the Piano roll.

Figure 6.32 Fruity Dance.

Figure 6.33 The character is set to flash between visible and invisible based on the notes in the Piano roll.

Mirror Horizontally will flip the character's dance movements on the vertical axis. This is great for adding two instances of the Fruity Dance and having a mirror image dancing to the same moves as your original.

Sync Changes means that the dance move that the character is performing will complete before switching to the next move that you have designated in the Piano roll. Turn this off if you are looking for immediate, on-point changes, though keep in mind that they might seem a little jerky when jumping from one move to another.

Visible toggles whether or not you can see the character, but remember that the Piano roll will have priority for this control, so if you deselect Visible, and the Piano roll has a show note that plays, the character will appear when the show note is triggered.

Keep in Front will place your character on top of all open windows. On Desktop will keep the character on your screen even after minimizing FL Studio.

Blend will smooth the transition between dance moves, and Speed will increase or decrease the character movement by a multiple of the tempo that you have set for your project. You are able to create your own animations using PNG or GIF files, but this lies outside the scope of teaching you how to successfully create music within FL Studio, so I will just mention that FL Studio recommends using image editors with layering and transparency abilities when creating your image sheets. To get a better idea of what the files look like, you can navigate to FL Studio > Plugins > Fruity > Generators > FruityDance > Artwork or simply open the help file (F1), navigate to Fruity Dance, and check out Making Your Own Animation.

Fruity DrumSynth Live

Fruity DrumSynth Live (see Figure 6.34) is a great plug-in for making beats and is extremely flexible with adjusting your sounds. The compact style of the plug-in allows you to keep it in view most of the time for easy editing. A standout feature of this plug-in is the ability to morph two sounds into one another, which I find useful for creating your own drum sounds or when you just need to add a little extra to your sample.

Figure 6.34   Fruity DrumSynth Live.

The DrumSynth is based on the manipulation of sound waves and will literally combine the two selected sounds and then allow you to mix them using the mod wheel to the left of the virtual keyboard. The Wave section, located in the upper left of the plug-in, allows you to mix between sample sounds and the built-in noise generator that is directly to the right of these settings.

All of the darker knobs that have – and + as values are velocity controllers. Remember that this doesn't always refer to volume, but typically that is what it will affect. The Tune knob will adjust the tuning (pitch) of the sample, and the Mix knob will control the blend of sample sound and noise generator.

What Is an LFO? LFO stands for low-frequency oscillator. An LFO in FL Studio modulates sound parameters using oscillations that play at frequencies typically lying beneath the human threshold of hearing (roughly 20 Hz). However, the purpose is not to create a deep sound; rather, the oscillation is meant to affect other parameters. For example, volume can have an LFO applied to it so that sound goes back and forth from loud to soft. Even a filter cutoff can have an LFO applied to it so that the tone of the sound goes back and forth from brighter to muddier. Almost every synth native to FL Studio will have an option for adding an LFO to a parameter of your sound.

The first oscillator allows you to select a frequency for generating a tone, and the slider beneath it will cause the note to sweep down when pulled left and sweep up when pulled right if the Noise button is deactivated. The Harmonics wheel allows you to distort the waveform by adding odd harmonics when turned left and even harmonics when turned right. The Decay knob will be familiar, but remember to use it! If that bass drum kick sound is lingering too long when played, lower the decay for a tighter punch—just know that this only applies to the first oscillator.

When Noise is not selected, the Sweep knob will determine how quickly the tone created sweeps across the frequency range set by the Frequency slider above. Invert will invert the phase of the two oscillators, so if you are getting that flat, lifeless sound from two waves cancelling each other out, select this switch to prevent phasing problems between them.

The second oscillator will have similar settings, and it has the ability using the first knob to ring modulate Oscillator 1 with Oscillator 2.

The Trig area in the bottom-left corner is similar to the Cut by Cut Itself options that we have seen in the Channel settings. When Mono is selected for a sound, the sound will cut any previous sounds that were playing. When Poly is selected, the sound will play without cutting, and the Group settings will allow you to group sounds into four available groups so that only the sounds in the same group will cut each other. This is important for hi-hat sounds, so if you have a closed hi-hat sound and an open one, usually grouping them is a good idea. When you place both in, say, Group Two, then whenever you play the open hi-hat, the closed hi-hat will stop the open hi-hat from playing and will give your music a more natural sound.

My favorite feature of this plug-in, as mentioned earlier in this section, is the sound-morphing ability. The Morph To drop-down displays a list of sounds that can be set to morph with the selected sound on the keyboard, and the mod wheel will control the mix between the two sounds.

One key thing to keep in mind when using this plug-in is that every note selection you make will give you a different setting for every section of the plug-in. When you play notes using your MIDI keyboard, DrumSynth Live will not automatically highlight a played note in the plug-in visually. This means that notes played on a MIDI keyboard will not change the settings display for the individual notes. Use the mouse to highlight the note for which you want to adjust parameters (which is indicated by the orange mark above it). If you can't see the note that is selected, click the Auto button in the lower-right corner, and the virtual keyboard will navigate to the highlighted note.

Use this plug-in to make your beats, but also use it for perfecting the sounds within your beats. Shorten, distort, re-create, and polish the sounds that make up the foundation of your song.

Fruity DX10

The DX10 (see Figure 6.35) is a synth that makes use of frequency modulation to create sounds similar to real instruments. By modulating the pitch of one oscillator to the pitch of another and then increasing the speed of these modulations, the once-simple tones take on a whole new life!

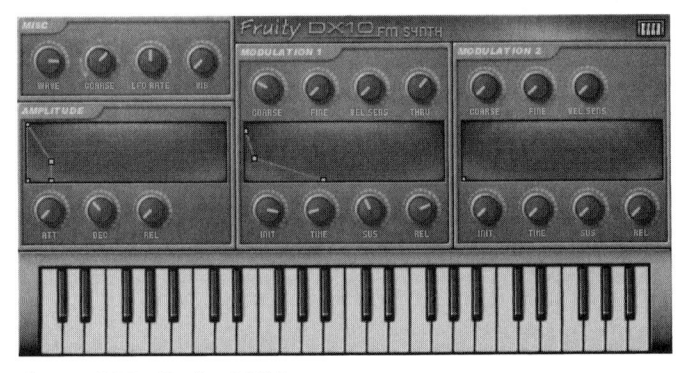

Figure 6.35   Fruity DX10.

There is a small set of presets to get you going, and if you are going for that '80s synth sound, there is plenty of flexibility within this plug-in for finding just the right tone. While you will see typical settings that we have dealt with in this book for the modulation settings, unfamiliar settings will lie in the first set of knobs in the Miscellaneous section.

The Wave knob acts like a tone brightness control and can be analogous to someone opening and closing his mouth while singing the same note. Turning left would be like someone closing his mouth, while turning right will open it. The Coarse knob adjusts the pitch of the sound by octaves, while the LFO Rate knob determines the speed of the vibrato, and the Vib knob controls the strength of the vibrato. This is a fun plug-in to explore and can generate some interesting bass sounds, background pads, and retro noises.

Fruity SoundFont Player

The Fruity SoundFont Player (see Figure 6.36) is a great way to put your samples to work. The first time I opened up the SoundFont Player and loaded a string sample into it, I was impressed by the quality that came out. Although the quality is not guaranteed, there are tons of online sites that offer free .sf2 files—just always be careful when downloading anything off the Internet. You can load your .sf2 files by clicking on the folder icon and navigating to them, and once they are open, you will be able to choose the patch and bank of the selected SoundFont file. If you click on the name, you will see the full list of available instruments.

Figure 6.36 Fruity SoundFont Player.

The Reverb and Chorus switches allow you to use the built-in reverb and chorus of the plug-in. The Send To selectors (see Figure 6.37) will allow you to route the output of the plug-in to any of the four send tracks. You will still need to insert an effect on the send track if you want the sound to be processed, so I suggest leaving this section alone unless you want to use the built-in effects. For creating sends, just use the Mixer so that you develop a pattern in your workflow, rather than varying your methods of routing.

Figure 6.37 Reverb and chorus sends.

The lower settings only need to be used if you want to change the envelope, LFO, or cutoff settings of the sound. Raising the attack adjusts the instrument so that it produces a smooth, swelling string sound, while adjusting the Mod knob applies modulation to the currently loaded instrument.

This is a very simple and powerful generator that has great quality, so definitely take the time to experiment with some of the sounds available and try routing the audio to a reverb send or chorus send to see how much easier this setup makes it.

Fruity Envelope Controller

This is an ADSR envelope that generates automation, makes no sound by itself, and can be linked to nearly anything in FL Studio. Remember, automation is nothing more than something automatically happening, such as a channel panning from left to right. This plug-in is great for softening the attack of a punchy snare or helping a note to sustain longer where needed. We have seen the controls for this type of envelope and do not need to go over what each parameter does, but it is worth mentioning that each envelope can be added to a certain part of the MIDI keyboard. (Don't worry; it doesn't affect your actual MIDI keyboard, it just tells the sounds how to play for certain note ranges.) Each articulator (which is a fancy way of saying "the different envelopes") can be assigned to a finite range on the mini-keyboard (see Figure 6.38). Use the mouse to select your range so that only those particular notes will respond to the envelope that is created.

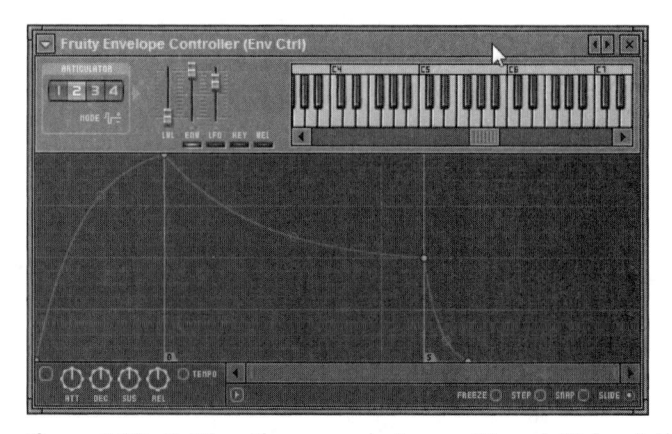

Figure 6.38 Setting the range between C4 and C5 for Articulator 2 in the Fruity Envelope Controller.

Fruity Granulizer

The Fruity Granulizer plug-in, shown in Figure 6.39, will load like a sampler channel but without the actual sample. You can put any sound that you want into this plug-in, and the sample will be "granulized." Typically, it is difficult to describe sound changes when those changes do not affect pitch and are envelope based, but the Fruity Granulizer is reminiscent of sounds used by the movie *The Matrix*. When phone calls are made and the voices have a choppy effect on them, that is similar to what you can do with the sample you load.

Figure 6.39 The Fruity Granulizer.

For this short example, I dragged a random choir sample to the Granulizer's sample window from the project Browser (see Figure 6.40). A great use for this plug-in is linking an external MIDI fader or knob to the Pan, FX.D (effects depth), and FX.S (effects speed). This will allow you to adjust stereo separation, the rate of choppiness, and the intensity of the effect, all at your fingertips. You can move the knobs live by clicking and dragging the mouse, but I have found that I am able to locate that perfect sound within seconds when using linked controllers.

This effect essentially splits up the sound into a bunch of tiny pieces and plays them at rates you determine. Although you know what the Effects section does, it is good to understand that the Grains section will only affect how the grains themselves play back.

The Attack wheel will create a fade-in to and a fade-out of the sample. The Hold will determine the length of each piece of audio. G.SP, or grain spacing, will determine how long it takes between playback of each grain. Turn it to the left, and the sample will play more quickly than when it is turned all the way right, because this will place a good deal of space between grains, thereby slowing down the overall sample.

Transients show up in digital recording and are basically little spikes of sound that can cause the overall sound to clip and be distorted during recording or playback. This is one of the many reasons for leaving plenty of headroom when recording, because when a drummer hits a cymbal, the initial transient in the waveform could cause the signal to clip if the volume or amplifier gain is turned up too much. They seem to jump off of the waveform, and when they occur, the Granulizer detects them and assigns grains to them.

Figure 6.40   Dragging a sound into the sample window of the Granulizer.

The big Hold knob will determine the length of those specific transient grains. When off, the switches will ignore transients. When Use Regions is highlighted, they will load sliced samples if they were pre-sliced, and when Detect is selected, they will cause the Granulizer to find the transients automatically and assign grains. Keep in mind that we are talking about small differences that are hard to notice without adjusting the knobs yourself. The difference is there, but it is not night and day, so it helps to really listen for that perfect sound.

The Time section will allow you to loop your sample, but if the sample has a fade-in, ending, and silence at the end of the sample, this will be noticeable. The Hold switch creates a freezing effect on the sound, and when you press it, it actually sounds like your soundcard has locked up.

The Key To drop-down menu will cause your keys to map to a certain behavior based on your selection. The default mapping is Pitch, so as you climb up the keyboard, the sample gets higher in pitch. Key To Percent means that C5 to C7 represents where the sample starts, so if you play C5 it will play normally, but C7 will start from a later portion of the sample.

When Loop is engaged, this can be difficult to hear. Key To Step will cause every key after C5 to progressively offset the sample by steps, and Key To Transient will cause the start time to be based on slices as you go up the keyboard from C5.

The Start wheel is just when the sample should start playing from. Turning this knob to the right will cause the sample to play past the absolute beginning. It will not delay when the sound starts, it will cause the sample to actually play from a later position but still in time. For example, if the statement "I drove my red car down the street" was recorded, as you slide that Start knob to the right, the talking would begin at the same time but would start with different words, such as "ove my red car down the street," "car down the street," and so on.

Fruity Keyboard Controller

The Fruity Keyboard Controller plug-in (see Figure 6.41) can be thought of as an internal controller. This plug-in, much like MIDI, will only send information and doesn't make any sound on its own.

Figure 6.41 The Fruity Keyboard Controller.

The possibilities with this plug-in are nearly limitless, because anything that can be linked can be controlled. To better understand this, we will map the keyboard controller to the bass and midrange controls of the BooBass plug-in that we already discussed. When both plug-ins are inserted on the Channel window, open BooBass, right-click the Bass knob, choose Link to Controller, and then select Kb Ctrl (Kb Ctrl) - Note from the Internal Controller drop-down menu (see Figure 6.42). This tells the Bass knob to react to anything the Keyboard Controller tells it to do based on where the Keyboard Controller's Piano roll notes are placed.

Next, right-click the Mid knob, select Link to Controller, and choose Kb Ctrl (Kb Ctrl) - Velocity from the Internal Controller drop-down menu. Now you have set the Midrange knob to react to the note velocity of the Keyboard Controller's Piano roll.

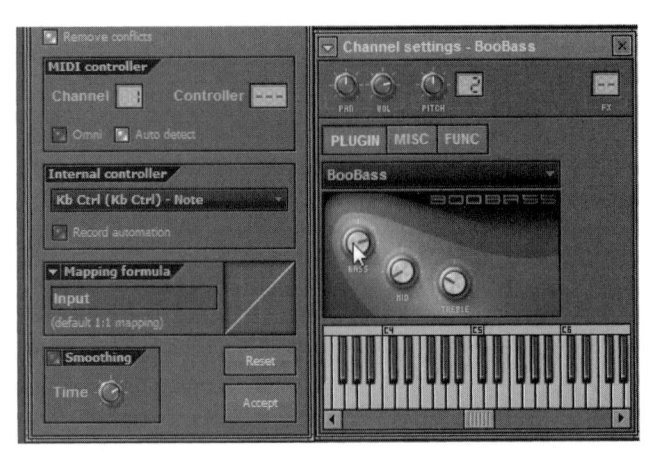

Figure 6.42 Linking the Bass knob to the Keyboard Controller note value.

Now that everything is linked, how do you get the Bass knob to move by using the Keyboard Controller? I'm glad you asked, because the rest is easy and only dependent upon your creativity and needs.

In this example, let's say that we want to have the bass play with power for one bar and then cut down the bass and boost the midrange for the second. Start by selecting the Keyboard Controller in the Channel window and opening the Piano roll for the Keyboard Controller. (Right-click the Keyboard Controller channel and choose Send to Piano Roll.) The range on the graphic of the Keyboard Controller will determine what keys will affect the linked Bass knob, and as you can see in Figure 6.43, the range that is being used is C4–C6. This means that if we put notes on the Piano roll higher or lower than this range, the Bass knob will not be affected. C4 is the lowest value of the Bass knob (with this knob, it means the bass will be lowered to zero), while C6 will be the highest (the bass will be turned all the way up).

Figure 6.43 The range of the keyboard graphic (the highlighted area between C4 and C6) determines what notes will be in use by the Keyboard Controller.

Because we are working with the bass first, let's place a note on the Piano roll near the upper part of the range for one bar and then a second note in the lower part of the range for the next bar (see Figure 6.44). The notes will determine the knob position, because the Keyboard Controller only tells the knob what to do, rather than making any sound. When you play the project, you will see the knob move between the two different positions.

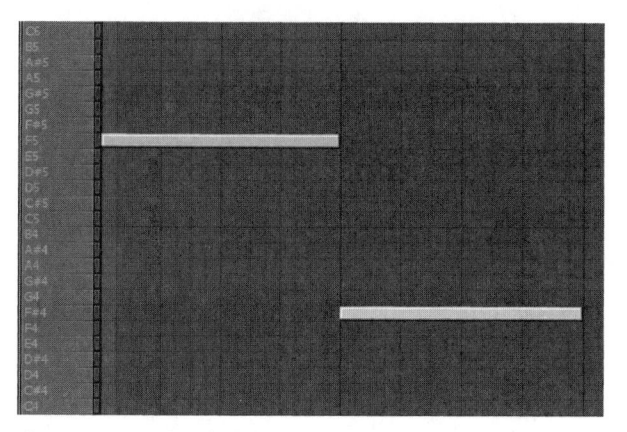

Figure 6.44 The first bar containing an F5 and the second bar containing an F#4 note.

Now let's do the same thing with the Midrange control. The difference here is that the Piano roll note velocity will control the Midrange knob rather than what note is in the Piano roll, so when you change the velocity of the note, the Midrange knob will move with those changes. We want the midrange to be stronger in the second bar, so lower the velocity of the first note and raise the velocity of the second note.

At this point there are still no notes in the Piano roll of BooBass, and you have only entered in notes on the Keyboard Controller Piano roll. Now that you have this set up (see Figure 6.45), try pressing Play in Pattern mode. You will see the Bass knob turn up for the first bar and turn down for the second bar, while the Midrange knob does the opposite. Select the BooBass channel so that it is active and try playing a few notes on your MIDI keyboard. Or, press Ctrl+T and play a few notes on your typing keyboard. Now you can hear the changes and see that the Keyboard Controller basically tells the controls what to do.

The controls available in the Keyboard Controller include an ability to cause the Keyboard Controller to auto-map your keys or auto-map your keys while only using the white keys. Next to the auto-mapping drop-down is the current note selected on the keyboard graphic, and the knob next to that will allow you to adjust individual values of each note by selecting any note on the graphic and turning the knob.

To keep it simple, I would leave this alone and use the auto-mapping, because changing different notes' values will mean that the control (the Bass knob, for example) will not react based on a descending or ascending range. What I mean here is that if you change C5 to be a value of 1 (the available range of all notes is between 0 and 1) when your selected range is C4–C6, then C5 will move the knob the same amount as C6. When you play notes going upward on the

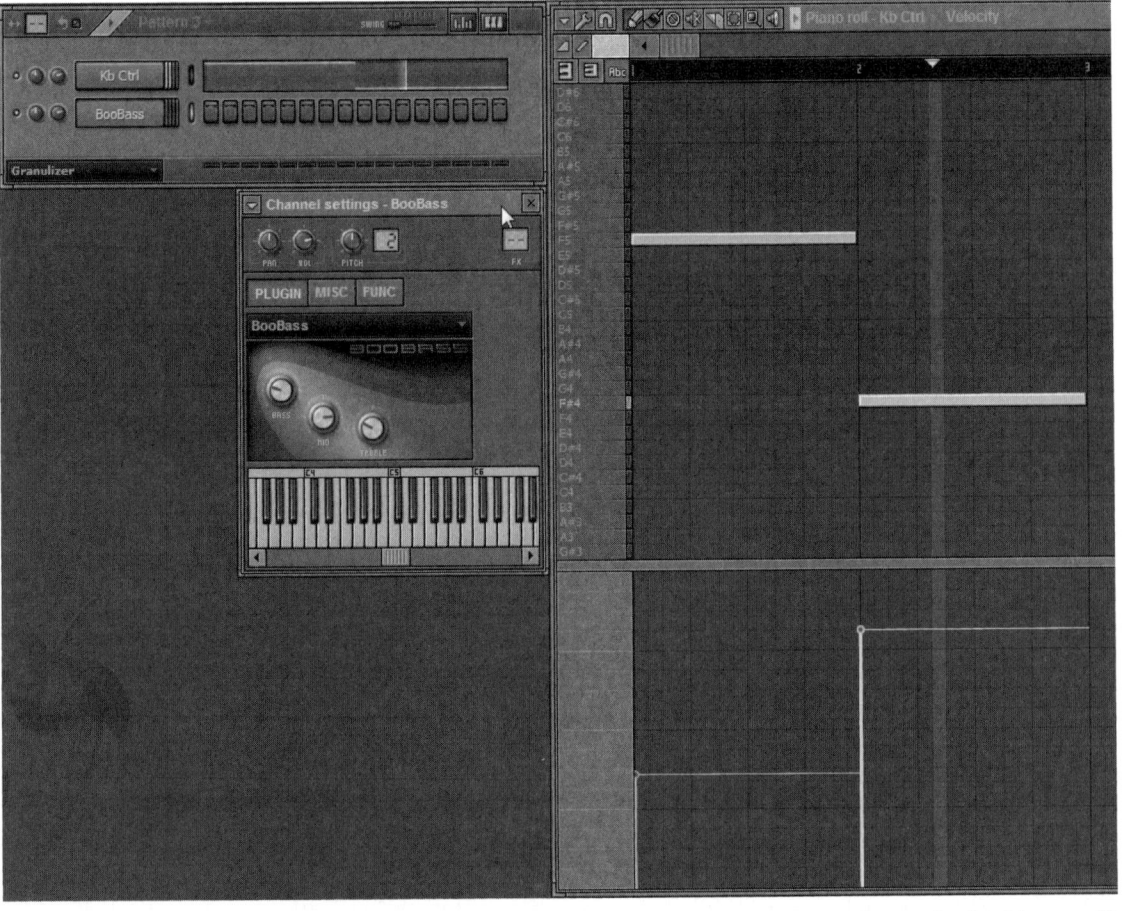

Figure 6.45 An example of using the Keyboard Controller to change the Bass (notes in the Piano roll) and Midrange (velocity of the notes in the Piano roll) knob positions.

Piano roll of the Keyboard Controller, as you pass C5, the note will spike to the extreme (Bass knob will turn all the way up) and then go back to the normal progression when you press C#5, D5, and so on. The Release toggle switch will cause the note value (0–1) to jump back to the position of the Value for Auto Release knob (located to the right of the toggle switch) when a note is released (when a note on the Piano roll ends). The smoothing option will determine how quickly changes happen between notes (in our example, how quickly the bass drops out).

I wanted to use a basic example to illustrate how this plug-in can work for you and make changes (especially in third-party plug-ins) to any parameter that you need altered. The Piano roll makes it easy to map out tempo-perfect changes to your filters, volume, panning, and anything else you can come up with. Don't be afraid to experiment with this one, because if you don't like what it is doing, you can simply remove or mute the Keyboard Controller, and it will stop controlling knobs and parameters without you having to go back to find what was controlling which specific knob.

Fruity Slicer

The Fruity Slicer is a simplified version of the plug-in Slicex and is a great way to turn your audio into playable slices. You can load any audio sample into the Fruity Slicer by selecting a sample from the Browser, right-clicking the sample, and sending it to the Fruity Slicer or dragging the sample itself over to the Fruity Slicer sample window. Fruity Slicer will attempt to slice the audio itself unless there is preexisting slice information, in which case the sample will be sliced according to that data.

In Figure 6.46, you can see that the sliced pieces are placed on the Piano roll as MIDI notes. This means that as the song plays, the notes will trigger that part of the sample (the sliced piece). After loading a sample, press Play on the main transport to see the Fruity Slicer in action.

Figure 6.46 The Fruity Slicer with the Channel window and Piano roll showing.

The basic interface is fairly simple to use, especially when the beat is sliced properly, and creating interesting sounds or rhythms using the different slices can add real depth to your music.

This is a great place to create multiple layers in your music, such as vocal stutters or extra drum hits, using clips that are already in your project.

At the top of this generator is the BPM and Beats display. It is important to know that these are linked to each other, so if you lower the BPM, the beats will drop as well. The first option in the Fruity Slicer is the Open Sliced Beat Groove, which lets you import a groove file (.zgr) that tells the plug-in where the cuts in a sample should be made. It is important to know that there is no audio data in this file, and it only imports the slice information (basically draws the notes on the Piano roll), but it will try to find the original sample to import.

The Open and Slice a Sample button will allow you to load a wide array of audio (MP3, WAV, REX, and so on). Save the Original Sample will save the audio with no sample slicing information, and Save Processed will save the audio with the slice points. To avoid navigating the project Browser, use Load Sample to bring in your audio when opening the Fruity Slicer if no sample has been loaded or you want to change the audio currently loaded.

In the event that the slicing seems off or poorly timed, you can press the Beat Slicer button (third in the row of four) to open a list of options for setting slice points in your audio (see Figure 6.47). Use Sample Built-In Slicing will place the slice points back where they belong, using the slice markers that were saved with the sample from a program such as Edison or ACID. The Dull, Medium, and Sharp Auto-Slicing options place slice points in the audio, where Dull is a lower number of slices, Medium will have more slices, and Sharp will have the greatest number of slices.

The beat selections change the slice points (MIDI notes on the Piano roll) of your audio based on the project tempo. So if the original slice points had a faster part that, for example, hit twice consecutively on the 1/4 note, and you select 1/2 beat, then that particular section will have the two 1/4-note hits in one slice (MIDI note).

As a visual example, compare Figure 6.46 to Figure 6.48, where in Figure 6.46 I selected 1/2 beat from the Slicing menu. You can see that the two quick little 1/4 notes that were near the third bar are now one 1/2-beat note.

The No Slicing option will remove all slices, and the audio will be mapped to one note on the Piano roll. Zero-Cross Check Slices will nudge the start and end points of the slices to the closest zero-crossing (where the waveform of the audio is not making any sound). Use this if there are pops and clicks in your audio, but keep in mind that if the slice points are way off, you might still hear distortion between slices.

The Edit portion of this menu gives you options to export individual slices. Choose Open in Edison to send your selected slice to an instance of Edison. Choose Open in BeatSlicer to send the slice into an instance of BeatSlicer.

The Stretching Method options are presets that will determine positioning of slices and stretching of the audio. Each can be adjusted by moving the PS (pitch shift) and TS (time-shift, or length

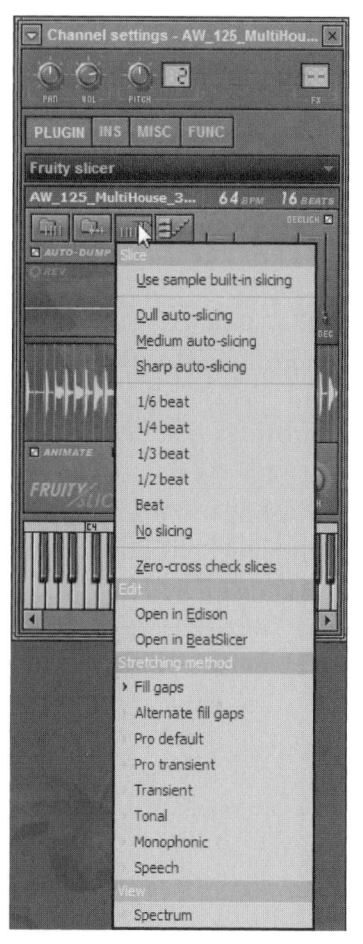

Figure 6.47 The Slicing menu.

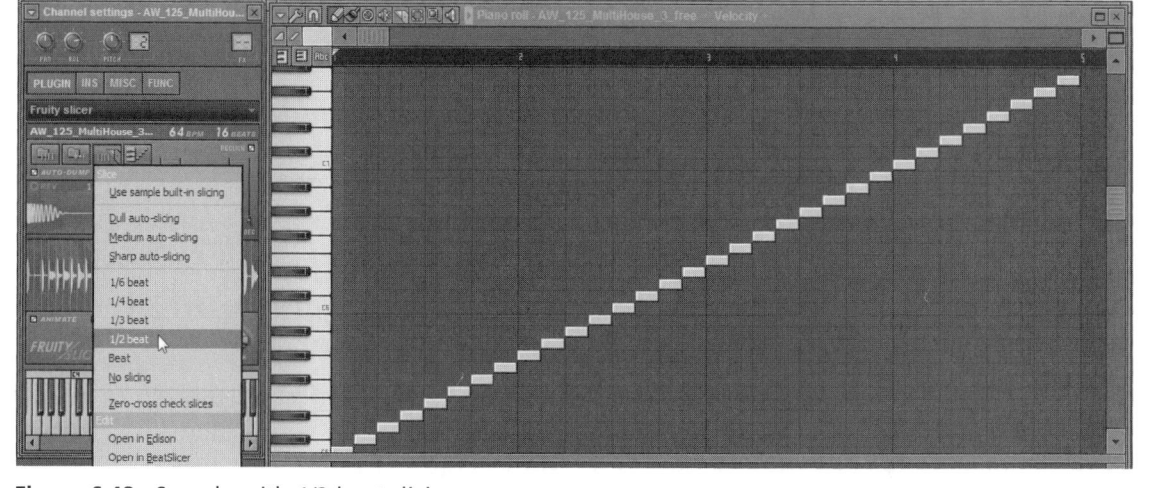

Figure 6.48 Sample with 1/2-beat slicing.

of the slices) sliders. Pro Transient is great for drum samples, because the initial waveform spike from a drum hit is taken into account when the plug-in makes slice points.

The View option will allow you to toggle between spectrum and waveform views, which is nice for those who prefer spectrum-style editing.

The Dump Beat to Piano Roll button (see Figure 6.49) will place MIDI notes on the Piano roll that will determine when slices are played. Reverse will reverse the position of the MIDI notes on a vertical axis, so the slices will play in reverse order, but the sound of each slice will still play normally and not reversed. Random will move the MIDI notes to random positions on the Piano roll. Because this is random, it is worth trying it out a few times, because a new rhythm can be created, even with vocals!

Figure 6.49 Dump Beat to Piano Roll menu.

The Flatten option will dump the notes into the Piano roll in a straight line, so that the slice points are preserved, but will only play the first slice. This can be great if the slice points you have make up a rhythm that you want, because you can use the Flatten option and the slice points remain, but now only the first slice plays, creating a rhythmic stutter.

Shift Up and Shift Down will move the slices to their next slice point. The easiest place to see this change is in the Piano roll. Quantize will snap your slices to the grid that is chosen in the Piano roll, and Swing will add a swing to the slice positions. Remember that this doesn't add swing to the audio, but rather to the rhythm of when the notes are triggered, although in many cases I have liked the Swing setting more than the imported slice data.

Accentuate Beat will cause the notes that lie on each first beat to play at a higher velocity, while Pitch Up Beat will raise the pitch of every other beat starting with the first one. Widen Stereo will alternate left to right panning of each slice (MIDI note), while Crazy will change a little bit of everything (of the note in the Piano roll) and is a new setting each time it is selected.

The Stutter effect options will break each slice into two pieces (Half) or four pieces (Fourth) and are great for giving your audio a choppy sound. Original Length will place notes on the Piano roll that match the original sample speed if it was different from the project tempo.

The Attack and Decay sliders act like a respective fade-in and fade-out for each slice of the sample, but these are global controls, so all slices will be affected. The Auto-Dump is, by default, highlighted and will drop the note slice selections into the Piano roll. Turn this off when you just want to play the slices using your MIDI keyboard or typing keyboard.

Auto-Fit Switch will cause the sample to fit to the current project tempo when you load it in but will not change a current sample if turned on after a sample has been loaded. Animate will provide a visual representation of the slice being played in the Fruity Slicer, and Play to End will cause the slices to play to the end of the loop.

The Low and High knobs affect where samples are sliced by altering the sensitivity to low notes and high notes. This is nice when you are getting slices from a low note that should not be a slice. By moving the Low knob, you can cause Fruity Slicer to ignore that low note and remove the slice point.

The individual slice editing can be accessed by right-clicking in the Slice Preview window, which is located above the Sample Preview window (see Figure 6.50). Here you can remove the slice (which takes away the slice point at the start of the audio), split the slice (which adds a slice point to where your cursor is in the Slice Preview window), and copy to audio clipboard for use with pasting into the Playlist or anywhere that can accept the audio slice.

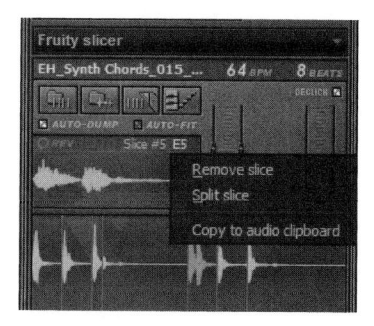

Figure 6.50   Editing a slice in the Slice Preview window.

The Reverse button will reverse the audio of the selected slice. Keep in mind that accuracy can be difficult to achieve, and if you are having trouble getting the precision you need, I suggest using Slicex, which we'll look at later in this chapter.

Fruity Vibrator

The Fruity Vibrator plug-in (see Figure 6.51) allows you to alter your sound using a force-feedback device. The force-feedback effects are in the form of .ffe files, and the Vibrator takes these effects and maps them to the Piano roll (or MIDI keyboard if you are using one), and they respond based on notation and velocity.

Figure 6.51 The Fruity Vibrator.

Microsoft has a force editor tool that allows you to create these effect files for placement on the Piano roll. This editor, along with help using it, can be found on the Microsoft website in the latest DirectX software developer kit. Creating these files lies outside of the scope of this book, and while using .ffe effect files can add interesting texture to your music, learning the coding is not necessary when you are able to create effects and adjust them in real time using other FL Studio tools.

Layer Channel

The Layer Channel is a plug-in that produces no sound; rather, it helps control multiple sounds in different ways. The concept is simple, yet powerful: Use a channel to control multiple channels. The easiest way to see this in action is to add two different instrument channels and a Layer Channel. Now make sure that the Layer Channel settings are in view and highlight the two channels that the instruments are on (see Figure 6.52). Now select Set Children in the Layer Channel settings, and those two instruments will be controlled by the Layer Channel. Remember that you can still control them individually if you click on the specific instrument channel, but now when the Layer Channel is selected and you play notes, both instruments will react.

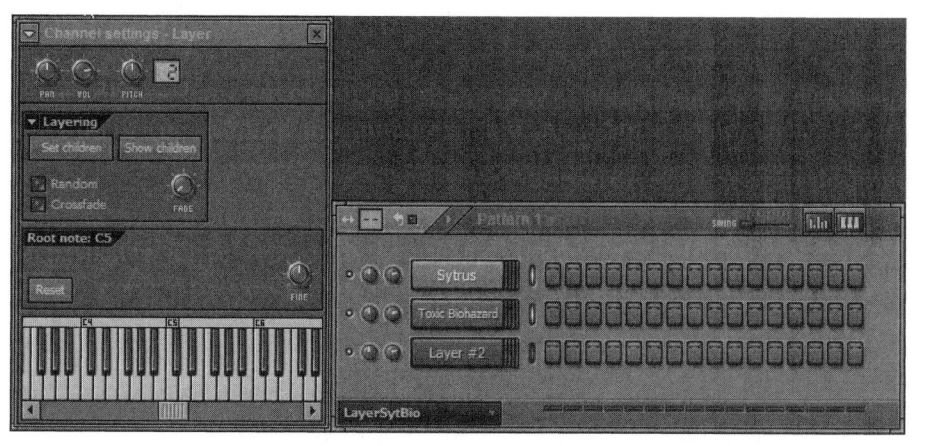

Figure 6.52 Setting the children of a Layer Channel.

The Show Children option next to Set Children will highlight linked channels (children) in the Stepsequencer and de-select all other channels, allowing you to double-check which channels you linked to a Layer Channel.

Figure 6.52 demonstrates the ability of the plug-in to layer multiple instruments, but there are many uses for a Layer Channel. Let's explore another example where we use layering to give our samples a more variable feel, such as replicating the dynamic playing of a live drummer. Add three Fruity Kick plug-ins followed by a Layer Channel and then link the three kick channels by again highlighting the three kick channels and then selecting Set Children (see Figure 6.53) in the Layer Channel settings.

Figure 6.53 Setting three slightly differing kicks as children for a Layer Channel.

After you set the children, open up each kick plug-in and make small adjustments to the kicks so that each sample sounds unique. Now select Random in the Layer Channel settings and press one key a few times on your keyboard. As you probably hear, the Layer Channel is randomly playing the children, which in this case are the three kick sounds. When you only have slight adjustments, this can produce a more realistic sound for percussion, but experiment with all types, because you might find an interesting combo of random sounds.

The Crossfade toggle switch will cause the Fade knob to control which linked channels (children) play. When the Fade knob is turned all the way left, you will hear the first linked channel (child), and as you turn the knob to the right, the Layer Channel will run through the linked channels until reaching the linked last channel when the knob is all the way to the right. This is a fun plug-in to experiment with and can make a great tool in your creative arsenal.

MIDI Out

Recalling our discussion on MIDI, you will remember that MIDI doesn't make any sound on its own; rather, it tells MIDI instruments when to play, and the MIDI Out plug-in is no different. As you can see in Figure 6.54, I have Harpsichord selected, but when I press the keys on my MIDI keyboard, there is no sound. This is because nothing is set to receive the MIDI data coming from the MIDI Out plug-in. When an instance of LSD is loaded into the Mixer track that the channel containing the MIDI Out plug-in is linked to, then you will hear sound. We will discuss the LSD in greater detail in Chapter 7, "Effects Plug-Ins," but for now understand that the only thing coming out of the MIDI Out plug-in is MIDI information.

Figure 6.54 The MIDI Out plug-in.

When sending MIDI to an external device, it is important that the device port number (in the Options menu, F10) matches the MIDI interface port number (set in the MIDI options, F10) so that they communicate with each other. The channel and bank output can be selected at the top of the plug-in, so if your external device has a great sound on Channel 3, Bank 54, you can drag the mouse over these boxes to match that number, and the MIDI Out plug-in will send MIDI information to that channel and specific bank. This plug-in is great when you need MIDI to be sent to an external device—just make sure that you have researched how to set up that device so that the sound you are looking for is played.

Plucked!

The Plucked! generator, shown in Figure 6.55, is an example of physical modeling synthesis and creates a plucked string sound that is common in many electronic styles of music. With the right effects and EQ, the Plucked! synth can add a haunting melody to nearly any track. The sound played can be adjusted using the controls, where Normalize will make the decay (length of each sound) the same for all notes, and Gate will remove the decay, causing the audio of each note to suddenly stop near the end of the sound.

Figure 6.55   Plucked!

The Decay knob will adjust how long the audio of the triggered note plays after being released, and the Color knob will change the tone from muffled (left) to bright (right). The Widen option, when selected, will create a wider stereo sound for the instrument. This instrument is simple, but I think that is its strong point, because you know the sound that you have to work with and how to easily adjust it to your taste.

SimSynth Live

SimSynth Live is a synthesizer that brings us back to the '80s by using oscillating waves to create sounds. This plug-in has three oscillators (see Figure 6.56), allowing you to really tweak your sound and achieve perfect results. The Oscillator sections have knobs allowing you to adjust sounds they make by changing the oscillation type, the speed, the frequency, and the volume. The last three switches are a little less familiar, but the 1 and 2 switches just add a wave to the oscillator one or two octaves above the original, and the Warm button lightens the intensity of the oscillator. All the oscillators feed into the Amp section, which has the familiar ADSR envelope to adjust, and then the sound moves into the SVF (State Variable Filter) section.

Figure 6.56 SimSynth Live.

The first set of ADSR controls will control the envelope of the filter that is placed on the sound, so if you raise the attack of the SVF section and keep the Amp section set to have a quick attack, the sound will still play fast, but the filter will take longer to activate. The LFO knob will determine the amount of LFO effect you place on the sound, but this is based on the settings you make in the lower LFO section, so without enabling this, you won't hear anything. The Track Switch button just means that the filter sound will be made using the Amp ADSR envelope instead of the one in the SVF section.

The Cutoff, High-, and Low-Pass knobs are types that we have seen, but the EMPH knob will cause the frequencies near the set cutoff to have emphasis, so with many sounds, it will create a sharper, brighter sound when turned right.

The LFO section allows you to place an LFO on your sound before it plays through the final output, and there is also a Chorus toggle switch, allowing you to widen the sound. The only unfamiliar portion in that section is the Retrigger button, which will cause the LFO to start every time there is a note played, rather than continuously running. Try adjusting this to see whether you get better rhythmic results. SimSynth Live is great for creating original sounds when you are looking for a retro synth, and it is especially useful for creating automation clips with filter sweeps.

Slicex

Slicex (see Figure 6.57) is the big brother to the Fruity Slicer and allows for a much wider range of editing abilities. The concept behind this plug-in is to take one or two audio samples and create new rhythms from the sliced samples by mapping each sample to MIDI notes on the Piano roll. You can also use the Slicex to simply play slices with your MIDI keyboard as well, but many big advantages over the Fruity Slicer include multiple articulators, multiple audio sources, and Edison-style editing capabilities.

I will say that my preference in audio slicing is this plug-in, mainly due to the ability to turn any audio loop into an instance of the FPC while being able to edit the sound itself. If you have a

Figure 6.57 Slicex.

clean drum loop and you like the instruments, but the loop is stale, load it into Slicex! Slicex will determine the points where each part of the drum beat starts and break them up into slices. Now you can create a new drum beat using those same sounds with notes placed in the Piano roll, or you can play the new beat live and record using your MIDI or typing keyboard. Slicex even allows you to drag regions or slices of samples into the other deck by using the Drag Sample option, and then you can replace a region in the other deck. You can totally rebuild a beat using this drag-and-drop feature. We will start with a look at the main features of the interface and then dig into using multiple samples and layering sounds.

Main Panel

We'll begin our tour of Slicex with a look at the master panel (see Figure 6.58). The first four sliders are global to everything in Slicex, so use caution when adjusting these values, because they will affect all slices. The first slider is a master volume control, followed by a randomness amount, a master LFO, and a master pitch. Again, these sliders will affect all sound, so don't try to use these to change the pitch of one slice.

Figure 6.58 Slicex main panel.

Next to the sliders is a graph that will control X-Y modulation based on where you move the point inside the graph. This will be discussed further as we run into cases where it can be used, but for now, know that the values can be responsible for controlling different parameters in Slicex. The Layering drop-down menu allows you to determine how different layers will react to each other (see Figure 6.59), but it is important to note that two slices must share the same trigger key to use layering.

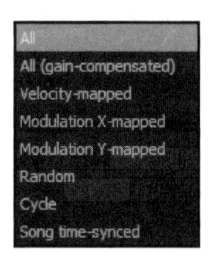

Figure 6.59 Layering options.

All means that all regions or slices assigned to the same note will play as is. All (Gain-Compensated) is great for drums or sounds that are boosting the audio too much, because it will pull down the volume when two regions or slices are playing so that they don't go above the original volume of one region playing alone.

Velocity-Mapped means that the velocity of the notes will determine which region will play, so if you want to make a certain region play instead of another region that is linked to the same MIDI note, you can use the velocity of the note in the Piano roll to determine which region will play.

Modulation X-Mapped and Modulation Y-Mapped will cause the Modulation control at the top of the screen to act as a crossfade between layered regions (where left to right is X and top to bottom is Y on the graph). Random will cause layered regions to crossfade between each other at random. Cycle will alternate between layered regions on playback, and Song Time-Synced will select the closest region to the tempo of your project.

When the same deck option is not selected, both layers from each deck will play when they are triggered at the same time. However, when same deck is selected, Deck A is triggered by odd-numbered MIDI channel notes, and Deck B is triggered by even-numbered MIDI channel notes. In Figure 6.60, the usual Piano roll dump from Deck A is present (using by default the green

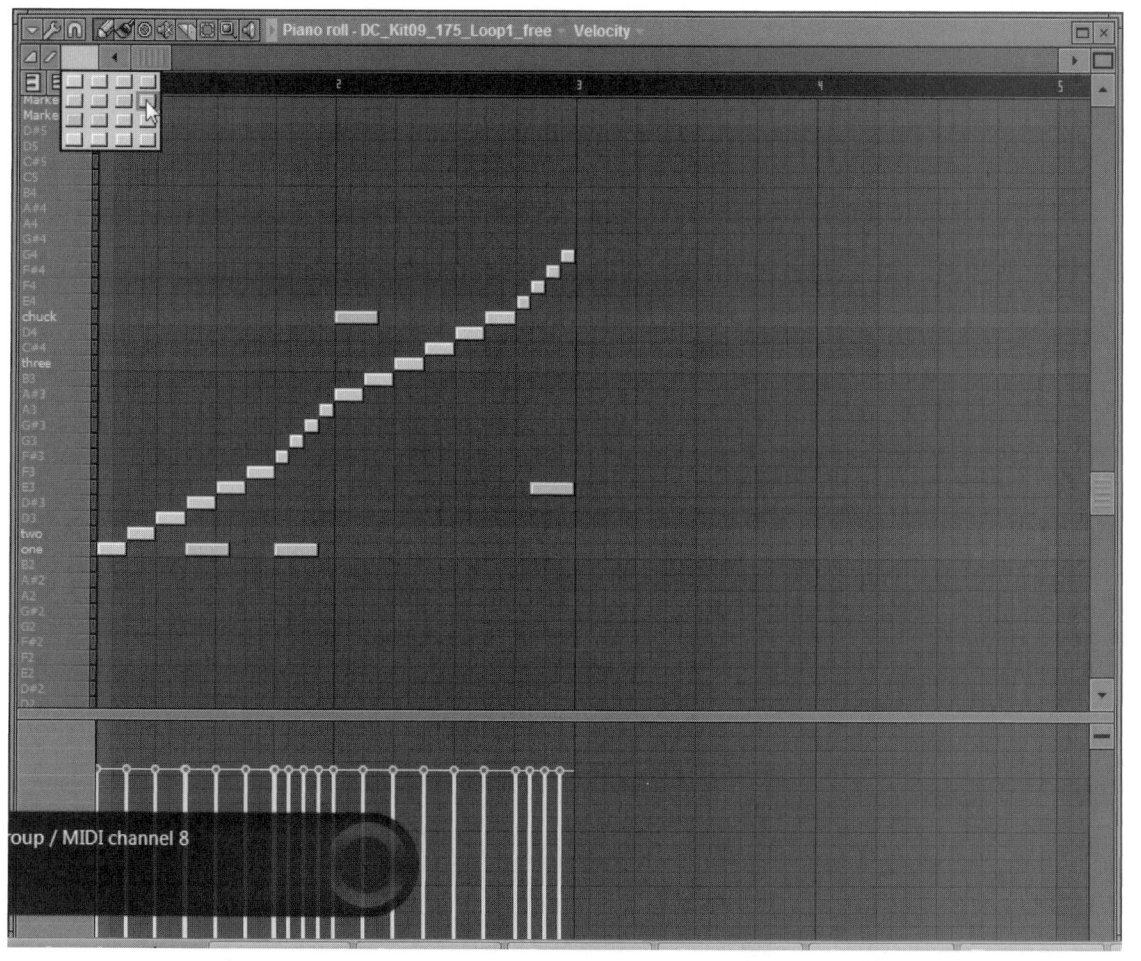

Figure 6.60 Layers in Deck B are triggered by the notes on the Piano roll set to trigger on MIDI Channel 8.

MIDI channel notes), but when I select Same Deck and have linked layers, the notes that I have drawn in pink (MIDI Channel 8 or any even number) will trigger regions (slices) from Deck B based on their selection. It's important to know that when using this, unlinked notes will not play anything from Deck B. The last note (in pink, MIDI Channel 8) in this example has no name, is not linked, and will not trigger anything from Deck B, so placing a note in the Piano roll does nothing.

The Crossfade Curve option will allow you to choose from five different available crossfades when the layers between Deck A and B are set to crossfade between each other. The down arrow beneath Same Deck will open a drop-down menu with a list of deck options and general settings (see Figure 6.61).

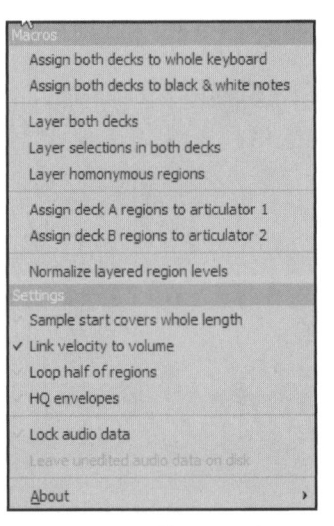

Figure 6.61 Slicex options.

The Macros portion of this menu begins by allowing you to determine how the slices relate to the keyboard notes. Assign Both Decks to Whole Keyboard means that as you go up the keyboard, Deck A slices will be mapped to each note consecutively, so that when the last slice from Deck A plays, Deck B will be the next series of keyboard notes. You can see a visual example of this in Figure 6.62, where Deck A is the short, choppy notes and Deck B is the longer notes. Assign Both Decks to Black & White Notes will place Deck A slices on the white keys and Deck B slices on the black keys.

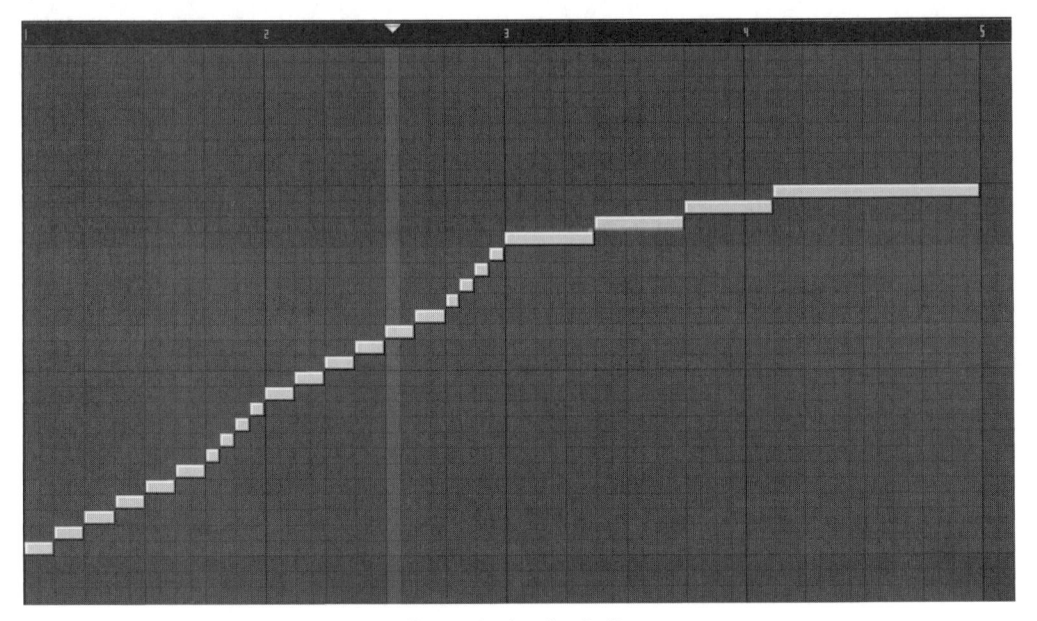

Figure 6.62 MIDI roll notes controlling playback of slices.

Layer Both Decks will cause corresponding regions (Region 1 in Deck A with Region 1 in Deck B, Region 2 in Deck A with Region 2 in Deck B, and so on) to layer with each other so that they are parallel on the keyboard. Layer Selections in Both Decks will link the two slices you have selected (one in Deck A and one in Deck B) to the same MIDI note in the Piano roll. So when you play the note to which both slices are linked, you will hear both slices play at the same time.

Layer Homonymous Regions is an ultra-fancy way of saying link regions with the same name. For example, rename a marker in Deck A Kick and then rename a marker in Deck B Kick as well. Then select Layer Homonymous Regions. You can see that both regions trigger at the same time.

One thing to remember is that this is not a toggle switch (on/off), so if you rename new regions after selecting the option, they will not automatically link. You will have to select Layer Homonymous Regions every time you want regions with the same name to link to each other.

Assign Deck A Regions to Articulator 1 and Assign Deck B Regions to Articulator 2 will cause the regions (slices) in each deck to be affected by their respective articulators, while Normalize Layered Region Levels will normalize the audio in each slice.

The Settings section contains a variety of toggle switches that will affect different parts of Slicex. When turned on, Sample Start Covers Whole Length means that when adjusting an envelope for the sample start section, that envelope will affect the entire slice of audio. When this is turned off, however, the envelope will only affect roughly the first 100ms of the sample.

In Figure 6.63 I have Sample Start Covers Whole Length turned on, and you can see in the upper highlighted area where I have a velocity curve on the sample start. It gradually fades in over the sample start, but when the sample start covers the length of the entire region, the velocity fade-in is applied to the whole slice.

In the lower highlighted area of Figure 6.63, you can see that Marker 4 (as well as all the other regions) has a long fade-in, and the only audio that really plays is highlighted within Marker 4.

When selected, Link Velocity to Volume will cause your slices to play as loud as the velocity of the note played. This means that when you play your MIDI keyboard softly, the slices will play quietly, and playing hard will cause the slices to play loudly.

Loop Half of Regions will cause your loop points to only encompass the latter half of a region. HQ Envelopes allows you to set envelope points, curves, and lines with more precision. Lock Audio Data will freeze all editing so that you can clearly see any envelopes that you have drawn by removing the control points, and it protects you from accidentally changing something you don't want to.

The Auto-Dump toggle switch will place notes on your Piano roll that correspond to the slice points in audio when a sample is loaded into Deck A. Deck B behaves differently, and the MIDI notes corresponding to the slices can only be inserted by choosing Dump to Piano Roll from the wave editor menu bar.

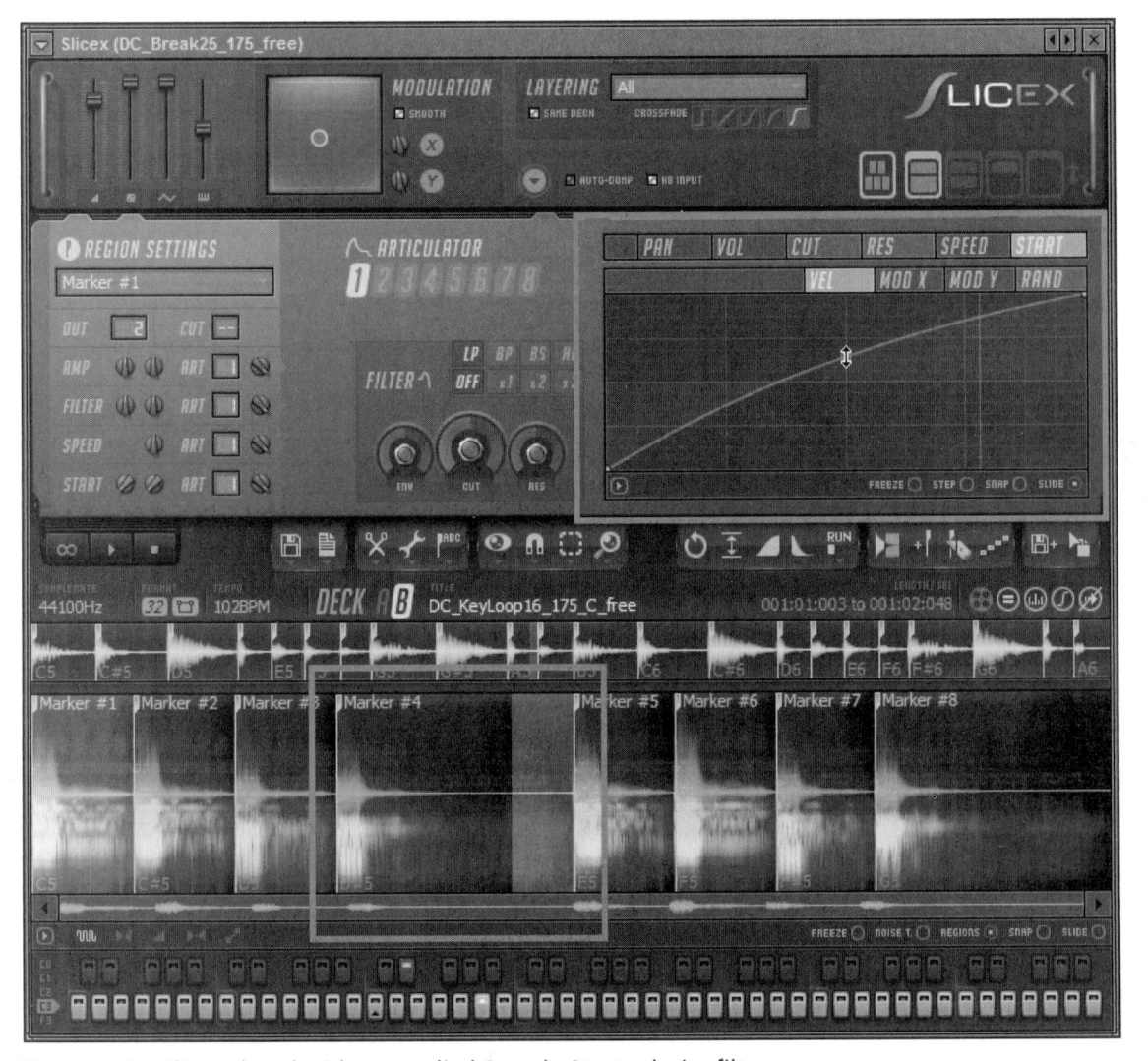

Figure 6.63 Slices played with an applied Sample Start velocity filter.

The KB Input button will turn on the keyboard shortcuts for use in Slicex. It is worth taking the time to learn some of these to speed up your audio editing, but keep in mind that this will make Slicex play instead of the main transport when you're pressing the spacebar and Slicex is focused. This is one reason to leave it off, but the main reason is for the capability to use the Typing Keyboard to Piano Keyboard feature.

To the right of these settings are five toggle switches that allow you to change what portions of Slicex to view. You can have the entire plug-in open or go down to just the master panel, which only affects how the plug-in looks and the space it takes up on your computer screen. All envelopes, effects, and audio slices are still active regardless of the window appearance selection made here.

Articulation Panel

This section of Slicex, shown in Figure 6.64, will control filters, envelopes, and any modulation effects that are linked to a marker or region. The first drop-down menu on the left of the articulation panel will determine which region will be affected by the settings. For example, if you select Marker #2, then the region between Marker #2 and Marker #3 will highlight, and the envelopes that you set will only affect that region. So if you pan the audio to the left with Marker #2 selected, only the selected region will pan to the left when it is triggered from the keyboard or Piano roll. A cool feature of the marker names is that if you rename them, those names will show up in the Piano roll when Text Display is selected, making finding the right notes associated with your slices much easier.

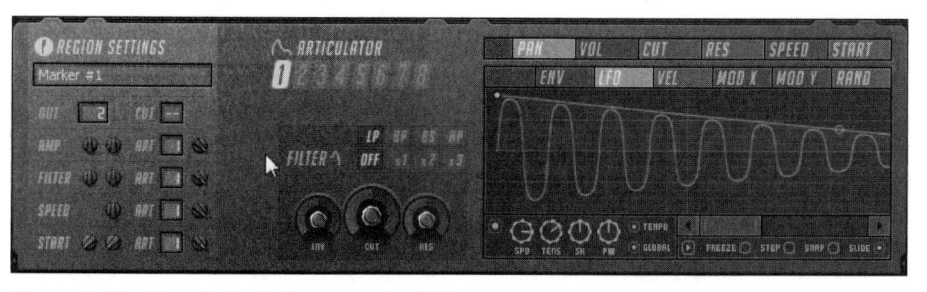

Figure 6.64 The Articulation panel of Slicex.

In Figure 6.65, I have done this to Marker #2 using Articulator #3 so you can see the resulting playback on Insert 2, where the audio is panned over to the left. When you select an out, the marker will play out of the Mixer track that is the selected number of positions to the right. In Figure 6.65, the output of Marker #2 is set to one, so it is one output right of the Mixer track that is linked to Slicex in the Channel window.

The Cut option will prevent other regions with the same cut number from overlapping. To better understand this section, keep it running through your head that the knobs below the Region (marker) selection drop-down only affect the selected region (marker). The Amp knobs will control panning and volume of the selected articulator, and Filter will adjust the cutoff frequency and resonance of the selected articulator. In Figure 6.66, I switched the positions of the envelope controls to give you a better visual of what the knobs in Slicex control.

The Articulator selection allows you to specify the articulator to which you want to add an envelope or filter. Think of the articulators as individual placeholders for settings, and the articulator numbers chosen in the region settings will determine the amount of those settings placed on the region. The Filter controls beneath the Articulator selector will allow you to place frequency filters on articulators, which in turn will affect the linked region. So to put a low-pass filter on a single region, select it from the Region Settings drop-down list and adjust your filter.

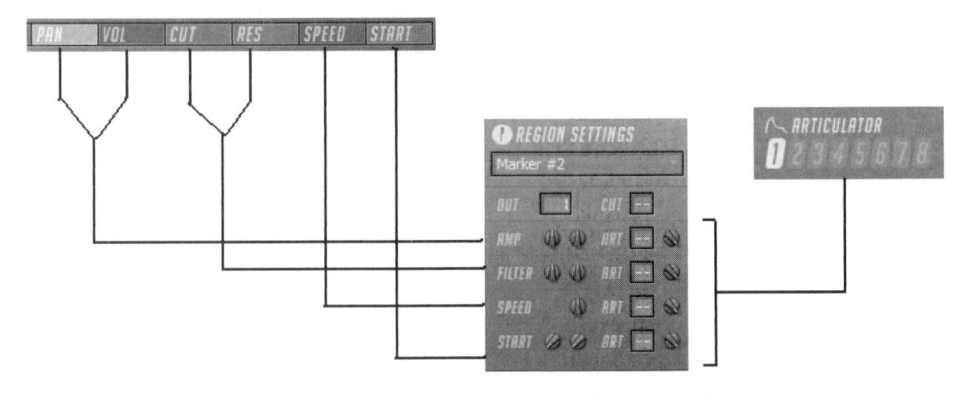

Figure 6.65 Setting Marker #2 to pan left, using Articulator #3.

Figure 6.66 A broad view of the knob signal path for the region settings.

Then turn on the articulator to which that filter is linked by selecting the articulator number to the right of Filter in the Region Settings menu.

The envelopes have been discussed in many different parts of this book, and the Start Sample section was discussed earlier in this chapter, but it important to note that in order for an envelope to work, there must be two points on the graph of the Envelope section. Many that you will open will not have the straight line to edit, in which case you must draw new points on the graph by right-clicking to add a point.

Wave Editor

Most of the options in the wave editor (see Figure 6.67) are identical to those discussed in Edison, so I will just highlight the differences, but feel free to go back to Edison in Chapter 4 to review what each button does. The only real differences in this window are two selections. One is the toggle switch between Deck A and Deck B, and the other is a toggle switch to display either both decks or only one at a time. To save room, flipping this into Single mode allows you to only have one deck in view at a time, but you can still use the Deck A/B selector to choose which one you want to look at. The envelope displays will also allow you to put an envelope (post-articulation) to the entire sample that is loaded into Slicex.

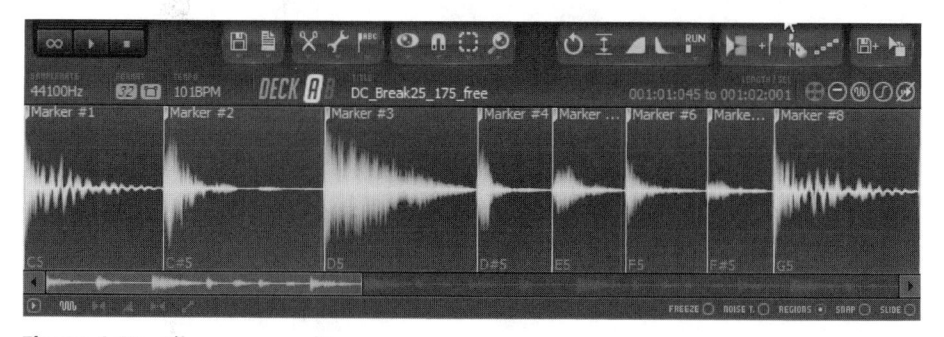

Figure 6.67 Slicex wave editor.

Use the Tools and Build Your Own!

Here we will look at adding two decks and adjusting a few parameters so you get a basic step-by-step example of using Slicex. Begin by adding Slicex to an empty channel and linking it to a track in the Mixer. Now insert a drum loop into Deck A and a music loop into Deck B. In this example I am using the free loops downloaded from the Image-Line online section (Loops > Loopmaster David Carbone DandB Masterclass > Free > DC_Kit09_175_Loop1_free for the drums in Deck A and DC_KeyLoop16_175_C_free for the music loop in Deck B).

Go up to the arrow drop-down menu and select Assign Both Decks to Black & White Notes so that Deck A uses the white notes and Deck B uses the black notes. The first thing you will notice is that the slices from Deck A are assigned MIDI notes and dropped onto the Piano roll (see Figure 6.68). The reason why I used this example is because, as you can see, the Piano

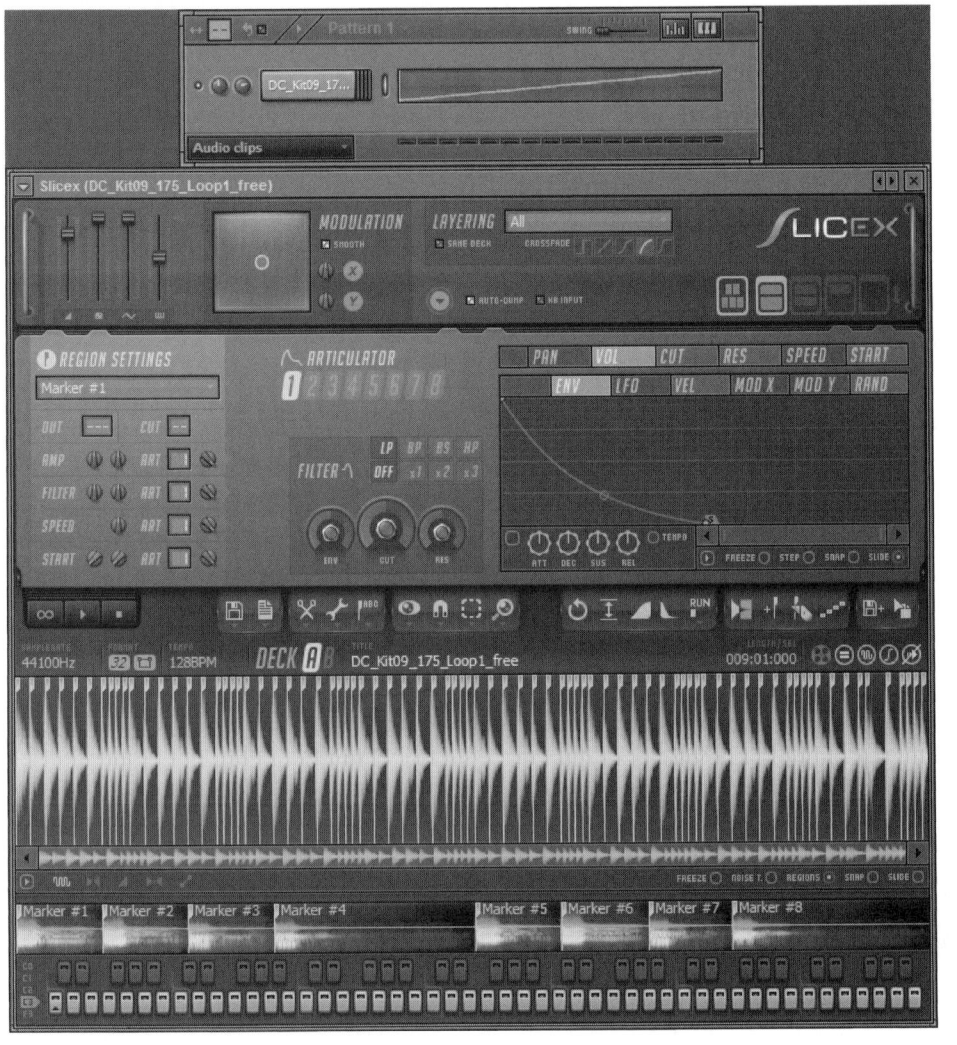

Figure 6.68 Slice points in the audio of Deck A automatically dropped into the Piano roll.

roll hits the ceiling, and the notes overlap each other. This can happen when there are too many slices for the Piano roll range.

In our example, the loop actually is the same loop running a few times, so you can remove unnecessary notes. Do this by selecting the area after two bars in the Piano roll (see Figure 6.69) and deleting the selected area. This will leave you with a clean two-bar loop. If you'd like, you can select the unused audio in the sample and delete that, too, leaving you only with a clean loop in Deck A.

Before adding effects, let's get Deck B playing with Deck A by linking selections. Let's link Marker #1 in Deck A with Marker #1 in Deck B. Do this by right-clicking anywhere in Marker #1 in Deck A and then right-clicking anywhere in Marker #1 in Deck B so that they are both

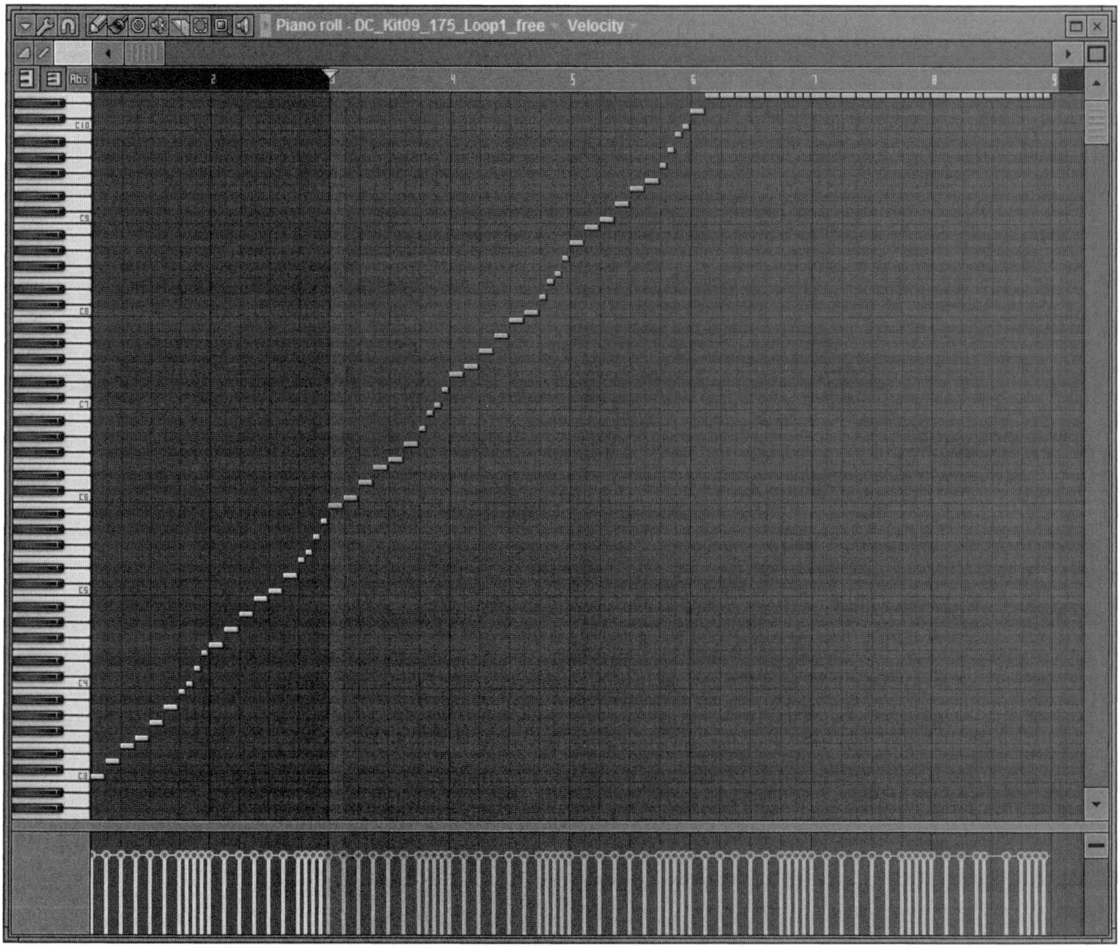

Figure 6.69 Selecting unnecessary notes in the Piano roll to simplify the loop in Slicex.

highlighted (see Figure 6.70). Now go to the down arrow drop-down menu and select Layer Selections in Both Decks (see Figure 6.71). When you play the pattern, both Marker #1s will play from Deck A and B at the same time.

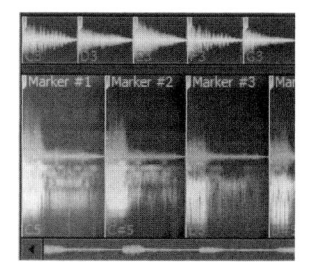

Figure 6.70 Highlighting markers from different decks for linking. The top deck is in wave view, while the bottom deck is in dual view mode.

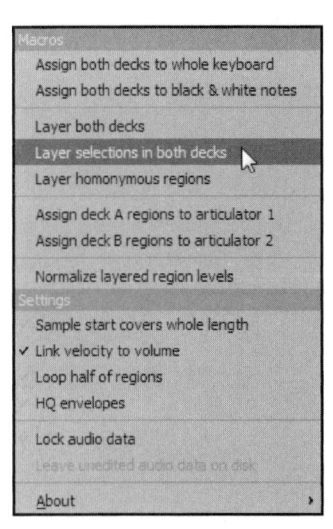

Figure 6.71 Choosing layer selections.

Now link Marker #13 in Deck A with Marker #4 in Deck B. This is where we will stop with linking selections and move on to adjusting parameters of different selections.

For this example, we will put a pan on the two triggered slices in Deck A that follow the triggered Deck B slices to create a widening effect, and we will want the different slices to play in individual Mixer tracks. Start by right-clicking on Marker #2 in Deck A to select it and go up to the Region Settings. Make sure that Marker #2 is selected and change the output (Out) number to 1. Choose 2 for the Articulator Number selector box (next to Amp) and then highlight Pan and Vel.

At this point you will see a red line in the envelope graphic display (see Figure 6.72). Drag this line down to the bottom on both sides and then select Marker #14 from the Region Settings drop-down menu and select Articulator 2 in the box located to the right of the Amp knobs. The same pan will be applied to this marker.

To give one of the slices a cutoff filter, we will start by selecting Marker #6 from the drop-down list, choosing Articulator 3 next to the Filter knobs, and making the output (Out) 2. Feel free to experiment with the different settings, but for this example we will choose LP (low-pass filter) and x1 (single-filter mode). In the graphic display, choose Cut and LFO, then have the line go from high to low (remember that if there is no line, right-click in the graph to create a point) and turn up the Speed knob until the oscillations are abundant (see Figure 6.73). Now you will hear a definite difference in the way that the sliced audio plays, and your different pieces of affected audio are now playing out of different Mixer tracks.

Slicex is a monster in the world of plug-ins, and although it can seem complicated at first, don't be afraid to load samples and mess with them as much as you like, because you can always load the same sample in a different instance of Slicex or turn off the articulation controls. Similar to FL Studio's general use of linking, a good understanding of how Slicex links these different

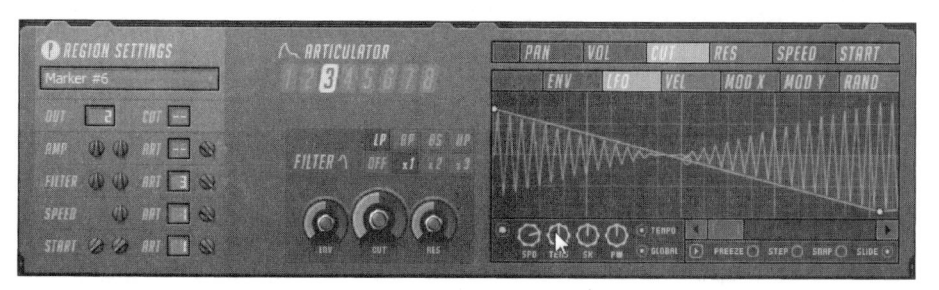

Figure 6.72 The Pan control becomes active when Pan and Vel are selected.

Figure 6.73 Speed knob turned up to create multiple oscillations in the graph display, which in turn affects the audio of the selected marker.

parameters is key to being able to utilize all of the tools available. However, keeping it simple and playing live slices that are recorded into Edison for later editing is perfectly acceptable.

If adding filters using plug-ins is more your speed, a final option could be to send each region or marker to a different output, then individually mix each slice in its own track, and then record the final audio into Edison. This way you get all of your effects on each slice, but after rendering it to one file, you will save a ton of space and memory because no plug-ins for the slices will need to be loaded.

Synthmaker

Unfortunately, the Synthmaker plug-in lies outside the scope of this book. Synthmaker (see Figure 6.74) is a program within a program, and the documentation and available tutorials could fill an entire book by themselves. Start with the basic tutorials to get into building your own synths, and trust me, I know it looks like an unreachable task at first look, but even learning the basics gives you the foundation of knowledge for how many of the synths you have actually work. As you start adding parts and throwing filters and effects on your plug-in, you can start to see the signal flow and how things work (or don't work) with each other.

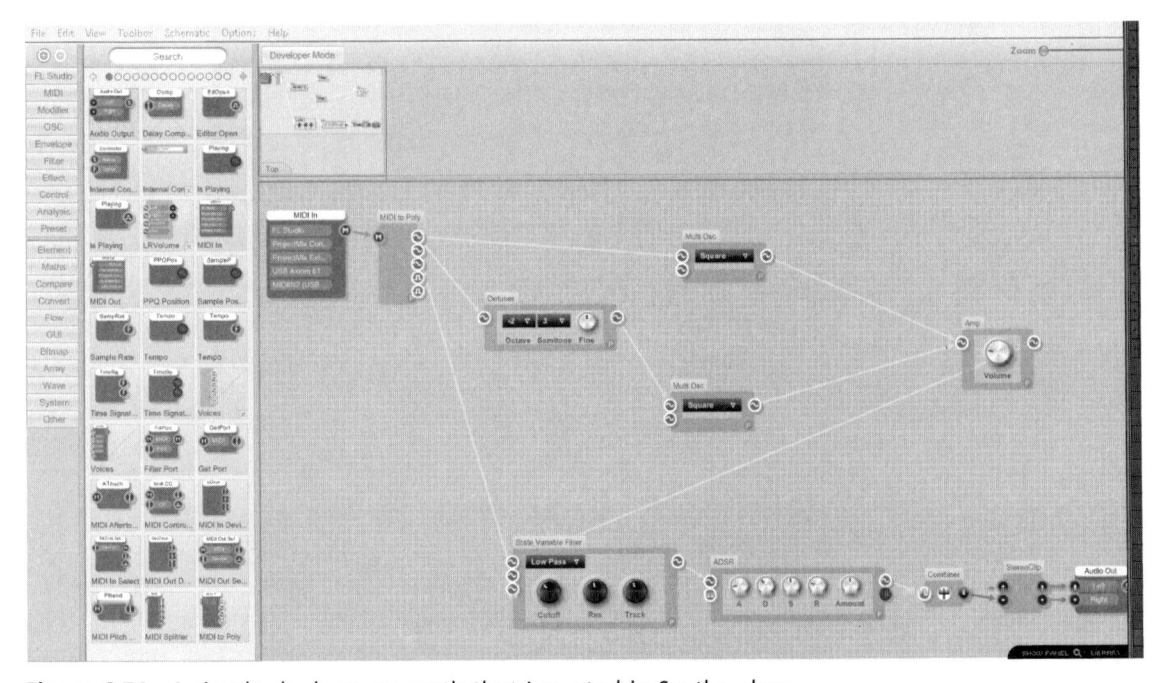

Figure 6.74 A simple dual-square synth that I created in Synthmaker.

This is not a program to be mastered in five minutes, so be patient and take your time when something doesn't work right away. Once you begin gaining confidence in Synthmaker, the plug-in becomes a playground of creativity, and this time you can tell people that not only did you write the music, but you made the synth that's making the sound!

TS404 Generator

The TS404, shown in Figure 6.75, is a bass synthesizer that can resemble classic synth sounds and has the ability to create its own original sounds. The layout of this plug-in is simple, and

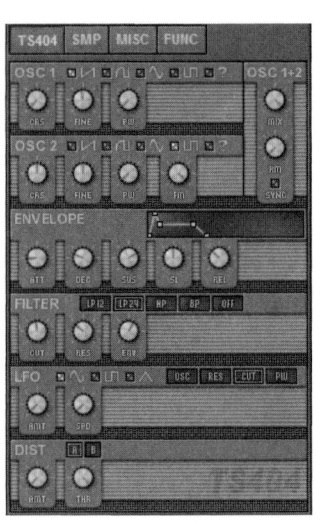

Figure 6.75 The TS404 bass synthesizer.

the audio can be controlled by the two oscillators; their settings; the mix between them (Osc 1 and 2); the envelope control similar to many discussed previously; a cutoff/filter with low-pass, high-pass, and band-pass controls and LFO; and finally, some general distortion. Although these controls are seemingly simple, the number of combinations and settings is nearly limitless.

When you open the TS404, it will load the default sound, but there is no accessible preset list inside of the TS404 plug-in. To get to your presets, open the Browser and navigate to Channel Presets > TS404. This immense list will get you started creating bass synthesizer sounds and give you an idea of the variety of sounds available with this plug-in. When I am thinking of a certain sound, what I will do is pick out the closest preset to what I have in mind and then adjust settings where they are needed. Understanding what each knob does helps in finding the right sound, but the best way to understand the different controls is simply to listen and tweak knobs to see how the different parameters affect the sound.

WASP and WASP XT

Even the defaults of WASP (see Figure 6.76) and WASP XT (see Figure 6.77) sound identical, so we will be discussing the updated and more refined WASP XT. This synth pulls from the influence of '80s synths but steps into the more modern style of synths. You will hear familiar saw sounds, but the deep ambient noises that can be created in WASP XT are spectacular.

Built into this plug-in is a filter, three oscillators, a ring modulator, a frequency modulator, two ADSR envelopes, and even a distortion setting. The KB Track knob in the Filter section allows you to spread the cutoff range, and the remaining options are all ones that we have seen plenty of times now.

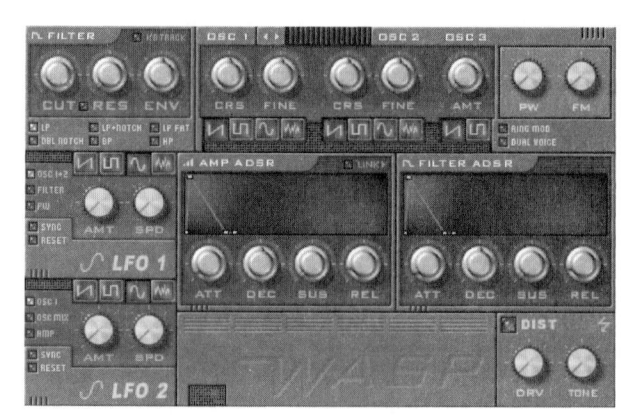

Figure 6.76 WASP.

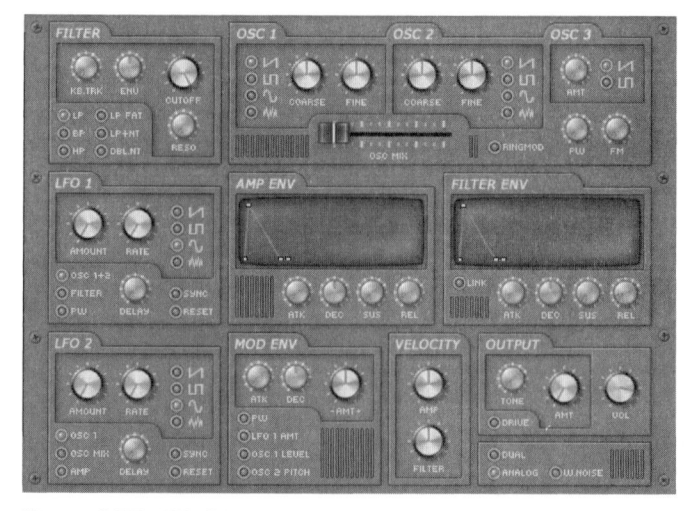

Figure 6.77 WASP XT.

The slider beneath OSC 1 and OSC 2 acts like a crossfader between the two oscillators for the final output, and to enter in a third oscillator, just turn the Amount knob under OSC 3. The PW knob is the pulse width, which only works on square-shaped oscillators (the symbol that looks like a sideways, squared-off S). It will alter the shape of the oscillation, and the result will depend on the other settings and oscillations. In some cases, I was able to get a softer sound that was less scratchy by turning this to the right.

You know how to operate the LFO settings and remember that the amp envelope feeds into the filter envelope, and a quick way to make the filter envelope identical to the Amp section is to click the Link button, and it will basically duplicate the settings. The Modulation section will control modulation of a chosen destination where your choices are modulating the pulse width, LFO modulation amount, OSC 1 volume, or frequency response of OSC 2.

The Amp and Filter knobs in the Velocity section control the modulation velocity of each specific envelope, so you can boost the specific modulation of an envelope. The Output section has an old-school Tone knob that will brighten or darken the sound, while the Amt knob will control the distortion amount when Drive is turned on.

Dual will double the oscillators and detune one so that you get a richer sound, which comes in handy for quickly beefing up your synth. Analog will add randomness in an effort to more accurately mimic hardware, where the oscillators are not perfectly linked. W. Noise uses actual random white noise in the oscillators instead of the sound generated from the plug-in.

Most of this plug-in will come down to taste and experimentation, so it is worth the effort of at least going through the presets to hear the available sounds. After this, lock on to a preset you like and try trashing the sound a bit to see whether you get an even more desirable result. You will find that, through training your ears to hear what the knobs do to sound, you will be able to quickly create the sounds you want anytime you need them.

Wave Traveller

The Wave Traveller (see Figure 6.78) is great for altering sample playback, but most will use this plug-in specifically for the vinyl scratch simulation. This plug-in allows you to create those scratched vocals that sound like you pressed them to record and scratched it yourself live. The quality when scratching is superb, allowing playback adjustments to be extremely broad.

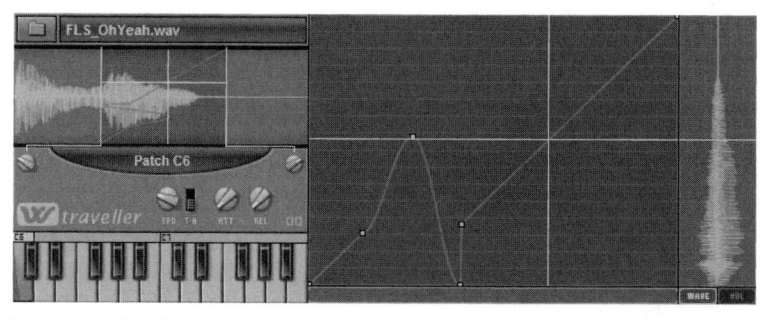

Figure 6.78 The Wave Traveller.

Get as creative as you want with the samples (try synth sounds, live instrument recordings, and so on), but for reference, I will assume that a vocal is loaded into the Wave Traveller. To load a sample, click the folder icon and navigate to an audio file. Underneath this is the preview window that displays the sample, how much of it will be played, and the spline (the red line affecting the playback direction and speed of the sample).

Every key on your MIDI keyboard can cause the sample to play through the Wave Traveller, and the best part is that each key can have its own individual settings, allowing you to make multiple scratches of the same sample and play them using a MIDI keyboard or trigger them in the Piano roll.

The Patch area will let you select a note from C0 to B9 to create a spline setting, or you can click the virtual keyboard of Wave Traveller. The knobs on either side of the Patch Selection drop-down determine the start and end points of your sample. This is great for taking a vocal phrase and assigning different words out of that phrase to different notes. The Speed knob will determine generally how fast or slow a sample will play back based on tempo when the T-A switch to the right is flipped up, whereas playback will be based on absolute value (as a percentage of the original sample speed) when T-A is flipped down.

The Path Definition panel on the far right of the plug-in is where you draw the spline that affects your audio. The spline that is created here is represented by time on the horizontal axis and sample position on the vertical axis. A good way to wrap your head around it is to just think that the steeper you draw the slope of a section of the spline as the plug-in moves from left to right, the faster your sample will play in either direction. As you make the spline more of a gradual slope, the playback (again, forward or reverse) will slow down as it passes across that adjusted section of the spline.

It's important to know that the speed at which the sample plays back is also affected by the Speed knob and the T-A switch. The key is adding in sample position, where the height of the spline represents the playback position of the sample. So if you start your spline at the top on the left side of the graph (Path Definition panel) and make a straight line that gradually goes to the bottom right of the graph, then the sample will play in reverse (see Figure 6.79). This is because you are starting the spline (period of playback) at the end of the sample and gradually bringing it back to the beginning while keeping the direction constant.

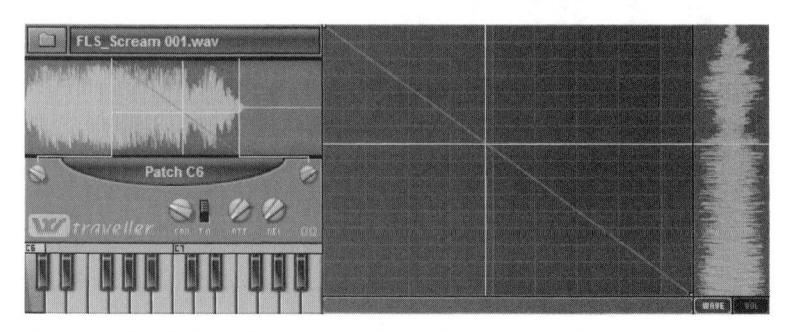

Figure 6.79 With this spline setting, the sample plays in reverse.

The Wave Traveller can take a little practice to get the hang of, but the effort is well worth the reward of being able to quickly add scratch effects to your samples. From vocals to kick drums, your imagination is the only limit.

We have taken a deep look into the available instruments and generators included with FL Studio. Where possible, I omitted repetitive information so that you don't have to read about attack and decay in 20 parts of the book. Remember that key to getting the right sound out of your instruments is experimentation with everything. Save your project as a new file, play with settings of a generator, and try to get a desired sound using your own detective work. You get quite an exhilarated feeling when you create a sound all on your own and you are not using a preset. The sound becomes yours, and while the settings may have been used in the past, it is not incredibly likely with most plug-ins because of the range of choices.

In the next chapter, we will look at more plug-ins, but we will focus in on the effects plug-ins included with FL Studio. These plug-ins are what make your final product have echo, reverb, distortion, and a wide array of other sonic changes. I will demonstrate how you can even use effects channels to put live effects on inputs, such as a voice or a guitar, and explain the routing process of the effects channels that can be loaded into each individual Mixer track.

7 Effects Plug-Ins

Most of the songs on the radio and professionally produced CDs have that shimmer to the sound, and everything seems to fit sonically. Many of the sounds will have reverb to help the music sit nicely in your mix, and some have delay so that voices repeat a few lines after the initial lyrics are sung, but where does it all come from? The final phase of FL Studio—the effects plug-ins! At this point, you have a running project, and everything is at the right point in the timeline, but it just doesn't sound right. That's fine, because we are going to take an in-depth look into the effects plug-ins and their capabilities. Ideally, after this chapter, you will be able to use almost everything that FL Studio has to offer and will possess a thorough understanding of what tools to use when you are looking for a particular sound. Many of these will deal with frequency and range of sound, so the best way to work is to open up a plug-in as you read about it. Link the sound from any channel to a Mixer track and insert the plug-in to see what it will sound like. Although I will be explaining what they do and generally what will change about the output after the sound runs through the plug-in, your ears will always be your best guide when using these tools.

EQUO

The EQUO plug-in (see Figure 7.1) allows you to affect individual frequencies of the sound that is playing through the Mixer track EQUO is placed on. Don't think of this as a final EQ on your tracks, think of it as a dynamic EQ adjuster for while the song is playing. This plug-in allows you to affect the volume of frequencies and even the frequency amount in each side of a stereo output. So you could drop the bass in just your left ear, leaving the right side playing normally. EQUO is great for creating a sweeping effect using automation clips. Remember that you can automate nearly everything, so it's as easy as right-clicking a knob and choosing Create Automation Clip. So let's look at what the controls do and then apply our new knowledge!

The left side of EQUO is a graph that has low frequency on the left and high frequency on the right. At the top of this graph is a drop-down menu with Random, Flat, and Interpolate options. Random will generate a random EQ curve for the selected bank. Remember that if you have master selected (M), this will only affect the final output and will not be used for the sweeping effect for which this plug-in was intended. Flat will bring the EQ line back to the middle (default), where there will be no noticeable effect, and Interpolate will automatically draw the

227

Figure 7.1 EQUO.

in-between curves on Banks 2–7 when you draw a curve on Bank 1 and then a curve on Bank 8. I enjoy this option because when you have a certain sweep in mind and you know the start and the end of the sweep, the Interpolate option will draw the curves that are necessary in between to create a smooth transition between the first and last bank curves.

The mode buttons to the right of the drop-down are Pencil, which allows you to move single frequency blocks up and down; Line, where you can click and drag straight lines to make a curve; and the Curve option, which is the default behavior. When you click and hold the Analyze button, it will draw a curve based on the audio that is playing through EQUO. The Bank Select down at the bottom allows you to draw a different curve for the bank you select. The Volume, Pan, and Send buttons will allow you to change frequency volume for a bank, the frequency amount in the left or right channel using Pan, and the frequency send amount for the bank that you have selected.

The Morph knobs are where all the action happens for the frequency changes. The Shift knob will slide the currently drawn curve to the left or right, depending upon the position of the knob (see Figure 7.2). This is the knob that you will want to automate.

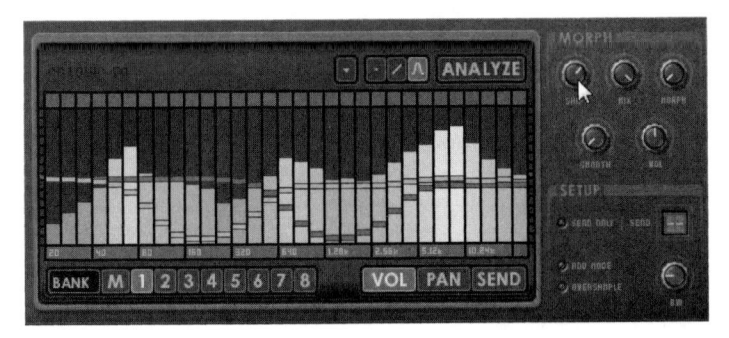

Figure 7.2 EQUO with a frequency curve shifted to the right.

The Mix knob will determine how much of the curve is added to or subtracted from the original sound. It will be turned to the right by default so that the curve you draw will have maximum effect on the sound playing through EQUO. Turning it to the left will affect the sound in reverse, so if you have a pan curve that drops the bass on the left side when the Shift knob is turned, the Mix knob, when turned to the left, will cause the bass to drop in the right side. I find it best to leave this knob alone unless you want to create a frequency sweep that goes from one extreme to the other. Remember that when the Mix knob is in the middle, that means the curve you have drawn will not affect the sound output.

The Morph knob will blend between Banks 1 through 8, where the knob turned left is the first bank, and the knob turned right is the eighth bank. This is also a desirable knob to automate.

The Send Only option allows you to mute the Mixer track output to the master, and then you can select a send track on which to place the sound. Remember that 1–4 means Send 1, 2, 3, or 4, so select accordingly. If you have music or a different instrument on the track to the right of EQUO and you choose to send to one, the send output will play on that track. This can cause trouble because you can't see why the EQUO is playing on that send through internal routing, so use caution with this option.

Add mode means that the effected signal will be combined with the original output, rather than just the effect playing through EQUO's output. This is good for when you need the original curve to play with your effected sound. So if you have a curve that cuts out the midrange, with Add mode on, when the curve passes over the higher frequency to cut it out, the higher frequency will still play (see Figure 7.3).

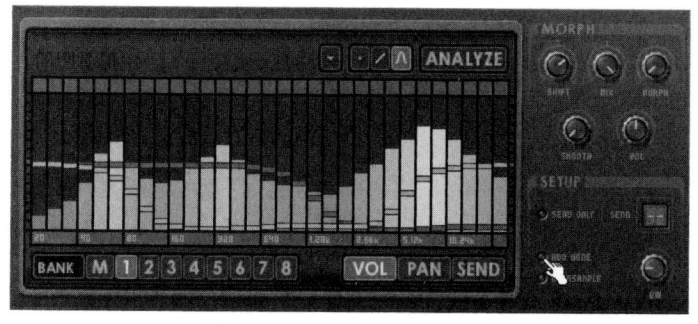

Figure 7.3 Add mode engaged in EQUO.

Oversample will improve the quality of sound that comes out of EQUO, and the Bandwidth knob will adjust the amount that the curve will affect the sound. So if you raise the bandwidth, your EQ curve will have a more subtle effect on the audio playing through EQUO.

In one of your Mixer tracks, open up an instance of EQUO, select Band 1, and draw a simple dip in the middle of the graph. Because we are only dealing with Band 1, make sure the Morph knob is all the way to the left and the Mix knob is all the way to the right. Now right-click on the Shift knob and choose Create Automation Clip (see Figure 7.4). In the Playlist, you will see an automation clip appear in the first empty space available (see Figure 7.5). Draw a line that starts from the top and gradually drops to the bottom over time. Now hit Play, switch back to the EQUO window, and you can see the plug-in making the changes to the sound and how the frequency is affected.

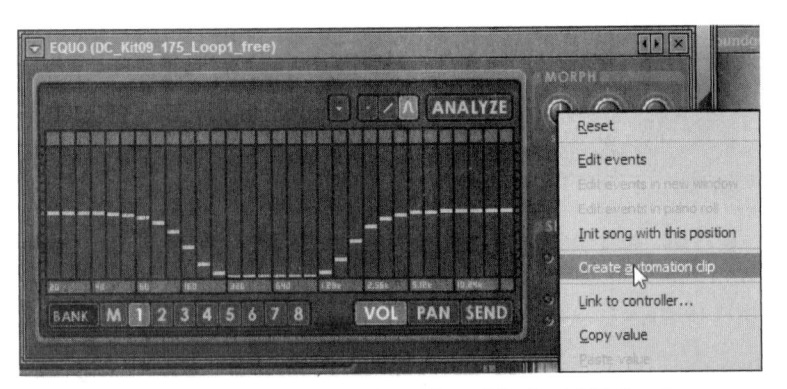

Figure 7.4 Creating an automation clip with the Shift knob.

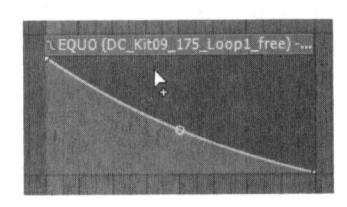

Figure 7.5 An automation clip of the Shift knob in the Playlist.

This is only scratching the surface, and you can create eight different banks and automate the Morph knob for a completely custom sound. This effect is great for muffling a drum beat in the beginning of a song, and then as the main verse starts, you can bring all the frequencies up to normal. One thing to note is that you should get your EQ settings where you want them using the Fruity Parametric EQ before making changes with this plug-in.

Fruity 7 Band EQ

Fruity 7 Band EQ (see Figure 7.6) is a simple EQ that has preset frequency values so you can only alter the amounts of those specific frequencies. There is no tension control, so you can't etch out a specific tone, but for general quick EQ that calls for mild precision, this is as simple as they come. Think of the same graph that we dealt with in EQUO, and you will get the idea. This is one of the fastest ways to automate a quick bass removal by linking

Figure 7.6 Fruity 7 Band EQ.

the low-frequency knob to an automation clip. Remember that you can always use the integrated Mixer track EQ for the speediest EQ changes, but this is easy to forget about, and a plug-in is easier to turn off for comparing settings than having to go back and completely readjust the built-in EQ. This plug-in is great for understanding what specific frequencies are affected when you raise or lower them, but I think that you will find the other EQ options to be much more flexible.

Fruity Bass Boost

Have you ever made a song and had the bass seem lifeless and lacking that "force to be reckoned with" feel? Fruity Bass Boost (see Figure 7.7) is the plug-in that can give your sound that needed boost. This is an even lighter version of an EQ and only deals with one specific frequency that you choose. You can then boost that frequency to give your bass or even kick drum a warmer, heavier sound. Keep in mind that you will most likely need to lower the volume so that the sound doesn't become distorted. When boosting a frequency signal, typically the volume increases as well, but I want to mention here that boosting a frequency is not always the way to go. Usually, cutting unwanted frequencies and using multi-band compression to boost bass frequencies is key to a great mix. Finding the right tone takes practice, but the more you pay attention to which frequency works with which sounds, the easier it will be to apply those effects to future projects.

Figure 7.7   Fruity Bass Boost.

Fruity Blood Overdrive

This will distort any audio signal that it passes through and is great for getting a crunch sound to your guitar if you're playing directly into FL Studio (see Figure 7.8). The PreBand setting will control the amount of frequency filtering on the distortion, so when you only need distortion for the low or high end, this is where you set it. The Color knob will tell the PreBand what frequency to affect (how much to boost the distortion of that particular frequency). The PreAmp knob is essentially the distortion itself and the amount that audio is overdriven. The ×100 knob will literally multiply the preamp by 100, which is great for distorting an instrument but will typically yield terrible results when you apply this much distortion to a collection of tracks or sounds.

PostFilter allows you to further fine-tune the frequency response of the sound after it has gone through the distortion, and the PostGain is essentially the final volume control. If the sound is clipping, lower this knob, because lowering the PreAmp will remove distortion in your sound. Try plugging in a guitar or even singing into this plug-in for gritty sounds that usually require an effects box.

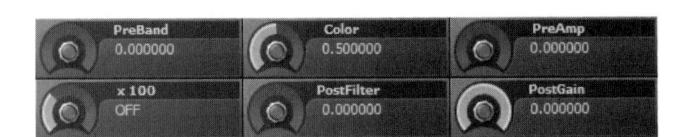

Figure 7.8 Fruity Blood Overdrive.

Fruity Chorus

Chorus (see Figure 7.9), which is similar to Unison found on many synths, will take a sound, delay it, and detune it slightly so that it seems as if two or more sounds are playing. When you copy a vocal and place the two on top of each other, it just sounds like a louder vocal. The Chorus effect takes that vocal and modifies it slightly so that you can hear the difference and they sit together better in the mix. While this is great for vocals, you also can add chorus to anything you want to thicken up. Try duplicating a vocal and placing the Chorus effect on one, then panning one copy to the left and one copy to the right. You may get some results that will surprise you.

Figure 7.9 Fruity Chorus.

The Delay knob will determine the delay between chorus voices, while the Depth knob will affect the chorus modulation. This one takes a little tinkering to fully hear what is going on, but when you adjust the delay to a low setting and the depth to a high setting, you will get a thicker, heavier chorus effect.

The Stereo knob will adjust the left and right modulation effect from the chorus and, in changing values, will affect the stereo image of your sound. The LFO controls allow you to set a modulation speed and type of wave that the LFO uses.

Cross Type is an important knob because it will determine what range of sound the chorus will affect—Process HF will work on higher sounds, such as flutes and female soprano voices, and Process LF will be better suited for bass and baritone male voices. The Cross Cutoff determines at what point in the frequency spectrum the sound is affected by the chorus. This is basically the fine-tuning of the Process knob.

Wet Only should be turned on when you are using the chorus as a send track to affect sound. So if you have vocals that are going to the main output, but you want a little chorus, add the Fruity Chorus to a send track and then route the vocal track to the send track and select Wet Only. This will make sure that the chorus track only plays the affected audio through the master and doesn't add in the original sound, which can cause clipping.

Fruity Compressor

Fruity Compressor (see Figure 7.10) is the simple version of FL Studio's compressor and is a great tool for understanding how compression works. The use of compression is highly debated, especially today, with engineers pushing (or being told to push) songs to their absolute maximum volume. The use of heavy compression takes away the dynamic range of a song. In other words, parts of the song that are supposed to be soft play at the same volume as the loud parts. This doesn't mean your volume knob no longer has an effect; it just means that the music that is playing will no longer have quiet parts and loud parts, but it will be a wall of sound that will always play at the volume level you set.

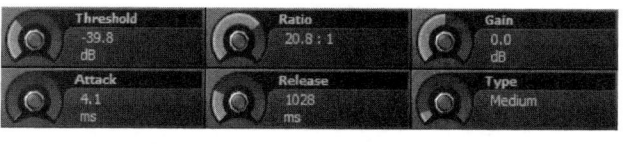

Figure 7.10   The Fruity Compressor.

Compression is a way of automating the volume of a signal by reducing the dynamic range of a sound. It seems counterintuitive that compressing something can make it louder, but compression more accurately compresses sound so that you are able to turn it up. When a sound has quiet and loud parts, if you turn up the whole sample to better hear the quiet parts, the loud parts get too loud and can cause distortion. Compression lowers the distance in volume between the loudest and softest notes so that as you turn up the volume, the loud parts do not clip, but you are able to hear the quieter parts more clearly. Those in favor of heavy compression argue that it brings their song up to one constant volume or gives their music a distinct sound that no other has, which in their opinion sounds better. It is my personal opinion that compression, when used properly, can give a song the punch it needs and fix slight volume problems, but there should be no rules to how you use it, because if everyone thinks it sounds good, you can argue that! However, I am not the final say on what you like, and as with anything in FL Studio, experiment and see what you find appealing.

To understand what this plug-in does, it is usually best to start with a drum track that has cymbals, a kick, and a snare so that you have a range of volume within the sample. Place the Fruity Compressor on the drum track as you go through the settings so you can hear the difference when adjusting. The Threshold knob determines at what volume the compressor should start affecting the sound. With the threshold all the way up, there will be no compression because there is no volume ceiling that the sound needs to hit in order to activate the compressor.

The Ratio knob is the amount of compression, where the number on the left is how loud (in decibels) the sound needs to go above the Threshold setting to allow a 1-dB increase. So if your threshold is set at −10 dB, and the ratio is set at 15:1, then a sound that plays 30 dB louder than your −10-dB threshold will cause the compressor to only allow a 2-dB increase in the volume of the sound (because a 15-dB increase only allows a 1-dB increase in the output, so a 30-dB increase allows 2 dB). The gain is the volume control of the output after it has been run through the compressor.

The Attack and Release are similar to the ADSR envelopes that we discussed, but rather than a sound, the compression is affected. The Attack controls the amount of time before compression starts. For long, droning notes that gradually increase in volume, like a break in a song, where a single pad plays a long note and gets louder, a long attack means that the compression will kick in slowly. For sounds such as a kick drum, it is usually necessary to apply a quick attack so that the compressor catches the drum before it clips the audio.

The Release switch is how fast the compressor stops affecting the sound, so in the example of a drum kick, if there is a long release, after the drum kick hits, the compressor will still be active and can affect other sounds in the track, such as a hi-hat that gets compressed undesirably. For kicks and quick-burst sounds, a faster release works great, but don't be afraid to experiment with these settings, because adjusting the attack and release to extremes may give your music a crazy breathing effect.

The Type knob will allow you to switch the knees of the compression. The knee is the time it takes the compression to reach the maximum setting that you determine (from the Ratio knob), starting from a 1:1 compression ratio. Hard means that once the threshold is passed, the compressor kicks in full, medium allows 6 dB where the compression is applied, vintage allows 7 dB, and soft will apply the compression over 15 dB of sound. So if you have a soft knee, the compression of the sound will increase to your set ratio gradually over 15 dB.

Sidechain Compression I want to give you an example of how useful compression can be. Sidechaining by itself is nothing more than using one signal to affect another signal. The ducking effect created from sidechaining compression can be heard in many popular songs today, and the idea is to sidechain the signal from one sound source to control the compression of another signal. In Benny Benassi's "Satisfaction," the bass seems to breathe with the kick drum. This effect is actually pretty easy to achieve in FL Studio, and this section will demonstrate how. Start by loading a simple bass instrument and a kick instrument and then linking them to individual tracks in the Mixer. Place some kicks in the Stepsequencer and a single note in the bass channel, as in Figure 7.11. Now insert a Fruity Compressor on the bass track in the Mixer and a Fruity Peak Controller on the kick track in the Mixer. Feel free to experiment with the Ratio, Attack, and Release controls on the compressor, but first right-click the Threshold knob in the compressor and select Link to Controller. From the dialog box that pops up, select Peak Control - Peak for the internal controller and then select Inverted for the mapping formula (see Figure 7.12). This will cause the bass to quiet when the kick hits rather than play with the kick. Adjust the Peak Controller settings so that the peak tension is raised up, the Base knob has a low setting, and the

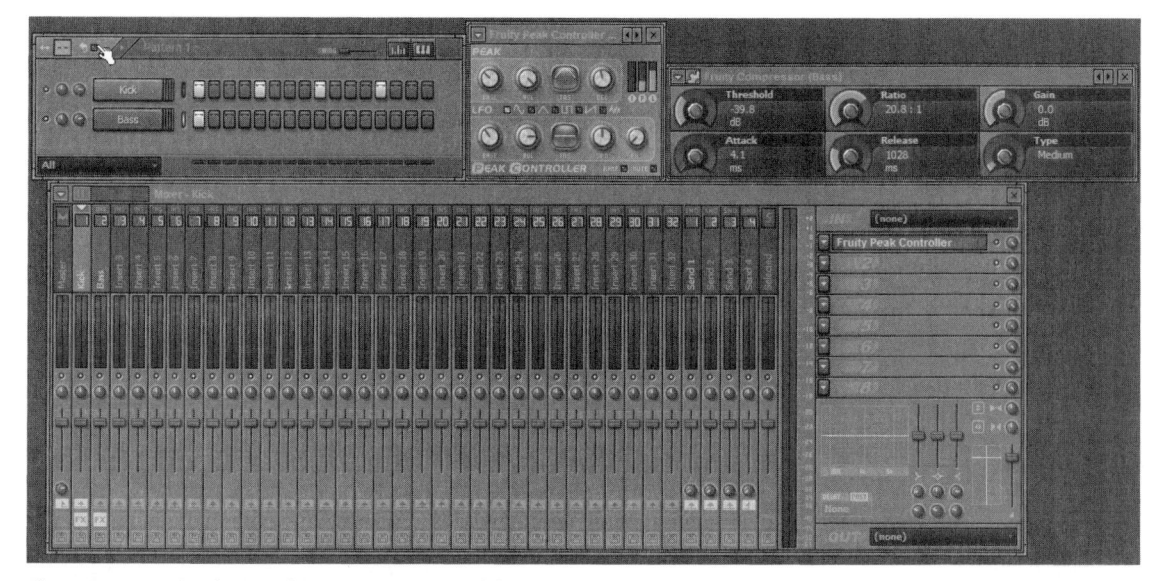

Figure 7.11 The bass is being compressed from the kick signal using the Fruity Peak Controller.

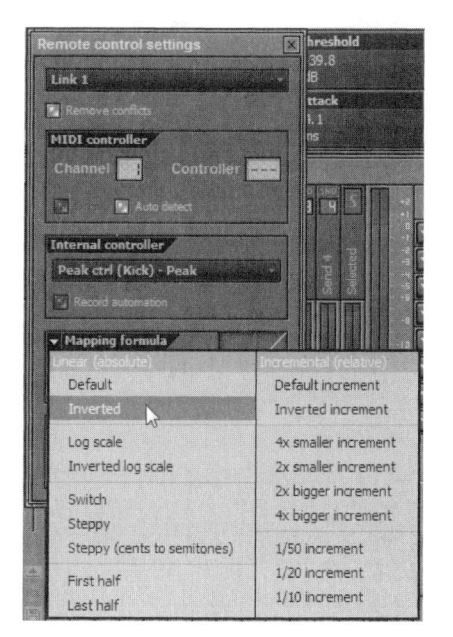

Figure 7.12 Select Inverted to cause the threshold to lower the bass volume when the kick drum triggers the compression.

decay is set near the middle. Make sure that Mute is not selected on the Peak Controller in the bottom right; otherwise, the kick will be muted. Press Play, and you will hear the bass being compressed from the signal of the kick drum.

Fruity Delay

Fruity Delay (see Figure 7.13) is what will give any sound that feeling of slowly fading away. It works great on vocals when you want a line to repeat for emphasis. You can automate the controls here, too, and have the tempo increase while the volume drops so that the voice repeats faster and faster while dropping in volume. Putting delay on instrument pieces such as a hi-hat can produce an interesting backbeat that is better than what you initially made.

Figure 7.13 Fruity Delay.

The Input knob will affect the volume of the original sound and how loud it plays into the plug-in. Feedback is the volume of the echoes created by the delay. Be careful, because turning Feedback all the way up will cause the echo to repeat endlessly. Consider that this could be used to create the rhythm of a song with just the constant repeating sound and then automated to stop repeating at the end of the song. There are many creative ways to utilize this plug-in.

Similar to other plug-ins, the Cutoff will affect the frequency of the echoes that come out of Fruity Delay. Tempo by default is set to Auto so that the echoes will automatically lock to the tempo. This is usually the desirable setting so everything is crisp, but feel free to change this setting and try automating it, because many different types of music incorporate specific tempo-synced delay for interesting percussion and melody.

Steps will affect how often the echoes play, and Mode will affect the stereo image of the echo. The Normal setting plays the output like the original, and Inv. Stereo will swap the left and right channels so that the right channel will echo on the left and vice versa. Ping Pong will alternate between using the left and right inputs to echo, so if you have a constant hi-hat in the left channel, it will still play in the left channel, but it will echo in the left, then right, then left, and so on.

Fruity Delay 2

A more compact and very similar plug-in, Fruity Delay 2 (see Figure 7.14) is the refined uncle of Fruity Delay (1). The input controls are the same, where volume is the amount of input from the original signal and panning will determine how much of each side of the input has delay. So if you pan it to the left, you will only get echo out of the left side because that is all that is coming into the echo. Normal, Inverted, and Ping Pong will work as described in Fruity Delay, and the

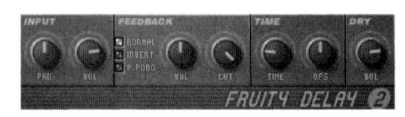

Figure 7.14 Fruity Delay 2.

second Volume knob and Cutoff knob both affect the output of the delay plug-in. Remember that, when turned all the way up, the Volume knob for the output means that the delay will continue endlessly.

The time wheel locks to the tempo, so the values you choose here will be based on fractions of the original beat. This ensures that echoes are in time with your project and allows you to make different echoes without worrying if they get out of tempo. The Stereo Offset knob (OFS) will cause the left and right outputs to offset each other. Although this can deliver a wider sound, overkill with this can make your audio sound distorted or just plain wrong, so use caution when adjusting this.

The Dry knob will determine how much of the original input comes out of the plug-in output. If you have the delay on a send track, then turn the Dry knob to the left so that only echo plays out. This way, you can determine the amount of dry signal you want by using the regular volume control in the Mixer.

Fruity Delay Bank

Now we are getting into a much more flexible delay plug-in. The Fruity Delay Bank plug-in (see Figure 7.15) allows you to have multiple echoes running, which can come in handy when you're creating soundscapes or sound designing for a film. Multiple delays can give the perception that a sound is everywhere in the mix but dynamically moving around. This is definitely a plug-in to experiment with when you start getting ideas for delays in your music. For the basic delays, the prior plug-ins discussed will work great, but if you're looking for more, this is the plug-in for you.

Figure 7.15 Fruity Delay Bank.

The tabs at the top of the plug-in represent the different delays you can have running, and they will have identical settings for each one. At the top right is a set of controls that will be global to the delay effects. The Oversample feature is like many of the oversampling options on other plug-ins and will increase the quality of the audio that comes out of the delay plug-in. The Wet and Dry levels will affect the amount of delayed sound (Wet) versus the amount of original sound (Dry) that plays out of the output. The In knob will determine how much of the original signal (volume-wise) will play into the delay plug-in. Turn this up if your sound isn't getting enough delay response. The Feedback knob will determine the overall feedback of the delay plug-in and affects all running delays.

The next series of sections in this plug-in will look the same regardless of which tab you select. Just know that if they are turned on, they are active even if the tab is not selected. This is good to keep in mind in case you are getting a rogue delay signal, because you may have left a delay turned on that you didn't want.

The In section houses the On switch for the selected delay, so if you highlight this with Tab 2 selected, then the second delay will be activated. By default, only the first delay is turned on, so that you aren't overwhelmed by a wall of sound when sending signal into the plug-in.

The Solo switch will isolate the selected delay so you can fine-tune each delay one at a time. The Volume and Panning knobs will affect the input signal, not the output, so remember that this is for getting your incoming signal up to a certain level or panned to a certain side before applying the delay. Unless you are having trouble getting the delay plug-in to react to the sound, I would leave these alone and adjust the output settings for panning, but feel free to experiment with how the plug-in reacts to different input levels.

The Filter section allows you to apply filtering to your signal and decide whether you want the signal to be affected prior to the delay effect or after. Selecting the Post option will cause the filter to be placed on the signal after it has gone through the delay effect. This comes down to preference and listening, because the difference between pre and post can give your music interesting results for final mixes.

If you mouse over where it says Off, you can click and drag through a list of different filters to place on your signal. Try selecting an HP (high-pass) filter and then automating the Cut (cutoff) knob. This can give your delay a disappearing effect when the automation causes the knob to go from 0 to 100%. The numbers next to the filter select will essentially determine the severity of the cutoff filter, with 3 being the most intense.

The Gain knob will control the output volume of the filter (not the signal) all the way up to 200%, so you can really boost that effect if you need to. The Cut knob is the one I suggested automating because it controls the cutoff frequency amount for the feedback of the delay, so if you have an LP (low-pass) filter selected, and you slowly turn up the knob to 100%, the high end will drop out, leaving a murky, muffled delay.

The Res knob will increase the volume of certain frequencies that are close to your selected cutoff amount and can produce a shiny ring sound, but to best understand this one, try adjusting the Res knob to hear the difference.

The Feedback section will control your actual echoes that play from the initial signal. So if a vocalist says "Hey" into the mic, and it runs through this plug-in, every subsequent "Hey" that repeats after the first one can be controlled in this section.

Echo processing just determines whether the first echo will have effect on it. So if you need the first echo to be lower than the rest of the vocals, and you want it to hide more in the music, make sure that Process First Echo is selected. I have to admit that it is very hard to see the difference between the two visually, but clicking the box with the vertical lines will cause the image to change slightly. The important part in the image is the second line, and if the second line is the same height as the first line, that means the first echo will mimic the original signal before going through processing.

Next to this little toggle switch is a series of different feedback modes, including Inverted (INV), Normal (NORM), and Ping Pong (P.PONG). The Off setting will disable your feedback, which essentially removes the echoes. Remember that this is there so you can apply filtering on one tab with no echo and then place a different echo on another tab, all using the same plug-in.

The Tempo-Based Time switch will cause the echoes to sync with the set tempo of your project. In most cases you should leave this on, because it will make producing that tight echo sound incredibly easy. However, for more ambient echoes that don't stick to the tempo, turn this off and experiment!

The Time fader will affect the time between each echo, and with multiple echoes going, the Tempo-Based Time switch makes incorporating multiple echoes easy. The Offset fader (OFS) will determine how far apart (left to right) the echo seems on playback and is another control that I highly recommend experimenting with.

The Separation fader (SEP) will offset the left or right channel to give the sound a richer, wider sound by delaying the echo of one side. This section also has a Volume and a Pan knob and affects the actual feedback (echoes).

Don't get confused by all the Volume and Panning knobs—they are just there to affect specific sections of the plug-in so that you can decide where in the signal path the panning or volume should change. For example, if you only want echo playing out of the left side for this tab (selected delay effect), then you can adjust the Pan knob in the Feedback section, and that particular echo with play out of the left side. The difference is that if you adjusted the input panning to the left, then only the signal from the left side would have an echo (which you can pan either left or right). So if a great vocal was mostly in the right side, panning the input to the left would mean that most of that vocal would not play in the delay echo because it is using the signal from the left side.

The Feedback Filtering has the same set of controls that the Filter section had, only these control the already affected echoes (feedback signal). The Grain section allows you to slice your echoes into small audio pieces. You can then adjust how far apart these grains play using the Division slider (DIV) and how smooth the grains sound by using the Shape slider (SH). Try automating the DIV slider after finding a good SH setting and go from off to 10 on the DIV slider over a span of time. It may not be what you are looking for, but changing up the grain division can add that little extra spice that may have been missing from a project.

The Output to Next Delay Bank knob (NEXT) allows you to send the signal from the selected tab (bank) into the next one for further processing. The Pan and Volume knobs will affect the overall output of that selected tab (bank) to the main output. A lot is happening with this plug-in, so take a little time to create different delays, because you will find that you can create a much richer mix using multiple echoes.

Fruity Fast Distortion

Fruity Fast Distortion (see Figure 7.16) is a very simple distortion plug-in that can quickly add that needed grit to any signal. Although it can be used with a guitar, I found that stacking two of them will produce a better sound but can really muffle the original signal. However, try using it on a bass guitar for a fuzzy, warm sound or on any single-note instrument. With vocals, I noticed that it helps create that screaming radio sound that many bands use, so try running your vocals with this—you might like the results.

Figure 7.16   Fruity Fast Distortion.

The Pre wheel is basically the amount of distortion, so moving it to the right will boost the distortion. The Threshold knob will determine what frequency is affected by the distortion, but to simplify, turn right to increase the amount of distortion.

The A/B switch changes between the two distortion types. I found that A is calmer and works nicely with instruments, while B is grittier and has a nastier breakup of sound when boosted.

Mix will determine how much of the original signal plays with the distorted sound. So if you only want distortion, turn it to the right.

Post is the volume of the distorted sound, so if the sound is perfect but clipping and too loud, turn this knob down, because turning down the Pre will remove distortion.

Fruity Flanger

Fruity Flanger (see Figure 7.17) will give your audio that spacey sound that is similar to someone singing a single note while opening and closing his or her mouth. This tool is particularly popular with DJs as a transition effect. When mixing from one song to another, a flanger is placed

Figure 7.17   Fruity Flanger.

on the outgoing song, and it seems to widen and dissipate from the mix when combined with lowering volume levels. In FL Studio, the Flanger is a great way to add body to your sound and make it move within the mix. While DJs use it to transition between songs, you can use it when transitioning between a chorus and a verse or any number of places in your project.

The Flanger basically takes the input signal (the track that you put the Flanger on) and creates multiple copies that are slightly delayed to cause phase cancellation. So certain frequencies in the signal get removed because at certain points the sound wave is cancelled by a sound wave that is an opposite shape. It is hard to imagine that two sounds can create silence, but that is what phase cancellation is all about. When you have two identical waveforms playing, they will just make the sound louder, but if one is inverted, then all sound will cease. There is a lot of math involved, which I will spare you, but it is good to have the basic idea of what is happening with this plug-in and why it makes the cool sound that it does.

The Delay knob will determine the minimum delay between the copied signals, so if you want a separated, wild sound, raise the delay, but for a crisp flanger, keep it at 0. The Depth is the modulation of the flanger delay, so increasing this will give your effect a chunkier sound. The Rate is the modulation speed of the effect, and you can hear the difference by turning this knob while running the effect.

Phase will allow you to manipulate the stereo sound of the effect. Using a lower setting here will give you a stereo sound that is simple and barely noticeable, while increasing it will create a widening effect on your audio. Damp will pull out some of the higher frequencies of the final output when you increase the value, and Shape will determine the shape of the oscillation. So if you want a choppier, more abrupt flanger, move this setting more toward the Triangle (TRI) setting.

Feed will set your feedback amount, but be careful when boosting this one, because it can easily cause clipping when not adjusted properly. Invert Feedback and Invert Wet will invert both of their respective signals and allow you to create a different sound, depending upon the other settings of the Flanger. These two settings are good to experiment with, but leaving at least one turned on will ensure that you still get more of a flange effect as opposed to a chorus effect. The Chorus effect will produce a copy of the original signal that simply plays slightly delayed and has no modulation. Dry and Wet are the output volume controls for the Flanger effect (wet) and the original sound (dry), while Cross is a version of the wet signal that has had its left and right channels inverted.

Fruity Flangus

Fruity Flangus (see Figure 7.18) is a simple version of Fruity Flanger, but it produces results just as stunning. This is a great tool to use for a quick flanger effect when you start understanding where and when to use the Flanger in your music. One thing I want to point out is that there are no rules, and if it sounds good, then by all means insert the effect and make it work!

Figure 7.18   Fruity Flangus.

The first setting is the Order window (ORD), which can be adjusted by clicking and dragging up or down. This will add thickness to the flanger as you increase the amount of flangers running and give a smoother sound to the effect overall. The Depth slider will give your output sound a deeper feel to it by increasing the amplitude of pitch oscillation for the flangers. The Speed (SPD) slider will determine the speed of the pitch oscillation, and the Delay slider (DEL) will control the delay applied to the flangers.

The Spread slider (SPRD) is a smoothing tool for the flangers, so if you are hearing something that you don't like about how the flangers are working with each other, try adjusting this setting. The Stereo Cross slider (CROSS) allows you to send more of the left channel into the final output when slid up or more of the right channel to the final output when slid down and will be a mixture of both when sitting in the middle.

The Dry and Wet sliders are similar to other plug-ins, but when both sliders are in the middle, no sound will play. The top (100% dry or wet) is the signal being sent to the output normally, while the bottom of the slider (–100%) is the inverted signal being sent to the output.

Fruity Formula Controller

The Fruity Formula Controller plug-in (see Figure 7.19) is an internal controller and allows you to link different controls to nearly any parameter in FL Studio. We have taken a look at linking using the Peak Controller, so now we will look at using this controller, which allows for a greater deal of flexibility. Bear in mind that this controller can get deep into mathematics, but for the purposes of this book, we will stay on the music-making path without getting too deep into mathematical functions. For a complete list of the syntax, functions, and objects that are supported by the Formula Controller, press F1 when the Fruity Formula Controller is highlighted in FL Studio.

Figure 7.19   Fruity Formula Controller.

This plug-in should be inserted onto an effects track, and once it is placed, then you can right-click most knobs or sliders and link them to the Formula Controller. One of my favorite uses of this program is the ability to use your mouse like a fader or a slider. We will take a look at creating panning for a track using the mouse and the Fruity Formula Controller.

Begin by placing an instance of FL Keys in an empty sampler channel and then inserting an instance of the Fruity Formula Controller on the FL Keys track in the Mixer (see Figure 7.20). (Remember to link the channel in the Channel window and the track in the Mixer using Ctrl+L.) Now right-click on the Pan button in the FL Keys Mixer track and choose Link to Controller (see Figure 7.21). From the Remote Control Settings window that comes up, choose Formula Ctrl (Keys) - Out from the drop-down menu in the Internal Controller section (see Figure 7.22) and then click Accept.

Figure 7.20   FL Keys with an instance of the Fruity Formula Controller.

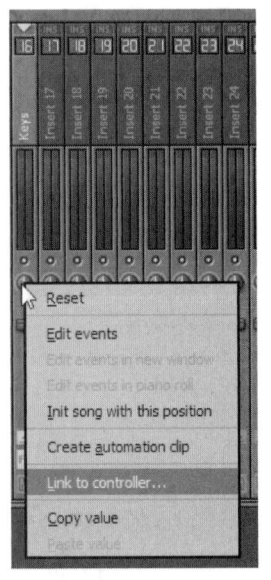

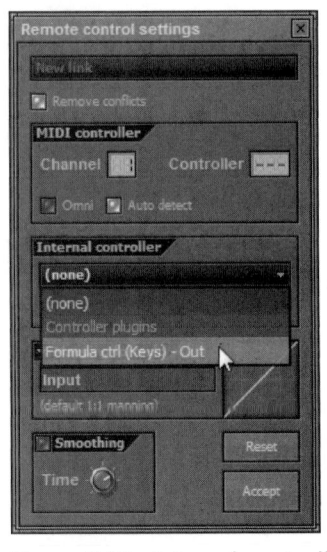

Figure 7.21 Linking the Pan control to the Fruity Formula Controller.

Figure 7.22 Internal controller selection.

Now the Pan knob is linked to the Fruity Formula Controller, but we don't have the Fruity Formula Controller set to respond to anything yet. Now go to the Fruity Formula Controller and, from the Presets menu, select Mouse Position (see Figure 7.23). When you move the mouse, you will see that the Pan knob moves with it. This is a great way to give your mixes that human touch to automation, because you can record the results as you change parameters live. The mouse can act like your very own XY joystick controller!

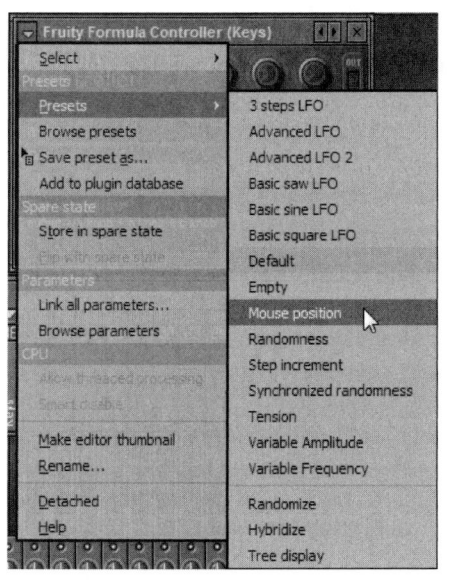

Figure 7.23 Presets menu of the Fruity Formula Controller.

To control a different parameter, you can insert another instance of the controller, but this time after linking the parameter to the new Fruity Controller, make sure that the formula says mouseX instead of mouseY in the Formula section of the Fruity Formula Controller. Now this parameter will be controlled by the X movement of the mouse (left to right), while the first setting (Y movement up and down) remains the same.

The knobs can be made to control custom parameters of your project, and the formulas for combining them again are located in the Help file. The different formulas can be typed into the Formula section, and if they are acceptable, after pressing Compile, you will get a message stating "Compiled OK," which lets you know that your formula worked.

The Meter tab will display the reaction of the plug-in in a graphical representation. Don't let the math part scare you, because the presets are typically what you will need, but I encourage you to try and enter in some of your own formulas and combinations. The possibilities are endless with this plug-in because you can link nearly anything, so your imagination is really your only limit. There are a few more controllers that we will take a look at, but definitely experiment with all of them and see which best suits your needs.

Fruity Limiter

We took a look at compression with the Fruity Compressor and what it can do for your music, so you should have a good foundation of knowledge on the subject at this point. The Fruity Limiter (see Figure 7.24) is similar, but it contains more features for fine-tuning a final mix or perfectly dialing in compression or limiting of your project. I prefer this plug-in when compressing pretty much any sound that needs it, and it works great as a final limiter for your overall

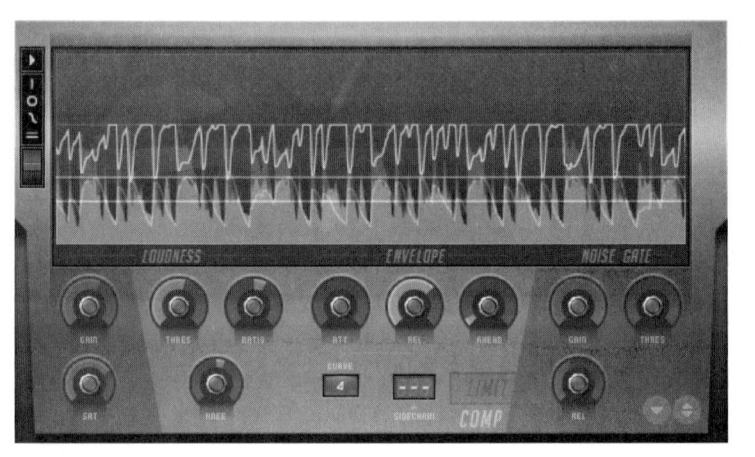

Figure 7.24   Fruity Limiter hard at work.

mix. For compression of certain frequencies, such as compressing the bass in someone's voice without affecting the rest of the vocal, you will want the multiband compressor, which we will look at later, but for now let's take a look at compressing and limiting signal with this powerful plug-in.

A good thing to understand is how the Fruity Limiter works and the order of operations that happens within it. When a signal goes into the Fruity Limiter, the first thing to affect the sound is the compressor, then the gain controls, then the limiter with the gate controls, and lastly the saturation setting before being sent to the output. It is good to know how this works just so you know why certain settings can change the sound based on the order in which they are adjusted.

The Limiter opens up on the limiter settings, which is not surprising being that it is the name of the plug-in, but to keep with the signal flow of the plug-in, we will start by looking at the compression settings. So that you aren't confused and stuck looking at the limiter settings, change it to compression settings by clicking the letters COMP that lie below the LIMIT letters on the plug-in.

The first knob you see is the Gain knob, which will affect the output of the compressor after compression has been placed on the input signal. So keeping with our signal path, this gain will determine the amount of signal that goes into the limiter. The Threshold, Ratio, and Knee knobs will set the compression parameters as discussed with the Fruity Compressor, and the Saturation knob is actually a threshold setting for saturation, so lowering it will increase the amount of saturation placed on your signal. This particular setting is very subtle and good to play with when precision-tuning your mixes.

The Envelope section is again an envelope for the compression, where the Attack and Release relate to the compression of the signal, but the severity of the attack and release slope is controlled by the Curve setting. Curve 1 will produce a steep slope, while Curve 8 will produce a relaxed slope.

Billing Address:
Frank M. Salinas
1181 Valelake Ct
Sunnyvale, CA 94089-2032
United States

SDNw4w6RFR

Shipping Address:
Frank M. Salinas
1181 Valelake Ct
Sunnyvale, CA 94089-2032
United States

Returns Are Easy!
Visit http://www.amazon.com/returns to return any item -including gifts- in unopened or original
condition within 30 days for a full refund (other restrictions apply)

Your order of November 13, 2009 (Order ID:102 — 1404861 — 1249846)

Qty	Item	Item Price	Total
	IN THIS SHIPMENT		
1	FL Studio Power!: The Comprehensive Guide (First Edition... (** P-2-I33B7 **) 1598639919 1598639919 1598639919 Paperback	$26.39	$26.39
1	Talk Is Cheap (** P-2-C9B19 **) B000000WGL B000000WGL B000000WGL Audio CD	$8.99	$8.99
1	Live at the Hollywood Palladium (December 15, 1988) (** P-1-A57H12 **) B000000WID B000000WID B000000WID Audio CD	$11.98	$11.98
1	Main Offender (** P-4-M25F4 **) B000000WJ2 B000000WJ2 B000000WJ2 Audio CD	$11.98	$11.98

Subtotal	$59.34
Shipping & Handling	$6.96
Order Total	$66.30
Paid via Visa	$66.30
Balance Due	$0.00

This shipment completes your order.

Have feedback on how we packaged your order? Tell us at www.amazon.com/packaging.

1671 (4 of 4)

SDNw4w6RFR

amazon.com
and you're done.

15/DNw4w6RFR/-4 of 4-//CP/std-n-us/5320480/1114-01.00/1113-18:17/sp112691671/1-1 1A3

The Sidechain box allows you to select a track to control the compression envelope. We discussed one way of creating sidechain compression earlier, but this option allows you to place a Fruity Limiter on a Mixer track and then select a different track to control the compression. Imagine that you have two tracks—one bass and one drums. In this example we will place the limiter on the bass track and then select the drum track, right-click the send on the bass track, and select Sidechain to This Track (see Figure 7.25). The reason for this is so that the kick will show up as an option in the sidechain list for the bass when we right-click the sidechain box (see Figure 7.26). Now when you adjust the compression threshold and ratio, it will start to affect the bass based on the signal coming in from the kick. Another cool thing to consider is that if you

Figure 7.25 Setting up sidechain compression with two tracks and the Limiter plug-in.

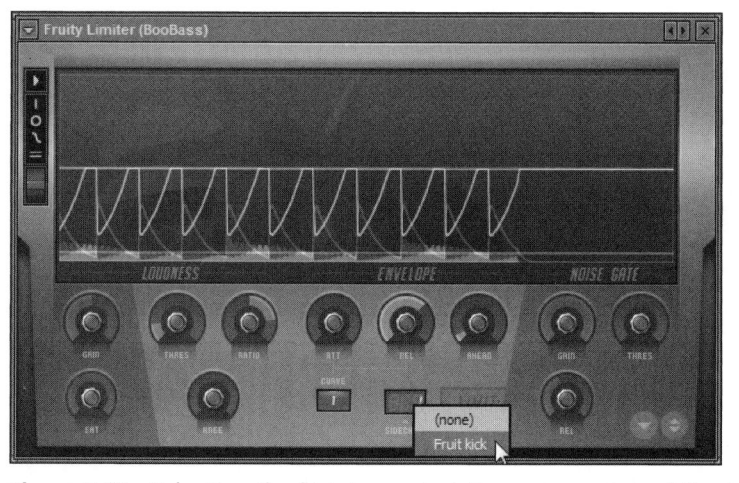

Figure 7.26 Selecting the kick to control the compression of the bass.

disable the send of the kick track to the master output, then you will only hear the bass affected by the kick signal, but the kick itself will not play.

Now let's look at the limiter settings, because the noise gate settings will still follow these in the signal path of the plug-in. Gain and Saturation will work in the same manner, but the Ceiling knob is the one to pay attention to here. The Ceiling setting will determine where the overall volume needs to be attenuated, or pulled down to prevent clipping or getting too loud. So if there is a part in your music that gets too loud for a brief moment, you can bring down the ceiling, and when the loud part plays, the actual volume will remain under the ceiling that you set. This is great for that final mix when you just need to make sure that no rogue sounds cause your audio to clip and you need to ensure that all of your songs play at the same volume.

The Envelope settings will react similarly to the Envelope settings of the compressor and will affect how the limiter reacts to the input signal. To only use this plug-in as a compressor without limiting, raise the ceiling to its maximum setting.

The final set of controls is the Noise Gate controls. These are very effective with single sounds because you can create a gate that stops sound from playing after it drops below a certain level (volume). The Gain control in this section will determine how much gating effect is placed on the output signal. The Threshold knob will tell the limiter when to let sound play and at what volume to stop playing it. The Release time affects how quickly the gate will close, so if you want the sound to gradually fade out, you can put a longer release on the gate, and this will produce that effect.

Try taking a single-hit sound and placing reverb on it (see Figure 7.27). Now open an instance of the Fruity Limiter and adjust the Gate effects. This is the best way to hear the gate in action. Typically, when there are a lot of sounds playing, the effect is not noticeable because there is always sound triggering the gate to open.

Figure 7.27 Here you can see the gating effect on a single sound that has a reverb tail on it.

The last section that I want to mention is all visual. The selections to the left of the Limiter will display the input and output peaks, analysis and gain envelopes, and level markers, and the bottom icon will allow you to adjust the scroll speed of the plug-in. One thing to take note of is that this plug-in will drain more power from your computer than the Fruity Compressor, but in my opinion, if your computer can handle it, this is the way to clean up your final mixes.

Fruity Love Philter

The Fruity Love Philter plug-in (see Figure 7.28) is arguably the most powerful effect plug-in available from FL Studio and can create a multitude of effects on your sound. Much like the Fruity Delay Bank, this filter has eight filter settings that can play into each other, allowing you to create an infinite amount of filtering, gating, and delay effects.

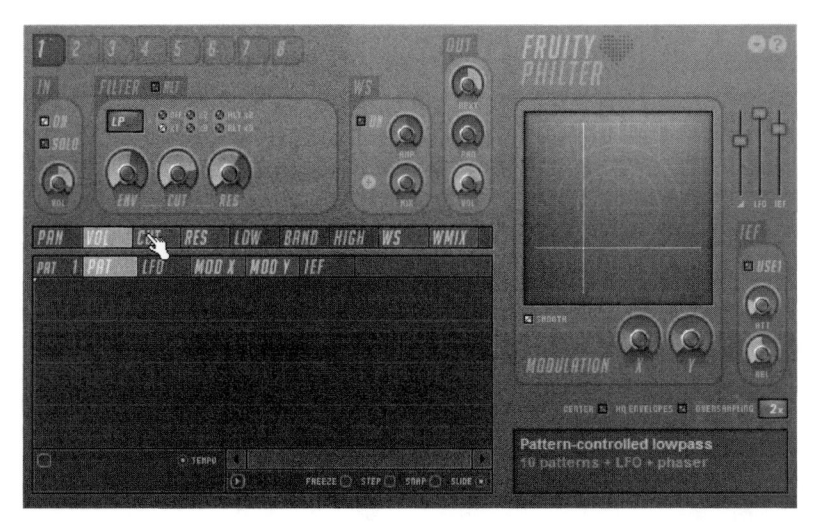

Figure 7.28 The Fruity Love Philter.

At the top of the plug-in are the different banks you can use to create your effects. By default the first two are turned on, so keep that in mind when adjusting your filter settings. Also remember that they play in order, so if you turn off the first bank, no audio will play out because this is essentially stopping the audio chain.

To hear a single bank, use the Solo switch in the Input section. The Filter section is similar to filters that we have dealt with already, with the x1, x2, and x3 settings causing the filters to be more severe as the multiplier goes up. The Waveshaper section (WS) will add distortion to the input signal, and the Amp setting will determine the amount of distortion, while Mix will mix the affected signal and the original signal.

The Out section applies to the currently selected filter, where Next will determine how much signal is sent to the next filter, Pan will determine the panning output of that filter, and Volume will determine the volume of that specific filter.

Below these settings are articulators similar to the ones that we explored with the Slicex plug-in. Most are familiar, aside from the Waveshaper (WS) and Waveshaper Mix (WMIX) selections. The Waveshaper selection allows you to create a distortion curve where the X-axis is the input and the Y-axis is the output, and the Waveshaper Mix will determine the blend between affected signal and original signal.

Try creating your own distortion curve for the Waveshaper and make sure that you enable the Waveshaper. You will most likely find many uses for this part of the plug-in, especially when using random sounds in your audio. This distortion can make a sound purposely jump out of a mix when you need it to stand out for a brief period in your project.

Beneath these articulators are settings that determine how the different modulators will affect the selected parameter (for example, using an LFO to determine panning of the selected filter). You can draw your own pattern using the pattern selection, and if you click and drag over the pattern number, it will change between the available 10 pattern slots that you can draw. The Mod X and Y selections will dictate how the XY controller that is also part of the plug-in will control the selected parameter. So in Figure 7.29, you can see that the panning has a sharp bend to the left when the X controller is moved from left to right along the X-axis.

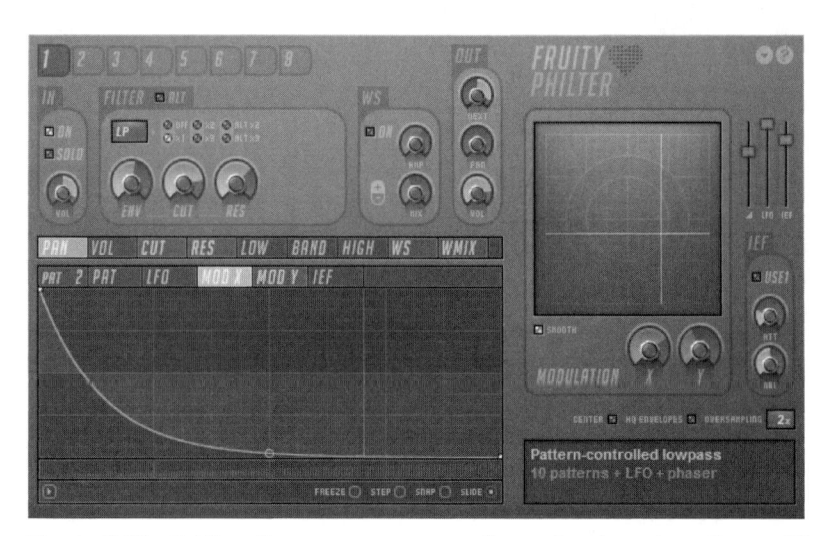

Figure 7.29 Setting the response curve of panning based on the position of the XY controller on the X-axis.

The IEF selection acts like a smoothing device for your envelope, and the harder your envelope attacks and releases, the more response you will see from this setting. An envelope follower will take the incoming signal and create an envelope based on the volume levels of the signal. So as the volume of the input increases, the changing envelope created will affect the selected parameter (such as panning or volume).

At the bottom left of the Envelope area is a menu that allows you to make some changes to the envelope itself (see Figure 7.30). The first set of options will allow you to open, save, copy, and paste an envelope state. This is great for when you have taken the time to build your own envelope and want to recall it for different projects. Flip Vertically will invert the current envelope that you have, and Scale Levels will allow you to pinpoint the envelope center point and tension of the curves and change the values of the envelope points.

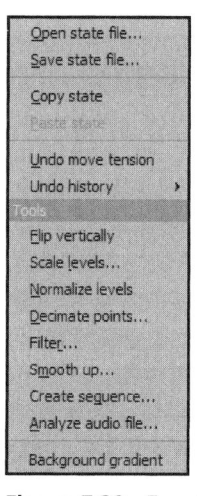

Figure 7.30 Envelope menu.

Normalize will work similar to how it does with audio, but rather than the volume reaching a peak amplitude target, the envelope's highest and lowest levels will reach that target. This quickly adjusts your envelope to create a more extreme effect. Decimate Points will let you determine the number of control points on your envelope, Filter will allow you to fine-tune the filter of your envelope, and Smooth Up will smooth abrupt changes and calm down any spikes in the envelope lines. Create Sequence will allow you to create a sequence for your envelope using the Envelope Sequencer tool, and Analyze Audio File will mimic the volume envelope of an input sound file.

To the right of this menu and below the envelope, you can choose Freeze to stop any editing of any envelopes, so when you have the sound you want, select this option so you don't accidentally change something that you didn't want changed. Step allows you to freely draw curves in the envelopes, while Snap will cause the envelope points to snap to the closest step when drawing your envelope curve. We discussed Slide before, but to reiterate, this option keeps the distance between control points relative to each other when moving them around. Disable this if you need to move a control point without the rest of them moving with it.

The XY controller is a built-in controller to which you can link different parameters, as in the example in Figure 7.29, where the panning of Filter Bank 1 is linked to the X-axis movement of the XY controller. The Input Envelope Follower section (IEF) has a toggle switch where you can have the output of the first filter be the signal that creates the envelope for your selected parameter. So if IEF is selected for panning, then choosing this option means that the output from the first filter will determine how the envelope controls the panning. Keep in mind that the IEF can work for any bank because it bases the created envelope off of the input signal so you can apply that envelope to the first bank as well. You can fine-tune the reaction of the IEF by adjusting the Attack and Release knobs. This is a big one to experiment with, because you can create a multitude of perfectly timed effects. Because the modulation is based on the input signal of the first filter or the general input, the modulation of the envelope will react to that signal, which basically keeps it in time with itself.

The final set of controls is at the top right, and the three faders allow you to control overall volume output, LFO amount, and IEF level. The big thing with this plug-in is to take your time. This is a very complex plug-in, but once you start to understand how the sound flows through it, you will be able to add incredible depth to your projects and will never be limited by what you can do with envelopes in FL Studio.

Fruity LSD

The Fruity LSD effect (see Figure 7.31) acts like a generator for MIDI files. It still needs to be inserted into a Mixer track as an effect, but it can receive MIDI and play sound using your soundcard's synthesizer. In my case, my Project Mix is just an audio interface, so the synth that is used is Microsoft's built-in MIDI synth. To get it to work properly, I had to open an instance of MIDI out and then send that MIDI signal to the LSD effect, and after properly routing the signal, I was able to hear the built-in synth play sounds based on the MIDI notes I placed in the Piano roll of the MIDI out instrument.

The LSD is typically what you will use to play MIDI files if they have specific instruments assigned to the MIDI notes. The Bank button at the top will open a window allowing you to change the DLS bank so that you can use a different bank for creating your sounds. Leave this setting as is if you do not have a DLS file that you want to specifically use.

Figure 7.31 Fruity LSD.

The Port window is where you link the MIDI out port and the LSD port so that the MIDI signal sent from the MIDI out generator properly makes it to the LSD effect plug-in. Don't use Port 0, though, because that is the main MIDI out of FL Studio and can cause a heap of trouble when trying to get your MIDI sounds to play properly. The 16 available channels contain instruments that can be changed by clicking on them and selecting from the list that pops up, but remember that if your MIDI out instrument is sending a certain instrument, then the LSD will automatically switch back to that instrument. So, change the instrument in the MIDI out, and the LSD plug-in will follow suit.

The last control is the main volume output of Fruity LSD. The drop-down menu will allow you to select the device you want to use for synthesis, and in my case I am only able to select the Microsoft Synthesizer. The Reverb and Chorus buttons are both global effects, but keep in mind that the chorus will not work with the Microsoft Synthesizer. As I like to reiterate, MIDI is *not* sound, so MIDI alone will not produce music without a synth using the MIDI information to trigger sound.

Fruity Multiband Compressor

The Fruity Multiband Compressor (see Figure 7.32) is my favorite tool for adjusting problem areas with certain frequencies. I prefer using multiband compression to an EQ in many different cases. Vocals is a big one—I don't like to remove frequencies with vocals, because it can create a muddy or lifeless sound. When you use a multiband compressor, you are merely attenuating certain frequency ranges so that they are not as pronounced by using compression. This plug-in works similarly to a compressor, but rather than compress the entire sound, the Multiband Compressor specifies certain frequencies that will receive amounts of compression. This is great when a sound is perfect but just has a little too much high end on it. By using the Multiband Compressor, it will calm the high-frequency response and give the sound a more relaxed EQ that brings the offending sound (frequency) down in volume.

Figure 7.32 The Fruity Multiband Compressor.

The first thing to think about when looking through the settings here is that the compression controls are no different than the compression controls for the Fruity Limiter or Fruity Compressor, but the three sets of the same controls that you see apply to the specific frequency ranges. They compress the lows, the mids, or the highs. The Limiter button is a quick setting that will not allow the Multiband Compressor output to go over 0 dB, which prevents clipping, but it is best to deal with your levels prior to adding a limiter so that the overall mix doesn't sound squished.

The Filter Type button will toggle between a Butterworth IIR filter (IIR) and a LinearPhase filter (FIR). The FIR setting is recommended for use with mastering your audio, and I invite you to investigate deeper into the filters, but be prepared for quite a bit of complicated math.

The Speed slider will determine the pace that the compressor visualization runs or, when all the way left, will display the frequency ranges. These frequency ranges for compression can be set by turning the frequency knobs located beneath the graphic display. These will tell the compressor what specific frequencies to compress when certain sections are active. Adjust these when the compression seems to be happening to too much or too little of a frequency range. For example, if you need heavy compression in the low end of your sound, but you don't want to cut out too much midrange, then try moving the low-frequency knob to the left a bit so that the low-frequency compression will happen to a smaller frequency range.

We know how the different knobs will affect the compression of the different frequency ranges, and now we know how to set those ranges, but what if we need to listen in to one frequency or have no effect on another? The buttons at the top of each compression section include Active (compression is working), Muted (the output of that frequency is turned off), and Bypass (the output is the original and is not affected by the compression for that frequency range). So if you need to listen to a specific range to find what needs to be compressed, then mute all but the needed range, and then you can adjust the frequency range knobs to include or exclude the sound you want.

If you need absolutely no compression on a certain frequency—for example, you only need compression of the lows—then you can bypass the mid and high frequencies, and only the selected low range will have compression applied to it. Trust me when I say that practicing with this plug-in will come in handy, because this is the plug-in that will add that extra crispness to your projects and can boost your mixes to a professional-sounding level when used properly.

Fruity NoteBook

The Fruity NoteBook (see Figure 7.33) is a cool plug-in that you will see used in many of the tutorial projects as well as the projects from the "cool stuff" folder, all found in the Browser (F8). This can be used to explain portions of a project, to display notes on a project for another

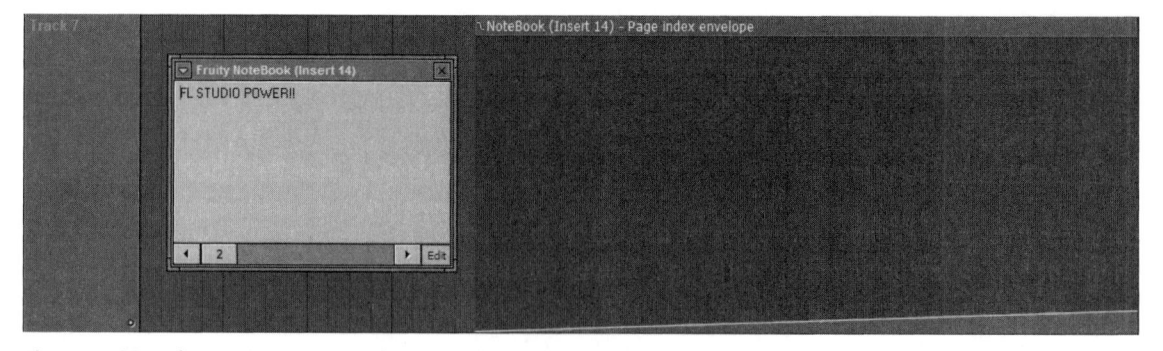

Figure 7.33 The Fruity NoteBook with an automation clip that gradually turns the pages.

artist who may be remixing your project, to leave yourself project notes for reminders, or even as a fun way to pass the time. All you have to do is right-click the page turner button and choose Create Automation Clip, and the line will represent pages as it goes up the Y-axis. Draw in your control points to tell the NoteBook when to change pages. I found that I was even able to create a small animation using typing characters and quick page turning, but I was forced to come to terms with my nerdiness and move on. This is a great plug-in for conveying messages that react to your automation clip and making projects appear well put together when the page turning is in time with the music. If the pages are turning too quickly, you can use the automation clip channel Min/Max settings to slow down the page turning in the Piano roll automation clip editor.

One final tip is that you can right-click the control points in the automation clip for the NoteBook to select Hold Point mode from the list. This will allow you to edit the automation in steps. Remember that none of this is necessary for improving your music—it is just for fun or function and will in no way affect the sound of your project.

Fruity Parametric EQ

This is the light version of FL Studio's parametric EQ, but it works great for quick EQ changes to your audio (see Figure 7.34). This plug-in is not resource intensive, so it will not be a drain on your computer when active. This makes it easy to dial in your EQing, because you can stack instances of this plug-in to give you greater control over your EQ settings.

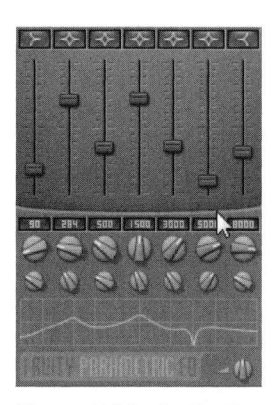

Figure 7.34 Fruity Parametric EQ.

The sliders will affect the amount of frequency that is played to the main output for the track that has the parametric EQ. The top row contains different band settings, allowing you to create a low pass or high pass so only those frequencies play. Here you can automate the controls to achieve that old radio effect by taking out the bass and some of the higher frequencies for the effect and then bringing the levels back to normal when you want the sound to play as it originally sounded.

The larger knobs below the sliders will affect where the frequency is pinpointed, so if you need to boost the midrange in a different area, move one of these knobs until the pinpoint is at the frequency you want. The smaller knobs beneath those are the bandwidth knobs, commonly referred to as the Q. This determines how much of a certain frequency is affected by the height of the sliders, so if you are trying to isolate a certain frequency and notch out an undesirable sound, you can turn this knob to the right, and it will create a narrow area that drops when you lower the Frequency slider.

The graphic representation of the EQ can be used by left-clicking to move the center point of a frequency (dragging left to right) and right-clicking (and moving left to right) to change the bandwidth, while both will move the Frequency slider amount up and down. Remember to experiment using automation with this plug-in, because you may find that creating the sound you want only requires a little EQ adjustment that you are able to draw in the Playlist.

Fruity Parametric EQ 2

Fruity Parametric EQ 2 (see Figure 7.35) is the big brother to the Fruity Parametric EQ and will do the same essential functions as the parametric EQ, but it offers high-quality options that will strain performance. Don't fear using this plug-in, though, because unless you are near the minimum requirements or you have a ton of plug-ins running, it shouldn't be an issue.

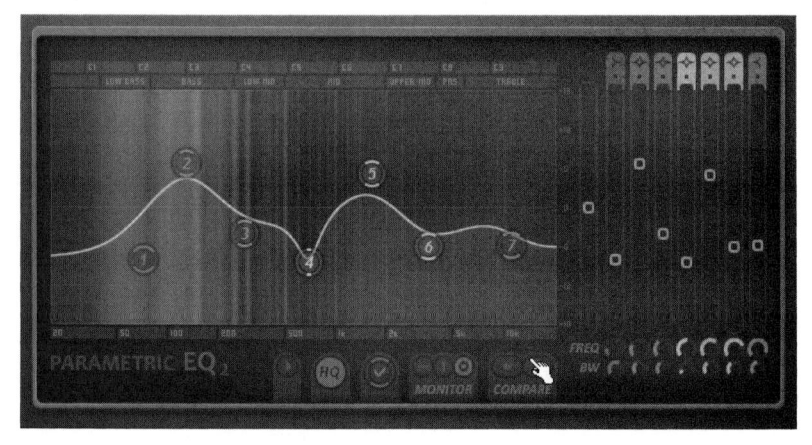

Figure 7.35   Fruity Parametric EQ 2.

A huge advantage to using this EQ is that you can see incoming and outgoing frequencies represented by spectral monitoring, so when a frequency is playing with intensity, there will be more graphics playing with the music in that specific range. So if you have a deep kick drum and you place the Parametric EQ 2 on that track, then you will see activity in the low end of the spectrum from the spectral monitor. The top-right multicolored buttons will allow you to select the band type and slope for the particular "token" that is represented by the same color on the graph. Below that are the Frequency sliders, and below that are the frequency center points and the bandwidth.

This section will most often be used to adjust the bandwidth because the actual tokens in the spectrum on the left side can be clicked and dragged to any point. For intricate adjustments, hold the Ctrl key while adjusting knobs, and you will get more precise value changes.

At the bottom are the Options menu, which will open up information on the plug-in, and the high-precision Monitor setting, which will increase the resolution of the spectral monitoring. (Keep in mind that this affects performance slightly.)

The HQ button will also affect performance, but it will increase the overall audio output quality. View Band Tokens will remove the large tokens, but you will still be able to see the frequency center points. The Monitor switch allows you to change between no visual monitoring and a visual of the input or output signal.

A great way to use this plug-in is to just drag the tokens to roughly where you want the EQ to be and then fine-tune using the bandwidth and band types. The EQ can also be automated using the sliders on the right, so getting a dynamic change in frequency is actually very simple.

Fruity Peak Controller

The Fruity Peak Controller (see Figure 7.36) is another one of the internal controllers available in FL Studio, and a useful example can be found in the "Sidechain Compression" sidebar earlier in this chapter, but here we will look more closely at the features and abilities of this plug-in.

Figure 7.36   Fruity Peak Controller.

The Fruity Peak Controller can be looked at as a plug-in that uses the signal of an input, its own internal LFO (see "What Is an LFO?" in Chapter 6), or the combination of both to control something. One of the more common uses is the sidechain compression that we discussed, but it can control nearly every parameter in FL Studio. The peak control is the upper half, and the LFO settings make up the bottom half of the effect plug-in.

The first thing to pay attention to with this plug-in is the Mute switch, because it will silence the input signal. This is on by default, so unless you are only using a signal to control a parameter (such as a kick drum used to compress a bass signal, but the kick is never heard), then uncheck this option to unmute the track that has the peak controller.

The Peak Control section in the upper part has a Base knob that will determine the base value of the peak controller. This is useful when you need to specify a range that the peak controller will react to, such as a volume range of an instrument that will send signal.

The Volume knob will determine how the peaks of volume from the input signal will affect the controller. So if the input volume is not producing the desired effect, try raising or lowering the Volume knob to have more or less signal affecting the peak controller.

The green box with the line running through it is the tension level. This will affect how the input volume reacts to the peak controller and can give you sharper or duller response, depending on what you need.

The Decay knob will determine how long it takes the peak controller to stop controlling a parameter after the input signal stops or drops below the base range.

The three bars to the left are visual representations of what is going on with the peak controller. The first bar is the input signal, the second bar is the peak controller value, and the third is the LFO. Think of the peak controller and LFO bars as knob positions. When they are at the top, they are at maximum, and when they are at the bottom, they are at minimum. So if you have the input signal going up and down, the peak controller value will also go up and down, and for whatever you have linked to it, that knob will go from its highest point to its lowest point. This is just a generalization, and the settings that you make will determine how the peak controller values react to the input signal, but this is the basic idea.

The LFO section allows you to use an LFO to affect the controller value, so if you need a panning effect to continuously go from left to right, then you can set up an LFO and link the panning to the LFO (not the peak) of the Fruity Peak Controller. In this case you are not using the input signal at all.

The five LFO shapes to choose from include Sine, Triangle, Square, Saw, and Random. The Base knob is similar to the peak control Base knob and will set a range for the controller to react to the LFO, while the Volume knob will adjust the amplitude of the LFO.

The Tension section is identical to the peak tension and will determine the curve that is used to link LFO values to the LFO controller values, so try adjusting this knob for a more dramatic effect. The Speed wheel will determine the speed of the LFO, and the Phase wheel will tell the LFO where to start.

The Ramp switch helps to remove clicks and pops if you are hearing them in your audio from abrupt changes from the controller.

Fruity Phaser

The Fruity Phaser (see Figure 7.37) is very similar to the Fruity Flanger because it also uses multiple delayed versions of the incoming signal, but the phaser creates a sweeping effect that has more impact on your sound.

Adding a phaser to a vocal right before a breakdown or to an instrument that plays in the background can produce impressive results. Again, remember that adding that little extra to your

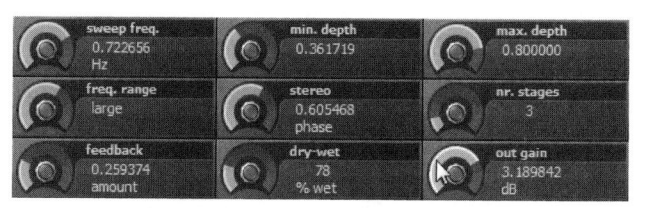

Figure 7.37 The Fruity Phaser.

projects can push them well above the rest of the music out there, and I highly recommend experimenting with this plug-in!

The Sweep Frequency knob allows you to choose the frequency of the LFO that will control the phaser. The available values of this knob depend on the frequency range setting. The Min and Max Depth settings will determine the range in which the phaser operates, and the Frequency Range, as mentioned before, will determine the available values for the Sweep Frequency knob, where a small setting allows for a range of 0 to 2 Hz, and a large setting allows for a range between 0 and 10 Hz.

The Stereo knob will set the synchronization of the left- and right-channel LFOs, which can create a wider sound in your mix. The Stages knob will determine the number of phasing stages active on your sound. For a subtle effect, keep this number low, and for really wild phasing, you can crank this number up to 23.

Feedback is the amount of signal that gets returned to the phaser, and when turned up to a higher number, it can create a more intense effect on the sound. The Dry-Wet knob will mix between the original sound and the processed output (wet). The Out Gain knob will increase the volume of the output signal, so if the effect is right but not quite loud enough, turn it up here. Remember that this will not affect the phaser effect, and it only controls the output volume of the already affected signal.

Fruity Reeverb

Reverb is a way to create space in your music. If you have ever recorded your voice and played it back, in the mix it sounds like it is a person talking right next to you, rather than blending in with the rest of the music. In a large auditorium, when you yell, you hear your voice repeat because sound waves bounce off of surfaces and reflect until they are absorbed by the walls. Each time the sound waves bounce off of a surface, that surface takes some of the volume off of the sound. If you were to yell in a small room versus a large room, you would get very different reverberations because the sound waves travel at a constant speed, so when they bounce off of a surface more quickly (as is the case in a small room) and return to you, you get the sense that you are in that small room. Even in pitch black, you can tell roughly how big a room is by yelling and listening for the sound waves to bounce back.

The Fruity Reeverb plug-in (see Figure 7.38) takes the sound and adds that reverb so that it sounds more natural and closer to a live sound. Reverb is great for many different instruments as well as vocals and can be used on any sound that you feel needs it. Before plug-ins like these and their hardware counterparts existed, to get reverb in the vocals, record companies would set up a speaker in a long underground tunnel that ran beneath the studio. A mic was placed in the tunnel to record the vocals as they played through the speaker, and they bounced all over the tunnel. This was mixed with the original vocal recording and is the premise of how reverb works today.

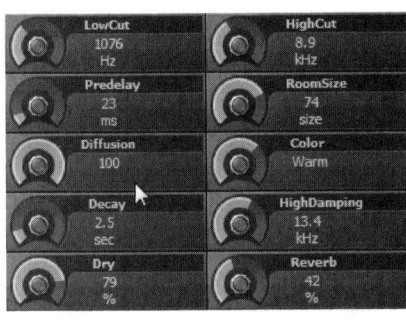

Figure 7.38   Fruity Reeverb.

We no longer need tunnels and a wild array of equipment; we can create our reverb simply by adding this plug-in to a track. In my personal opinion, unless you need specific reverb for a specific sound, you can insert reverb on one of the send tracks and send any of the tracks to the reverb track to add reverb to it. This also helps create a uniform reverb sound with your mix.

The LowCut and HighCut will allow you to EQ the reverb output, so if you are getting a booming sound in the reverb, adjust the LowCut to a higher setting until the deeper sound is gone.

Predelay allows you to tell the reverb to wait a specified amount of time before activating the first reverberation. This can help you create a huge room sound, but it can also cause the sound to overlap and create an unpleasant result. Usually I leave this set to a low value or zero unless I specifically need a sound to wait before starting to reverberate.

The RoomSize setting will shape the sound of the reverb and is great for creating a big room sound or giving your sound a more intimate (small room) feel. Diffusion will cause you to go from being able to hear the individual reflections to hearing a seeming white noise where the reflections are indistinguishable.

The Color setting will affect how much bass is in the reverb, where a bright room takes out some of the bass and a warm room leaves it in. The Decay is how long the reverb will play until it is inaudible, but it is good to note that a small room with a long reverb (decay) will not sound natural, so adjust between RoomSize and Decay accordingly.

HighDamping emulates a room that absorbs the higher frequencies and gives the reverb a warmer, murky sound, so if you want all of your high end in the reverb, set this all the way to the right, and the damping will turn off.

The Dry knob will determine how much of the original signal plays through, and it is good to remember to lower this to zero if you're using the reverb on a send track so that you only have reverb playing out of the send.

The Reverb knob will set the amount of reverb (wet signal) that will play through the output of the plug-in. Reverb will make any vocal sound better within reason, so try experimenting with adding subtle amounts to different parts of your projects, and you will see how useful this effect is in music. Keep in mind that reverb is an effect that is easily overdone and can be the culprit of washed out, muddy tracks when every track has reverb on it.

Fruity Reeverb 2

Now that we have taken a good look at what reverb is and how it works, we can look at the updated version of FL Studio's reverb effect. The Fruity Reeverb 2 effect (see Figure 7.39) is particularly helpful in understanding how the settings of the reverb work because of the room graphic spinning on the left side of the plug-in. The size of it changes (representing room size), the number of walls varies (representing diffusion), and the colors even change (indicating a frequency change or adjustment in delay).

Figure 7.39 Fruity Reeverb 2.

The Mid/Side switch will allow you to toggle between MID processing, which is a left and right signal summed into a mono signal, and SIDE processing, which will allow for stereo control of the signal. Keep in mind that if you have a mono signal coming into the reverb, choosing SIDE will not do anything, so a vocal recorded with one mic will usually require the MID setting. For most of your reverb needs, the MID processing will work just fine.

The knobs bear a striking resemblance to those in Fruity Reverb and control the same reverb adjustments. Remember that these settings don't affect the dry sound; they only affect the wet output of the reverb.

HighCut (H.CUT) will take out the brightness of the reverb and give the audio a clouded sound. The LowCut (L.CUT) knob will remove the low-frequency noise in the reverb, so if your reverb has a deep thundering sound or even a random low bass note, adjust the LowCut to a higher setting until the noise is gone.

The Predelay (DEL) knob for this plug-in has a switch next to it that will allow you to make the predelay adhere to the project tempo. This can create a cool effect when you choose this and then have a long predelay setting, because the following reverb will wait a set amount of time, but those numbers will be linked to the tempo. This means that if you have a setting of 2 for the Predelay knob and then you increase it to 6, the reverb will delay a great deal more, but it will still be in sync with the tempo when it plays. Using the predelay with a sharp-sounding or fast and short synth can give the instrument a call-and-response type of sound, because the note plays and then the reverb follows later, while keeping in time. To really get creative, you can even create an automation clip of the predelay so the reverb responds to the initial sound at different times.

The Room Size knob (SIZE) will give the reverb a bigger sound, while the Diffusion knob (DIFF) will control the number of reflections in the reverb. As the reflections go higher, the sound blends into a white noise, and each reflection disappears into another.

The Bass Response knob (BASS) will give your reverb a warmer or thinner sound by increasing or decreasing the lower frequencies. The Bass Crossover knob (CROSS) will pinpoint the lower frequencies that the Bass Response will boost or quiet. So if you wanted a more intense and bass-filled reverb, you could turn up the BASS knob and set the CROSS knob to roughly 50 Hz.

The Decay knob (DEC) controls how long you hear the reverb, and the High Dampening knob (DAMP) will determine how quickly the high frequencies leave the reverb sound. So if you want your reverb to last a bit, but you want the higher sounds to leave quickly, this knob should be turned to the left. If you don't want any of the high end to get cut out of the reverb, turn it all the way to the right, and it will turn the dampening off.

The Dry slider will control the amount of original signal (dry) that is mixed with the final output of the plug-in. The Early Reflections slider (ER) will determine when the first reflections occur in the reverb, and the Wet slider will control the amount of processed signal (amount of reverb) that will play through the output.

The Stereo Separation knob will allow you to widen the reverb sound or bring it into the center. Take the time to explore this plug-in, because you will find many uses for it when trying to get that natural sound to your mixes, especially with band recordings and vocals.

Fruity Scratcher

The Fruity Scratcher (see Figure 7.40) is a cool plug-in to quickly scratch a sound that you might have by using your mouse to perform the scratching. You can set the sensitivity, so the speed that your mouse moves won't matter. You will get the most use out of this when scratching vocals, instrument hits, or other short sounds. Loading a full song into here works, but not very well, so stick with shorter samples.

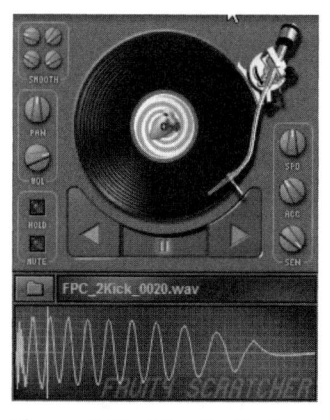

Figure 7.40 The Fruity Scratcher.

The four smoothing options will allow you to adjust the sound that the Scratcher outputs when affecting the signal. So for a grittier, less natural sound, try lowering these knobs.

The Pan and Volume knobs both affect the master output of the plug-in, and the Hold light will indicate when the record is being held, or it can be clicked to stop the sound from playing. The Mute switch will turn off the output of the effect, which can be helpful when you are getting sound trailing from the record not completely stopping.

The record itself can be controlled to scratch the sample by left-clicking and dragging up and down or by left-clicking on the waveform where the sample is located and dragging left to right.

The green buttons beneath the record are reverse playback, pause, and forward playback controls. When in Play mode, the sound will still stop if you click on the record and begin to scratch, but it will continue playing after you release the mouse button.

The Speed button (SPD) will determine how fast the sample plays back, and the Acceleration knob (ACC) will control how fast the turntable accelerates up to the speed you set. The Sensitivity (SEN) is where you set how fast the turntable will move based on the mouse movement, so if you feel like you are flying over a sample too quickly, lower this knob.

The lower portion of the plug-in is where you can see the waveform of the sample that you will be scratching. The folder icon allows you to load any sample that you have on your computer in the event that the sound you need is outside of FL Studio. Within FL Studio, you can drag any sound into the sample window. This is a great tool for simple scratching, but for serious manipulation and precise scratching, use the WaveTraveller.

Fruity Squeeze

The Fruity Squeeze (see Figure 7.41) is a fun plug-in that can add mild character or completely destroy the input signal and create a broken transistor sound where it cuts in and out. This is a fun one to randomly add to vocals or the entire mix to create a brief grit effect.

Figure 7.41 Fruity Squeeze.

Squarize will cause the sound to get grittier and choppier as you turn up the dial, while lowering this will smooth out the effect. The Preserve knob will control how much of the sound (in samples) is left unaffected by the plug-in, and the Impact knob will determine how much of the sound (in samples) is pushed to a nominal level.

The Relation knob allows you to select the ratio of impact samples to preserve samples, and adjusting this will move the Impact knob based on the Preserve setting. The Amount knob will determine how much effect the other Puncher settings will have on the sound, so if you have this turned all the way up, you won't hear any change when adjusting the Puncher settings.

The Filter settings allow you to place a filter on the plug-in output, and you can select the filter type by clicking in the small box and dragging up and down and then adjusting the Frequency and Resonance knobs to taste.

The Pre and Post switch will allow you to insert the filter before the puncher (Pre) or after the puncher (Post). The Mix slider will control the amount of original signal versus processed signal that plays out of the main output of the plug-in, and the Gain slider will control the final output volume. Keep this one at the ready, because there are plenty of situations in which the broken sound can come in handy when putting together creative electronic music or even sound designing for a movie.

Fruity Stereo Enhancer and Stereo Shaper

Both of these plug-ins allow you to affect the stereo image of your sound, and we will look at the simple version first. The Stereo Enhancer (see Figure 7.42) will allow you to create a basic stereo widening effect by using phase offset between the left and right channels. The Stereo Separation knob will determine the amount of separation placed on your sound, where all the way to the left will be a mono output, the middle will leave the sound unaffected, and the extreme right will add maximum separation.

Figure 7.42 The Fruity Stereo Enhancer.

When Pre is selected, the phase offset effect will be applied prior to the other parameters affecting the sound in the plug-in, whereas Post will cause the phase offset to be applied after the sound has been altered.

The Phase Offset setting will allow you to delay the phase of the left and right channels up to 500ms. For a simple stereo widening effect, move this knob slightly left or right rather than a large amount. (Try a setting between 20 and 40 ms.)

The Invert switch will allow you to invert the phase of the left or right channel and turn off the inversion effect when None is selected. The Pan and Volume knobs are for the main output of the plug-in. This plug-in can be placed on a mono signal, such as a guitar that was recorded through a mic or with a direct input, and by bumping the Phase Offset a small amount, you can give your guitar a richer sound.

The Fruity Stereo Shaper (see Figure 7.43) is a more flexible version of the Stereo Enhancer and definitely takes time to fully understand. The idea is that the stereo image of a sound is made up of left, center, and right, where the center channel is the combined left and right channels mixed into a mono signal that will output as left and right but be identical, thus creating the "center" feel to the sound.

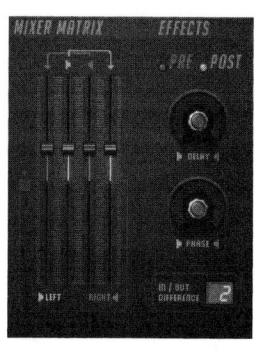

Figure 7.43   The Fruity Stereo Shaper.

The Matrix sliders from left to right will control the right channel amount that feeds into the left channel, the left channel volume, the right channel volume, and the left channel amount that feeds into the right channel. Pre and Post settings will cause the Delay and Phase knobs to have effect prior to the stereo matrix (Pre) or after the sound passes through the stereo matrix (Post).

The Delay knob will delay the left or right channel, depending on which way it is turned, and the Phase knob will control the phase offset of the left and right channels. The Sidechain Out option can be used to send a sidechained signal to a selected Mixer track so that the difference in signal between the original sound and the processed sound plays through the sidechain track.

The presets for this plug-in will typically be all that you need to create the sound you desire, but make sure you experiment with the settings so that you familiarize yourself with how the phases can create the stereo-widening effect. To dig deeper into the math involved with this plug-in, press F1 while the plug-in is highlighted, and you can see the formulas used to create the stereo imaging. For a speedy stereo widening of a guitar or vocal, select Delay from the Preset menu, and you will immediately hear a difference.

Fruity Vocoder

The Fruity Vocoder (see Figure 7.44) is a popular effect used on vocals in many different types of music today. The Vocoder by itself will not do anything, because it processes two or more incoming signals to create the plug-in output. The two signals include the modulator (the sound used for vocoding), which is usually a human voice, and the carrier (the sound being vocoded), which is usually a synthesizer. The way it all works is that the Vocoder detects certain frequencies in the modulator and filters the carrier based on these detections. This causes the carrier to take on characteristics of the modulated sound. This is how we can get synths to have a voice in them or give our voices a synthy sound, however you see it. First we'll take a look at the features of the Vocoder, and then we'll look at a specific example using our own voice.

Figure 7.44 Fruity Vocoder.

The Formant slider will affect the pitch of the vocoder-modulator to vocoder-band relationship. Slide this up and down for a more feminine or masculine sound. Adjust these Min and Max knobs to set a frequency range for the output of the plug-in.

The Scale knob will determine where the frequency center point is, so sliding this left will give your output more low end, and sliding it right will give you more high end.

Invert will switch the modulator frequencies, so if you are getting a low-frequency response, a quick way to get a high response is to select Invert, and the frequency of the modulator will invert.

The Bandwidth knob will determine the number of frequencies that are allowed to output from the carrier sound and can be great for tweaking the output to get just the right sound.

The Envelope knobs are fade-in (Attack) and fade-out (Release) controls for the envelopes of the different frequencies to which the modulator responds. The Mix sliders allow you to change the amount of dry signal from the modulator and carrier that plays in the final output, and by clicking the L and R buttons, you can quickly swap the modulator and the carrier to get a completely different sound.

The Hold button will allow you to freeze the modulator signal while the carrier signal still holds. Automating this can create an awesome stopping effect with a vocal that holds the words, but the carrier that is creating the melody continues playing.

The Bands selection will determine the output quality of your overall sound, but a low Bands setting can give your modulator a gritty sound to it and is worth experimenting with.

The last set of options allows you to select between different filters, and selecting a larger number will produce more rigid frequency response.

Let's look at how we can do this with our own projects! Start by naming three tracks in the Mixer (F2), where the first track is Modulator, the second is Carrier, and the third is the Vocoder (see Figure 7.45).

Figure 7.45   Setting up the Modulator, Carrier, and Vocoder tracks.

Now turn off the send to the master for the Modulator and Carrier tracks and route both the Modulator and Carrier to the Vocoder. The way that the Vocoder works is that it combines the left input as the modulator and the right input as the carrier, so after routing these, pan the Modulator track to the left and the Carrier track to the right.

Now insert an instance of the Vocoder on the Vocoder track, and everything will be routed properly. In an empty sampler channel, insert an instance of 3xOSC and link the 3xOSC channel to the Carrier track (Shift+L when the track and channel are highlighted).

Now draw a few notes in the Piano roll of the 3xOSC (see Figure 7.46). When you hit Play, you should see signal in the Vocoder track, but you won't hear any sound because there is no modulator to help produce an output.

Now on the Modulator track, select the input that you are using for a mic and press Play. Now when you speak into the mic, you can hear that your voice is causing the 3xOSC to mold with your voice. Try adding more instruments and linking them to the Carrier track for even more complex sounds.

Remember that this is only one example of how to use the Vocoder, and I suggest trying multiple instruments separately and combining them to get new sounds. Try adjusting the band settings to get a choppier sound with low bands and a more defined sound with higher bands. This

![Screenshot of FL Studio showing the Piano roll, 3xOSC, Fruity Vocoder, and mixer windows]

Figure 7.46 Drawing notes in the Piano roll of 3xOSC that will ultimately affect the Modulator signal.

plug-in can give your vocals that awesome effect that is very popular in many different types of music, and each instrument you use will affect the vocals differently. You can even sing in a monotone voice and use the Carrier (instrument) to give melody to your voice from the notes drawn in the Piano roll.

Wave Candy

Wave Candy is a visualization plug-in that allows you to analyze your sound based on looking at an oscilloscope, spectrum analyzer, peak meter, and vectorscope (see Figure 7.47). The visualizations will give you accurate readings of what the different frequencies in your mix are doing and can be very useful in the mixing and mastering stages of music creation in FL Studio.

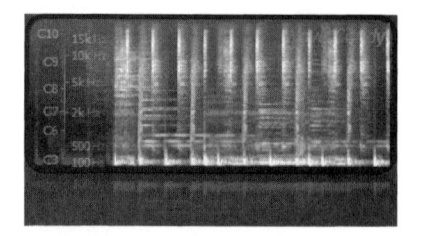

Figure 7.47 Wave Candy.

Remember that this is a visualization plug-in, so your sound will not be affected by the plug-in—rather, the appearance of the plug-in will be affected by the sound. With all visualizations, you have options to adjust the window of Wave Candy so that it is small, opaque, or even has a blurred effect when using Vista. You can also set the background color of the visualization in the Background section of the plug-in. The only options that change when selecting between the different visualizations will be specific to the chosen visualization. These options will allow you to fine-tune the accuracy of the visualization as it relates to the sound playing through the plug-in. When you are first experimenting with this plug-in, a great place to start is by inserting it on the Selected Mixer channel.

Fruity Wave Shaper

The Fruity Wave Shaper is a distortion effect that determines how strong a signal will play based on the input and the curve setting that you create on the graph (see Figure 7.48). The X-axis represents the input, while the Y-axis represents the output. When signal is playing into the plug-in, you will see a thin white line that moves to the right as the input signal gets louder.

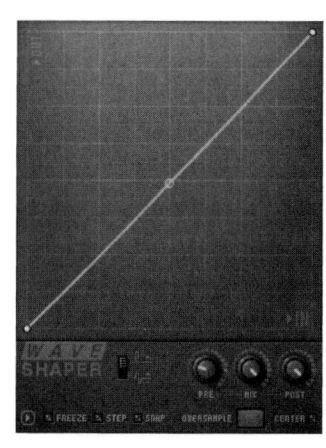

Figure 7.48 The Fruity Wave Shaper.

A quick way to understand the relationship between the X and Y axes is to place the Wave Shaper on your master track and then adjust the curve. Start by dragging the middle point down so that the curve takes a while to move up the Y-axis (see Figure 7.49).

The input increases while the output stays the same longer, rather than the two increasing at the same rate. Because it takes more power from the input signal to get the same output, distortion is introduced into the overall sound.

The Unipolar mode will cause the bottom of the graph to be 0 dB for the signal, and the Bipolar setting will cause the middle of the graph to be 0 dB, allowing for offsetting the signal in reverse by dropping it below the 0-dB setting.

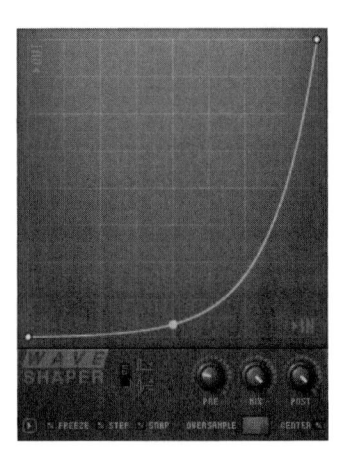

Figure 7.49 Adjusting the Wave Shaper curve.

The Pre knob will determine how much signal goes into the plug-in from the original. Mix will control the amount of input signal versus processed (wet) signal, and Post is the final volume output.

The bottom row includes a Freeze option, which will prevent further editing of the curve; Step, which will allow freehand drawing of a curve; and Snap, which will cause any control points that you draw to snap to the graph grid lines.

Oversample will improved the quality of the effect and can remove pops and clicks in some instances, and the Center toggle switch will remove DC offset from the output of the plug-in. This is one of the stranger plug-ins from FL Studio, but don't be afraid to randomly place it on a vocal or an instrument and automate the Mix knob to create warped effects on your sounds.

Fruity XY Controller

The Fruity XY Controller (see Figure 7.50) is another of FL Studio's internal controllers that you can map to nearly any parameter in FL Studio. What I love about this plug-in is that if you have a joystick controller (even one resembling a videogame controller) and it connects to your computer, you can map the X-axis controls of the XY Controller to the X-axis controls of your joystick, and the same applies to the Y-axis. This makes creating a simple surround-stereo fade-in/out very easy and practical because you can link the Y-axis to volume and the X-axis to panning. By linking these controls, you can spin the position of the crosshairs in the XY in a circle, and the sound will respond as if you are creating a surround pan, because as you increase the Y-axis, the volume gets louder (as if you are getting closer), and as you increase the X-axis, the signal will pan right (as though the signal is moving to your right side).

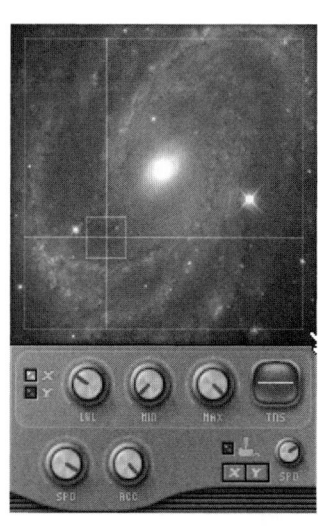

Figure 7.50   The Fruity XY Controller.

Remember that this is only an example for when you link the volume and panning of the same track—the X and Y axes can be linked to anything! The X and Y buttons in the plug-in will determine which settings you are affecting when adjusting the Level, Min/Max, and Tension settings.

The Speed wheel and Acceleration wheel both affect the movement speed of the crosshairs on the XY Controller graph, but the Speed wheel determines the overall top speed of the cursor, and Acceleration will control how fast that top speed is reached. If you want to use a joystick or an external controller that has XY capability, highlight the joystick box, and a menu will pop up allowing you to select your joystick. After selecting your joystick, you can choose which parts of the joystick will control the X and Y axes, and the joystick Speed knob will set the sensitivity of the plug-in to your joystick.

Remember that if you are using a MIDI keyboard that has faders, you can link the X-axis Level knob to one fader and the Y-axis Level knob to another fader, which will give you the same control without the need for a joystick.

The final cool feature that I want to mention with the XY Controller is that you can change the background as I did in Figure 7.50 by right-clicking anywhere in the graph and selecting a background from the menu.

Soundgoodizer

The Soundgoodizer (see Figure 7.51) is a multi-band maximizer that uses presets from Maximus for bringing out the best in your sound, and the best part is that it is simple! The settings for the Soundgoodizer are based on presets for the Maximus plug-in, which we will briefly discuss in the next chapter. The four available presets should each be tried when you are trying to boost the overall sound, because the best judge of what sounds good is your own ears.

Figure 7.51 The Soundgoodizer.

Clicking and dragging the dial in the middle of the Soundgoodizer will add or subtract the effect. I have found that placing this on a master track is a quick way to brighten up or thicken your mix, and it works well for creating more depth with many different sounds, including vocals. Try adding the Soundgoodizer to what you considered to be a final mix, and the results may surprise you.

Vocodex

The Vocodex plug-in (see Figure 7.52) operates with the same idea as the Fruity Vocoder, but it allows for more flexibility and options. In this version you can use a single track, set the input of the track to be your mic and use a preset from the immediate section in the Vocoder menu, and use your MIDI keyboard (or even the Typing Keyboard to Piano Keyboard option—Ctrl+T) to instantly affect your vocals! (See Figure 7.53.) This is possible because the Vocodex plug-in has a built-in synth that acts as a carrier for the modulation signal (your voice).

If you want to get more precise using the Piano roll or the Stepsequencer, then you will want to add a Mod track like in the Fruity Vocoder example, but this time have the output of the Mod track sidechain to the Vocoder. (With the Mod track selected, right-click on the Send button on the Vocodex track and choose Sidechain to This Track.)

Remember to disable the Mod send to the master track so that the original signal doesn't make it to the mix, because if you want the original to blend in, you can use the settings of the Vocodex. Now send the output of your carrier (instrument or channel making the sound) to Vocodex by linking that channel to the Vocodex Mixer track directly rather than using the Send knob. The more you use this plug-in, the more you will get familiar with its features and realize just how powerful it is.

Many of the features have similar effects that have been discussed in other effects plug-ins descriptions and the "Fruity Vocoder" section, but there are a few settings that are specific to Vocodex. The first slider that you see is a Soundgoodizer slider (SG) that is integrated into the

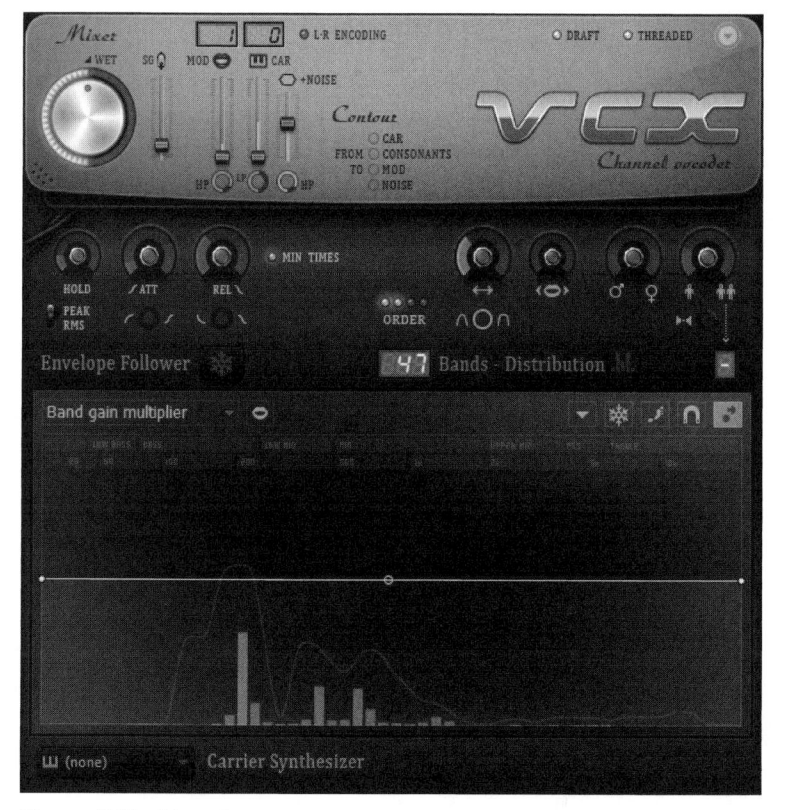

Figure 7.52 Vocodex.

plug-in. If your output has the perfect tone and frequency but is peaking too loud and causing clipping, the Soundgoodizer can help add the right compression to prevent these audio spikes.

The L.R. Encoding toggle switch will cause Vocodex to act like the Fruity Vocoder and will use the left channel as the modulator and the right channel as the carrier if this is easier or makes more sense to you. Once you understand how the Vocodex works, though, I doubt you will ever need this selection.

The Noise slider will add general noise to the carrier signal if it is not rich enough. Increase this slider value when you want the different sounds of your voice, such as S and T sounds, to output with more clarity.

You'll learn much about this plug-in by changing settings and listening to the end result, because the settings are all going to be your preference. Much like the Vocoder plug-in, try sending in multiple carriers to create a more complex effect on the modulator (your voice) and play with the Bands settings to get different responses for the overall output. Vocodex has the ability to create almost any vocoder effect that you will hear in today's music, and with your experimentation and exploration, it will create sounds never before heard that you can call your very own!

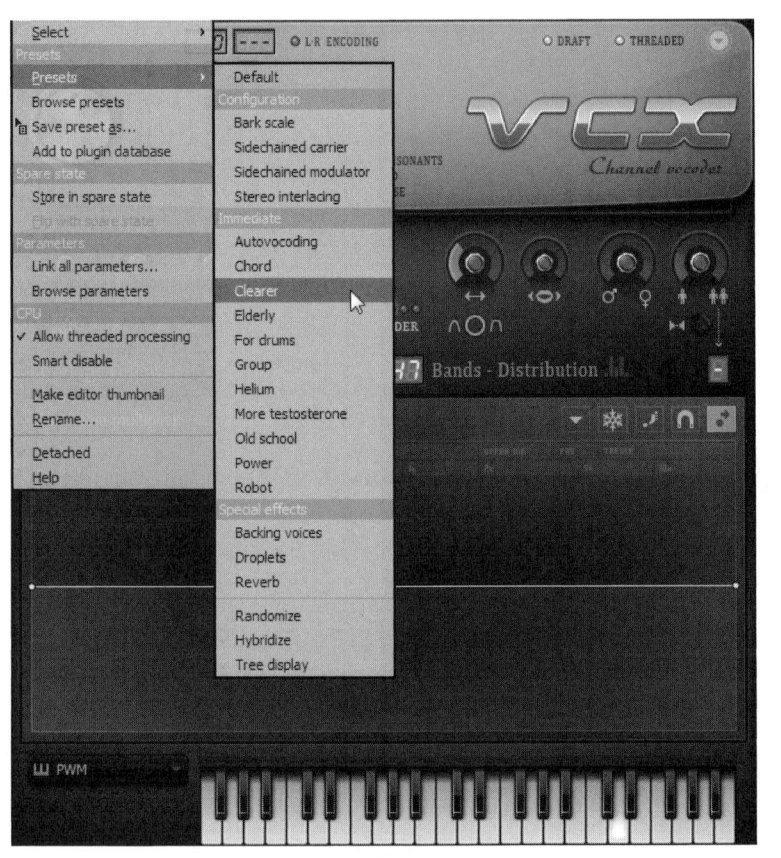

Figure 7.53 Selecting the immediate option for live effect of the modulator using notes played on a MIDI keyboard.

We have taken a detailed look at the effects plug-ins that FL Studio has to offer, and by now you should be developing a good idea of where to use the plug-ins and how to create the sounds you need. I have to remind you that with these, experimentation and an attentive ear are key to successfully using these plug-ins with your own projects. A great way to build a foundation of knowledge is to try to copy effects from other songs using the tools you have, and naturally you will come up with your own settings that you can save for future projects.

In the next chapter we will take a brief look at the plug-ins that are not included with the purchase of FL Studio so that you can decide whether they are right for you and whether they would suit your needs. The idea is to give you the basic knowledge of what they do and how they work so you can make a purchase based on need rather than curiosity.

8 Extra Generators and Effects Plug-Ins

This section is dedicated to the plug-ins that do not come included as full versions with FL Studio when you purchase the Producer Edition. The easiest way to spot these is that they will have the word DEMO at the top of the plug-in, and if you open the help file (F1), there will be a green letter D next to the name of the plug-in. As you go through this chapter, keep in mind what your needs are when making music and if the plug-in would be useful to you. While I believe that you can make nearly any type of music using the stock tools of FL Studio, there are more tools available that will make your music-making much easier. The idea of this chapter is to give information to help you make an informed decision on what plug-ins you want to add to your arsenal of music-making tools, so for that reason, we won't get bogged down in discussing every feature available for every plug-in. Rather, we will look at what these plug-ins can do and how they can be used to enhance your FL Studio experience.

Extra Generators and Instrument Plug-Ins

The generators and instruments are what create sound and offer you ways to alter those sounds. The only exception is the Video Player, which we will also discuss. Remember that making a project your own can come down to setting that sound just right so that it has your trademark sound on it. With a limited supply of instruments, you may find yourself searching for something more. In some cases these plug-ins can take your existing sounds and samples, increase their flexibility within your music, and completely rearrange them to create a brand-new sound!

DirectWave

DirectWave (see Figure 8.1) is one of my favorite plug-ins available for FL Studio. The plug-in initially installs as a player version, so you are able to troll through the menus and use the DirectWave files that are available to gain an idea of this plug-in's capabilities. Since it installs as a player, you can test out the included piano sample to hear the quality and try out some features. Try clicking on the Samplefusion drop-down menu to explore downloadable presets and sample banks.

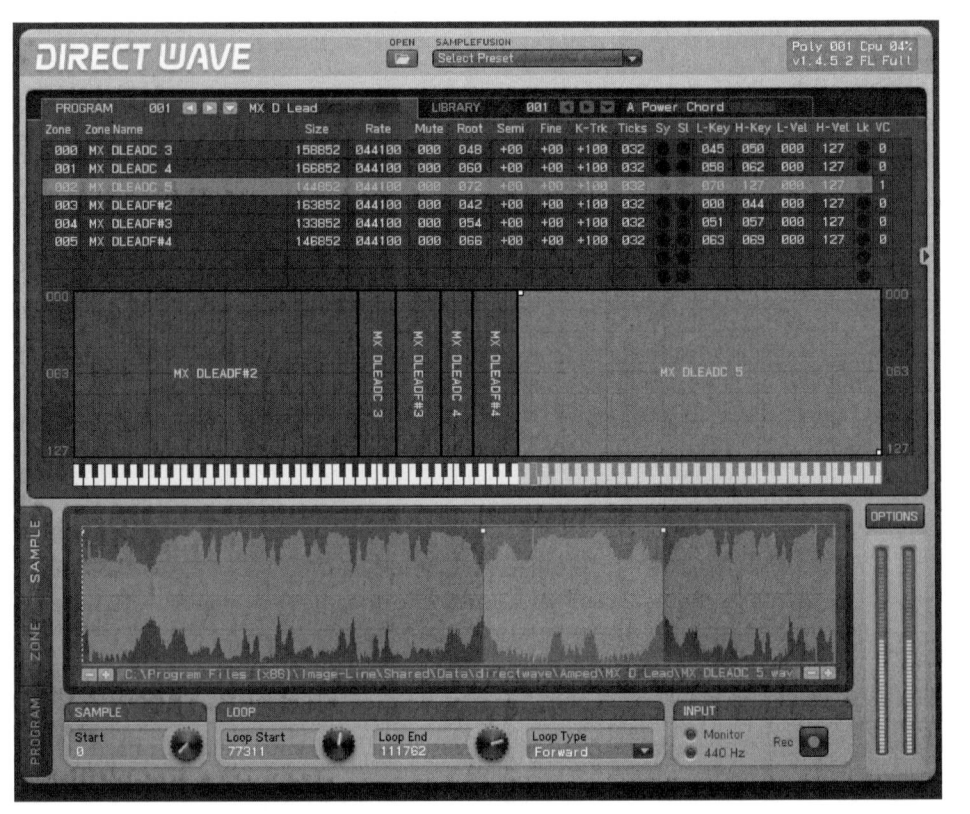

Figure 8.1   The DirectWave plug-in looping a sound.

When you have Program selected at the top left of the plug-in, you can see the samples laid out across the virtual keyboard. If you are using a MIDI controller, when you play the notes on the keyboard, the graphic will show you what key you are pressing and how hard you are pressing that key.

Below this are the sample properties, where you can set looping points and a start point for the sample, and you can even record your own sample from the input selector. With this, you can record your own snare hit, adjust the sample so that it plays perfectly on time, and you have built your own sample that can be placed anywhere in the Playlist or played live through DirectWave. It makes those sample CDs seem like they aren't worth the cost when it is this easy to make professional loops and sounds!

The Zone section (see Figure 8.2) allows you to apply tuning, filters, an LFO, phaser, delay, chorus, reverb, and even quantization to the sounds loaded into DirectWave. With the Current Selection versus Global option, you can individually add sounds and effects to each loaded sample in the Direct Player. This means that if you have one horn sound playing at C3, you can load that in, stretch it across a few octaves so it plays different notes rather than the single C3 note, and change filtering or effects for each note of that stretched sample.

Figure 8.2 The Zone options for DirectWave.

The Program section (see Figure 8.3) opens to reveal the different settings for the available effects that are built right into DirectWave. Here you can set your sounds to play with polyphony so that multiple notes can play at once or create a glide effect so that the note changes bend into each other. And they can be global settings or individual sounds, depending on your zone selection.

Figure 8.3 The Program section of DirectWave.

It is good to know that this player will only accept WAV and Ogg files, so those MP3s won't directly import. However, you can always export them as WAV files so they can be immediately imported, but remember that the reason for not bothering with MP3 files is that they are low quality, and their compression removes most of a waveform's digital information. This is why it is a good idea to try to find WAV-quality sounds for maximum quality and stretching ability.

There is a large list of acceptable programs that will import into DirectWave, including Battery, Kontakt, and ReCycle files, but remember that with the ability to record a sample inside of DirectWave, this means that if sound plays at all through FL Studio, you can use it!

A solid structure and fluid workflow make this plug-in ideal for electronic and hip-hop artists that love using pieces of music to create their projects. In many cases, loops are pre-cut so that keys on your MIDI keyboard will play parts of the sample, and you can create a new groove live using the slices individually. Try playing with the included sounds so that you can see what the DirectWave player is capable of, while keeping in mind that you can record your own samples to make instant loops, and you may find that this is a purchase you can't live without.

Fruity Video Player

The Fruity Video Player plug-in (see Figure 8.4) is pretty straightforward and allows you to play videos alongside the music in your project. This is great when you are trying to score a film or create a music sequence for a commercial.

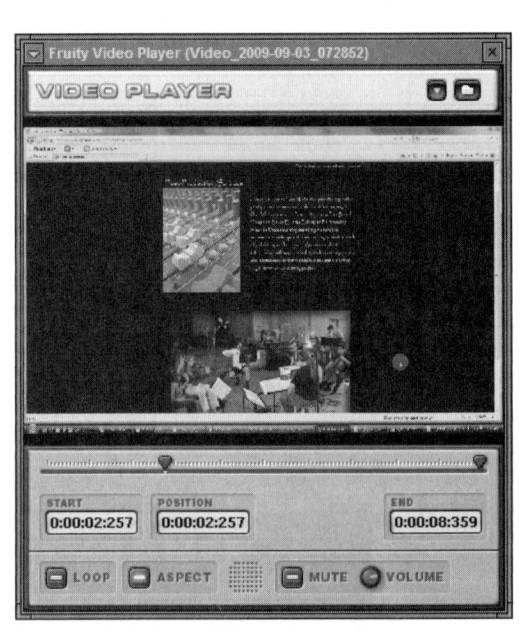

Figure 8.4   The Fruity Video Player.

FL Studio is not video editing software and will not export a video; it is only used to time your music with a video clip. The Video Player can set loop points so that the video repeats over a certain period, allowing you to fine-tune your musical cues. Another great feature is that you can actually pull audio out of a video clip and place it into FL Studio for further editing. Especially if you are going to be scoring a movie and you need to play longer clips, purchasing this plug-in is a must.

Morphine

The moment Morphine (see Figure 8.5) opens up, many initial reactions don't reach beyond "Whoa...." This synthesizer allows you to create an endless array of sounds and blend them into each other using a morph option similar to the one we saw in the DrumSynth Live plug-in, but Morphine has the ability to morph between four internal generators. The blending between generators can even be controlled by an envelope that is linked to the session tempo!

There really is very little that this plug-in is unable to do, and it is leaps and bounds beyond many others when you consider ability and control. Being based on additive synthesis, the simple sounds, such as basses and strings, sound great, but this plug-in caught my ear for its ability to create amazing soundscapes and atmosphere sounds. I used the morphing ability to start with a

Figure 8.5 Morphine.

simple sine sound and blended it into a complex array of two combined atmosphere sounds. They moved seamlessly into one another, and the effort was minimal, with incredible results. In my opinion this speaks to nearly every artist, aside from those who only use live instruments. I can see placement of the available sounds in every genre of music out there, so it's definitely worth your time to give this plug-in a try.

Ogun

Ogun (see Figure 8.6) is another additive synthesizer that allows for a wide range of sound adjustments. Particularly specialized toward metallic sounds, Ogun is great for creating single-shot percussive sounds and droning high-frequency pads. It has an XY controller, allowing you to map out different parameters to be controlled, and it has built-in filter, envelope, chorus, delay, and reverb effects that you can place on your sounds. You can even create an envelope based on the input signal of an audio clip by dragging it into the graph in Ogun, and it will draw lines that ultimately affect your final output.

In the presets, you will find a decent list of available sounds that you can tweak to make your own, and most will tell you if they are mapped to the XY controller. Ogun is closely related to Autogun, and the two plug-ins can share presets. This is a great plug-in when you need that extra spice in your project and the typical synth sounds aren't cutting it. Start by loading a preset and

Figure 8.6 Ogun.

altering the XY controller and then drag an audio clip into the graph to affect how the synth will play. Remember that dragging an audio clip only affects the graph and does not morph with the sound that plays.

Poizone

Poizone (see Figure 8.7) is a synth that can have up to 32 voices running at once and is incredibly flexible in its use. This is my favorite plug-in containing a built-in arpeggiator. The multitude of not just sounds but patterns of sounds that you can make is astounding. In many different forms of music today, you will hear arpeggiators running in the background, and in some cases they are the main hook.

Navigating through the controls can seem daunting at first, but the layout is very user friendly once you understand what their purpose is. The setup includes two subtractive synthesis oscillators, a noise oscillator, delay, chorus, gating, and the ability to control the arpeggiation of your sound. Most of these controls are automatable, so you can cause the arpeggiating sound to change octaves and even directions mid-song. For electronic and pop artists, this will be an indispensable tool in your music-making.

Figure 8.7 Poizone.

There are a great deal of available presets to go through, so start by working with the single sounds and then move on to creating arpeggiating sounds that play in your project, and you may find that you can't be without Poizone.

Sawer

Sawer (see Figure 8.8) is another synthesizer that was modeled after a 1980s Soviet synth called a *Polivoks*. This synth is reminiscent of '80s synth sounds in some respects, but due to the rarity of the synth that it was made to mimic, you will hear sounds that you most likely have never before heard.

There are incredibly warm sounds capable of playing through this plug-in, as well as stripped, empty filler sounds for ambience. Sawer also has a built-in arpeggiator that you can use for any number of sounds that you create, or you can place it on any of the presets. Again, the number of knobs and faders can seem overwhelming, but taking it piece by piece, you see that it is a familiar set of ADSR envelopes, filters, glide knobs, oscillators, and effects that are common to adjusting the sounds. To investigate, start with a simple bass sound and then include arpeggiation and add a phaser. Try using one of the preset pads to add warmth and depth to one of your songs.

Sawer tends to be a CPU hog, so be certain that your system is powerful enough to run it successfully. Any dual- or quad-core system should have no issues. Sawer is for anyone looking for a synth that is rare in tone and very close to the original analog synth.

Sytrus

I must admit that once I started getting the hang of using Sytrus (see Figure 8.9), I really started having fun with the sound-designing abilities. This plug-in is nearly limitless in its ability to

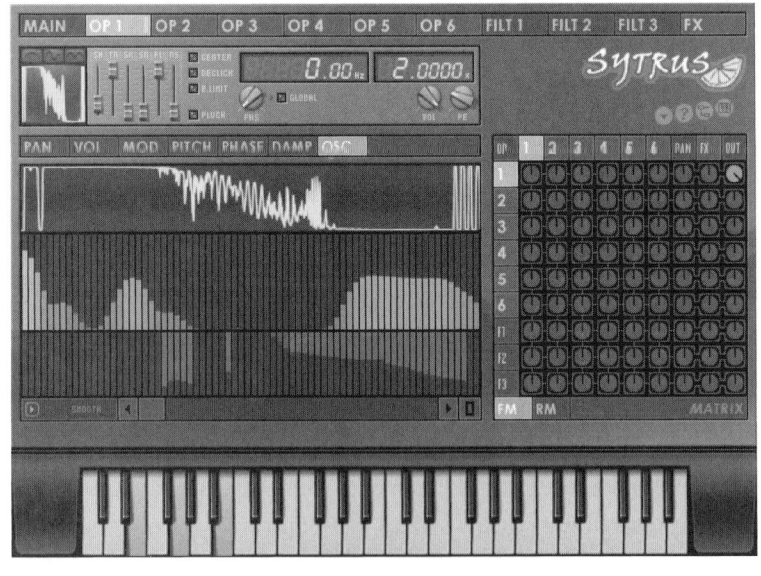

Figure 8.8   Sawer.

Figure 8.9   Sytrus.

create sounds because of its ability to use a combination of frequency modulation (FM), ring modulation (RM), and subtractive synthesis. Anything from a long, spacey drone to an entire drum kit can be created in synth form using Sytrus.

Sytrus has six operators that act as oscillators for your sound. A number of different filters and envelopes can be placed on each operator, allowing you to create nearly any sound you could need using effects, frequency modulation, and ring modulation.

In my opinion, the best way to see what the controls do is to start with the default sine wave that sounds like a simple beep and adjust controls from there. You can even build a quick arpeggiator in the Vol > Env tab of any operator.

The key and seemingly confusing part is the matrix of Sytrus. The idea is that the top row feeds signal to the left row based on what knob you turn to activate, and then the output is controlled by the last vertical row. So if you turn the knob that is below Operator 3 and to the right of Operator 2, this means that Operator 2 is feeding signal to Operator 3. To get the output of Operator 3 to play, just turn the knob that is under OUT and to the right of Operator 3.

Again, this is only a starting point; for full exploration of Sytrus, press F1 with Sytrus selected, and a full explanation of every feature will be displayed. This plug-in creates high-quality sounds that you can manipulate and change using different operators that feed into each other. It is difficult to find a more flexible and powerful software synthesizer.

Toxic Biohazard

Words that come to mind when describing Toxic Biohazard (see Figure 8.10) are gritty, dirty, nasty, dark, and extreme. This is a very impressive instrument and sonic sequencer. There is an ongoing list filled with uses for this plug-in, and using nearly any of the presets, you can add a raw edge to your project that it may have been missing.

Many times when you are working on a project, it seems as if it is missing punch or impact, especially with electronic and hip-hop music. This plug-in has the ability to add that ferocity to your music while keeping the CPU usage low so there is no fear of inserting more than one instance into your projects.

Based on frequency modulation (FM) and subtractive synthesis, Toxic Biohazard has six ADSR generators that are each linked to an individual oscillator, giving you incredible flexibility over your sounds. The surrounding effects are very familiar, including chorus, reverb, delay, and a flanger, and there is even a built-in master EQ to polish your overall output.

The sequencer portion contained within the plug-in will allow you to build a complex or basic arpeggiator for your sound and instantly adjust how the arpeggiation reacts. To give it a good test run, try selecting a sequence from the Preset menu and changing the arpeggiation and then the actual sound that is being arpeggiated. There will be very few (if any) artists who will not be able to use this plug-in for creating sounds, fills, or even an entire groove.

Figure 8.10 Toxic Biohazard with a sequence set to play.

Extra Effects Plug-Ins

These plug-ins don't make sound, but the things they can do with it are astounding. In this section we'll take a look at the missing plug-ins in your FL Studio experience that allow you to alter your audio for remixing, distorting, and even mastering. These plug-ins have different purposes, but keep in mind how you could use them in your current projects (including the ones you might have thought you finished).

Grossbeat

Prior to having all of these digital recording toys, manipulation of sounds was all done manually, so if somebody wanted a sound to play backwards, he would have to actually set it to play in reverse and then record the result. If he wanted a stutter effect where the volume cut in and out, he would have to adjust the volume sliders manually to achieve the effect (although I doubt this technique was very popular way back when).

Grossbeat (see Figure 8.11) allows you to create these audio stutters and time-shifting changes using an array of envelopes and settings contained within one plug-in! The most impressive part of this plug-in is that it can operate on the audio-stream, so as your voice passes through the plug-in, you can make it scratch certain words by setting a time-adjustment curve in the graphic display.

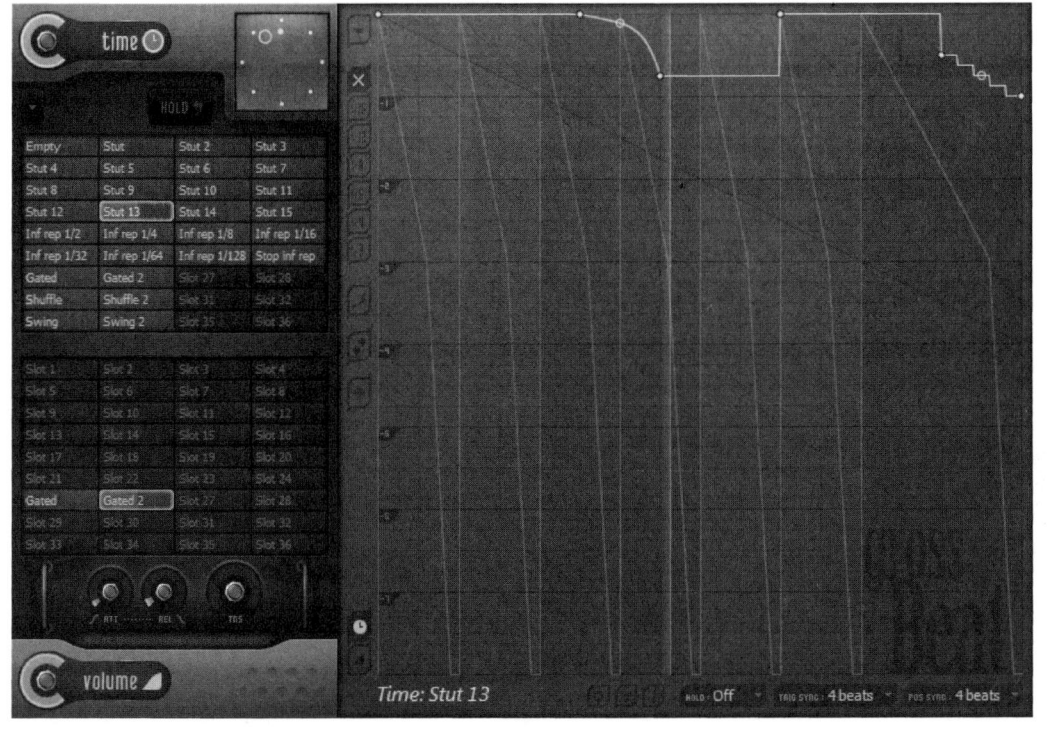

Figure 8.11 Grossbeat.

Any sound can be reversed, scratched, or stuttered using the controls in Grossbeat, and you can combine the time adjust with the gating effect. One thing to keep in mind is that Grossbeat affects sound based on where the time position marker is in the plug-in, so in order to hear any effect, your project must be playing.

Once you understand the playback direction on the graph, you can start recording vocals that have a tempo-based scratch to them, so the scratch will always happen precisely when you want it to. Combined with the gating effect, there is no genre of music that wouldn't receive benefit from using this plug-in. Especially for those creating rap and hip-hop, this will become one of your most used polishing tools for your vocals and other percussive sounds. There is no better plug-in for creating that perfect scratch or stutter in your audio, and Grossbeat comes in at the top of my list for extra purchases.

Hardcore

The Hardcore plug-in (see Figure 8.12) takes thousands of dollars worth of guitar pedals and crams them into one easy-to-use plug-in. Guitar players who have used multiple effects pedals will be intimately familiar with this plug-in before launching it because of the graphic display. It is set up to look identical to a guitar pedal chain with a few extra abilities.

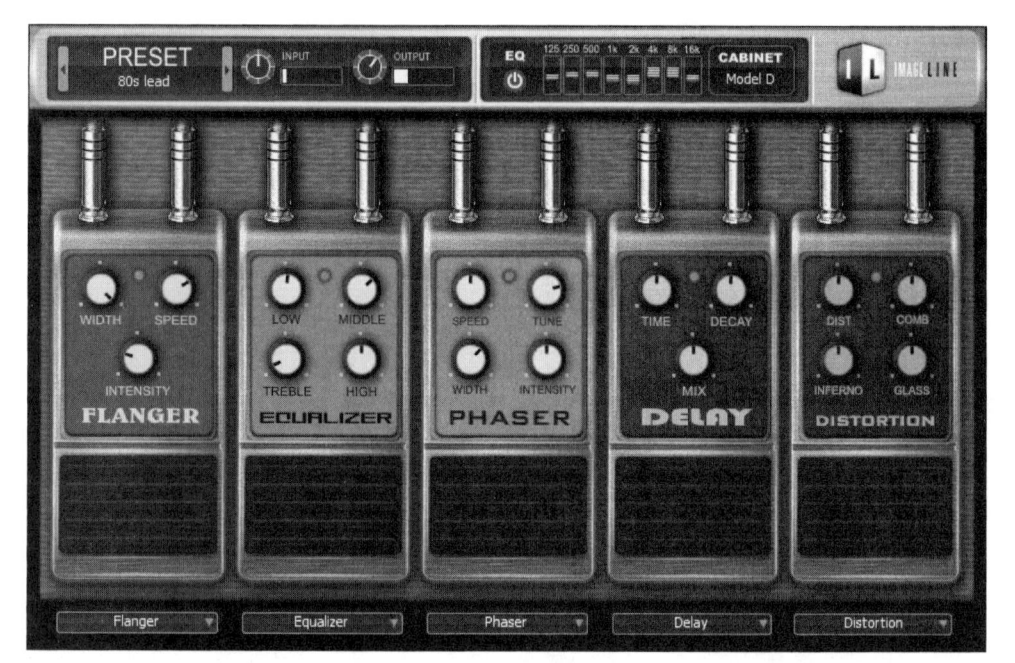

Figure 8.12   Hardcore.

This plug-in is designed with guitar playing in mind, but don't hesitate to experiment with vocals and other sounds or instruments. The built-in cabinet modeler replicates the recorded sound of different types of speaker stacks along with an EQ, so you can get that realistic guitar distortion or clean phasing. Remember that the purpose of this plug-in is to affect any sound, and it will not produce any sound without an input signal. Whether it is a live instrument, a mic, or a routed channel, this plug-in will create the effects that you look for in guitar pedals. This plug-in is a must for singer/songwriters, rock bands, and anyone who plays the guitar live. I have found this plug-in to be best suited for guitar sounds, but again there are no rules when making music, so experiment with adding this effect on different sounds.

Maximus

Have you ever listened to a track and wondered, "How do they get it up to the perfect volume without it getting too loud and causing clipping or distortion?" Maximus (see Figure 8.13) provides a prime example of how digital audio has made it easy for the home studio musician to create full, loud mixes that beef up weak parts and calm down volume spikes. The secret to this amazing plug-in is its use of three multi-band compressor/limiters that affect the low, mid, and high frequency ranges and a master compressor/limiter for your main output. This allows you to place compression on the lows to address those deep notes, such as bass and kicks, but place a different amount of compression on the mids and highs. Then you can place a final compressor/limiter on the entire output to pinpoint the mix for which you have been searching.

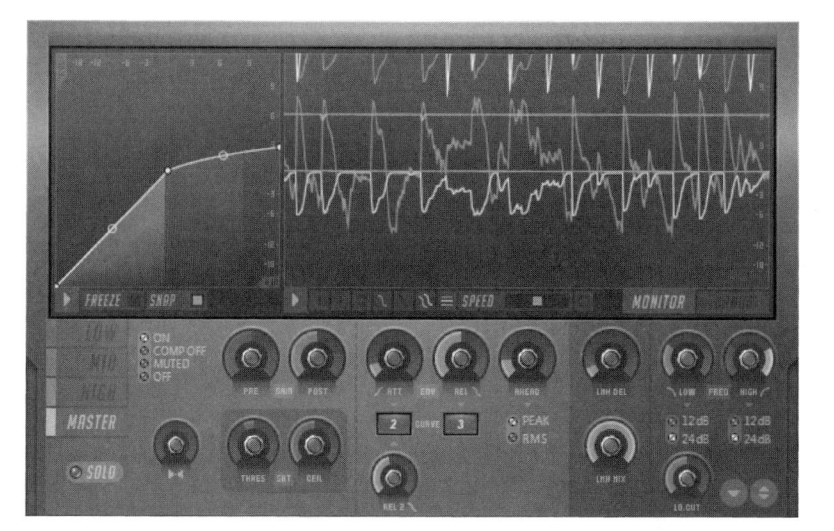

Figure 8.13 Maximus in action.

This borders on the argument of loudness versus dynamic range, where engineers make their mixes so loud that there are no perceivable soft parts—this is commonly referred to as the *loudness wars*. Many professionals argue against heavy compression because they assert that it takes away from the range at which a song should play, while proponents for making it louder claim that their mixes get heard more easily by record companies. Some bands even have their engineer mix their songs at a maximum volume so that all sections are the same volume, including the quiet breaks. I feel that this is a decision for you to make, and coupled with opinions from friends, you will find your happy medium.

Remember that it is all about experimentation through trial and error when trying to create what you think is the perfect mix. Maximus, although great for limiting and compression, is best suited for the master track in the Mixer because it addresses all of your volume problems for the entire project in one plug-in. One effective use of Maximus on a single track, however, is for de-essing vocals, which takes out the prominent sibilance in your words (S sounds that have heavy midrange frequency response). For the most part, though, this will be the last thing that you place on your final mix, and the intention of the plug-in is to bring your projects up to professional status. Everyone can and will benefit from this plug-in, and for those trying to get their songs on the radio, this can give your track that crisp edge it needs.

We have taken a look at everything that FL Studio has to offer, and I hope that you have gained a much stronger understanding of not just using, but *effectively* using the software to meet your needs. Remember that you can always refer back to sections in the event that you get lost or need a little extra info, but the best way to get better at using the program is to actually build projects inside of it. The more you try to use different effects, generators, and general abilities of the program, the more you will find that creating a project is no longer about creating a beat slowly from pieces, but it becomes a fluid workflow that is only hindered by your own imagination.

My strongest words of wisdom are practice, practice, practice! FL Studio has managed to create a program that competes with—and in many cases exceeds—the abilities of professional-level software available today.

I have worked on professional setups and duct-taped home studios, but regardless of how expensive the equipment was, the only concern was whether music could be made. With this software in your possession, you not only have the building and editing tools, but there are even a few that aid the completely tone deaf. Even the Randomizer can help you create the hook you need without having to do anything aside from hitting a button. FL Studio is truly limitless, and you will find that mastering the capabilities of the software will allow you to create more music than you ever thought possible. Now stop reading, and start making some music!

Index